# Lean Enterprise Value

# Lean Enterprise Value

## Insights from MIT's
## Lean Aerospace Initiative

Earll Murman
Thomas Allen
Kirkor Bozdogan
Joel Cutcher-Gershenfeld
Hugh McManus
Deborah Nightingale
Eric Rebentisch
Tom Shields
Fred Stahl
Myles Walton
Joyce Warmkessel
Stanley Weiss
Sheila Widnall

*I hope you enjoy these findings & insights, and look forward to many discussions.*

*Earll*

palgrave

First published 2002 by
PALGRAVE
Houndmills, Basingstoke, Hampshire RG21 6XS and
175 Fifth Avenue, New York, N.Y. 10010
Companies and representatives throughout the world

PALGRAVE is the new global academic imprint of
St. Martin's Press LLC Scholarly and Reference Division and
Palgrave Publishers Ltd (formerly Macmillan Press Ltd).

ISBN 0–333–97697–5 hardcover

This book is printed on paper suitable for recycling and made from fully managed and sustained forest sources.

A catalogue record for this book is available from the British Library.

Library of Congress Cataloging-in-Publication Data

Lean enterprise value : insights from MIT's Lean Aerospace Initiative / Earll Murman ... [et al.].
     p. cm.
   Includes bibliographical references and index.
   ISBN 0–333–97697–5
   1. Airplanes, Military—Design and construction—Costs. 2. Massachusetts Institute of Technology—Research. 3. Industrial efficiency. 4. Aerospace industries—Cost effectiveness.
   I. Murman, Earll M., 1942-.

TL685.3 .L38 2002
658.5'15—dc21                                   2001059824

Editing and origination by
Aardvark Editorial, Mendham, Suffolk

10  9  8  7  6  5  4  3  2  1
11  10  09  08  07  06  05  04  03  02

Printed in Great Britain by
Creative Print & Design (Ebbw Vale), Wales

*We dedicate this book to the men and women of the US aerospace community –
whether in industry, government, organized labor or universities, including our
graduate students and MIT faculty colleagues – who have inspired this book
through their contributions to the Lean Aerospace Initiative, and whose
talents and dedication are helping to shape the future of aerospace*

# CONTENTS

# Contents

# List of Boxes

# List of Figures and Tables

## Figures

# List of Figures and Tables

## Tables

# FOREWORD

This book is an outgrowth of the Lean Aerospace Initiative (LAI), a unique partnership between industry, government, labor, and academia created in 1993 to help transform the US Aerospace Enterprise. LAI's very existence, we believe, speaks to the book's central message: *an enterprise must **create value** to achieve lasting success in an environment of fundamental change*. We propose this central message – and the cumulative learning experience out of which it has grown – to help guide the transformation of *any* enterprise or industry, at whatever level it is defined.

To understand the genesis of the Lean Aerospace Initiative and the evolution of the thinking reflected in this book, let us take a step back to the early 1990s. This was a period of considerable uncertainty for the US defense aerospace community, in the aftermath of the demise of the former Soviet Union. Massive cuts in defense spending and shifting defense priorities, along with a stagnant international market in commercial aerospace, created a depressed business environment. Affordability, rather than performance at any cost, became the new defense acquisition imperative. To survive and succeed in such a radically new environment, the industry had to remake itself. It was also at this time that the Department of Aeronautics and Astronautics at MIT was thinking strategically about the future needs of the aerospace industry.

LAI was launched in this environment and in response to these challenges. In mid-1992, Lt. Gen. Thomas R. Ferguson, Jr – then the Commander of the Air Force's Aeronautical Systems Center (ASC) at Wright-Patterson Air Force Base, which is engaged in the acquisition of all aircraft systems for the US Air Force – was confronted with rising costs when budgets were being drastically reduced. He had just finished reading *The Machine That Changed The World*, a book summarizing the results of MIT-based research on the world auto industry during the previous five-year period under the auspices of the International Motor Vehicle Program (IMVP). The book introduced the principles of lean production as a fundamentally new and different system of manufacturing, one that accounted for the significantly superior performance of some Japanese auto producers. The lean concepts evolved at Toyota had produced outstanding results in the auto industry in terms of cost, quality, time to market, product diversity, and affordability, propelling Japanese auto companies to the front ranks of industrial performance worldwide.

Lt. Gen. Ferguson explored with Professor Daniel Roos of MIT, then the IMVP Director, whether lean principles could be applied to the defense aerospace industry. A 'quick look' study was undertaken. The results were briefed to Lt. Gen. Ferguson and the presidents of 29 aerospace companies on November 5th, 1992, at the annual ASC Presidents' Day meeting in Dayton, Ohio.

Following a transition period in order to structure what became a unique partnership, the Lean Aircraft Initiative was born in May 1993. It was organized as a consortium between MIT and major US aerospace companies in partnership with the US Air Force and other federal agencies. Led by the MIT Department of Aeronautics and Astronautics in close collaboration with the Sloan School of Management, the program was based in the Center for Technology, Policy and Industrial Development (CTPID), an MIT-wide interdisciplinary research center that also served as the IMVP's home base.

The consortium defined for itself a bold charter: *to help bring about fundamental change in both industry and government operations in defense aerospace in order to achieve greater affordability of systems, increased efficiency, higher quality, enhanced technological superiority, and a stronger US defense industrial base*. This basic charter, later modified to include *enhancing the effectiveness of the national workforce*, continues to guide the Lean Aerospace Initiative. With the addition of the space sector to the consortium in early 1998, the name was changed to Lean Aerospace Initiative. And when the Boeing Commercial Airplane Group joined the program a year later, the progressive change in the program's scope became complete, covering all aspects of the aerospace industry.

As a first approximation, the 'quick look' study in 1992 characterized the US military aircraft industry essentially as a 'craft system with a mass production mentality'. Clearly, the challenge would be greater than identifying known lean principles from the auto context and simply applying them in an aerospace context. While the problem-solving thrust of the effort was centered on defense aerospace, its intellectual scope would have to embrace a broader domain that included commercial aerospace. Also, to focus only on conducting research, and to expect industry and government stakeholders to implement the results, would be too limiting. LAI determined that developing implementation tools would be essential.

The solution was to structure an open, inclusive, and evolving process to foster the development of a learning community. Today, LAI brings together key stakeholders from industry, government, organized labor, and MIT, all united around a common vision. An Executive Board consisting of senior representatives of all member organizations provides general direction and oversight. The stakeholders work together within a partnership framework, with well-defined roles and responsibilities. As partners, they jointly determine broad research directions and priorities. Clearly established success criteria guide overall progress.

Objective and systematic research is central to LAI's mission. Research is conducted by a number of teams – with membership from all stakeholders and chaired by industry, government, and MIT co-leads – in areas such as product development, manufacturing systems, supplier networks, people and organizations, acquisition, and enterprise topics. Researchers from other universities participate in these teams as well. The sponsoring organizations provide support to specific research projects, making the real world our laboratory. The resulting stream of research products has raised awareness and enabled implementation through a variety of means – implementation tools, workshops and conferences, and pilot projects for testing out new ideas. This, in turn, has contributed to greater understanding, generating new research questions and hypotheses. The many graduate students who have actively contributed to research and later sought careers in aerospace continue to help shape the industry's future. A virtuous cycle – which has proven successful to the present day – has been set in motion to create lasting value.

The Lean Aerospace Initiative has taken root, grown, and flourished as a new model of industry, government, labor, and university partnership. Accelerating lean implementation has produced enormous – and documented – payoffs. Still, transforming the US Aerospace Enterprise is a complex undertaking. Changing the established culture has proven to be the greatest transformational challenge. Although much has been achieved, much remains to be accomplished.

MIT itself, as a stakeholder, has also changed in important ways. The need for rapid deployment of research results into action has engendered new ways of interaction between MIT researchers and practitioners. Research issues not only span many engineering disciplines but also cover challenging management and policy issues, fostering a growing emphasis on integrative, multidisciplinary research that cuts across different schools and departments. The School of Engineering and the Sloan School of Management have become engaged in LAI. Following its first three-year phase, LAI extended the program's co-directorship to include a senior faculty member representing the Sloan School. More recently, a new co-director, representing the sponsoring partners, was appointed to ensure the delivery of value for all stakeholders.

Like other key stakeholders, MIT has also realized value from its engagement with LAI. An important benefit has been creation of basic knowledge on principles governing fundamental industrial change, performance, and competitiveness. MIT's degree programs and academic curriculum already reflect this new intellectual capital. In addition, working alongside industry, government, and labor has enhanced MIT's basic mission to educate tomorrow's leadership in engineering and management and to advance the common good through public service. A further benefit has been educating the educator. LAI is an important investment in MIT's academic future.

The successful collaborative model represented by the Lean Aerospace Initiative has also been adopted internationally. One notable example is the UK Lean Aerospace Initiative (UK-LAI), a consortium of aerospace companies, government, and four universities in the United Kingdom (Warwick, Nottingham, Cranfield, and Bath). Another is the Lean Aircraft Research Program (LARP) in Sweden, based at Linköping University. University-to-university collaborative research alliances have been established between MIT and universities engaged in these two programs, to take advantage of synergies.

Further, within the United States the concept has more recently been extended to create the Lean Sustainment Initiative (LSI) and the Labor Aerospace Research Agenda (LARA), both companion programs at MIT. LSI, which began in 1996, seeks to help achieve fundamental transformation of the logistics, repair, and maintenance system supporting the US Air Force into a cost-effective, quality-driven, reliable, and responsive sustainment enterprise in the 21st century. This initiative, too, is being pursued as a partnership between the US Air Force, other government agencies, major commercial repair organizations and suppliers, and MIT. The LARA partnership between organized labor and academia seeks to strengthen future aerospace workforce capabilities – labor and professional – through an agenda of research and derived recommendations. LARA, started in 1998, draws upon LAI member organizations as well as non-aerospace companies for its studies.

Looking back is also instructive in looking forward. The path the Lean Aerospace Initiative has taken since 1993 – mirroring the cumulative learning experience we have tried to convey in this book – has been extraordinarily enriching, energized, and purposeful. We have learned important lessons and believe the insights gained can be of value to other industries facing fundamental change, as well as to similar partnership initiatives between industry, government, labor, and academia. Here are several insights we would like to share.

First, the Lean Aerospace Initiative represents the emergence of a *learning community*, initially focused on 'low-hanging fruit' (that is, short-term benefits), but progressively acquiring a wider perspective and valuing longer-term solutions.

Second, the creation of a *neutral forum* facilitated by MIT has provided a unique platform for dialogue, knowledge sharing, and mutual learning in an open setting.

Third, the development of a *common vocabulary* has been crucial to fostering communication among all stakeholders, and to bridging sectoral and cultural differences, as well as chasms between functional specializations, organizational layers, and competing interests.

Fourth, the generation of a *common knowledge base* through systematic research by an impartial party has proven critical in accelerating the process of fundamental change.

Fifth, the presence of a *trusted change agent* has been indispensable to the implementation of research-driven change strategies by all member organizations and across much of the aerospace supplier base.

Sixth, the program's *governance structure* and the terms of engagement of all stakeholders cumulatively have provided a self-correcting and adaptive mechanism that has proven essential in creating and delivering value to all stakeholders.

Seventh, the *transparency* of the entire consortium process has helped create trusting relationships across otherwise competitive enterprises, while ensuring that proprietary information has been safeguarded.

Eighth, the *collective commitment* of all stakeholders to work, share, learn, and build together has been essential to the program's progress and overall impact.

The journey taken by the Lean Aerospace Initiative, like the journey presented in this book, continues. Gen. Lester L. Lyles, Commander of the Air Force Materiel Command, likened LAI to the building of the continental railroad in the 19th century. In a keynote address to the program's Executive Board in December 2000, Gen. Lyles noted that we have not yet driven down the golden spike. A great deal has changed since the program's inception, as have the nature, magnitude, and composition of the challenges. We plan to continue the LAI journey with renewed energy and vision, by both widening and deepening the stakeholder community.

One final note: as we completed our writing of this book, the terrorist attacks of September 11th, 2001, took place. These attacks are a tragic reminder of the seriousness – and diversity – of threats to national security. They also raise new demands for safe air transportation and remind us of the impact on our daily lives of instantaneous global communication and information dissemination.

We can't predict how those events will shape the future, but we suspect that the future will be quite different than the one we took for granted on September 10th, 2001. In the preceding months, as we were writing the book, we anticipated that aerospace would be called upon to contribute future value to society and to face future challenges – challenges that would be even more compelling for the transformation already underway. We are confident that the underlying processes for determining lean enterprise value will benefit the national and international communities affected by these events as they enter uncharted waters and respond to new threats. Efficient use of resources is needed, whether in times of crisis or in times of calm. The underlying principles of creating lean enterprise value apply equally.

THE AUTHORS

# Acknowledgements

We would like to extend our profound thanks and appreciation to the many organizations and people whose support and contributions, often given unstintingly over many years, made this book possible.

First and foremost, we recognize the member organizations of the Lean Aerospace Initiative listed in Appendix A, which have provided both financial support and encouragement. As a learning community, they joined us to give inspiration, form, and substance to this book. They also provided data and support for the research that underpins our findings and insights. We deeply appreciate our association with members of related initiatives: the Labor Aerospace Research Agenda at MIT; the Lean Sustainment Initiative at MIT; the UK Lean Aerospace Initiative at the Universities of Warwick, Bath, Cranfield, and Nottingham; and the Swedish Lean Aircraft Research Program at Linköping University.

Much of our thinking reflected in this book can be traced to the cumulative research conducted by more than a hundred talented and dedicated graduate students, many of whom we have personally supervised. In important ways these students are the enduring products of the Lean Aerospace Initiative as they pursue careers in the aerospace industry, government, or other sectors. Already 56 students have completed their thesis research with LAI support and another 25 students have participated or are currently participating in LAI research as part of their studies. An additional 27 students enrolled in graduate MIT degree programs, mostly supported by their companies, have contributed to LAI research. Their names are given in Appendix B.

We also gratefully acknowledge our other MIT colleagues who have been engaged in the LAI research program over the years, some of whom have supervised these students: Charles Boppe, David Cochran, John Deyst, Charlie Fine, Dan Frey, Stan Gershwin, Ed Greitzer, Tim Gutowski, Wesley Harris, Daniel Hastings, David Hoult, Sandy Jap, Jan Klein, Harvey Sapolsky, Jerry Shapiro, Duncan Simester, Anna Thornton, and Dan Whitney. We would like to recognize, in particular, the earlier leadership and guidance provided by our MIT colleagues Dan Roos and William Pounds.

A number of people in industry, labor, government, and academia contributed to or reviewed various sections, case studies, or vignettes within this book to ensure their factual accuracy and that our wording did justice to their reality. We are grateful to the contributions, reviews, and comments provided by Norman Augustine, Sam Autry, Lt. Col. Keith Birkholz (USMC), Rich Briggs, Tyson Browning, William Bullock, Dennis Bush, Greg Caires, Paul Carter, Chris Cool, Eugene Covert, Charlie Davis, Greg Drohat, Chuck Ebeling, Jerry Gannaway, Gary Goodman, Andrew Gore, Allen Haggerty, Don Handell, Cliff Harris, Wesley Harris, Daniel Hastings, Bob Hoffman, Sarah Hotaling, Brian Ippolito, Tom Keider, Bill Kessler, Thomas Kochan, Vicki Kygar, John Paul MacDuffie, Andrew Martinez, Theresa McCauley, Don Meadows, Joe Mize, Mike Nipper, Curt Newill, Gordon Ramsbottom, Leon Silva, Ed Schein, Lt. Gen. Richard Scofield (USAF, Ret.), Robert Seamans Jr, Steven Sleigh, Joe Stout, Bill Wansing, Heidi Wood, Randle Wright, and Bob Zwitch.

At any given time, the Lean Aerospace Initiative typically has well over six hundred active participants, and we fear that we may inadvertently have failed to recognize one or more of them and their contributions to this book. If this is the case, we sincerely apologize.

As noted in the Foreword, the Lean Aerospace Initiative was conceived and organized by the US Air Force. Key members of the Manufacturing Technology Division of the USAF Research Laboratory's Materials and Manufacturing Directorate provided support and leadership that made this book possible: John Cantrell, Ken Feeser, Bill Kessler, Alan Taylor, and Gary Waggoner.

We would not have been able to complete this book without the support of many people at MIT. We would like to acknowledge, in particular, the staff of the Lean Aerospace Initiative, the staff of the Center for Technology, Policy and Industrial Development (CTPID), the Deans of Engineering and the Sloan School of Management, our successive Provosts and, of course, our President.

Producing a book with thirteen authors has been a challenge and a learning experience. We are grateful that the book has brought us closer together – in our thinking and in our regard for one another. Being able to truly speak with one voice, however, was only possible with the expert editorial and writing support provided by Scott Cooper. He is a rare professional who understood our shared visions, asked us challenging questions, reconciled our diverse (and sometimes divergent) writing styles, and added new clarity to the concepts.

Finally all facts, statements, opinions, and conclusions expressed herein are solely those of the authors and do not in any way reflect those of the Lean Aerospace Initiative, the US Air Force, the sponsoring companies and organizations (individually or as a group), or MIT. All but the authors are absolved from any remaining errors or shortcomings, for which the authors take full responsibility.

| | |
|---|---|
| ACC | Air Combat Command (USAF) |
| AFB | Air Force Base |
| AFSOC | US Air Force Special Operations Command |
| ARBG | Acquisition Reform Benchmarking Group |
| AWAC | airborne warning and control (plane) |
| BCAG | Boeing Commercial Aircraft Group |
| BRAC | Base Realignment and Closing |
| BTP | Build-To-Package |
| CAB | US Civilian Aeronautics Board |
| CEO | Chief Executive Officer |
| COMSTAC | US Commercial Space Transportation Advisory Committee |
| DARPA | US Defense Advanced Research Projects Agency |
| DoD | US Department of Defense |
| DSB | US Defense Science Board |
| FAA | US Federal Aviation Administration |
| FARA | Federal Acquisition Reform Act |
| FASA | Federal Acquisition Streamlining Act |
| FBC | 'Faster, Better, Cheaper' |
| G&A | general and administrative |
| GAO | US Government Accounting Office |
| GDP | gross domestic product |
| GE | General Electric |
| GPS | Global Positioning System |
| HPWO | high-performance work organization |
| HR | human resources |
| IAM | International Association of Machinists and Aerospace Workers |
| ICBM | Intercontinental Ballistic Missile |
| IMVP | International Motor Vehicle Program |
| IPPD | integrated product and process development |
| IPT | integrated product team |
| ISO | International Standards Organization |
| JDAM | Joint Direct Attack Munition |
| JIT | just-in-time (delivery) |
| JPATS | Joint Primary Aircraft Training System |
| JSF | Joint Strike Fighter |

| | |
|---|---|
| LAI | MIT Lean Aerospace Initiative (originally Lean Aircraft Initiative) |
| LARA | Labor Aerospace Research Agenda |
| LEM | Lean Enterprise Model |
| LESAT | Lean Enterprise Self Assessment Tool (LAI) |
| MILSPEC | Military Specification |
| MIT | Massachusetts Institute of Technology |
| MRP | Manufacturing Requirements Planning |
| NASA | National Aeronautics and Space Administration |
| NAVAIR | Naval Air Systems Command |
| NRO | National Reconnaissance Office |
| O&M | operations and maintenance |
| PPBS | Planning, Programming, and Budgeting System |
| R&D | research and development |
| S&P | Standard & Poor's (index) |
| SLEP | Service Life Extension Program |
| SPC | statistical process control |
| SPO | System Program Office |
| SPI | Single Process Initiative (DoD) |
| SST | supersonic transport |
| TQM | total quality management |
| TTL | Transition-to-Lean (LAI) |
| UAW | United Auto Workers – International Union of Automobile, Aerospace and Agricultural Implement Workers of America |
| UK-LAI | UK Lean Aerospace Initiative |
| USAF | United States Air Force |
| USAFR | United States Air Force Reserves |
| USCG | United States Coast Guard |
| USMC | United States Marine Corps |

# PART I

# Higher, Faster, Farther

From air races to moon races, the mantra of aerospace has always been 'Higher, Faster, Farther'. The field has been driven by, and has thrived on, the technical challenges of air and space flight. Since 1915 in the United States, when the National Advisory Committee for Aeronautics (NASA's predecessor) was formed, the national and international prestige of aerospace and the need for military superiority have driven national investments.

Aerospace is, and will continue to be, a 'flagship' industry of the United States, as well as of many European, Asian, and other countries of the Americas. And it promises continuing excitement and challenge. But aerospace also promises to be much different in the future from how it has been in the past. That is the subject of Chapter 1, 'The 21st-Century Enterprise Challenge'. It is a challenge some industries have already faced, and that others will face in the future.

A fundamental understanding and implementation of what we term *lean enterprise value* is central to the transformation of aerospace. Focusing on aerospace surfaces new insights about the concepts of 'lean', 'enterprise', and 'value'. In Chapter 1, we lay out five fundamental principles for creating lean enterprise value. These principles, and the resulting value creation framework, can be applied at the level of an individual program or platform, and apply as well at the level of a corporation or government agency – what we call the multi-program enterprise. These principles apply even at national and international levels, where the concept of lean enterprise value is not normally used, but provides new insights.

Many industries undergo developmental periods that establish a set of values and a culture that dominate thinking and behavior – even when that thinking is no longer 'right'. Take the automobile industry. When a number of the present authors were young adults, each new year brought new model cars that were longer, wider, more powerful, and more stylish. The US automobile industry perceived that these cars responded to value consumers desired – and failed to realize the shift that came when consumer values changed to smaller, more fuel-efficient, more reliable, and safer cars. It took a 'wakeup call' from Japan – a story well known to all.

Part I of *Lean Enterprise Value* captures the wakeup call for aerospace and the ensuing response over the past twelve years. That wakeup call began as a whisper in the 1970s, and grew to a shout with the end of the Cold War in 1989. But many did not hear. The aerospace field, with its legacy of high technical performance – epitomized by the Apollo program – was ill equipped to respond to the challenges of affordability and global economic competition.

Chapter 2, 'The Cold War Legacy', briefly recounts the background leading to this aerospace crisis and lays out the conditions that created the post-Cold War 'Monuments and Misalignments' of Chapter 3. There we recount the consequences of this legacy that became apparent as the 1990s unfolded. In all, Part I establishes the context for our prescription for how a major industry must change to survive: *lean enterprise value*.

# CHAPTER 1

# The 21st-Century Enterprise Challenge

The core challenge for industries in the 21st century involves identifying and delivering *value* to every stakeholder. Meeting that challenge requires *lean* capability at the *enterprise* level.

Aerospace provides a 'living experiment' for our discussion of this challenge and how it can be met. Aerospace brings together the hopes and dreams of a nation, employing complex technologies on challenging missions in air and space. When such an industry finds its core business models and guiding principles called into question – which is exactly what is happening to the US aerospace industry today – the lessons are important for every sector of the economy.

The end of the Cold War, the rise of global competition, and the maturity of core products such as engines and airframes are powerful forces driving the challenge to aerospace. Other industries have their own unique mix of precipitating forces, often including the latter two. In every case, the core challenge comes back to what we call *lean enterprise value*.

These are our book's three key themes – lean, enterprise, and value. Translating all three into action is a powerful antidote to what 'lean' has come to mean in too many cases. Applications of 'lean' have too often focused on just eliminating waste – a perspective with dangerous limitations. In contrast, *our* view of lean is centered on the elimination of waste with the goal of *creating value*. This means delivering what customers want and need; tangible returns on investment that shareholders rightly expect; and job satisfaction and lifetime learning that workers deserve. It means concrete sharing of the total benefits that suppliers need if they are to continue operating as full partners in good times and bad. It means delivering value to society that reflects its broader desires and concerns. The *enterprise* perspective we bring makes it possible to see entire 'value streams' as well as interconnected levels of activity that reach across national and international boundaries. That perspective stands in sharp contrast to 'lean' as narrow change efforts in only one part of an organization, such as manufacturing or the supplier network.

Ultimately, we will show that creating *lean enterprise value* goes well beyond figuring out better ways to 'do the job right'. It involves 'doing the right job'.

In focusing on lean, enterprise, and value, we build on nearly a decade of sustained research and action by a unique consortium. The Lean Aerospace Initiative (LAI) brings together leaders from major US aerospace companies and suppliers, government agencies, representatives from organized labor, and MIT. We have collaborative agreements with similar consortia in the United Kingdom and Sweden. This book reports on the results from an ongoing cycle of learning that has taken place in the LAI consortium – conducting research, applying the principles, taking stock of progress, and constructing tools for broader dissemination and transformation. While the story derives from the LAI experience, it reaches much further: to massive change initiatives and policy restructuring in government and industry. Our story contains lessons for any industry that employs leading-edge technologies in a complex national and global environment.

Twelve years ago, another book came out of MIT that focused on an industry facing a profound crisis. *The Machine That Changed The World*[1] introduced the concepts of 'lean' manufacturing as instrumental to the future of the world auto industry and also relevant to many other sectors. Our new thinking here on 'value' and 'enterprise' comes directly from our efforts to apply those concepts to aerospace. Our findings bridge across the many change initiatives that emerged in LAI member companies and throughout the industrial landscape – Total Quality Management, Reengineering, Six Sigma, and other formulations – to offer an integrated framework for action.

This book speaks directly to organizations that are on the journey of change. While our focus is aerospace (which includes aircraft, engines, avionics, launch systems, missiles, satellites, and more), the keys to transformation in this sector of the economy are applicable *wherever* there is a need to refocus on lean enterprise value.

## Lean Enterprise Value

In a 1994 speech at the Air Force Chief Scientists Group dinner, Gen. Merrill A. McPeak, then Air Force Chief of Staff, looked ahead to the year 2020 and urged a fundamentally new way of thinking.[2] He pointed out, for example, that the aerospace industry has always focused on pushing the frontier for air speed. A former jet pilot, Gen. McPeak said that he well understood that 'speed is life' mindset. But he expanded its scope to include speeding up the air tasking order process, tightening the loop between intelligence and operations, and shortening the development times for aircraft and spacecraft. In other words, he illustrated how 'faster' is not just a technology frontier centered on better defense capability, but is a requirement for all parts of the aerospace industry – indeed, for all industrial sectors. And it means completely different capabilities.

The promise of 'lean' principles and practices resonated with many US aerospace leaders. Government officials saw in these concepts not only the ability to increase defense capability, but also an opportunity for increased affordability in an era of declining defense dollars. The systematic elimination of waste driven by the lean mindset would support the very cycle time gains urged by Gen. McPeak. Industry executives also knew that traditional cost-cutting measures would be inadequate in a post-Cold War era marked by global competition. But there were also concerns. Would a model pioneered in the auto industry really work in the aerospace context – with its low-volume, high-complexity products, and significant sources of instability? And what about fears over job security? The workforce often perceives 'lean' as 'mean', with jobs eliminated in the name of 'efficiency improvements'.

To answer these questions, we must first understand the historical legacy of the US aerospace industry, which for decades was dominated by the constant imperative to go 'Higher, Faster, Farther'. As we highlight in the balance of Part I of this book, there was a national consensus that put a man on the moon, drove the designs for commercial and military aircraft, and 'won' the Cold War. Some of the innovations during this era foreshadow what we now see as lean principles and practices – such as Lockheed's fabled 'Skunk Works' operations (detailed in Chapter 2). But the dominant historical legacy of this era is a culture and practices that are less functional now that key parts of the industry have matured and the global threats have completely changed. It is common for industries to reach a 'dominant design' phase – and the particular history of aerospace parallels many sectors of the economy.

As in so many industries, infrastructure, institutions, and even mindsets have become misaligned with the environment and are now 'monuments' blocking forward progress. Attempts to address these barriers through downsizing, outsourcing, mergers, acquisitions, and regulatory reform all fail to engage the root cause of the challenge. What's needed is a fundamentally different orientation to creating value for the many stakeholders in this industry, other sectors, and society at large – over the lifecycle of a wide range of aerospace systems.

While 'traditional' lean principles and practices represent a key point of departure in developing this new orientation, the experience in aerospace points to broadening the way lean is typically understood. As we see in Part II of the book, lean can't be approached as a list of things to *do*. It is a different way of *thinking*. Lean is not just the elimination of waste; lean is also the creation of value.

While powerful, we must admit that 'lean' is also an awkward word. It is powerful in capturing an almost counterintuitive notion – that becoming lean results in more capable organization. A lean organization is a more flexible and adaptive organization. Reducing inventory, removing unnecessary steps, and eliminating other forms of waste can clear the path to continuous improvement. At the same time, though, the word carries baggage. There is a risk of placing too much emphasis on cutting costs. Worse still, lean is sometimes seen as a code word for eliminating jobs.

Our approach of pairing 'lean' and 'value' confronts these problems head-on. Eliminating waste must always serve a larger purpose – it must be oriented towards value creation. Accordingly, we have a new definition of becoming lean: *Becoming lean is a process of eliminating waste with the goal of creating value.*

Many aerospace and other industrial leaders attracted to lean were drawn initially to so-called 'low-hanging fruit' – improvement opportunities both easily visible and relatively easy to address. Aerospace examples will resonate with readers familiar with other industries: developing integrated product teams; involving suppliers early in the design process; reducing in-process inventory for materials in a factory; introducing visual displays on job processes; coordinating procurement functions; training workers in statistical process control principles; or introducing preventive maintenance practices.

These types of improvement opportunities are often addressed through 'kaizen events' – one-time 'blitz' efforts involving multiple stakeholders. But the Japanese word *kaizen*, so common in lean parlance, translates approximately as 'continuous improvement based on knowledge' – which contradicts the notion of a one-time effort. And even if successful, such efforts always risk creating isolated 'islands of success'. Each improvement effort may be a significant accomplishment, but it may also remain isolated and not represent the priority at the *enterprise* level. At that level, the priority might be to change policies and procedures to focus on life-cycle value, or to engage the workforce fully in pursuit of continuous improvement. Rather than such *kaizen* events, it may be more important to establish true long-term partnerships with suppliers, or to have fully integrated product and process design teams, or even to assess the overall direction and product mix in a given enterprise.

These tasks are more difficult than picking the low-hanging fruit. And it is a far greater challenge to undertake these activities in an *integrated* way, so that they mutually reinforce the overall objectives of the many stakeholders in a given enterprise. A truly lean enterprise would succeed from the points of view of end users, shareholders, the workforce, suppliers and partners, and society.

We report on increasing evidence of this broader enterprise mindset, and the benefits that accrue. Experience in the aerospace industry really drove the focus to the enterprise level, given the relatively small role played by manufacturing compared to new product development, supply chain integration, and lifecycle sustainment.

Before moving on to 'value', let's make clear what we mean by 'enterprise' (Chapter 6 provides a much more detailed description). First, there are individual programs that constitute distinct enterprises, each comprising a core and an extended enterprise. The USAF/Lockheed Martin F-22 Raptor fighter jet is one example: a multi-billion dollar program where we see the systematic integration of first-tier suppliers into every phase of development, production, and deployment. Boeing's Joint Direct Attack Munition (JDAM) is another: a much smaller program that has achieved major savings by adopting a lean enterprise approach.

## Programs, Projects, Platforms, and Products

What the aerospace industry calls 'programs' might, in other sectors, be termed 'projects', or 'platforms', or even 'product lines'. Whatever word is used, these are the key building blocks for the creation of value. Each can be thought of as a distinct 'value stream' in which various activities transform raw materials and information into finished goods or services to serve best a set of customers and stakeholders. The key point is that there is a defined organizational structure, with clear lines of assigned responsibility and accountability.

We use the word 'program' throughout the book, but our discussion applies to projects, platforms, or product lines.

It is significant when a leader in aerospace or any industry asserts that a given set of activities – regardless of scale – *must* be viewed as an interconnected whole. That interconnected whole is an *enterprise*.

Beyond the individual program enterprise, there are divisions of large corporations, government agencies, and other entities that we call multi-program enterprises. Here we find all the complexity of a lone program multiplied by the many interdependencies that exist across different programs. There will be a set of individual program leaders, as well as leaders for many support functions. There may be a single multi-program enterprise leader, such as a CEO or government agency director, but more likely there will be a distributed set of leaders who must coordinate their efforts. Again, it is significant when a leader asserts that this full range of activities must be seen as an interconnected enterprise – one in which the focus is on optimizing the entire system as a whole, not just on the separate parts.

Beyond the multi-program enterprises are the national and international enterprises, such as what we term the US Aerospace Enterprise, the European Aerospace Enterprise, and emerging counterparts in other parts of the world. Lean principles extend to national and international enterprises as well. As a call to action, this book urges nothing less than a lean enterprise transformation at every one of these levels.

The concept of enterprise teaches us something about 'true north'. It was Toyota that identified the customer as 'true north'. This notion of being customer-focused – with the customer providing clear guidance and direction to the application of lean principles and practices – is still at the core of lean, but serving the customer or end user alone is insufficient. At the enterprise level, it is just as important to serve the shareholder, the workforce, the acquirer (in aerospace, usually different from the end user), suppliers and partners, and society. So, while the principle of finding 'true north' still holds, aerospace teaches us that it must be an orientation not only towards serving the customer, but towards creating value for *all* enterprise stakeholders.

## Value as 'True North'

Even if persuaded of the urgent need for change, aerospace – like other industries – must confront big questions. How will direction, leadership, and support be provided? How many resources should be devoted to a high-stakes enterprise such as the Joint Strike Fighter? How much capability should be built around developing information technology support systems? Are the jet transport and communication satellite businesses primarily manufacturing or service businesses? These types of question all concern something beyond doing things right – they focus on hard choices about the right thing to do. And the answers require a systematic understanding of value and its creation – again, for end users *and* multiple other stakeholders.

In Part III, we detail our value-creation framework and its three phases: value *identification*, value *proposition*, and value *delivery*. Classical lean concepts as represented in *The Machine That Changed The World* or *Lean Thinking*[3] include identifying customer value. However, most implementations of lean principles and practices have centered on the third phase and focused on eliminating waste. Those efforts largely to 'do the job right' serve customers and often ignore other stakeholders. The focus of the value identification phase, though, is the imperative to 'do the right job'.

Consider, for example, the contrasting strategies of Boeing, with its proposed near-sonic cruiser, and Airbus, with its new A380 megajet. These products both reflect attempts to identify value long before the application of traditional lean practices and principles. Airbus appears to believe that there is more value in the long-haul hub-to-hub markets, while Boeing seems to believe that greater value lies in faster and more frequent point-to-point service. Such pivotal choices are part of any systematic effort to create lean enterprise value.

Value delivery is possible only where there is mutual agreement (tacit or explicit) among the key stakeholders, which is reflected in our second phase on establishing the value proposition. Consider here, for example, the very different value propositions associated with the large, wide-body jets built by Boeing and Airbus, and those for the smaller regional jets built in the United States, Canada, Brazil, and Europe. For wide-body jets, the value proposition might include low-cost transportation between population centers, a steady revenue base, stable jobs in a known business, and export gains. The value proposition associated with the regional jets goes well beyond the ability of an airline to fly a plane with lower direct operating costs. It could represent the revitalization of under-used airports or route segments, job growth in a new region, a change in status and skills for airline staff, and a potentially important building block in efforts to provide true 'intermodal' transportation service to travelers. Again, any focus on creating lean enterprise value must take into account these very different value propositions. Only then can the more traditional lean tools be applied to the third phase, value delivery.

Linking our three-phase model to the three levels of enterprise creates something like the three-by-three grid in Figure 1.1.

**FIGURE 1.1** Value-creation framework for three levels of enterprise

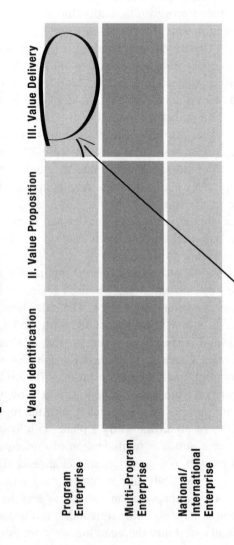

I. Value Identification  II. Value Proposition  III. Value Delivery

Program
Enterprise

Multi-Program
Enterprise

National/
International
Enterprise

Most lean principles and practices have been focused here

FIGURE 1.2 | **Value creation iterates and adapts**

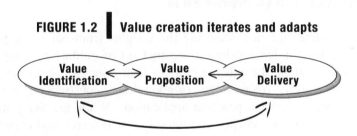

As Figure 1.1 indicates, most applications of lean principles and practices have focused on 'value delivery' at the program enterprise level. (In Chapters 8–10, we explore *all* parts of the grid.) Each phase of the value framework is iterative and dynamic (see Figure 1.2). The goal is to create value, and lean principles and practices are enablers throughout the value creation process.

Understanding the value-creation process begins at the program enterprise level. This involves seeing the *full* value stream, not just separate functions or 'chimneys' of activity. It also highlights the long forward shadow cast by value identification and value proposition efforts. Again, 'true north' for an enterprise at any level is not just a matter of serving the customer, but also of finding value for a wide range of other stakeholders.

The same three phases of value creation can be seen at the level of corporate or government organizations – our multi-program enterprises. Here we find a constant struggle around aligning the infrastructure to support multiple programs and preventing the suboptimization that could result from focusing on any single program. This is also where we see some of the tension between market forces and organizational structures.

As the analysis moves up to the national and international level, we see that identifying value and constructing value propositions is as much a tacit, invisible process as it is an explicit, visible negotiation. Here we find that institutional arrangements, public policies, strategic alliances, and numerous other mechanisms either support or undercut value creation.

Again, the challenge of creating lean enterprise value applies across the many diverse segments of aerospace as well as other industries and sectors. We cannot stress enough that the creation and delivery of value requires first identifying stakeholders and constructing robust 'value propositions'. For most sectors of the economy, this requirement points to new guiding principles and a fundamentally different infrastructure.

## Principles of Lean Enterprise Value

One great challenge in assembling the insights from our research is to codify the lessons learned into a succinct set of guiding principles that build on and extend the existing body of lean principles. Such principles have to meet all the rigorous tests of good theory construction, as well as equally rigorous tests of practical application.[4] While the five principles we present below are deeply grounded in our research and experience, these propositions have yet to be fully tested in aerospace or other sectors.

Before we get to the principles, though, let's return to the two words 'lean' and 'value'. Taken literally, each has an almost opposite connotation – 'lean' with its connotations of taking away, particularly with respect to eliminating waste; and 'value' as adding or creating, particularly around something beneficial. Our definition joins the concepts together in two ways. First, it is not enough simply to eliminate waste – again, there must be a focus on eliminating waste with the goal of creating value. Second, there is a virtuous cycle whereby effective elimination of waste can increase capability to identify and deliver value, while value creation brings additional needed resources and motivation to tackle ever deeper forms of waste. We join the two words together – 'lean value' – to refer to this broader conception of lean and this focused approach to value.

Our first principle is easy to state, but hard to do. It is a simple message to take lean implementation much further than it has typically gone.

---

### *Principle 1*

#### CREATE LEAN VALUE BY DOING THE JOB RIGHT
#### *AND* BY DOING THE RIGHT JOB

---

Doing both together – doing the job right *and* doing the right job – establishes a constructive, dynamic tension. Each enables the other. With that in mind, let's turn to the full value-creation framework.

---

### *Principle 2*

#### DELIVER VALUE ONLY AFTER IDENTIFYING STAKEHOLDER VALUE AND
#### CONSTRUCTING ROBUST VALUE PROPOSITIONS

---

There is a precedence order here – delivering value will be constrained by poorly structured value propositions, and enabled by robust, well-structured propositions. And of course, *robust* value propositions cannot be structured around poorly identified value.

Having identified this 'lean value' dynamic, let's now place it in context – which brings in the concept of 'enterprise'. Any attempt to foster the lean value dynamic below the enterprise level risks suboptimization; hence, our third principle.

## *Principle 3*
### FULLY REALIZE LEAN VALUE ONLY BY ADOPTING
### AN ENTERPRISE PERSPECTIVE

While one part of an operation, such as manufacturing or purchasing, may become lean, the overall net gain will be limited if lean is not integrated as part of an overall *enterprise* strategy. Note, though, that the meaning of 'enterprise' is not always clear. Leaders and others have to assert the *interdependence* of various stakeholders, and make clear that they are part of a *common enterprise*. This is a non-trivial aspect of operating at an enterprise level.

Our fourth principle builds on the concept of different levels of enterprise: program, multi-program, and national or international.

## *Principle 4*
### ADDRESS THE INTERDEPENDENCIES ACROSS ENTERPRISE
### LEVELS TO INCREASE LEAN VALUE

These interdependencies are dynamic – as program enterprises get the lean value dynamic going, they provide a better foundation for lean efforts at the multi-program level. Lean capability at the multi-program level can, in turn, be more responsive in providing the enabling infrastructure at the program level – again, a virtuous cycle. The same is true between the multi-program level and the national and international enterprise. The reverse is also true: deterioration at one level risks contagion at other levels.

Institutions can either accelerate or undercut these lean enterprise value dynamics, depending on the degree to which they are aligned or misaligned. Because institutions are often slow to change, the risk of misalignment is great. But institutional infrastructure can be an essential enabler, and can minimize dependence on charismatic leaders.

Finally, we offer a proposition on the underlying mechanism for sustaining lean enterprise value, which focuses on people's knowledge, capabilities, and new ways of thinking.

## *Principle 5*
### PEOPLE, NOT JUST PROCESSES, EFFECTUATE LEAN VALUE

Lean enterprise value is constrained when knowledge is withheld or when people are not appreciated for the knowledge that uniquely resides in their roles and experience. Achieving lean enterprise value begins with value identification, flows through agreements involving the value proposition, and extends through value delivery. It is knowledge and capability at all three enterprise levels that enable the elimination of waste in order to create value.

Organizations frequently state that 'people are our most valuable resource'. But when it comes to investment in capability, retention of human resources in a downturn, or even establishing basic principles of respect in the way that people are treated on the job, reality falls well short of such declarations. In the mass production model, the greatest value is placed on a small number of leaders and experts, often identified through forced competitions. Full application of this fifth principle would involve creating mechanisms to maximize the ability of all people in a defined enterprise to understand and help effectuate lean value.

Antoine de Saint-Éxupéry wrote more than half a century ago: 'As for the future, our task is not to foresee, but to enable it.'[5] Our view is that we create the future with our actions today. These five principles of lean enterprise value are meant to guide action, and will enable future success for the entire aerospace enterprise and for other industries in the 21st century.

Let's take a brief walk through some of the specifics of the aerospace context that illustrate why the framework of lean enterprise value is so critical. That context includes multiple sectors, a product mindset, challenging complexity, global dynamics, and workforce anxieties – characteristics that will be familiar to readers from any industry in today's economy.

## The Aerospace Challenge

The challenge in aerospace is enormous. This industry is among America's largest exporters in global markets. Significant numbers of the nation's scientists and engineers work in this industry – this *is* rocket science. During the 20th century, the aerospace industry played a central role in four core missions – valuable to the nation, and in many respects, the entire world:

- enabling the global movement of people and goods;

- enabling the global acquisition and dissemination of information and data;

- advancing national security interests; and

- providing a source of inspiration by pushing the boundaries of exploration and innovation.

Without exception, none of these will ever be routine; they will always stretch the capabilities of technologies, challenge the vision of engineers, and inspire society. But the principles that guided past success in each of these missions are not the same principles needed for the future. There is no guarantee that the firms currently leading this industry will drive future success or that the missions will even remain in the domain that we think of as 'aerospace'. Consider the full scale and scope of the challenge facing this industry – and so many others.

## Multiple Sectors

Enterprises in most industries often span multiple sectors – or at least must deal with dynamics across very different sectors. In the case of aerospace, achieving lean enterprise value requires attending to the similarities, differences, and interdependencies across the military and commercial sectors.

The military side of the industry is committed to ensuring global peace and security for today and tomorrow, but must deal with the half-century legacy of having defined itself in relation to the Cold War. After having always been driven to go higher, faster, and farther than a single defined enemy, how can this industry redefine itself to address a much more complex mix of threats, from asymmetric challenges mounted by contending nations, terrorists, and rogue nations to instabilities created by ethnic conflicts?

US Department of Defense efforts to procure new military aerospace systems to meet changing security needs and circumstances have been complicated not just by the decline in defense dollars. Other factors have included fits and starts in funding, acquisition practices, the industrial base, and programs, which together have created an environment of constant instability and have undercut the ability to 'do the job right'. The costs of instability are significant – wasted resources, displaced workers, the loss of skills, and even the risk of entire companies exiting the industry. Further complicating the challenge is the distribution of aerospace facilities across nearly the entire United States and in the home countries of nearly every customer – a distribution that reflects political pressures to share out the work associated with each military product.

The commercial side of this industry has set a global standard for the design, manufacture, and support of aircraft and spacecraft – enabling a global revolution in air travel, data collection, and telecommunications. But the US aerospace industry has found itself facing head-to-head competition from a combined set of European businesses and governments joined together under the Airbus umbrella, as well as emerging competitive pressure from parts of the former Soviet military complex, China, Japan, and other nations. This includes the rapid growth of regional jets in countries such as Canada and Brazil. Again, there are challenges both in doing the job right and in doing the right job, and these in turn raise issues of competition and cooperation in an increasingly interdependent worldwide aerospace industry.

Within the broad commercial and military sectors, segments of the industry are in different stages of maturity. While 'dominant designs'[6] have emerged for airframes and engines, there are dramatic breakthroughs occurring in materials technology, avionics, information technology and design methods. Further, aerospace products are increasingly integrated into larger mission-capable systems to ensure successful performance in fighting wars, space exploration, or air transportation, thereby blurring traditional boundaries and distinctions. Issues include integration with communications, surveillance, and other systems. All of these systems must work together if aerospace is to deliver value in terms of any of the overarching missions highlighted above. Moreover, critical, leading-edge information technology is now more likely to be imported from outside the industry than to derive from R&D within aerospace. This requires a change in mindset from that instilled in the education and training of most of the aerospace workforce.

## A Product Mindset

Many industries face the challenge of shifting from producing discrete products or services to offering complete customer 'solutions'. In aerospace, the producers of airframes, engines, and many satellites – where the 'dominant design' has been well established over many decades – face this challenge in particular. What these firms make are treated primarily as products, with a focus on a relatively narrow slice of their lifecycle value stream. It is how engineers think about their career paths. It is the way much of the military is organized – from acquisition through field sustainment. But this narrow focus is highly limiting, unsuited to the challenge of creating lean enterprise value.

Today's US Air Force – the customer for many defense aerospace products – faces a parallel challenge: to see itself not as a collection of pilots and platforms but as an *integrated network* of military capabilities. Today's F-16 pilots need to understand that they and their planes are the warfighting front end of a complex support system of information and other resources needed to carry out their military missions. Speed, precision, flexibility, timeliness, reliability, adaptability, efficiency, and interoperability within a framework of reduced lifecycle costs would be key characteristics of a successfully integrated system of capabilities. We're not quite there.

Shifting to thinking of multi-use platforms is a step in the right direction. It enables increased attention to interdependencies across an enterprise. The focus on fleet management and integrated reservation systems is also indicative of enterprise thinking, but more is needed. For example, in a recent book reflecting on his years of service,[7] US Army Gen. Wesley Clark (Ret.) points to the billions of dollars invested in an aircraft, without corresponding investment in planning cycles to ensure flexible, timely, and effective use of these resources. In other words, Gen. Clark is pointing to the challenge of shifting to a lifecycle management approach. Similarly, consider the infrastructure needed to support investments in sensor, planning, communications, and other information technologies – none of which is specific to any single platform. This really requires focusing the entire industry on fulfilling defined missions, not on narrow adherence to a specific way of flying the missions.

## The Challenge of Complexity

Industries that produce complex products, in complex organizational settings, and with substantial government regulatory control, can learn a great deal from aerospace.

Aerospace systems are complex *internally*, containing functional relationships and interactions that exhibit a challenging array of design features, technical specialties, materials, manufacturing processes, and assembly methods. The challenge here is not just the many elements, but the fact that they interact in ways that are not always straightforward. Plus, aerospace systems are typically quite complex *externally*, as they interface with a great number of other elements comprising larger systems, such as air traffic management or communications. This complexity is intensified by the fact that individual aerospace products are typically error-intolerant – they must function perfectly in extremely adverse and challenging operating environments where failure of a single part can spell catastrophe.

Product complexity is exacerbated by the fact that many aerospace systems have service lives extending for decades. For example, the grand-children of an original B-52 pilot might well be piloting today's B-52s, which feature whole new generations of technologies introduced since the basic platform's introduction decades earlier. This effective regeneration of aerospace products over time (by embodying new technologies) presents a transformational challenge, that is orders of magnitude greater than that for stable or newly developed products.

The sheer complexity of aerospace products and systems is mirrored by another key characteristic that is instructive for any industry – the complexity of organizational relationships among partners and suppliers, competitors, government agencies, and others within the industry. The aerospace industry draws upon a broad, deep, multilayered, and multi-faceted supplier base cutting across many industries. As much as 60–80 percent of the end-product value of aerospace products derives from this supplier base, drawing materials, parts, components, and subsystems for integration into the final product or system. Suppliers also participate in the design and development of new products. Firms are linked together as suppliers, customers, and even partners of each other. The same firms can be competitors in a different market segment or program. These extensive and deep relationships represent both a constraint to the industry's transformation – due to its complexity and interdependence – and a source of energy spurring new ideas and opportunities.

The aerospace industry operates within a complex sociopolitical, regulatory, and institutional environment. The relationships between the industry and government, and indeed the distinctly 'visible hand' role of government in the industry's fortunes (serving in important cases as its principal customer), further add to the complexity. The government, in fact, has played a significant role in the industry's evolution since its early beginnings – as regulator, customer, and enabler of a stream of technological innovations.[8] Over many decades, military–commercial 'spillover effects' – from the development of the jet engine to advances in electronics, computers, and materials technologies – have been the fountain-

**FIGURE 1.3** | **20 years of consolidation in aerospace**

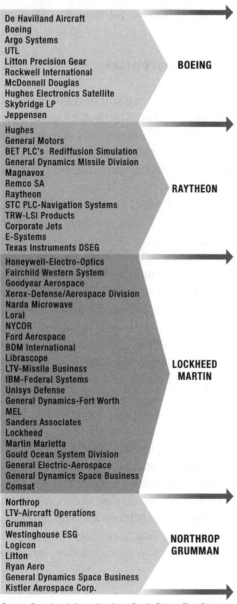

De Havilland Aircraft
Boeing
Argo Systems
UTL
Litton Precision Gear
Rockwell International
McDonnell Douglas
Hughes Electronics Satellite
Skybridge LP
Jeppensen

**BOEING**

Hughes
General Motors
BET PLC's Rediffusion Simulation
General Dynamics Missile Division
Magnavox
Remco SA
Raytheon
STC PLC-Navigation Systems
TRW-LSI Products
Corporate Jets
E-Systems
Texas Instruments DSEG

**RAYTHEON**

Honeywell-Electro-Optics
Fairchild Western System
Goodyear Aerospace
Xerox-Defense/Aerospace Division
Narda Microwave
Loral
NYCOR
Ford Aerospace
BDM International
Librascope
LTV-Missile Business
IBM-Federal Systems
Unisys Defense
General Dynamics-Fort Worth
MEL
Sanders Associates
Lockheed
Martin Marietta
Gould Ocean System Division
General Electric-Aerospace
General Dynamics Space Business
Comsat

**LOCKHEED MARTIN**

Northrop
LTV-Aircraft Operations
Grumman
Westinghouse ESG
Logicon
Litton
Ryan Aero
General Dynamics Space Business
Kistler Aerospace Corp.

**NORTHROP GRUMMAN**

*Source:* Based on information from Credit Suisse First Boston and Morgan Stanley.

head of innovation benefiting the commercial industrial base. However, as traditional aerospace technologies have matured, less R&D funding has been forthcoming. This reflects the diminishing returns to be realized – to the consternation of many aerospace enthusiasts.

## Increasing Impact of Financial Markets

Financial markets have always been important stakeholders, but their impact has grown in a variety of sectors. In the case of aerospace, industry leaders were shocked in the late 1990s to find that the combined valuation of the largest US aerospace companies was well below that of Microsoft. Wall Street rewards profit margins, predictability, and growth, none of which has been a characteristic of this industry.

In this context, the past few years have seen dramatic restructuring and merging of what were once powerful and distinct companies. Notable is the emergence of Boeing, Lockheed Martin, Northrop Grumman, and Raytheon as the major US aerospace companies. This industry concentration (see Figure 1.3) reflects attempts to address overcapacity in airframes, avionics, and related business areas. Similar concentration took place within European nations a generation earlier, and is now occurring at the regional level in Europe.

Beyond the mergers, acquisitions, and other structural changes in organizations, aerospace companies are changing their very business models. They see value not just in delivering products, but also in delivering services. Just as many automobile companies have found great business opportunities through their financing divisions, engine companies such as Pratt & Whitney and General Electric see higher profit margins associated with taking total lifecycle responsibility for their products. This goes well beyond building jet engines to include maintenance, upgrades, leases, recycling, and many other ways of providing value to customers. Concurrently, we see investments in new leading-edge information and communication technologies with the promise of higher returns through integration with traditional aerospace products. This includes everything from providing internet and satellite communications on airplanes to new configurations for cockpits.

## The 21st-Century Workforce

Today, this industry finds itself challenged to attract and retain the workforce it will need for the 21st century – as do many other economic

# FIGURE 1.4 | Declining opportunities in military aircraft programs

**Legend:**
- Vertical Bars: Military Aircraft Program Starts
- Horizontal Bars: 40-Year Career Span

Experience: 5 Programs
Experience: 3 Programs
Experience: 2.5 Programs
Experience: Less than 2 Programs
Experience: ? Programs

**X-axis (Start date of career):** 1950s, 1960s, 1970s, 1980s, 1990s, 2000s, 2010s, 2020s

**1950s**
XP5Y-1, A2D, XC-120, F4D, F3H, X-5, B-60, B-52, A3D, X-3, S2F, X-2, F10F, F2Y-1, F-100, B-57, F-102, R3Y-1, F-104, A4D, B-66, AO-1, F11F, C-130, F-101, T-37, XFY-1, F8U, P6M-1, U-2, XY-3, F-105, X-13, C-133, F-107, B-58, F-106, F5D, X-14, C-140, T-2, F-4, A-5, T-39, T-38, X-22, X-26B, C-5A, X24

**1960s**
A-6, E-2, SR-71, XV-4A, X-21, X-19, C-141, B-70, XC-142, F-111, A-7, OV-10, X-22, X-26B, C-5A, X24

**1970s**
F-14, S-3, YA-9, A-10, F-15, F-16, YF-17, B-1A, YC-15, YC-14, XV-15, AV-8B, F/A-18

**1980s**
F-117, F-20, X-29, T-46, T-45, B-2, V-22

**1990s**
YF-22, YF-23, X-31, C-17, F-22, X-32, X-35

**2000s**
JSF, X-45A, GLOBAL HAWK

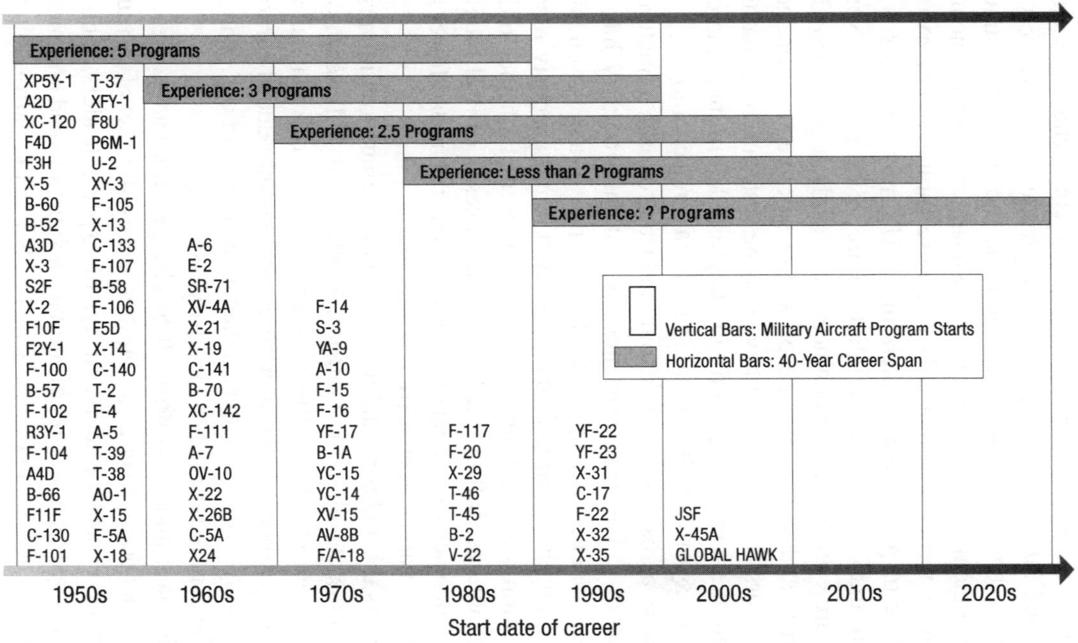

*Source:* Jeffrey A. Drezner, Giles K. Smith, Lucille E. Horgan, Curt Rogers, and Rachel Schmidt, 'Maintaining Future Military Aircraft Design Capability', RAND #R-4100 (Santa Monica, CA: RAND, 1992), pp. 48–9. Note that 'experience' relates to average design team experience.

sectors. In a recent survey, nearly five hundred US aerospace engineers, managers, production workers, and technical specialists were asked about this statement: 'I would highly recommend that my children work in this industry.' Only 17 percent of the engineers agreed or strongly agreed. The numbers were similar for the other groups; and overall, four out of five people in the aerospace industry would *not* recommend it to their children. In individual interviews, people said that while they were very proud of the industry and their own contributions, the instability, among other factors, led them to what for them was a heart-wrenching conclusion.[9]

In human terms, aerospace is a mature industry. For example, the average age of production workers in the US military sector is 53 years, with more than 20 percent eligible to retire in the next five years.[10] The numbers are even higher for engineers; one study suggests that 33 percent of scientists and technicians are or will be eligible for retirement in the next few years.[11] Not only will key skills be lost, but the remaining work-force is unlikely to have the mix of skills needed to meet the challenges ahead. This is particularly critical in information technology.

Of course, aerospace is not the only industry to reach a 'mature' stage of development.[12] The real issue here is that this industry has always – correctly – seen new aerospace products as part of a never-ending frontier of new possibilities. Aircraft and spacecraft simultaneously represent the transportation and communications backbone of both the 'old' and the 'new' economies. Sitting on this divide poses a central challenge. As Figure 1.4 indicates, each generation of engineers has had fewer and fewer chances to be part of new airframe programs.

So long as this industry and its customers continue to think primarily in terms of discrete airframe/platform products, it will seem as though possibilities are shrinking. But a different view – one that takes respon-sibility for *all* aspects of the four core missions introduced earlier – opens up a vast array of possibilities, linkages, and interactions. The challenge goes to the core mindset of the industry's workforce.

Why is that mindset so difficult to change? It's hard to see, let alone embrace, what doesn't yet exist. Further, the existing set of institutions and infrastructure creates blinders. Arrays of experts, leaders, lobbyists, and staff are focused on a process of military acquisition and commercial sales rooted in outdated assumptions. This has led to the narrow interpretation of 'lean' centered on reducing waste and cutting costs within current oper-ations. Labor unions representing many of the professional, technical, and production workers are caught in their traditional contentious battles with employers while simultaneously working to develop high-performance work organizations. Given the many points of tension, it becomes clear that strong labor–management partnerships and high levels of employee commitment depend on a 'true north' orientation towards creating value.

## Global Dynamics

Aerospace has become a global industry. There is international competition in every product line, as well as increased collaboration to develop new technologies and unlock new markets. Some product lines also feature excess capacity. For strategic reasons, the United States can ill afford to exit any of these lines of business. At the same time, success in these new domains is increasingly a point of national pride for other countries – whether it is Europe merging three of the Airbus national companies into a single shared organizational headquarters, Japan developing its own launch vehicle, Brazil building regional jets, China establishing expertise in aircraft subassemblies, Russia commercializing the space station, Turkey building F-16s, or any of numerous nations negotiating offset agreements to have a share of the parts production for planes they are buying. What is at stake here is the ability of every nation to establish a foothold or even a strong presence in the aerospace industry.

Beyond increased global competition, the aerospace industry over the past several decades has seen a rise in collaboration among firms, both domestically and internationally, in order to compete more effectively. These collaborative arrangements have taken a variety of forms, encompassing joint ventures and other types of closely knit interfirm relationships involving substantial contributions by partners of capital, technology, or other assets.

## Current Successes and Future Prospects

While clearly there is cause for concern in this industry, there are also rays of hope and innovation. This industry has pioneered satellite communications (including television and internet access directly to homes via satellite), placed a successful robotic vehicle on Mars, developed the safest and fastest form of transportation (while dramatically decreasing jet aircraft community noise), and delivered to the warfighter the most advanced stealth aircraft. Properly structured, with its missions and technology focused on future challenges, the aerospace industry has the ingredients to attract the best of the 21st-century workforce.

Beyond the technical achievements, this is an industry that includes many winners of the Malcolm Baldrige National Quality Award.[13] It is an industry with a number of customer-focused 'lean' factories. It is an industry that is pioneering new ways to think about product development – especially for the most complex and demanding products. It is an industry with labor–management partnerships centered on driving high-performance work systems and strategic alliances with suppliers to drive down costs and innovate for the future.

The many challenges in aerospace have forced people to look beyond just manufacturing or the supply network. They have driven a focus on adding value across the enterprise – taking into account the perceptions of value held not just by customers, but also by shareholders, employees, suppliers, communities, Congress, and other key stakeholders. From this enterprise perspective, we see time as a critical variable, crucial to a number of interdependent cycles. These include planning cycles, acquisition cycles, logistics cycles, development cycles, production cycles, sustainment cycles, and others – all of which require more than simple cycle-time improvement. The focus is not exclusively on speeding up existing operations or processes, but toward establishing entirely new capabilities – doing the job right and doing the right job. Simply put, creating future value depends on building today's lean enterprise capabilities.

## Moving Forward

This is a book about fundamentally changing an industry. Our example, aerospace, is an industry that is technically complex and committed to filling missions that will never be routine. Human safety, national security, and technological strength are at stake. Other industries share these characteristics. The principles of lean enterprise value we offer are not only for aerospace, but for others facing comparable challenges.

The complexity and the compelling forces within the aerospace industry have driven a broadening of the definition of 'lean'. The focus has been elevated to the enterprise level, with the aim of creating value – not just eliminating waste. We offer our own insights with a simple, but ambitious, objective. We believe that ideas combined with action can transform an entire industry. Aerospace and other sectors of the economy have embarked on this journey. We hope to accelerate the transformation wherever new ways are needed to create lean enterprise value.

## CHAPTER 2

# The Cold War Legacy

From its modest beginnings at Kitty Hawk – and even earlier, in da Vinci's sketches – the urge to defy gravity inspired what has since become the aerospace field. And from that moment when we were able to fly, humans have sought to go higher, faster, and farther. This quest was never more manifest than during the decades after World War II, as US national defense and prestige, along with increasing demands for transporting people and goods, drove tremendous growth in the US Aerospace Enterprise – that national community of aerospace firms, US government executive agencies and departments, Congressional committees, professional organizations, universities, and labor unions.

Almost every industrial sector comes of age with a period of rapid growth that establishes organizational cultures and value expectations of the stakeholders. For aerospace, that period was the Cold War. Aerospace has industrial features unique to its military legacy; other industrial sectors – particularly those with strong links to government or that face large market contractions – have similar characteristics. Appreciating the Cold War legacy will help us understand the aerospace response since the 1990s and how lean enterprise value principles apply to other industries.

The Cold War period stretches almost half a century, from shortly after the end of World War II to the dissolution of the Soviet Union. The list of accomplishments in those years is truly astounding. We learned to travel anywhere in the world in a single day, not to mention beyond Earth's atmosphere and into space. We created and deployed military aircraft and spy satellites with amazing capabilities. We developed instantaneous global communications that brought world events into living rooms and boardrooms, which most of us today take for granted.

World War II transformed the United States into a 'superpower', willing and able to take on global military and political challenges. After every previous US war, military infrastructure was drastically cut back. After World War II, though, the reductions were only temporary. What had been a 'hot war' with the Axis powers in Europe and the Pacific quickly gave way to a 'cold war' with the Soviet Union and Communism. To compete in this Cold War, and the conflicts that stemmed from it, required military prowess.

A partnership had been forged between the US government and the US aerospace industry to help win World War II, and now it took on the defense of the 'Free World'. The US Aerospace Enterprise was at the heart of that effort, efficiently creating and building high-tech aerospace systems designed to outperform any in the world. We routinely flew faster than sound – and we went to the moon.

The close-knit alignment of government, industry, and public priorities began to deteriorate in the late 1960s and 1970s. From the Vietnam War forward, the government put in place complex processes to centralize management of expanded defense budgets and large bureaucracies to oversee the aerospace industry. The industry's response was to create large, conservative, risk-averse complexes of engineers and administrators. The spirit of public–private aerospace partnerships built on trust was eventually lost and with it, quick, nimble, and efficient national responses to aerospace challenges. As one consequence, the US Aerospace Enterprise – steeped as it was in a 'Higher, Faster, Farther' culture – was slow to recognize the importance of affordability as an imperative for long-term industrial survival.

These inflexibilities were masked by the Cold War consensus on spending a third of a trillion dollars annually on defense – which bought, among other things, a high-technology aerospace force that was key to the 1991 ejection of Iraq from Kuwait in the most efficient war in US military history. We may not have liked the bureaucratic price of the US Cold War machine, but it delivered as promised when called.

Despite that Gulf War vindication, the US public shifted its priorities away from defense following the dissolution of the Soviet Union in the early 1990s. The precipitous collapse of the market for military equipment to half its Cold War high revealed huge government and corporate bureaucracies, complex regulations, and risk-averse cultures. Though essential to managing the Cold War military effort, those administrative relics hobbled the search for a new and vital equilibrium of relationships among the public and private components of the US Aerospace Enterprise.

To use effectively the concepts put forward in later parts of this book, we need to analyze the post-World War II events leading up to this aerospace crisis. There are many industries that must transform themselves in response to dramatic shifts in external market realities. An appreciation of the antecedents of the aerospace challenge will provide readers with the background needed to interpret the solutions we offer in the context of specific industrial circumstances. To that end, this and the next chapter examine the history surrounding the deterioration of the close government–industry aerospace partnership following World War II and the rise of government and industrial institutions that hamper the aerospace community's adjustment to post-Cold War market realities. Alongside that exposition is an appreciation of the special challenges to industrial change in technologically more mature markets, such as those for commercial aircraft and satellites. Those insights will help us to understand and apply principles of *lean enterprise value* in sustaining the US Aerospace Enterprise promise – to fulfill, efficiently and effectively, the four core missions introduced in Chapter 1.

## 1945–69: A Bullish Quarter-Century

### The Postwar Boom

World War II had an enormous impact on the US economy, with every citizen either directly involved or affected. At its peak, the massive war mobilization absorbed 38 percent of US gross domestic product, far exceeding the investment in any subsequent conflict (the Korean War peaked at 14 percent and Vietnam at 9 percent), but dropped quickly after final victory in the Pacific.[1] The aircraft industry produced fighters, bombers, and reconnaissance aircraft in numbers far greater than those of today (Figure 2.1). Those airplanes were essential to victory, capturing the public imagination with their clearly crucial role over the battlefield at the

FIGURE 2.1 | US military aircraft production

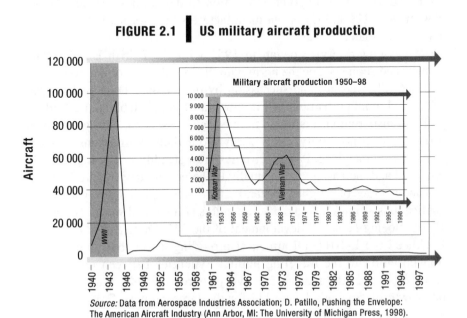

Source: Data from Aerospace Industries Association; D. Patillo, Pushing the Envelope: The American Aircraft Industry (Ann Arbor, MI: The University of Michigan Press, 1998).

Battle of the Bulge and in the skies over Asia, where they took the war to what was then the enemy heartland.

After years of Depression-era deprivation and wartime rationing and sacrifice, the United States enjoyed a booming post-World War II economy. With much of the world's industrial capacity in ruins, undamaged US factories thrived. Aerospace flourished, with the development of jet engines that enabled a new generation of civil transport and supersonic flight, and rockets that eventually propelled payloads to space and missiles to targets. In the general aviation industry, annual production of business aircraft and light personal planes eventually came to exceed ten thousand units, sustained in part by hundreds of thousands of World War II veterans and aspiring new pilots. Helicopters were developed to serve both military and commercial markets. And the whole new field of aviation electronics or 'avionics' for guidance, navigation, and flight and fire control engaged electrical engineers in large numbers. These developments led to a healthy increase in the number of aerospace companies.

Civil air transportation developed rapidly in the 1950s. The emerging commercial market quickly exploited airframe, jet engine, and avionics technologies developed with military funding. With airline competition limited by regulation, there was less focus on production efficiency and greater attention on introducing new aircraft to expand markets and win customers. The relationship between major airlines and aircraft manufacturers led to regular, ongoing interaction to define, develop, and launch new models. US and European manufacturers vied for market dominance and market share.

Jet passenger service began in 1952 with the British De Havilland Comet[2] and soon became the norm with the introduction of the Boeing 707 in 1958, followed in rapid succession by the Douglas DC-8 and Convair 880. Civil aviation had entered a new era of comfortable and affordable global transportation. Families, friends, businesspeople, and government officials were now only a day away from their destinations – nearly anywhere on the globe. Passenger-miles grew steadily, continuing virtually unabated and increasing exponentially to the present day (Figure 2.2).

The priorities of 'Higher, Faster, Farther' – forged in military aerospace applications – quickly found a home in this commercial world. By the late 1960s, Boeing launched development of the 747, Douglas its DC-10, and Lockheed the L-1011, all aimed at providing affordable long-distance transportation to the traveling public. Synergies between military and commercial development were everywhere: the 747 project was an outgrowth of Boeing's losing bid for the large military C-5 cargo plane won by Lockheed, and the Lockheed L-1011's fly-by-wire flight control grew out of technology developed for the military. National prestige also pushed aerospace and, by the end of the 1960s, the US aircraft manufacturers dominated the rapidly growing world market.

The lull in military spending after World War II was short-lived, and within a few years the large expenditures that were to mark the Cold War era began (Figure 2.3). Throughout the remainder of the Cold War – and

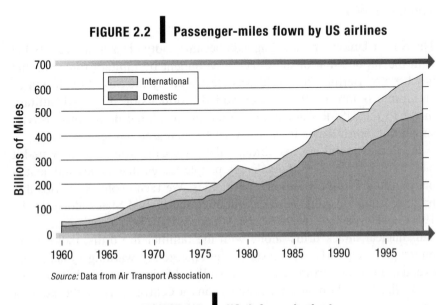

**FIGURE 2.2** | **Passenger-miles flown by US airlines**

*Source:* Data from Air Transport Association.

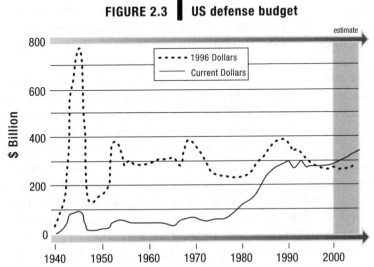

**FIGURE 2.3** | **US defense budget**

*Source:* Executive Office of the President of the United States, 'Budget of the United States Government, Fiscal Year 2001'.

even to this day – defense expenditures averaged nearly $300 billion, with peaks and valleys reflecting the changing national priorities we discuss in this chapter.[3] (Note that throughout this chapter we cite expenditures in the text in constant 1996 dollars, while figures present both constant 1996 and contextual current year dollars.)

## The Cold War

The Soviet Union's political agenda became sadly clear in the late 1940s with the suppression of the Czech government by military force and the blockade of Berlin. The world was electrified by the Soviet explosion of an atomic bomb in 1949, which added a dimension of global military threat to the USSR's apparent aspirations to global dominance. Soviet support of North Korea in the early 1950s increased our fears.

Readers who did not live through the early Cold War years may find it hard to comprehend just how deeply people feared that, at any moment, a nuclear attack might wipe out entire cities. We recall some scenarios that projected tens of millions of casualties in the United States alone. In the 1950s and even into the early 1960s people built bomb shelters, schools had 'nuclear attack drills' along with the familiar fire drills, radios were interrupted regularly with tests of the emergency warning system, and evacuation routes from cities were well publicized. These daily events made the Cold War and its implications a central part of the popular consciousness, shaping the priorities of individuals and reflecting society's priorities – leading elements of which were national defense against the Soviet Union and competition with the Soviets in arenas from the Olympiad to space.

On the military side, waves of new aircraft, for myriad missions and applications, followed one after another. Developed in less than a year, the North American F-86 SabreJet was one of the US jet aircraft used in the Korean conflict, along with the Grumman F9F Panther. At the same time, the Boeing B-47 multi-jet bomber was developed 'under forced draft' – that is, as quickly as possible – to carry atomic weapons. And there were more radical ventures, including the Convair/General Dynamics B-58 Hustler – the fastest airplane of its day carrying nuclear bombs. Time was of the essence; risks were understood as wartime risks. Defense budgets dominated federal outlays, and it was all strongly supported by the public.

In another aerospace domain, with intelligence agencies by the mid-1950s warning of a 'missile gap', there arose a national perception that the Soviets had amassed a superior nuclear missile force. The United States

### Spies in the Sky: The U-2

The Soviet nuclear and long-range ballistic missile threat in the early 1950s made it imperative to acquire intelligence data from behind the Iron Curtain. But the United States had no way of photographing sites, missile quantities, or deployment.

President Eisenhower, acting on the advice of a scientific task force led by James Killian of MIT and Edward Land of Polaroid, commissioned Kelly Johnson and the famous Lockheed Skunk Works to develop a long-range aircraft that could be the platform for high-powered cameras. It had to fly high enough to be invulnerable to Soviet interceptors and anti-aircraft missiles.

The Skunk Works (described in more detail later in this chapter) had successfully developed the P-80 Starfighter and the internationally used F-104 – in record time. The group, which operated under tight security with minimal constraints and oversight, was able to build – with only 23 design engineers – the first U-2 reconnaissance aircraft in just eight months. In 1956, it was operational – a mere ten months later.[4]

The U-2 was both a technological achievement and an acquisition gem. As Ben Rich wrote: '[A]t the end of the line we were actually able to refund about 15 percent of the total U-2 production cost back to the CIA ... because both the Skunk Works and the U-2 had functioned so beautifully. This was probably the only instance of a cost underrun in the history of the military–industrial complex.'[5]

The U-2 achieved mission-effectiveness for nearly four years before Francis Gary Powers' aircraft was downed on May 1st, 1960, by an indirect missile hit. The aircraft is operational today for military and civil missions – nearly a half-century after entering service!

responded by developing the Atlas and Minuteman Intercontinental Ballistic Missiles (ICBMs), as well as the U-2 and SR-71 spy planes and the Corona spy satellite to obtain more accurate intelligence data.

## Spies in Space: The Corona Satellite Program

Even before the downing of Francis Gary Powers, US military leaders considered Soviet missiles a potential threat to the U-2. They needed an alternative for photographic reconnaissance of Soviet ICBM sites.

In 1956, a Rand Corporation study urged development of a space satellite platform. Development began in February 1958, with the endorsement of President Eisenhower, as a dual classification project – that is, an unclassified research spacecraft program, Discoverer, and the top-secret recoverable film portion called Corona. After the U-2 incident, these efforts were accelerated.

Under the direction of the super-secret National Reconnaissance Office (NRO), Lockheed was given responsibility for developing the satellite and integrating a system comprising an Itek Corporation camera and a General Electric recovery capsule, developed from GE's re-entry vehicle designs. The system was to be launched on a Douglas Thor IRBM programmed for attaining low-altitude orbit, with the aid of the rocket motor originally designed as an augmenting propulsion for the B-58 – and which became the propulsion for the Agena satellite vehicle.

The project was difficult. It consumed 13 vehicles before one made orbit, performed a day's worth of picture taking, and returned the film safely to earth. That mission was followed by increasingly successful operations. By 1964, reliability was at 90 percent, thanks to major improvements made once some rigorous systems engineering practices were put in place. Corona became the most significant gatherer of worldwide optical reconnaissance information for the decade of the 1960s.

Aerospace capability during this era was intricately intertwined with national and global politics. The downing of U-2 pilot Francis Gary Powers on May 1st, 1960, led to a collapse of talks between Soviet Premier Khrushchev and President Eisenhower. And accountability for the 'missile gap' became part of John F. Kennedy's strategy against the Eisenhower administration in the 1960 presidential campaign.

These strategic missile and reconnaissance programs, shrouded in secrecy, enjoyed high-level political support and required significant technological breakthroughs. More important for this story, they showed the efficiencies and effectiveness that derived from close government–industry partnerships functioning as small teams that enjoyed substantial trust under minimal oversight. Waste, in the form of normal government and corporate red tape, was minimized. And developers were able to take prudent risks without threats of program cancellation from infrequent but inevitable failures.

Similar practices were effective in other, less secret organizations. The early postwar period was marked by an extremely competitive, almost frenetic pace, driving companies to accelerate time to first flight, aided and abetted by their customers. Organizations were 'lean', staffed by highly motivated people who thrived in small, multi-functional teams. There was a close working relationship between customers (government and civil) and suppliers (of aircraft and spacecraft). Specifications and regulations – both military and from the Civilian Aeronautics Board and the Civil Aeronautics Administration[6] – existed only at modest levels; later, they became restrictive and costly. The maxim was getting there first, with the best and the most.

## Skunk Works

Perhaps no organization better exemplified such infrastructure capability in the early Cold War years than Lockheed's 'Skunk Works', under the leadership of Clarence 'Kelly' Johnson. Lockheed's Skunk Works was organizationally hidden and separate from the main Lockheed divisions to protect it from the growing oversight and bureaucracy of the broader aerospace enterprise. This highly talented organization, run with what came to be known as 'Kelly's Rules', created military aircraft in record times at remarkably low costs. In many ways, Kelly's Rules align with today's lean enterprise practices (introduced in Chapter 6), suggesting a 'back to the future' quest for the current aerospace industry.

The essential practices of the Skunk Works seemed to be especially effective for programs with high levels of secrecy. The Corona development, for example, owed its success to the recognition by government customers that this new technology required a willingness to accept risks and sustain funding. The customer team organization also was patterned after the Skunk Works, which had produced the U-2 in utter secrecy. A very small government program office spent considerable time partnering with the contractors. And the contractors kept their teams small and highly

### Selected 'Kelly's Rules' for Lockheed Skunk Works[7]

- Strong but small project offices must be provided both by the customer and the contractor.

- A very simple drawing and drawing release system with great flexibility for making changes must be provided.

- There must be a minimum of reports required, but important work must be recorded thoroughly.

- The contractor must be delegated and must assume more than normal responsibility to get good vendor bids for subcontract on the project. Commercial bid procedures are very often better than military ones.

- Push basic inspection responsibility back to the subcontractors and vendors. Don't duplicate so much inspection.

- Funding a program must be timely so that the contractor doesn't have to keep running to the bank to support government projects.

- There must be absolute trust between the military product organization and the contractor with very close cooperation and liaison on a day-to-day basis. This cuts down misunderstanding and correspondence to an absolute minimum.

- Because only a few people will be used in engineering and most other areas, ways must be provided to reward good performance by pay not based on the number of personnel supervised.

integrated, benefiting from the security that was maintained for all but the basic Discoverer satellite. The response to needed changes was virtually 'on the spot'. Engineering, manufacturing, and procurement were housed together for all classified activities. There were competent management teams with extremely high expectations, motivation and morale.

Other than at the Skunk Works, though, this streamlined environment could only be sustained for a time. As we shall see, the numerous defense system programs initiated in the early Cold War years strained the DoD's management ability to prioritize expenditures and coordinate the interaction of various systems to achieve a harmonized military capability across the armed services. Many government–industrial organizations built around the concept of the Skunk Works ultimately could not resist the creeping penetration of government and corporate oversight by bureaucracies introduced to oversee large Cold War budgets and programs.

## The Sputnik Challenge

The launch of the Russian Sputnik satellite on October 4th, 1957, was perhaps the most important aerospace event of this period. Although small and of no direct military value, Sputnik catalyzed a national aerospace response to intensified fears of Soviet technological dominance. Within months, the US 'space mobilization' was underway. The Space Act of 1958 created NASA. Work on the DoD rocket and satellite programs accelerated, and the DoD established its Defense Advanced Research Projects Agency. New science and engineering curricula were introduced throughout the country's educational system, from universities down through secondary and elementary schools. And we saw the emergence of the Apollo program, perhaps the greatest technological achievement of the 20th century.

That humans might actually set foot on the moon seemed beyond reach in 1960. Yet, before the decade's end, 'rocket scientists' delivered civilization an incredible achievement, one so impressive that it became a common point of reference regarding society's ills: 'If we can put a man on the moon, why can't we solve [fill in the blank]?' Apollo attracted the best and brightest talent, as well as worldwide attention. Among its many 'firsts' was the use of live, worldwide satellite TV coverage of a major event – a sharp contrast to Soviet secrecy.

Yet, for all the good Apollo accomplished, there were negative side effects for the industry and society. It spawned engineering and flight heroes, but the program created a large bureaucracy and infrastructure. And as these grew, so too did the expectations of the many people who chose aerospace as a profession. New projects were exciting only if they matched or exceeded the Apollo challenge. Meanwhile, societal priorities changed during the nearly ten years of the Apollo mission. In the early 1960s, Americans came to see the US educational system as deficient in both size and rigor. There was a desperate shortage of engineers and scientists. But by 1970, a backlash developed – and thousands of those once desperately desired engineers and scientists were left unemployed. All this

## The NASA Budget: What Goes Up Must Come Down

Aerospace was truly in its heyday during the Apollo program. But could this momentum be sustained?

The NASA budget rose rapidly (Figure 2.4), reaching $5.93 billion – some 4.4 percent of the federal budget. By 1965, the 17 000 NASA employees of 1961 had nearly doubled to just over 33 000, and in all some 410 000 people throughout the country were working on NASA projects.[8] A national infrastructure emerged, radiating from centers in Texas, Alabama, Florida, and California, and supporting manned and unmanned missions, including probes to Mars – the forerunner of unmanned scientific missions to explore the universe. Apollo created a perception in the public and the Congress that it was the entire space program, drawing resources away from unmanned space exploration.

Following the peak expenditures of the Apollo program, the NASA budget declined by more than 60 percent. The early 1970s saw NASA's budget slashed by two-thirds, down to $10 billion and representing 1 percent or less of the federal budget – the level at which it remains today.

**FIGURE 2.4** ▎ **NASA budget as a percentage of the total US government budget**

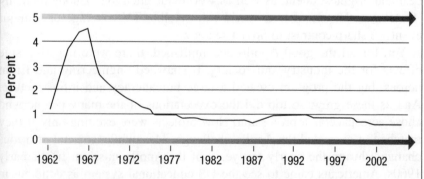

*Source:* Executive Office of the President of the United States, 'Budget of the United States Government, Fiscal Year 2001'.

contributed to a pattern of stifling institutionalization where once there had been innovation.

The Sputnik launch also opened the possibility of space-based systems for acquiring and transmitting data for communications, weather observation, and various other monitoring functions. By the end of the 1960s, such systems included both military and civil communication satellites, the first worldwide weather satellite systems (TIROS), as well as the initial Earth Resource Technology Satellite (ERTS). Commercial communications via space were recognized as a vital way to augment landlines, which led to a development program co-funded by the government with matching private investment from the formation of the Comsat Corporation.[9] In addition, the DoD established a series of reconnaissance spacecraft that provided imaging and electronic intelligence along with early warning of ballistic missile launches through infrared sensors aboard Defense Support Program vehicles. By 1969 – a mere dozen years after Sputnik – 635 satellites had been launched into low Earth orbit, and failed launches, frequent in the first 10 years, were infrequent. Another 42 successful launches into deep space to escape Earth's gravity had been made, though with 14 failures.

## Successes Foreshadow Future Crises

All told, it was a bullish quarter-century for aerospace – an era of mutually supportive priorities among government, industry, technology workers, and the American citizenry. The public priorities of national defense and prestige supported technology advances. Political events shaped responses, and institutions were created or shaped to meet needs. Patriotic, talented individuals were attracted to both national defense and civil applications. The total number of major US aerospace companies grew from 18 to 23 in the late 1950s, before consolidation in the 1960s dropped the number to 16.

With fresh memories of World War II, and with Cold War fears, society was willing to accept risk, understanding that failures were an inevitable step towards eventual success. Experimental aircraft were lost, but progress towards working systems accelerated even as brave test pilots gave their lives. Under those conditions, close working partnerships between government and industry teams – insulated from institutionalized waste and oversight – were able to execute aerospace projects at remarkable levels of efficiency and effectiveness.

Industry was not the only beneficiary of government Cold War spending. Funding flowed into university laboratories, which were considered essential partners in generating the requisite technology and intellectual capital to meet the nation's needs. New enterprises, new teams, and new knowledge – focused primarily on creating new products that could fly higher, faster, and farther – were rapidly shaping the entire US Aerospace Enterprise. This yielded a pioneering spirit that still has a profound effect on US aerospace culture.

The military–industrial complex spawned by the Cold War enabled the US Aerospace Enterprise to reach its heights. But at the same time, it began to undermine those practices that allowed us to do so much so well, and left a straitjacket on our ability to adjust quickly to changing international and national conditions, consequences that begin to emerge clearly only after the end of the Cold War era.

## 1970–89: Shifting National Priorities

### The Cold War (Part 2)

The big story of the latter half of the Cold War era was the rollercoaster in US military spending for new equipment, the bread and butter of the military aerospace industry. After a Vietnam War peak of more than $100 billion in 1969, the DoD's annual procurement budget plunged to $40 billion in the mid-1970s as the federal government lost public confidence in its handling of military matters following the debacle in Southeast Asia (Figure 2.5). After beginning to increase each year under President Carter, funding levels for acquiring weapon systems shot back up to $100 billion during the 'Reagan buildup' of the late 1980s, motivated by public concerns over the continued faceoff between NATO and the Warsaw Pact across the plains and forests of central Germany and the enduring strategic threats of Soviet nuclear weapons.

Continuing the trend established early in the Cold War, the DoD emphasized performance over cost in new equipment regardless of budget levels, citing the global life-and-death struggle with the Soviet Union. Growth in the complexity of military systems and aerospace organizations continued apace in the 1970s and 1980s as warfare became more complex and demanded technologically more sophisticated weapon systems, such as stealth aircraft and smart munitions. Development times and costs grew with product and institutional complexity. Cost overruns were solved by stretching schedules to postpone outlays. The time to develop major defense weapon systems increased by 80 percent during the latter half of the Cold War[10] (Figure 2.6). Consequent cost increases

## FIGURE 2.5 | DoD procurement budget

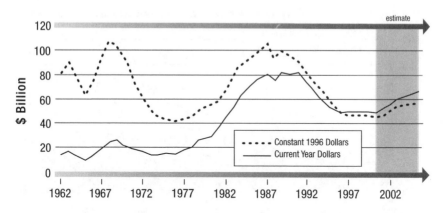

*Source:* Data from White House Office of Management and Budget (2000).

## FIGURE 2.6 | Development times for major US defense systems

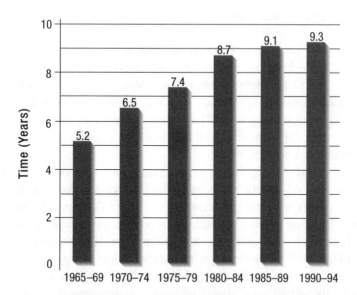

*Source:* Data from RAND SAR database. J.M. Jarvaise, J.A. Drezner, and D. Norton, 'The Defense System Cost Performance Database: Cost Growth Analysis Using Selected Acquisition Reports' (Santa Monica, CA.: The RAND Corporation, 1996), MR-625-OSD. Data (current as of December 1994) averaged over all major defense acquisition programs with available data. Note that 1970–74 may not contain some long-running program data that were not included in the SAR database, as they predated the SAR reporting requirements.

**FIGURE 2.7** | **US civil transport aircraft deliveries**

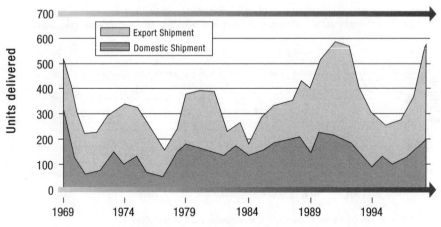

*Source:* Data from Aerospace Industries Association of America.

and related budget issues encouraged more government oversight, which reduced industry flexibility.

As the country progressed through the 1980s, defense components of the US Aerospace Enterprise regained public confidence and funding. While the valley of the defense budget revealed extraordinary administrative burdens from managing the Cold War military-aerospace efforts, the Reagan buildup starting in 1980 avoided the necessity for reform. But with that blessing came the curse of inflexible dependence on substantial federal spending, as we'll see later.

The commercial aircraft business rode its own rollercoaster through recessions in the early 1970s and mid-1980s (Figure 2.7). Without its pre-Vietnam era agility and with no technologies able to command recapitalization of airline fleets as the technology of jet transports compelled them to scrap their fleets, the commercial airplane business was badly hurt. Some companies left the business; survivors were left reeling.

In the civil aircraft market, the old priorities of speed and altitude became less important, and issues of cost, environmental impact, and consumer protection came to the fore. For civil space exploration, the nation opted for a budget-limited program over execution of a visionary Apollo-type plan as taxpayer priorities diverted public funding to other national issues.

We begin this section with the impact of the Vietnam War and end with the collapse of Communism and the victory in the Gulf War. Our aim is to show how US public priorities shaped the trajectory of the US Aerospace Enterprise and brought it to the end of the Cold War poorly prepared to cope.

## The Budget Valley after Vietnam

Just as World War II had transformed US society, so too did the Vietnam War of the late 1960s and early 1970s. The war grew out of concern for the spread of Communism in Southeast Asia – the so-called 'Domino Effect' – but strongly divided the country. Many questioned the legitimacy of the United States even waging a war against an enemy that did not directly threaten its own national security.

At the peak of the war in Vietnam, the defense budget was close to half that of the peak in World War II (Figure 2.3). Air power was prominent, with massive B-52 bombing, huge air interdiction campaigns conducted by Navy and Air Force fighter and attack aircraft, and Army Huey helicopters deployed for attack and rescue missions. This was the first 'televised war', and it was all broadcast 'live from the front' thanks to newly developed communication satellites. The public was brutally aware of daily events, and many who opposed the war saw the high-tech, high-performance aerospace weapons systems of the day as part of a needless conflict.

Tensions 'in country' and back home rose as troops fought and died with no victory in sight. On January 27th, 1973, the United States signed an accord ending the fruitless conflict. The final evacuation of American personnel in Saigon by helicopter from the US embassy roof on April 30th, 1975, was captured in pictures that live in history.

The United States had already been rocked by a decade of social upheaval when Saigon fell. National budgetary priorities had been called into question. US citizens from all walks of life reexamined personal and national goals and questioned institutions that had been established during the Cold War.

The new public priorities that emerged had a significant impact on the US Aerospace Enterprise and the expected value of its products and systems. The Cold War and the ever-present Soviet threat notwithstanding, a growing number of Americans no longer shared the national defense priorities of the military–industrial 'establishment'. Citizens saw little or no value in spending tax dollars on expensive military aircraft and spacecraft, and supported sharp reductions in defense spending. The political response was to take a third out of the defense budget in the 1970s.

Public impatience was not limited to actual dollars spent. In 1969, the Senate passed the so-called 'Mansfield Amendment', which forbade military funding for any research that did not have a 'direct or apparent relationship to a specific military function or operations'.[11] One among several results was a 40 percent drop in total funding for aerospace R&D by 1974. Defense-related work was curtailed or separated from universities. The number of students studying for aerospace engineering degrees dropped substantially from 1970 to 1975, creating a 'missing generation' that is felt today and will be for another twenty years.

## The Lost Opportunity to Get Lean

When President Kennedy took office in 1961, he appointed Robert McNamara, former CEO of Ford Motor Company, as Secretary of Defense. McNamara brought a cadre of 'whiz kids' to Washington, including Charles J. Hitch, who introduced new business practices for managing the development and coordination of the annual DoD budget called the Planning, Programming and Budgeting System (PPBS).[12] This included a disciplined, phased approach to developing and funding new programs aimed at unifying planning, programming, and decisionmaking across the military services and making it possible to do specific multi-year planning around alternative programs, rather than less specific planning around general functional areas such as manpower and material.

PPBS, while certainly effective in providing the armed services and DoD secretariat staffs with more precise options and better program information than ever before, was not without long-term costs. Its impacts included the demise of the close, mostly effective relationship between the military and contractors – a partnership that had fostered continuing informal discussion on program issues, with early visibility into problems and solutions. The new command-and-control approach was thus a paradigm shift from joint teams to an arm's-length relationship that established formal interactions between the government and industry, with all the institutional inefficiencies that have been recited so far in this chapter. A sizeable professional and military acquisition corps grew in time to support the PPBS process, and industry established its own counterpart infrastructure to protect its interests. This phenomenon contributed in part to a defense establishment culture that embodied inflexibility, bureaucratic complexity, and risk-averse behavior.

The severe budget downturn following the Vietnam War was an opportunity to unmask the expense of bureaucratic waste and to reform the processes symbolized by Hitch's PPBS. But this chance to move back to lean program and management practices successfully used in aerospace in the 1950s was lost. The public again supported defense spending. Defense budgets rose a decade after their Vietnam-era peak in 1979 and accelerated under the stewardship of Secretary of Defense Caspar Weinberger to record peacetime levels, never to turn down again in any significant way until the Cold War ended in the early 1990s. In the next chapter, we turn to the unfortunate impact on military aerospace industrial enterprises of a large government–industry bureaucracy trying to adjust to significantly smaller post-Cold War aerospace markets.

## Shifting Priorities in Commercial Aircraft

The US military aerospace industry was not alone in losing public support in the 1970s. The US Supersonic Transport (SST) program was a victim of changing public priorities in 1971, when the Senate terminated the US entry in that international competition. In the early 1960s, less than a decade after jet transports had entered the commercial arena, a government-funded international race began with the intent of producing supersonic transports that could travel two to three times faster than subsonic jets, at altitudes high enough to see the Earth's curvature. But this large and prestigious national project fell to the growing environmental concerns that developed after the project was well underway.

Meanwhile, jumbo jets that had been started in the 1960s – the Boeing 747, the Douglas DC-10, and the Lockheed L-1011 – entered service just as an early-1970s recession caused aircraft shipments to plummet (Figure 2.7). General Dynamics was driven from the commercial aircraft business. Technical delays on its Rolls-Royce engines hurt Lockheed's product, and the company permanently withdrew as a supplier of commercial transports after accepting government-guaranteed loans to avoid bankruptcy. Boeing reached the brink of bankruptcy, with employment declining by 100 000 workers – most from layoffs – in the 1968–71 period.

Aerospace companies addressed the growing emphasis on the environment and the impact of the oil crisis by developing high bypass ratio jet engines. These lower-noise engines, first introduced commercially on the 747 in 1970, provided passenger-mile fuel efficiencies comparable to the best automobiles – but in vehicles traveling ten times an auto's speed. Meanwhile, attention to flight safety made commercial air travel

## Supersonic Transports: A Victim of Shifting Priorities

Three contestants entered the supersonic transport (SST) race in the 1960s: the United States, the Soviets, and a British–French partnership. By the mid-1970s, the race was over and there was no clear victor. Why? There were technical challenges related to materials and aerodynamic design, but engineers love that stuff. No, the problem was broader. The aerospace enterprise of 'Higher, Faster, Farther' could not overcome the social challenges to SSTs – environmental concerns and economic factors.

From the start, there was considerable resistance to *any* US government investment in a commercial product like the SST. But the issue of national prestige and the prospects that the Europeans or the Soviets might dominate the commercial skies with SST was sufficient to build support within Congress and from the successive Kennedy, Johnson, and Nixon administrations. The program was crafted to provide a guaranteed 'loan' for funding the aircraft development, with the principal and interest to be paid out of the royalties on eventual sales.

On December 31st, 1966, Boeing was chosen as the winner of the US SST design competition, and proceeded to develop the final design and plans for development and production of a swing-wing B2707. However, trouble set in almost immediately and a new configuration was adopted. As detailed design proceeded, the weight of the aircraft steadily grew. With small payload fractions characteristic of supersonic planes, the operating economics worsened.[13]

Still, the international competition pressed on. The Soviet plane first flew in December 1968, and the British–French Concorde followed in March 1969. Meanwhile, development costs for the US program continued to rise. It was becoming increasingly difficult to justify the inherent higher operating costs of supersonic flight for the Americans.

The early-1970s shift in public priorities dealt the fatal blow to the US SST program. This national prestige project, with its irritating sonic boom and noisy engines spewing exhaust gases into the upper atmosphere, brought new environmental concerns to the national level – and this on top of the shaky economics. On March 4th, 1971, a prolonged public debate ended with a close vote to terminate funding for the SST program. *Time* magazine summarized the debate, which had centered on the changing priorities: 'It was obvious to winners and losers alike that something new is afoot, a questioning of old values, old landmarks, old priorities.'[14]

The Soviet SST, known as the Tu-144, made its maiden flight on December 31st, 1968, some two months ahead of the British–French Concorde, thus becoming the world's first supersonic transport to fly. The Tu-144's first passenger flight was on November 1st, 1977. Aeroflot withdrew the jet from passenger service in 1978 after 102 passenger flights. Meanwhile, the British–French Concorde entered revenue passenger service, which continued until interrupted by a tragic accident in May 2000. But unfavorable economics and lack of acceptance by the airlines and the public limited even that production to 20 aircraft.

the safest mode of transportation. Although public support for the high-technology SSTs was questionable, the public hungered for safe, comfortable air travel, and passenger revenue miles grew more than 11 percent per year in the early 1970s (Figure 2.2). This led to a recovery in the civil transport market, albeit part of the industry's cyclical upturns and downturns. A growing market for international sales also contributed to the aerospace sector's strong, favorable impact on the nation's balance of trade.

Other events profoundly influenced the civil transport industry. In Europe, the Airbus consortium of aerospace firms was formed in 1970 to challenge US dominance of the sizeable and growing jet transport market. The Airbus A300 series broke new ground, changing the basis of the company's competition from alleged subsidized price cutting to truly new technical applications that translated into economically competitive products. Initially, the Airbus impact was small, but by the end of the 1980s the consortium's market share made it a force to be reckoned with (Figure 2.8). It became an even more significant player in the subsequent decade as it forced a strategic focus on how to compete in a commodity market for airliners.

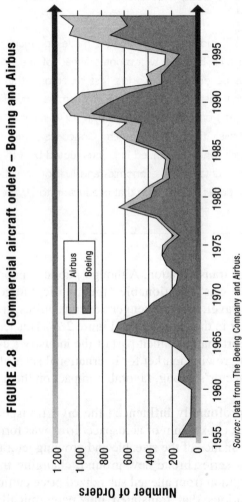

**FIGURE 2.8** Commercial aircraft orders – Boeing and Airbus

Source: Data from The Boeing Company and Airbus.

## Airbus Challenges US Dominance

For decades, US producers dominated the worldwide market for large commercial transport aircraft. That dominance flowed from a unique constellation of factors that spawned sustained growth and innovation, including extensive military–commercial spillovers. But beginning some three decades ago, previously unquestioned US dominance faced a growing challenge from Airbus Industrie, a consortium heavily subsidized by the French, British, German, and Spanish governments.

The consortium, originally formed in 1970,[15] is today a company owned jointly by BAE Systems of the United Kingdom (20 percent) and European Aeronautic Defence and Space Company (80 percent), formed through a July 2000 merger of Aerospatiale Matra of France, Construcciones Aeronauticas, SA of Spain, and DaimlerChrysler Aerospace of Germany. Airbus contracts with its industrial owners to design, manufacture, assemble, and support its aircraft.

Initially dismissed as unwieldy and likely to be saddled by parochial national interests, Airbus defied conventional wisdom, making significant inroads into the worldwide commercial aircraft market. Today, the Airbus series of large commercial transports – the A300-600, A310, A319, A320, A321, A330 and A340 – competes with its Boeing counterparts. The consortium's announcement of its A380, a double-decker jumbo jet available in March 2006 with a capacity of 555 to 800 passengers, moves competition with Boeing into the latter's stronghold. The A380 has at least 140 seats more than the largest Boeing 747, the model that helped Boeing monopolize the market segment for aircraft with more than 400 seats. This new Airbus entry promises to test Boeing's mettle and could determine the destiny of both rivals.

How has Boeing responded to the Airbus competitive threat? The firm introduced various models of its next-generation Boeing 737, the most popular in Boeing's product family, over the course of the 1990s, and rolled out the Boeing 777 – with which Boeing is determined to establish a benchmark for 21st-century aircraft – in June 1995. Boeing also decided in 1998, the year after its merger with McDonnell Douglas, to retain the MD-95, renamed and introduced as the Boeing 717-200, in an effort to preempt Airbus in the 100-seat market.

Boeing's early 2001 announcement of the near-supersonic 175-250 passenger twin-engine Sonic Cruiser (the 20XX), after scrapping earlier plans to develop a stretched version of the 747, is also an important competitive move, reflecting a decidedly different strategy in responding to future market opportunities. While Airbus is going with size with its A380, Boeing believes there is limited market potential for such a large aircraft. The company is opting for a smaller plane that emphasizes speed and range based on its assessment that passenger demand will force airlines to develop more point-to-point service structures in contrast to hub-to-hub route systems better served by ultra-large aircraft.

## General Aviation Encounters New Public Expectations

Public discomfort with established norms of responsibility in the post-Vietnam era brought pressure on aerospace from another quarter. Aviation manufacturers became more frequent targets of product liability lawsuits, even for indirectly caused defects throughout the lifetime of an airplane. This imposed the need for excessively costly insurance, virtually eliminating the flourishing general aviation aircraft industry. Annual production dropped ninefold in just five years (Figure 2.9). Cessna, Piper, and Beech, all famous names, disappeared as independent companies in the general aviation segment of the aircraft business. The civil helicopter industry felt a similar impact. By the mid-1980s, annual production dropped to about one-third of its peak at the beginning of that decade.[16]

These industries are still recovering from consumer litigation, which – coupled with public skepticism of defense projects – sharply altered the level of risk that government and industry were willing to take in developing new systems. It was a marked change from the early Cold War period.

FIGURE 2.9 | US general aviation shipments

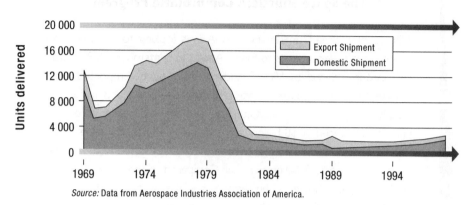

Source: Data from Aerospace Industries Association of America.

## Changing Public Constituencies for NASA

As the 1970s unfolded, public interest in space exploration also declined, driving reduced budgets for NASA (Figure 2.4) and a drop in college enrollments in aerospace engineering. However, there was growing political pressure to support the nation's capability and resources to undertake space projects, which had advanced significantly with Apollo. In 1972, bowing to this pressure, President Nixon authorized the start of the Space Transportation System, popularly known as the Space Shuttle. Human space flight was given a new breath of life. In addition, the scientific community succeeded in winning funds to initiate in 1976 the Great Observatories, which included the Hubble Space Telescope. With the first Shuttle flight in 1981, the public's interest in space began to grow again, thanks in large part to the striking images from Hubble.

However, the NASA budget grew only modestly in the late 1980s. There was widening Congressional concern over escalating expenditures, and debate continues even today on the benefits and priorities of unmanned versus human space exploration. In an odd twist, the Challenger explosion in 1986 in some ways reinvigorated the human space program. Reminded of the challenges of space flight, the public's interest increased, shifting support back to manned space programs.

## The Space Shuttle: A Compromise Program

With funding already in decline, NASA was looking to the future for bigger and grander projects to follow Apollo. In September 1969, a Space Task Group chaired by Vice President Spiro Agnew reported three possible long-range space programs for NASA: a manned mission to Mars by the mid-1980s, priced at $8 to $10 billion per year; an orbiting lunar station priced at $8 billion per year; and a 50-person space station that would orbit Earth and be served by a reusable shuttle, priced between $4 and $5.7 billion per year. Compared to the early 1960s and the Kennedy era, however, the mood – and the political landscape – of the country had shifted to value other priorities.

President Nixon, like Eisenhower, was a frugal government spender who viewed the big manned space effort as a 'stunt'. Also, he was much more interested in promoting cooperation with the Soviets and the Chinese. Further, space had become a secondary policy issue for the political establishment, and Congress had even reorganized the standing space committees out of existence.

This was the period when the last two Apollo flights were canceled, the Apollo Application Program was reduced to one Skylab, and – in a major blow to the Air Force – the Manned Orbiting Laboratory was cancelled. With Nixon's refusal to support any of the Agnew Space Task Group options, and waning Congressional support for any big new initiative, NASA's future looked cloudy.

The 1972 presidential election came to the rescue of the manned space program. Declining aerospace employment in California, Texas, and Florida – each with large numbers of electoral votes – forced Nixon to approve some program for NASA. He chose half of the lowest budget option – the Space Shuttle. With no funding for its destination, the Space Station, it was called 'a space truck to nowhere'.[17]

The characterization of the Space Shuttle as a cheap and ready vehicle couldn't be more inaccurate. It is a remarkable flying machine, much like a finely tuned racing car – laborious to prepare and expensive to use. But it was unable to achieve most of the affordability and reusability goals of its design. While society's mindset by the mid-1970s was one of performance at an acceptable price, NASA – living in the afterglow of Apollo – was poorly equipped to meet the changing fiscal priorities.

## Triumph and Vindication; Peace and Survival

To complete our understanding of the Cold War legacy, we must return to military aerospace, where the historic events and national responses surrounding the end of the Cold War have had enormous economic, business, and cultural consequences for the defense industry and, through it, for the entire US Aerospace Enterprise.

Just after defense budgets in the Reagan buildup reached historic highs in the late 1980s, the US defense establishment, built and operated to defend against the Soviet threat, handed the US and its allies a stunning victory against Iraq in the Gulf War.

For years, critics had sniped at the costs and complexity of military systems. They criticized large military space programs as too costly for their benefits. They characterized military aircraft system designs as too complex to be reliable and too expensive to counter forces armed with more, and cheaper, aircraft. On the eve of the Gulf War, some even predicted ignominious defeat of our complicated, fragile fighters that would be impotent in the face of sophisticated air defenses.

The outcome was quite the opposite – the war was a resounding success story for aerospace power. Authoritative postwar assessments said that the air campaign was the decisive factor in the war with Iraq, with the caveat that ground forces were necessary to eject the Iraqis from Kuwait. Another important finding was that the effective use of high technology was a key reason for the high level of performance of both air and ground forces, and for the minimization of US and allied casualties.[18]

Space sensors turned out to play a crucial role supporting air and ground warfare planning. CNN redefined global expectations for news coverage using communications satellite systems that grew out of national investments in space programs, including launch equipment.

There was no question that the US Aerospace Enterprise, along with the other components of the defense establishment, had fielded a well-trained, well-equipped fighting force that had skillfully applied high technology to win the most efficient war that the country had ever fought. The outcome of the Gulf War vindicated the expense of the complex of government and industrial organizations and processes created to oversee Cold War spending on weapons systems development and production. The public may have been impatient with the cost and speed of equipping, sustaining, and administering Cold War forces and their industrial tail, and it may not have liked the attendant inefficiencies of slow, risk-averse, heavy-handed, and expensive public and corporate bureaucracies, but by the time George Bush halted the Gulf War in February 1991 after only four days of ground combat, there was no argument about the success of that government–industrial team. This was the special national mission for which the US Aerospace Enterprise had been preparing for four decades – and it came through as promised. It was the high-water mark of the Cold War military–industrial establishment.

## Desert Storm: High-Water Mark for US Military Institutions of the Cold War

On August 2nd, 1990, Saddam Hussein shocked the world with Iraq's daring invasion of Kuwait. Encountering feeble resistance, Iraq quickly controlled a major portion of the world's supply of petroleum, an alarming and unacceptable situation for neighboring Saudi Arabia and the world's oil consumers.

The Bush administration forged a coalition of European and Persian Gulf allies, which immediately began assembling ground, naval, and air forces in Saudi Arabia and the Gulf. The United States dominated the Desert Shield force with a half-million soldiers, airmen, and sailors.

The war to liberate Kuwait began on the evening of January 16th, 1991, with a series of strikes against Iraqi air defense systems and strategic targets. More than 700 aircraft from the US, British, Kuwaiti, and Saudi air forces penetrated Iraqi airspace that night. Their missions spanned the full gamut of airpower: strike, air superiority, defense suppression, refueling, surveillance, reconnaissance, and electronic warfare. Together these required the use of myriad types of aircraft. Most notable was the first major combat appearance of the F-117A stealth fighter, equipped with laser-guided bombs. This strike aircraft attacked downtown Baghdad the first night, and every night, with impunity; an intense Iraqi air defense effort was impotent to defend the city. Dazzling CNN television images and sounds of bombs exploding in spite of bright blizzards of air defense gunfire in the night sky left an impression on the American public that vindicated, at a visceral level, its huge investment in the Cold War buildup.

Supported by a panoply of satellites, the air war continued for 28 days, first against air defense and strategic targets and then against Iraqi ground forces once the skies were secure. Finally, on February 24th, the ground campaign kicked off. Allied ground forces encountered severely degraded Iraqi resistance. Although accurate numbers will never be known, reliable estimates place 360 000 Iraqis on the ground as the air war began. By the time the ground campaign rolled into Iraq and Kuwait, half had deserted or been killed or injured, leaving 180 000 to oppose a force five times as large.[19]

On February 28th, 1991, after 100 hours of ground fighting with few allied casualties and with Kuwait liberated, President Bush ended the carnage by declaring a cessation of hostilities.

Ironically, just as military aerospace was fulfilling its historic promise, events elsewhere in the world were afoot that would again shift public priorities away from defense, just as they had after the Vietnam War. The fall of the Berlin Wall in October 1989 symbolizes the end of the Cold War. Practically, though, the West could not begin to be sure of the decline of the Soviet threat until Boris Yeltsin and unarmed civilians stared down the attempted military coup in Moscow in August 1991. A mere six months after the stunning aerospace victory over Iraq, survival of the democratic Russian republic set off events that would lead to a precipitous decline in public spending for defense and military aerospace. Just five years later, DoD funding levels for procurement and aerospace R&D would be at half their peaks near the ends of the Gulf and Cold Wars (Figure 2.5).

## Challenges of the Cold War Legacy

Central questions framing the substance of this book emerge from the Cold War legacy. How does a set of industrial enterprises focused on high-performance products sized to an annual market of $100 billion find business equilibrium as half of the industry becomes excess capacity in just a few years and affordability becomes paramount? How does an industry that has accommodated itself over decades to excelling in technology adapt to a new era in which efficiency of manufacturing and life-cycle support processes becomes dominant? How does an industry subjected to necessary but nevertheless complex, conservative, risk-averse government regulations and management transform itself into a nimble, agile, global competitor to survive in the new realities of a new century? And how do the government agencies and processes that impose these regulations transform themselves in an era when threats have changed and a revolution in business affairs is needed? How do the commercial aircraft, spacecraft, and launch industries respond to formidable global competition? How does society undertake bold space exploration projects when the American public appears satisfied with a space agency budget of about 1 percent of the federal budget? And what are the opportunities for innovation in these sectors when their core products have reached mature stages?

The next chapter explores the daunting obstacles faced by the US Aerospace Enterprise in its quest for a new equilibrium in the post-Cold War era. Our examination of these obstacles – similar to the types of barrier faced by many industries – offers insights that are an important prelude to subsequent sections of the book, where we delve into the expansion of lean thinking to encompass entire value streams and the entire enterprise.

# CHAPTER 3

# Monuments and Misalignments

By the 1990s, with the Cold War over, the US Aerospace Enterprise found itself in uncharted waters, and the institutions, accumulated infrastructure, and organizations designed for the successful campaign to thwart Communism were without a rudder. To make matters worse, a host of other destabilizing forces – which had been masked by the Cold War – suddenly appeared. The Cold War's end unleashed a wave of commotion that affected not only the military sector of the US Aerospace Enterprise, but also the commercial and civil space sectors. The once shared interests of aerospace customers, workers, and manufacturers had become misaligned, and products had matured. As the new millennium began, the US Aerospace Enterprise needed a new equilibrium.

The maturation of existing product lines posed a special challenge. Military aircraft technology, in particular airframe structure technology, today evolves much more slowly than in the glory days of the 1950s. We see the results in the fact that 40-year-old aircraft remain in useful service today, and in the lengthening of design cycle times for new aircraft. Spacecraft continue to evolve, but the basic designs of launch vehicles – and, in the case of the Space Shuttle, the vehicles themselves – go back two decades or more. Meanwhile, commercial jet aircraft have become a commodity; only aviation enthusiasts (and very frequent travelers) can name, or even care about, the make and model of the dependable, if crowded, jets on which they fly.

Typically, technology progresses along the type of curve represented in Figure 3.1. In all technology-driven industries, as the frontiers of knowledge are conquered, major innovations occur further and further apart – which has a significant, long-lasting impact. The maturity in the aerospace industry reflects this conquest of technological barriers.

The US Aerospace Enterprise is at a crucial juncture. The previous chapter highlighted the shift in shared interests among the constituents of the US Aerospace Enterprise. In this chapter, we build on these observations and show how the concurrent effect of product maturity and leftover norms from the Cold War continue the *misalignment* of the US Aerospace Enterprise with changing national priorities, new market conditions, the

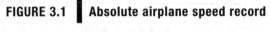

FIGURE 3.1 | Absolute airplane speed record

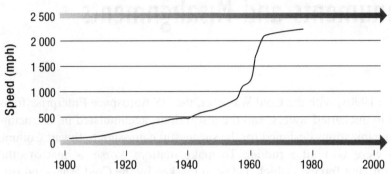

*Source:* Data from John H. McMasters and Russell M. Cummings, 'Airplane Design – Past, Present, and Future', presented at the 39th American Institute of Aeronautics and Astronautics meeting, Reno, Nevada (January 9th, 2001). © McMasters and Cummings 2001. Used with permission.

transformation of oversight bureaucracies, and the technological maturity of core products – all of which contribute to a significant transition in the industry.

In the first attempts at a new equilibrium, the aerospace industry seized on measures such as downsizing, outsourcing, mergers and acquisitions, and acquisition reform, seeking to establish a financially sound and efficient (albeit smaller) industrial base. While each resulted in some success, the institutions, organizations, infrastructure, regulations, cultures, and modes of thinking formed mostly during the Cold War era still act as barriers to the needed broader transformation.

To understand the origins of the present situation, we develop two lines of analysis. The first builds on the fundamental concepts of industrial innovation to help us understand the natural progression of maturing industries. The second identifies the barriers to constructive change in the industry. In lean parlance, such impediments are known as *monuments*.

## Dynamics of Industrial Innovation

Today, the US Aerospace Enterprise has lost the benefits that accompany a clear societal imperative, as it enjoyed in the days of the 'moon rush' or the Cold War. The changes in both the nature and predictability of the threats faced on the military side have given rise to a growing consensus that we need fundamentally new ways to define threats, develop the requirements, and choose the weapons systems. On the civil side, the aerospace industry has seen steady growth in demand for passenger and freight aircraft, telecommunications satellites, and launches for those satellites – but booming business has not translated into profitability. The aerospace industry has found itself unwittingly reduced to a commodity supplier in a new economy, with the commodity prices and profit margins that come with such status.

The 1978 deregulation of the airlines, which unleashed market forces artificially held at bay during the regulated era, offers one early example of this transition. The quest of earlier eras for aircraft flight performance gave way to low-cost, affordable transportation, and civil aviation transitioned to a commodity business. By the end of the 1980s, civil air transportation was booming, but not as a 'Higher, Faster, Farther' frontier. In fact, the speed and altitude of jetliners remained largely the same as that of the 707, introduced back in 1958. What did increase were range, reaching nearly half the circumference of the globe, and payload, exceeding 400 passengers.

The value metric for new commercial aircraft development made a tremendous shift. The breakthrough aeronautical technology of the early Cold War years gave way to safety, affordability, and comfort. As was heard so often in the hallways at Boeing by the 1990s: 'New technology has to earn its way onto the product.'

## A Shift Spurred by Airline Deregulation

The 1978 deregulation of US airlines marked a turning point in the evolution of the commercial aircraft industry. In the decades prior to this, the major domestic airlines that dominated the aviation industry enjoyed closely linked and mutually beneficial relationships with major aircraft manufacturers in launching new products, stressing technical performance and spurring continuous technological innovation. Airline deregulation, which came just as military–commercial spillover effects began to diminish and with military and civil technological requirements already on a divergent course, set into motion a chain of events that weakened those earlier dynamics of innovation.

Deregulation triggered greater market competition among airlines, cutting fares and reducing the profitability of major carriers. Lower entry barriers and an ample supply of aircraft invited fledgling new market entrants: this exacerbated market competition, making the financial performance of airlines even worse. Deregulation made it more difficult for established airlines to finance major innovations and become the first to launch a new aircraft. A tradition of innovation gave way to an increasing stress on affordability, the new driving criterion for choosing aircraft.

Post-deregulation shifts in market structure caused major aircraft producers to enter into cost- and risk-sharing arrangements, often as part of international collaborative ventures, to help underwrite the development of new systems. While the number of aircraft producers shrank, the number of airlines, the amount of leasing, and the demand for air freight transportation all grew worldwide, spurring overall demand for the products of these fewer producers. Another aspect of the commercial aircraft market changed, too. During much of the postwar period, domestic aircraft producers could engage in potentially ruinous competition with each other and take serious commercial risks, knowing full well that they could expect a steady source of profits from government procurement. That safety net simply vanished.

One way to understand how and why the US Aerospace Enterprise finds itself in today's situation is to look at the industry from the perspective of its history of innovation, using the model developed by James Utterback in his book *Mastering the Dynamics of Innovation*.[1] Aerospace is an industry characterized by innovation, but which is arguably entering a more mature phase. The sources of innovation and improvement in a mature industry will be different than in the industry's early days, as Utterback's model explains.

A unique set of external factors has affected the evolution of the aerospace industry in complex ways. For example, the Cold War and government space programs pushed technological innovations harder and longer

## Three Characteristic Phases of Innovation

Although the aerospace industry is unique in many respects, it is still useful to understand the lessons from other industries that have – with varying success – gone through the transition from one to another phase of innovation.

James Utterback proposes that industries pass though three such phases. First is the *Fluid Phase*, when product innovation is key. In this phase, product innovation is extremely rapid, and the variety of products and the firms building those products proliferate. At the end of this phase, a *dominant design* emerges, which – through a combination of usefulness, standardization, and/or market dominance – effectively ends competition based on wide product differentiation. Utterback points to the QWERTY-keyboard mechanical typewriter as a relatively low-tech example of a dominant design. A notable aerospace example would be the jet-powered, aluminum-tube-with-wings passenger transport.

Next comes the *Transition Phase*, in which innovation shifts to processes – that is, to design, development, and manufacturing innovation. The number of firms participating in the industry drops quickly, and continues to decline as greater linkage between product innovation and process innovation drives higher the cost of entry.

In the final *Specific Phase*, even major process changes are unlikely, and competition reduces to cost and customer satisfaction, achieved through incremental improvements.

Figure 3.2 is a generic depiction of the rise and fall of the number of firms making a given product over time. The patterns reflect the evolutionary phases reported by Utterback in numerous industries, and Figure 3.3 shows that the pattern applies to aerospace. Figure 3.4 compares the history of the aerospace industry with two other industries that make assembled products.[2] The drop in aerospace firms is typical for an industry that has a 'dominant design' and is in the Transition or Specific Phase.

## FIGURE 3.2 | Dynamics of innovation

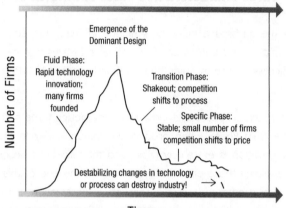

*Source:* Reprinted with permission from Entry and Exit of Firms in the U.S. Auto Industry: 1894–1992. Copyright 1987 by the National Academy of Science. Courtesy of the National Academy Press, Washington, D.C.

## FIGURE 3.3 | Evolution of the US aerospace industry

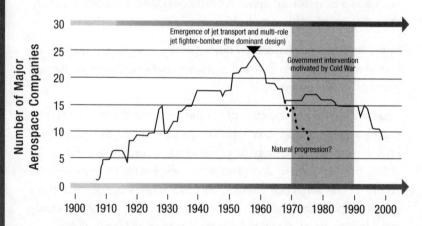

*Source:* S. Weiss and A. Amir, 'The Aerospace Industry', in Encyclopedia Britannica (Chicago: Encyclopedia Britannica, 1999).

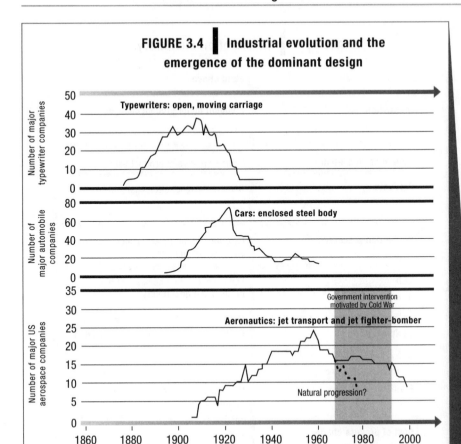

**FIGURE 3.4** | **Industrial evolution and the emergence of the dominant design**

Sources: For typewriters, based on data in George Nichols Engler, 'The Typewriter Industry: The Impact of a Significant Technological Innovation', University of California at Los Angeles, 1970; for cars, and reprinted with permission from Entry and Exit of Firms in the U.S. Auto Industry: 1894–1992. Copyright 1987 by the National Academy of Science. Courtesy of the National Academy Press, Washington, D.C. and J. Utterback, Mastering the Dynamics of Innovation (Boston: Harvard Business School Press, 1996) for aeronautics, LAI.

Table 3.1 shows characteristics of industries in each of these three phases. Those associated with the Fluid Phase are easily associated with the 'Higher, Faster, Farther' days of aerospace. And while the current situation varies with the specific sector of aerospace under examination, the characteristics listed for Utterback's Transition and Specific Phases are clearly evident in the industry's current state.

**TABLE 3.1**  █ **Phases of product lifecycle**

| | Fluid phase |
|---|---|
| **Innovation** | Frequent major product changes |
| **Source of innovation** | Industry pioneers; product users |
| **Products** | Diverse designs, often customized |
| **Production processes** | Flexible and inefficient, major changes easily accommodated |
| **R&D** | Focus unspecified because of high degree of technical uncertainty |
| **Equipment** | General-purpose, requiring skilled labor |
| **Plant** | Small-scale; located near user or source of innovation |
| **Cost of process change** | Low |
| **Competitors** | Few, but growing in numbers with widely fluctuating market shares |
| **Basis of competition** | Functional product performance |
| **Organizational control** | Informal and entrepreneurial |
| **Vulnerabilities of industry leaders** | To imitators, and patent challenges; to successful product breakthroughs |

than might have been the case in a strictly commercial industry. That delayed natural consolidation of the number of firms – indeed, the long, relative plateau from 1969 to 1992 in Figure 3.3 was sustained largely through government investment in aerospace technology and in the industrial base. Had market forces been in play, as in the commercial aircraft

| Transitional phase | Specific phase |
|---|---|
| Major process changes required by rising demand | Incremental for product and with cumulative improvements in productivity and quality |
| Manufacturers; users | Often suppliers |
| At least one product design, stable enough to have significant production volume | Mostly undifferentiated, standard products |
| Becoming more rigid, with changes occurring in major steps | Efficient, capital-intensive, and rigid; cost of change high |
| Focus on specific product features once dominant design emerges | Focus on incremental product technologies; emphasis on process technology |
| Some subprocesses automated, creating islands of automation | Special-purpose, mostly automatic, with labor focused on tending and monitoring equipment |
| General-purpose, with specialized sections | Large-scale, highly specific to particular products |
| Moderate | High |
| Many, but declining in numbers after emergence of dominant design | Few; classic oligopoly with stable market shares |
| Product variation; fitness for use | Price |
| Through project and task groups | Structure, rules, and goals |
| To more efficient and higher-quality producers | To technological innovations that present superior product substitutes |

Source: J. Utterback, Mastering the Dynamics of Innovation (Boston: Harvard Business School Press, 1996).

sector, we would probably have seen a much earlier shift to the characteristics of a more mature industry. A similar phenomenon occurred earlier with the deregulation of the airline industry – the removal of the artificial regulation barrier permitted market forces to reduce airfares and spurred airlines to demand cost-efficient planes from their aircraft suppliers.

Given that artificial constraints have largely been removed now that the Cold War is over, what does Utterback's model suggest about the future of the aerospace industry? First, as explained in the box and shown in Table 3.1, innovation in a given industry shifts from a focus on major changes in products (the Fluid Phase) to a focus on changes and specialization in processes (the Transition Phase). Then comes the Specific Phase, where innovation is often found in suppliers – smaller, more nimble organizations willing to take greater risk. Incremental improvements often dominate this phase, but not to the exclusion of occasional major changes in processes or even in products. And while industries in the Specific Phase seem very stable, they are vulnerable to being swept away entirely by major, often unforeseen, innovations. These innovations functionally replace the industry's own products while drawing on a different set of technologies and/or competencies that do not reside in the industry – for example, the replacement of typewriters by word processors.[3]

This scenario is already playing out in aerospace. With the end of the Cold War, there has been new emphasis on the critical role of processes, mostly in manufacturing, that have been largely neglected since World War II. Throughout the Cold War, the primary focus was on 'performance', and R&D investments were made to achieve breakthroughs in technical capabilities. By and large during the same period, aerospace production systems and practices evolved only incrementally from those of the World War II peak production period – at least until the mid-1980s, when commercial demands began to rekindle interest in this area of the business. With the end of the Cold War and the emergence of affordability as a key priority, leaders in aerospace and defense began to recognize the need to invest in manufacturing.[4]

Utterback's study looks at industries in the mass production era. It remains to be seen whether lean enterprise principles and practices, which we address in Part II of this book, might alter the dynamics of industrial innovation. Utterback briefly notes that Toyota, the central player in the lean production story, introduced revolutionary production systems in an industry deep in the Specific Phase, and thereby dramatically upset the stable balance of the automotive industry. For aerospace, the timing is crucial: lean is becoming widespread at the very moment lean is needed.

Utterback notes further that firms that are not major players in the dominant design often lead technical innovations. In this context, we must remember that aerospace includes many different technologies, which may be in different technology phases. Although the large commercial aircraft industry is clearly in the Specific Phase, new innovations in business and short-haul (regional) jet aircraft are, as we write, causing a breakout in that industry with characteristics of the Fluid Phase.

Still, most of the aerospace industry is only just beginning a painful transition from the era of 'Higher, Faster, Farther' to that of a more mature industry guided by the rules of 'Faster, Better, Cheaper'. This transition was delayed by the long struggle for military dominance and national prestige waged during the Cold War. Will the outcome on the other end of this transition be a mature industry that is also dynamic and flexible? As Utterback warns, stagnation is possible, and unforeseen changes in technology or world circumstances could send the industry into a permanent decline.

## Aerospace Innovation

Despite a more general maturing of the industry, it is important to note that many parts of the aerospace industry *are* innovating in technology, products, and processes. In fact, segments of the industry experience bursts of innovation, which thrive and reinvigorate the industry. Towards the end of the Cold War, stealth technology was a major breakthrough, revolutionizing tactical aircraft and missile development. Some prominent examples of innovation today are constellations of low Earth orbit satellites for navigation and communication, business and regional jets, many uses of information technology, and dramatic improvements in product development and manufacturing.

Take, for example, the emergence and extension of the Global Positioning System (GPS), which has revolutionized navigation for land, sea, and air travel, and which has applications in military, commercial, and even personal transportation. Preprogrammed maps coupled to GPS now provide auto-navigation for cars, boats, and even for farm equipment, in which the technology provides a means for robotic tilling, planting, and harvesting.

Innovations in business and short-haul (regional) jet aircraft are other good examples. Figure 3.5 shows rapid growth in the business jet sector. While only two companies worldwide supply large aircraft, four companies supply regional jets where there was one company building such jets only a decade ago. Some 15 new business jet models have been rolled out in the last decade. There has been similar growth in civil aviation,[5] as well as in small and/or low-cost launch vehicles.

Aerospace has always been innovative, and we fully expect that innovation will continue to thrive and be central to aerospace in the future. But it is important to recognize that innovation will probably occur in different areas than in the past. The more restrictive post-Cold War resources trans-

## FIGURE 3.5 | Rapid growth in the business jet sector

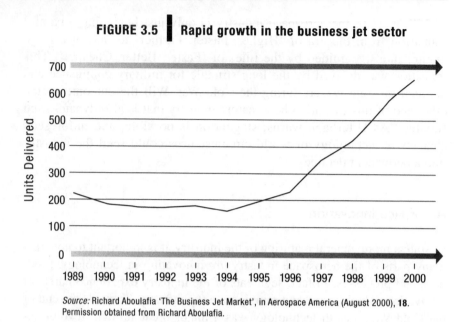

Source: Richard Aboulafia 'The Business Jet Market', in Aerospace America (August 2000), **18**. Permission obtained from Richard Aboulafia.

late into the need to be more selective in setting R&D priorities to gain the greatest benefit. For some, this reality has been difficult, as more mature areas may lose support. For others, it spells new opportunities.

### Actions and Reactions

The aerospace industry has tried several approaches in an effort to accommodate the new realities of the 1990s. These include downsizing/rightsizing, outsourcing, and mergers/acquisitions. Each approach has been aimed at reforming the infrastructure to reduce the direct and overhead costs associated with overcapacity or obsolete capability. And while each effort has had limited success in certain areas, none has solved the industry's daunting long-term problems.

For the government, DoD acquisition reform on the military side, and the NASA 'Faster, Better, Cheaper' programs on the civilian side, have encouraged new ways of doing business, often with dramatic results not fully appreciated or understood by the public. Many lessons have been learned. However, the successes have affected a limited number of programs, and the efforts have been slow to diffuse to other programs.

Let's take a brief look at the strengths and weaknesses of each of these general approaches employed in the 1990s by the industry and government – again, primarily (but not exclusively) in the defense sector.

## Downsizing or Rightsizing

A company faced with declining revenue may rationally decide to focus on its workforce. Unfortunately, the ideal of making a company more efficient and effective often translates into layoffs and early retirements.

Staff reductions have their downsides: a number of systematic studies in several industries have found no evidence of any increase in corporate performance as their result, for a number of reasons.[6] While layoffs and early retirements save money by reducing payroll, they can increase other costs. For instance, individuals who leave firms carry away not only valuable knowledge acquired during employment (and that must be regained), but many relationships as well. Some researchers have shown that even well-planned layoffs break up the corporate network in ways that can be quite difficult to repair.[7]

These observations are relevant to aerospace. *Aviation Week & Space Technology* has reported that 'some of the most talented, experienced engineers, managers, and factory-floor technicians are leaving the large aerospace companies – either on their own, or through ongoing downsizing campaigns'.[8] The space launcher segment illustrates this problem: 'Lessons learned from failures in the 1950s and 1960s are being lost, because there's no mentoring of these young guys. We've laid off the old and hired young workers, so the two never rub shoulders.'[9]

To make matters worse, layoffs create tensions with the remaining workforce if workers see the layoffs as unjustified, handled unfairly, or lacking assistance for displaced employees.[10] These sorts of tensions make it more difficult to win employee commitment to other changes needed to improve operations.

Michael Hammer, one of reengineering's leading advocates, has gone so far as to apologize publicly for advocating a one-dimensional approach to change – one that does not take into full account the loss of knowledge and capability.[11] Ultimately, all this raises a key question that we address later: whether the workforce is seen primarily as a cost to be cut or primarily as a source of ideas to drive improvement.

## Outsourcing

An increasing number of firms have turned to outsourcing to improve the bottom line.[12] By definition, outsourcing presupposes the existence of qualified suppliers with the requisite capabilities to assume the new responsibilities delegated to them by the outsourcing firm.

This strategy, which has been quite successful in the automobile industry,[13] is used increasingly in aerospace, where the costs of intellectual capital and infrastructure associated with maintaining a wide range of technical capabilities have put particular pressure on many prime contractors to consider outsourcing. The steadily rising investment requirements and financial risks associated with developing new products have motivated cost-sharing and risk-sharing partnerships, thus paving the way for greater outsourcing. And the increasingly global nature of the commercial aerospace sector in particular has pressured companies, through aerospace offset requirements, to outsource elements of production to indigenous companies within buying countries as a condition of sale. The result has been a steady rise in the percentage of work allocated to suppliers. For instance, Boeing Military Aircraft & Missile Systems reports that its suppliers' proportion of the work (in terms of total production costs), roughly at 60 percent in 1998, is expected to rise to 75 percent by 2016.[14]

However necessary or prudent, though, outsourcing has not been without problems. A firm that outsources some of its work may fail to accomplish a commensurate scaling back of its own plant and equipment infrastructure. Transferring more work to suppliers also entails greater transactional costs. An outsourcing firm typically must spread its overhead costs across a smaller base of programs, thus increasing costs to all customers. And there have been situations where 'economics' have driven decisions to outsource to suppliers without giving sufficient consideration to their capability or quality.

Suppliers as 'outsourcees' can also have problems. Comparatively more vulnerable to the broader cyclical shifts in the economy, suppliers are less likely to make long-term, productivity-enhancing investments. They have less access to the capital markets to finance new investments. Moreover, buffeted by the instability inherent in the defense acquisition process, many aerospace suppliers may well have sought a rosier future in the commercial sector, and may not be available for government contracts. For all these reasons, the expected efficiency gains associated with outsourcing decisions may not materialize.

A cautionary note about outsourcing comes from MIT Professor Charles Fine, who posits that supply chain design is the ultimate core competency.[15]

In highly integrated aerospace products, key knowledge and capabilities reside – to a significant extent – in the supplier base. A firm must be sensitive to whether outsourcing means greater dependence on suppliers for capacity or for knowledge – each with a quite different set of consequences. If a firm chooses to outsource a part or a subsystem, the prime contractor's knowledge embedded in that outsourced component becomes difficult, if not impossible, to recapture.

In a dynamic sense over many years, outsourcing decisions 'evolve far beyond the control of the initiator'.[16] These decisions tend to limit the initiator's future capabilities and choices. In the final analysis, dependence on outsourcing as the route to affordability has numerous pitfalls.

## Mergers and Acquisitions

For much of the 1990s, the Department of Defense encouraged a process of mergers and acquisitions for the major players in the defense aerospace industry, thus reducing their overall number to a handful (see Figure 1.3). All of these moves were part of a strategy to deal with reduced defense budgets and reduced new program starts, and often preceded new rounds of workforce reductions. The immediate aim was to stave off the short-term effects of declining business. Over the long term, the merged companies hoped to gain a larger piece of the shrinking pie, while achieving profitability through the efficiency of merged operations.

The approach was successful in the short run, at least by Wall Street standards. As Figure 3.6 shows, aerospace stocks during the first wave of 1990s mergers and acquisitions outperformed the market in general, despite the steep decline in defense budgets. But consolidation has not been an unqualified success. These horizontal mergers typically require assimilating two complete businesses into a single entity – which means two engineering components, two research-and-development components, two manufacturing arms, and two field-support organizations. The consolidated firm that results runs the risks of massive overheads and excess capacity – at the very moment that the budget or program pie is shrinking.

Another problem is that Wall Street analysts expected (and continue to expect) companies in this sector to maintain steady earnings growth. But the larger merged companies, often saddled with acquisition debt, could not meet these expectations. Failure results in large market-value losses for these firms, as investors find little reason to keep the stocks in their portfolios. Figure 3.6 also shows the collapse of aerospace industry stock values in the late 1990s, reflecting (at least in part) the market's opinion of how consolidation worked out.

# Lean Enterprise Value

**FIGURE 3.6** | **Post-Cold War market performance of aerospace stocks**

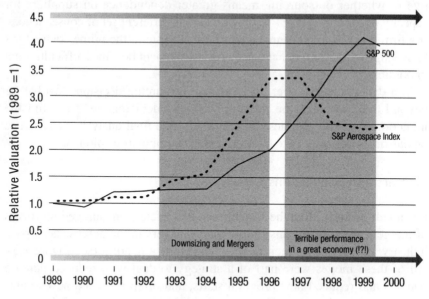

*Source:* Data from Thomson Financial Datastream.

## DoD Acquisition Reform

In a bold attempt to move away from the 'Higher, Faster, Farther' paradigm, the Department of Defense in the 1990s set out to employ more commercial-like acquisition practices aimed at putting greater emphasis on affordability and infusing commercial technology into military products. Each of the armed services established an acquisition reform office, and there has been an institutional effort to implement these initiatives through pilot showcase projects. Some have been extremely successful.[17]

Thanks to acquisition reform, approximately one-third to one-half of military specifications – known throughout the defense community as MILSPECs[18] – have been canceled. By 1998, the Single Process Initiative had converted at least 140 facilities to the ISO 9000 quality standard.[19]

Despite these improvements, though, acquisition reform suffers from the difficulty of diffusing the practices *throughout* the acquisition infrastructure. There has been no servicewide implementation of the initiatives. Many MILSPECs, though no longer required, are still used voluntarily; in some cases, they are the only standards available. Further, while some pilot programs, such as cost as an independent variable or acquisition

## 'Faster, Better, Cheaper' at NASA

NASA – with huge, ongoing commitments to programs such as the Space Shuttle, the Space Station, and the Great Observatories, but facing declining budgets – initiated a program for planetary exploration missions (later expanded) dubbed 'Faster, Better, Cheaper' (FBC). But while the goal – to push programs to carry through missions that produced greater benefits while requiring less money and less time – was fine, implementation was more of a problem.

A number of approaches emerged to satisfy the FBC vision, with different program managers adopting one or another. Under the 'constraint' approach, resources (time and money) would be reduced until it hurt. By some accounts, the constraints were imposed almost arbitrarily because the leverage points were unknown. Another approach, 'simplification', focused on reducing the mission scope of programs just getting underway, thus reducing the cost and shortening the development schedule. Both approaches put considerable stress on 'Faster' and 'Cheaper', but paid scant attention to 'Better'.

The third approach was 'calculated risk', with a scheme that guided management in deciding on adequate cost and schedule reductions, and with a focus on establishing challenging 'mission targets' that produced greater benefits – often through innovative measures. This approach has had the most success.

NASA's track record since 1992 under the FBC paradigm is impressive. Through early 2000, the agency had launched 146 payloads valued at more than $18 billion. Of those, total losses amounted to ten payloads valued at $500 million, or less than 3 percent of the total investment.[20] From most business perspectives, that reliability is quite high. Nevertheless, failures such as the Mars Climate Orbiter[21] and Polar Lander missions have threatened FBC, and the imposition of a 'mission success first' policy on top of FBC programs compromises the gains made thus far.

The move to implement FBC was a reaction to the times. NASA felt it had no choice. It is the continuous pursuit of FBC, even in the face of program failures, that will test the agency's true grit.

streamlining, have been very successful, most do not receive the high-level attention needed to challenge longstanding policies and procedures. Without this 'top cover', most programs end up resorting to risk-averse behavior to ensure their continuation. In an acquisition community whose uniformed members and top leaders change positions every two to four years, such bureaucratic procedural steps often hinder the advancement of innovative ideas and programs.

While these industry and government actions have experienced some success, the shift in national priorities and the maturing of the industry have highlighted *misalignments* in the US Aerospace Enterprise to these new conditions. Institutions, established to perform what were once worthy functions, are slow to change with the environment. Skill sets important in one era are less meaningful in another. Institutions may actually impede progress as their imperative shifts to survival rather than to modifying capabilities to meet changing goals. They become barriers to constructive change – known in lean parlance as *monuments*.

## There Will Always Be Monuments

The underlying theory regarding monuments is that the very institutions, infrastructure, and mindsets that enable success under one set of circumstances can become barriers under a new set of circumstances. For example, political scientists often point to civil service as a successful innovation in response to political patronage systems, but as a restraining force on innovation in a later era. Once addressed, though, system barriers or restraining forces have the potential to become enablers or drivers of change.[22]

In this spirit, it is important to note that we are not arguing for a future aerospace industry without institutions, infrastructure, or dominant mindsets. That would be inappropriate for any industry. In the case of aerospace, it is a very *different* set of institutional arrangements, infrastructure, and mindsets that is needed. Ultimately, we are making the case here that leaders at all levels, and in every enterprise, need to *understand* the historical value of current monuments in order to *transform* them effectively to meet future challenges.

## Barriers to Change

Utterback's model is useful for understanding the dynamics of innovation in the aerospace industry. However, it does not explain why, with the shifting realities of the 1990s obvious to all, *change* has been so slow in coming and so inadequate to the US Aerospace Enterprise's needs. Sure, there has been some concrete action. But why not more, and with a greater sense of urgency? The answer is simple: today's US Aerospace Enterprise is saddled with monuments from the Cold War days.

What is a monument? Again, it is something tangible or intangible – a strategy, an institution, a factory or other part of the infrastructure, or even a mindset – that was once useful, even vital. From the lean perspective, though, monuments may become impediments to much-needed change, and their existence can cause serious misalignments between where an enterprise is and where it needs to be.

This concept of monuments is far from unique to aerospace. The US auto, steel, and consumer goods industries spent much of the 1970s and 1980s struggling with the monuments of obsolete factories and attitudes none too friendly to consumers. Meanwhile, their Asian and European competitors took a new, consumer-focused approach, and captured large market shares.

The US Aerospace Enterprise, with its storied, often glorious past, is particularly rich in monuments. Understanding the forces that impede change in the US Aerospace Enterprise is key in understanding both the present conditions and the possibilities for paths forward. Here we will begin to construct a conceptual framework for understanding these forces. Aerospace *monuments* will be the substance of that framework.

Monuments exist at several levels of the US Aerospace Enterprise, and the examples we discuss are by no means exhaustive. Our framework draws attention to obsolete strategies for fighting old wars and defeating foes that no longer exist. There are institutions that were created to address once pressing issues, but that new circumstances have rendered inappropriate. There is the physical infrastructure, some of which dates back to World War II. And there are the mental habits: ideal for the challenges of past times, many of them are simply wrong for the fast-moving, turn-of-the-millennium world.

## National and Global Monuments

In the Cold War days, planning could be carried out using a clear set of action scenarios involving known enemies. Today, the US armed services have embraced this approach while struggling to develop one to match currently perceived needs. The publicly discussed rethinking of high-level US strategic policy after the Cold War involved a different scenario of fighting two 'medium-size' opponents at the same time – a strategy, say some, with the singular advantage of justifying *existing* force structures and procurement plans.[23] Recently, it has taken a noted bureaucratic warrior, Secretary of Defense Donald Rumsfeld, all of his expertise just to get the Joint Chiefs of Staff to budge off this strategy and consider a more realistic one, such as 'winning one war decisively while deploying peace-keeping troops in perhaps half a dozen other places'.[24]

How does Cold War-era strategy qualify as a monument? It is a leftover, misaligned with today's realities. We live in a multipolar world, with the United States occupying a uniquely powerful position as the sole 'megapower'. There are challenges from many directions, by opponents waging asymmetrical campaigns of terrorism, local destabilization, and other types of attacks.

Another possible strategy, for example, would be to develop force structures and operating methods that are flexible, highly mobile, and easily reconfigured. Yet, our military leaders are wary of such a strategic shift. And while their experience tells them that they must cope with today's threats with a diverse force structure that can be configured creatively, they know that fighting assets cannot be procured fast enough. Therefore, the military addresses these threats by pulling together equipment probably designed for other conflicts, but adaptable once in service.

Linked to this strategic monument is the DoD's Planning, Programming and Budgeting System (PPBS), introduced in the 1960s. Although PPBS allowed a more disciplined method for defense planning, programming, and decisionmaking, it has itself become a monument that hinders the swift input of requirements to address emergent threats. Defense programs take an average of nine years to reach the fighting forces once the requirements are identified, and the PPBS system is a major contributor to this outcome because it can no longer accommodate warfighter needs quickly and effectively in a fiscally constrained environment.[25]

DoD acquisition is a bureaucratic nightmare. The few new programs that are initiated are often aggressively scheduled and funded. But as reality sets in, schedules slip. Funds are diverted, mostly to other defense programs in the ramp-up phase. As a consequence, about half of all major acquisition programs take longer than their original schedule, with an average slip of 14 months.[26] Of course, this leads to ongoing programs with insufficient funding, which further exacerbates the problem with the portfolio of programs, causing multiple program stretch-outs or delays. The cycle seems endless.

The defense industry, charged with producing the assets needed by the fighting forces, is often plagued by budget and schedule instability. As with all instability, there are costs – higher-priced defense products for the taxpayers and layoffs or, at best, career stagnation for the defense industry workforce.

On the commercial side, the tendency to think only of the *product* – as opposed to the *capability* provided to the end user – can be considered a monument. Hughes recognized this problem and expanded to provide a variety of services directly to customers, from DirecTV™ for the public to bandwidth-for-hire for telecommunications companies. The Hughes example is interesting in that its satellite production facilities have been a victim of the corporation's success – they have been sold off as underperforming, at least in comparison to other parts of the company.[27] Aircraft engine companies also recognized this issue, and now sell 'power by the hour' to airlines, providing not only the engine, but spare parts and service to guarantee power as needed, within agreed-upon time limits.[28]

In the commercial jet transport sector, the product mindset combines with existing business relations between producers and airlines to create a 'boom and bust' cycle of supply and demand. Figure 3.7 illustrates that despite consistent growth in demand for air travel of some 5–11 percent annually, the industry is dominated by feast-or-famine cycles lasting 9–11 years.[29]

**FIGURE 3.7** | **Aircraft orders and deliveries compared with passenger seat miles**

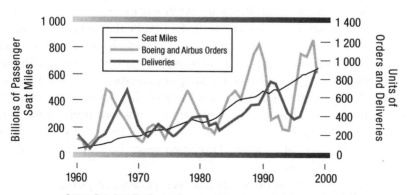

*Source:* Data from The Boeing Company, Airbus, Aerospace Industries Association, and Air Transport Association.

The industry has lived with this situation for many years, despite its harmful effects on long-term industry health – particularly the wellbeing of the workforce. The industry is moving towards more customer-oriented solutions, such as financing, leasing, and servicing packages, that would tend to dampen these cycles (or at least their effect on revenue), but not as aggressively as are the engine or telecommunications sectors.

Another monument in the commercial sector will be familiar to all air travelers – the elaborate hub-and-spoke system for moving passengers through complex routes. The aircraft, terminals, airports, routing and ticketing systems, and business plans of every major airline are tied to this monument. But the ultimate customer – the traveling public – may not be best served by this arrangement.[30] It's notable that the few exceptions to this hub-and-spoke approach by airlines have been quite successful – particularly for Southwest Airlines, which provides point-to-point service on many routes that the major airlines have largely ignored.

## Infrastructure and Institutional Monuments

One of the biggest monuments in the US Aerospace Enterprise is the phys-ical infrastructure – including military bases, outdated factories, and space-flight facilities – that remains from earlier eras. Our Cold War background demanded a large fighting force with large numbers of fighting assets – equipment such as airplanes, ships, tanks, and so on, as well as personnel. A great many facilities were required to produce, maintain, and operate these assets. The country also needed a surge capability to produce equipment during or just preceding a conflict. Production overcapacity, supported by an array of government-owned facilities, provided that surge insurance.

The picture has changed. Bases are extremely expensive to maintain and exist in greater numbers than are justified – despite the political pressure on members of Congress to maintain facilities in their home districts. The surfeit of military bases has been addressed in part by Base Realignment and Closing (BRAC) commissions, groups established through a bipartisan process that have been able to reduce some of the excess while deflecting the political consequences.[31] Countering the positive trend is the sorry environmental record of many of these facilities, a legacy of sites that must be cleaned up at great expense. This often severely slows the process of conversion to other uses.

The aircraft manufacturers themselves possess physical production capabilities that far exceed the production rates now needed, and many facilities date back to World War II when production was a hundred times

## Education as a Monument

Education in this country in the disciplines most directly relevant to the US Aerospace Enterprise remains based on an old model that evolved just after World War II and matured during the Cold War. There were several elements involved. The atomic bomb that ended World War II drove home the lesson that 'hard' science could translate into national power. And while it was widely assumed that the knowledge used by the Soviets to build their own atomic weapons at the beginning of the Cold War was stolen, Sputnik was a different story: many Americans were convinced that the 1957 launch of the satellite meant the United States was starting the 'space race' from the back of the pack. Government funding flowed to universities, subsidizing a curriculum heavily weighted towards scientific and technical skills. Scientists were rewarded for excelling in their specialties, and engineers were rewarded in a similar fashion for specializing in narrow technical disciplines.

The social sciences mirrored the experiences in the hard sciences, with management and other social science education similarly rewarding ever-increasing specialization. For example, the Academy of Management today has more than twenty separate divisions, each in fields with their own journals, specialized areas of study, and subdisciplines.

Times have changed, but the emphasis on narrow and deep technical education has not – putting curricula out of sync with the needs of modern industry. As industries shift from a focus on making technology advances to integrating those advances into products and services for customers, engineers are expected to play a new role – one where they interact with non-engineers, and even become marketers, strategic planners, managers, and customer-support people. The entrepreneurial boom of the late 1990s, while based on new technology, only intensified this trend, with engineers often thrust into the multifaceted roles of founders of or partners in small, rapidly evolving companies.

New definitions of today's industry needs in engineering education point consistently to the urgency of broadening technical education and including more of what is usually associated with the liberal arts and management.[32] A number of institutions are implementing changes to their curricula in response to these new definitions and new accreditation criteria.[33] Unfortunately, though, institutions of higher education are intrinsically rigid institutions – a disadvantage in times of change. Younger faculty, who might be expected to champion new things, are forced into specialized roles by the demands of winning tenure. Tenured faculty, while granted the freedom to champion new things, have little incentive to change from the specialization associated with their younger days. Because curricula and course structures represent the investment of a great deal of time and effort, changing them is very difficult. The fact that research staff and administrations live off the flow of research dollars, mostly distributed by discipline-specific organizations, only feeds the problem.

greater. The rationale for facilities appropriate to the production rates of World War II was waning even during the Cold War years; clearly, those facilities are surplus today.[34]

Infrastructure monuments pose a tough challenge, with disincentives for infrastructure reduction.[35] We've already mentioned political pressure external to firms. There's also the internal logic of the firms themselves doing business with the government: as the number of new programs diminish, it becomes increasingly important to win the remaining development programs, which in turn leads firms to reject infrastructure reductions out of fear that they might adversely affect their ability to win new programs. The Joint Strike Fighter program, with the potential for production of as many as four thousand aircraft over the next thirty years, is a good example. A program of such magnitude virtually assures the long-term viability of whatever firm wins. Firms have a disincentive to make prudent infrastructure reductions if they think they might lose because they're not seen as up to the task.

Today's infrastructure in the space sector, a monument developed during the heyday of the space race, represents a 'marching army' that has been difficult to trim as programs and their needs have diminished. The most severe example is the Space Shuttle, which requires a large and permanent force of people to run. By transitioning all launches to the Space Shuttle (up to the time of the Challenger accident), the US government effectively suppressed more competitive alternatives. This masked many problems: in particular, by forcing the assumption that all future US space traffic would fly on the Space Shuttle, the policy spurred erroneous predictions of high flight rates, which made the 'marching army' economical by spreading its cost over many flights. Today, it requires the same massive support as it did for the much higher rate of launches planned in the past – which makes the cost-per-launch unavoidably high.

If it had not been clear before, the 1986 Challenger accident finally demonstrated that the Space Shuttle would not satisfy the US Aerospace Enterprise's needs. Before that moment, though, pressure to keep up flight rates had led, indirectly, to the Challenger disaster – and created a monument. The misaligned policy also created a window of opportunity for the French Ariane launch system, the first of many to challenge US dominance in space launch capability, and has had a negative impact on funding and operations for almost all other NASA programs – including alternative US systems that missed many years of development.

## Cultural Monuments

The nonphysical, and hence least visible, monuments are perhaps the most debilitating. Within the US Aerospace Enterprise, these 'cultural monuments' include a mindset that focuses on best technical performance to the detriment of other considerations; a systematic aversion to risk; and disincentives to cost reductions. These all have a profound impact on the very core of the US Aerospace Enterprise, sapping the energy and innovation out of the workforce and potential entrepreneurs.

For much of its long history, the culture of best performance served the US Aerospace Enterprise well. In wartime – whether hot or cold – there are harsh penalties for falling behind in technology. But almost since the fall of the Berlin Wall, there has been widespread recognition among industry thinkers and government policymakers that aerospace needs to shift from its performance-driven culture, where cost is no object, to a focus on obtaining the maximum value for constrained dollars.

During the Cold War years, DoD acquisition practices were designed to 'pull' high-performance products from the industrial base using cost-plus-fixed-fee contracts. This resulted in bidders promising optimistic performance, unrealistically low costs, or both, to win orders – followed by inevitable renegotiations. After all, it's easier to deal with increased costs than with the politically difficult problem of eliminating programs (and hence jobs) or diminishing capabilities (and hence being seen as 'soft' on defense). The funding increases that result are compensated for by stretching schedules, which adds inefficiencies and costs associated with time on top of the increased costs to meet performance. The whole process – what some cynics call 'win and spin' – is a major cultural monument. Various acquisition-reform efforts are tackling this monument with some success, such as with the C-17 program (discussed in Chapter 8). However, it takes time to change government and corporate cultures shaped over more than forty years of doing business.

Current product-design practices represent another cultural monument, closely linked to the culture of best performance. Typical corporate and government product-development cultures are poorly adapted to creating value-based designs,[36] and product-development processes usually focus on meeting technical requirements and reducing technical, cost, and schedule risks – best achieved by a rigid system with formal procedures and numerous checks and reviews. Such a system, though, has severe limitations that can lead to misalignment. It makes it difficult to trade system characteristics against each other, or to handle flexible or variable requirements. It is also intrinsically slow and hence vulnerable to shifting needs.

Within this system, the most critical and challenging design functions are those related to performance. In aerospace, this has led to a culture where the product's technical design team is afforded more status, pay, and consideration than in other aspects of the enterprise such as manufacturing or quality.

Extensive risk aversion underlies these cultural monuments. At a time when shifting needs, emerging threats, and diminishing resources would suggest the need for bold new ideas, the US Aerospace Enterprise is instead retrenching to a few large systems that are 'too big to fail'. For instance, the only two new tactical aircraft systems on the horizon are saddled with a set of requirements established in a different era, and it may be difficult to address evolving needs and requirements. At the system level, this makes warfighters, system acquirers, and companies unwilling to risk innovation.

The history – and failure – of innovative programs such as the F-20 Tigershark helps us understand today's aversion to taking risks at the system level (see box), which permeates all levels of organizations. Success is usually defined as simply meeting the stated requirements, with no rewards for innovation or cost savings. Too often when there is a failure, energy is expended on assigning fault rather than on discovering the root causes and championing the learning that can be gained from that experience.

Government oversight, a component of the risk-aversion monument, often focuses on micromanaging costs to prevent the possibility of fraud

## F-20 Tigershark: A High-Risk Maneuver

At the start of 1980, Northrop found itself without an immediate successor to its T-38/F-5 series and was actively seeking opportunities to maintain the ability to produce complete aircraft. At the same time, Northrop was the principal subcontractor to McDonnell Douglas on the F/A-18 and was slated to be the prime contractor for the export version of the F-18 (F-18L). In the end, though, not a single F-18L was ever produced, and McDonnell Douglas continued to sell the F/A-18 abroad.[37] This placed even greater pressure on Northrop to find options for maintaining a future in military aircraft. The company rested it hopes on the *company-funded* F-5G, later called the F-20 Tigershark.

The F-20 was the largest commercial military project ever attempted. Designing it to compete with the F-16 for the export and domestic markets, Northrop invested $1.2 billion in the F-20, which first flew on 30 August 1982, powered by the GE F404 engine. Of the three prototypes built, two crashed during demonstrations and one now resides at the Los Angeles County Museum of Science.

The F-20 was one of the most advanced aircraft of its day. It was significantly less costly than the F-16, and the first to exploit fully the digital electronics revolution. Yet, the F-20 was abandoned after six years of sales attempts – with no customer. The lack of sales success was due, in part, to shifting political sands in Washington – difficulties unrelated to the aircraft itself (although it was conceded, eventually, that the test aircraft crashes also did little to spur business).

Theories abound as to why the F-20 didn't succeed. Perhaps it was the Air Force 'not-invented-here' syndrome; perhaps it was the government's changing export-sales policies; or perhaps it failed because it lacked merit. Whatever the answer, though, this notable venture has certainly soured the atmosphere for aerospace companies to take any kind of free-market approach to military aircraft development. Firms today are loath to put enormous levels of internal resources into system-level development before locking in paying customers.

(or embarrassing revelations such as that of the '$600 hammer' that came out during the DoD procurement scandals of the 1980s).[38] To many, it sometimes appears that ensuring that the books are in order takes higher priority than nurturing policies and procedures that will deliver value to the government and the warfighter.

How does this mindset play out in practical terms? With the reduction of procurement funding and a large infrastructure already in place, there is little incentive to make investments that would reduce the cost of producing products. The disincentives are compounded by the fact that the customer, with a 'cost-plus' mindset, often quickly absorbs savings from cost reductions.[39]

Political considerations make it difficult to embrace the notion that contractors should earn a rate of return that is reasonable by 'normal' business standards, and that they should be rewarded for improvements and cost savings. Those are true cultural monuments that cannot be addressed simply by 'granting' the industry higher profit margins on a cost-plus-more basis. As in any industry, such profits should be *earned* by saving money and delivering better products and services.

All of these cultural monuments are even more frustrating because they fly in the face of what has made the US economy so strong. Part of the energy that propelled the US growth economy of the 1990s came from taking large risks to realize potentially large rewards. The 'new economy' companies are a good example: while it is true that most fail, those that succeed create unprecedented new wealth. And beyond these examples, US businesses in diverse fields have captured or recaptured world leadership by accepting risk and embracing new technologies and business practices. Risk-taking and the flexibility it allows are key advantages in times, such as now, when rapid changes both in technologies and world political and economic systems are destabilizing established structures.[40]

Monuments cast a long shadow into the future. Moreover, the various types of monuments interact. So, the existence of strategic and cultural monuments induces the protection of infrastructure monuments, not their transformation. And when roles and responsibilities are defined relative to existing infrastructure and strategy monuments, it is difficult to identify cultural monuments that may be obstacles to change.

## The Challenge Ahead

To put it simply, the US Aerospace Enterprise *must* find a new equilibrium. The fall of the Berlin Wall symbolized a major change in the world situation. The Cold War was over, the West had triumphed, and the competition that mattered now was primarily *economic*. More than a decade later, the *full* implications of this change have not yet been revealed, but at least one thing is clear: US security and economic needs – the nation's *priorities* – are vastly different on this side of that event. This is reflected in new and unstable demands on the US Aerospace Enterprise – demands it is still struggling to understand and adapt to as it seeks to right its alignment with a new world situation.

The aerospace industry struggles with its own maturity. The characteristics of a maturing industry, which we presented earlier, suggest many of the things actually observed in aerospace today: the emergence of dominant designs and the consequent slowing of technological evolution, the diminishing number of large players, the emerging importance of production and manufacturing, and the concentration of innovation in niche markets, often led by new or small players. Yet, as we have pointed out, there are many opportunities for innovation. Any complicated industry should have similar experiences.

Understanding aerospace monuments provides a better grasp of the challenges ahead. The monuments cannot be ignored, but do not necessarily need to be battled. We think what is needed is for the US Aerospace Enterprise to recognize the monuments, understand how and why they became monuments, determine whose interests they still serve, see the behaviors these monuments reinforce, and appreciate what it will take to transform the monuments to allow for different behaviors. That's an approach relevant for any industry.

How can obstacles be surmounted and a new equilibrium established? Part II of this book takes up that question. For guidance, we look first to the lessons of an industry deep in Utterback's Specific Phase – the automobile industry. The lessons learned from studying the Toyota Production System, captured in *The Machine That Changed the World* and *Lean Thinking*, kicked off the lean movement, which has had a profound effect on automobile and consumer goods manufacturing.

The full scale and scope of the changes required in the US Aerospace Enterprise are even more dramatic than are those in automobile, manufacturing, or other industries. But as we will see in Part II, the initial steps on this journey have already been taken.

# PART II

# Better, Faster, Cheaper?

The response to new priorities in the United States was captured in the mantra 'Better, Faster, Cheaper', which was popularized by NASA Administrator Dan Goldin. No longer did society value massive endeavors like the Apollo program or the Supersonic Transport, so characteristic of the prior Cold War years. Military and non-military customers alike wanted better products, available sooner, and at a lower cost than in the past. For aerospace, that meant a new challenge – one for which its Cold War legacy had left it ill equipped.

While the United States was focused on Cold War priorities after World War II, Japan was focusing on economic challenges. Japan's needs centered on building an economically competitive industry with the least investment of resources. The paragon became Toyota and its 'lean' Toyota Production System. But automobiles and their consumers are so different from aircraft or spacecraft and their customers and users: could an industry such as aerospace quickly transform itself to such a radically different paradigm, and create the radically new culture that would be necessary? It was by no means certain – hence the question mark on our title for Part II.

Part II takes us on a journey. In Chapter 4, 'Lean Thinking', we delve into 'lean', explaining its origins, principles and practices, and relationship to major change initiatives such as Six Sigma, Total Quality Management, Reengineering, and others. Fundamentally, 'lean' is the elimination of waste from all activities related to the creation of products or services. But the underlying *reason* for waste elimination is to enable efficient creation of *value* for multiple enterprise stakeholders – the end user and the customer, the shareholder, the employees, the suppliers, and the partners, and the broader public and society.

After a decade of lean in aerospace, is there any evidence of applicability and improved performance? We provide an unequivocal answer –
*yes*. In Chapter 5, 'Islands of Success', we highlight many applications of
lean in multiple aerospace sectors – commercial and military aircraft,
engines, avionics hardware and software, missiles, and space launch
systems. In these examples (and many others not included in this book),
there have been major reductions of waste and creation of value. In most
cases, however, the full benefits of lean have yet to be realized, because
implementation has failed to encompass the entire enterprise.

In Chapter 6, 'Lean Enterprises', we introduce lean principles and practices at the enterprise level, and address what they are, how to implement
them, and how to assess enterprise progress on the journey to lean. We
define what it means to be a lean enterprise, and identify three levels of
interrelated and interdependent aerospace enterprises – program, multi-
program (corporate or government), and national and international. We
also address concepts of integrated enterprises, extended enterprises, and
stakeholders. Significantly, we present emerging evidence there (and in
later chapters) that major benefits are indeed realized when lean principles
are applied at the enterprise level – provided that they encompass a focus
on value.

The lessons of our Part II journey apply to many industries seeking to
become lean. But as we learn in Part III, being lean is not sufficient. It is
an enabler to creating *value*, the key to future prosperity.

## CHAPTER 4

# Lean Thinking

In early 1998, a group of managers, engineers, and union leaders from prime contractors and suppliers in the aerospace industry gathered as part of a special workshop on supply-chain integration. Among the invited speakers was Hajime Ohba, general manager of the Toyota Supplier Support Center.

Ohba made some brief comments. Then the group began to ask insistent questions about working with new suppliers: 'What is the first thing you do? What comes next?' But Ohba refused again and again to give any sort of a cookbook answer. When the questions continued, he finally emphasized that the group had to understand one thing. 'Lean', he said, 'is a way of thinking, not a list of things to do.' And Ohba elaborated: he had to meet with each supplier and understand how that particular supplier thought about its own production system. Only then could he begin to identify what would make sense in terms of how to focus the implementation of lean principles and practices.

What is the mystery here? Is there something particular about the concept of 'lean' that requires thinking in ways different from the 'norm'? Surely there must be a set of lean principles and practices that needs to be implemented in *some* kind of order?

To gain a full understanding of Ohba's approach to lean, we have to look back more than 50 years to a singular point in history: August 15th, 1945. That day, the Emperor announced to the Japanese people that his forces would surrender to the Allies of World War II. That day also marked a new beginning for Toyota, which faced a daunting strategic challenge.

US industry was, unambiguously, the world's dominant manufacturing force. Kiichiro Toyoda, then Toyota's president, posed the challenge this way: 'Catch up with America in three years.'[1] Given the economies of scale enjoyed by the large US automakers, which were looking to enter the Japanese market, Mr Toyoda felt that catching up was the only way Japan's auto industry would survive. He posed his challenge to Taiichi Ohno, then one of Toyota's key engineers.

Today revered as the originator of the Toyota Production System, Ohno had joined the company just two years earlier after a career in the textile industry. To accomplish their mission, Ohno and his associates determined that it was essential to know America and learn American ways. They centered on what today we would call the world benchmark of the time: the Ford Motor Company's River Rouge manufacturing complex located in Dearborn, Michigan.

Ohno quickly identified the sources of success enjoyed by the US automobile industry, as well as the system's underlying weaknesses. What he observed was *mass production* – high-volume, large-lot production, with vast warehouses to store inventory, and a highly vertically integrated operation extending from the iron ore mines all the way to the finished product. Ford had built a system well suited to meeting the needs of America's vast market. Ohno wanted a production system equally well suited to Japanese economic realities.

But Toyota faced many dilemmas in Japan: a small and fragmented domestic market, a workforce in short supply, scarce natural resources, limited land, and little capital available for investment – all the opposite of the US situation. Clearly, the mass production model exemplified by Ford's River Rouge facility would not work in the Japanese context. Even the variation on the mass production model that had emerged at General Motors, which had the advantage of a much broader range of product lines, was inadequate for the Japanese context.

A dynamic process unfolded over the next few decades – involving the emergence of what might now be called *lean thinking* – in response to the unique Japanese business challenges. A variety of solutions emerged to particular limitations of the mass production model: innovations such as just-in-time (JIT) delivery, in-station process control, total productive maintenance, integrated product and process design, *kanban* method for material pull, and others. The people involved in this process underwent deep and sustained learning. During the 1950s, their learning was driven by numerous visits to US factories to study 'the secret of American industrial productivity', aided by leading thinkers such as W. Edwards Deming and Joseph Juran.[2] The full impact of lean thinking became evident a few decades later.

Masaaki Imai tells the story of Toshiro Yamada, a retired professor who was a member of one of the 1950s study teams. Years later, Yamada paid a sentimental visit to some of the plants he had visited earlier, among them Ford's River Rouge facility. Back in Japan, at a banquet to celebrate the silver anniversary of the group's trip, he shook his head in disbelief. 'You know', he said, 'the plant was exactly the same as it had been 25 years ago.'[3]

The Japanese visitors, coming from the dynamic learning environment of their home country, were shocked. How could it be, they wondered, that US operations had not made advances with parallel intensity to those in Japan over the intervening half-century?

The application of lean thinking propelled Japanese firms, such as Toyota, to the front ranks of worldwide industrial excellence and competitiveness. Today, this way of thinking is squarely on the agenda across many industries in many countries. Celebrated leaders in the e-commerce world have taken the lean principles to new levels. Dell Computer Corp., for example, overtook much bigger rivals in the marketplace by using the internet to record orders and broadcast production schedules through a 'supplier supermarket', producing and delivering components on a just-in-time basis to factories that then build custom-made computers within a week of the original order. The company then ships these products to consumers overnight. Dell illustrates a unique mix of craft-type specialization on a high-volume basis, with almost no waste.

Lean thinking has been decades in the making – and is still evolving. While much of the history centers on the automobile industry, especially the evolution of the Toyota Production System (reflecting its pivotal role), lean thinking applies across many industrial sectors. This chapter recounts the journey to date and points the way forward. For the reader who is new to lean, this chapter will serve as a primer. For the more knowledgeable reader, the chapter offers frameworks and syntheses that we hope will trigger new insights.

## Lean Thinking Defined

Our definition of 'lean' in Chapter 1 centered on two key dimensions: eliminating waste and creating value. Both are essential elements that lean must incorporate. To focus exclusively on eliminating waste – cutting costs – is insufficient, and may not even produce a rise in revenues. To focus exclusively on creating value is also insufficient, because many improvement opportunities become visible only after focused efforts to eliminate waste (such as excess inventory, redundant inspection, sequential engineering, and so on).

What type of thinking is oriented along these dimensions? What has driven past Japanese success and now drives leaders in the world of e-commerce? Here's our definition of 'lean thinking', a synthesis derived from decades of scholarship and field observation.

Lean thinking is the dynamic, knowledge-driven, and customer-focused process through which all people in a defined enterprise continuously eliminate waste with the goal of creating value.

There are several key concepts embedded here, so it will be helpful to 'unpack' the definition. We will examine each of its elements briefly, in many cases building on the prior work of others. And we will more fully develop some of the concepts, such as 'enterprise' and 'value', in later chapters.

At the outset, it is important to note that lean principles did not emerge from the theoretical constructs of scholars, but are ideas first developed in practice and later distilled and codified by scholars and other observers. Taiichi Ohno, the father of the Toyota Production System, implies this very process in his foreword to a 1988 book on the subject: 'We are very interested in how [the author] Professor Monden has "theorized" our practice from his academic standpoint and how he has explained it to the foreign people.'[4] Even if the terms 'Toyota Production System' and 'lean' are of recent vintage, the underlying concepts and practices have been adopted and used over many decades.

'Unpacking' our definition of lean thinking involves reviewing a mix of scholarship and practice, beginning with two concepts: *customer-focused* and *knowledge-driven*.

## Origins of the Term 'Lean Production'

John Krafcik, then a graduate student at MIT's Sloan School of Management and a researcher in the International Motor Vehicle Program (IMVP), was the first to use the term *lean production system*. In his master's thesis, he highlighted that *lean production* uses less of everything compared with *mass production* – less human effort in the factory, less manufacturing space, less investment in tools, and fewer engineering hours to develop a new product. This makes it possible to produce a greater variety of higher-quality products in less time.[5]

The term *lean production* was introduced to a wider audience by James Womack, Daniel Jones, and Dan Roos in *The Machine That Changed The World*,[6] their book summarizing the first five years of work in the IMVP, an

MIT-based research initiative. Today, this book is widely regarded as one of the most successful business titles ever, and has been published in many languages. When it first came out, though, it created some consternation: its core was a comprehensive benchmarking survey of more than 90 automobile assembly plants in 17 countries, representing roughly half of the worldwide assembly capacity. The survey, conducted by Krafcik and then MIT doctoral student John Paul MacDuffie, examined issues of automation, manufacturability, product variety, and management practices – with striking and unexpected findings. And while the book may have masked the names of individual sites and many companies, the findings had unavoidable implications for specific firms and their facilities.

One key finding was that Japanese-owned assembly plants in Japan, on average, were 48 percent more productive (hours/vehicle) than American-owned plants in the United States. European-owned plants in Europe fared even more poorly. And in terms of product quality,[7] Japanese plants scored an average of 50 percent better than the US plants and about 47 percent better than the European plants. In the case of luxury cars, one Japanese plant examined required but 'one-half the effort of the American luxury-car plants, half the effort of the best European plant, a quarter of the effort of the average European plant, and one-sixth of the worst European luxury-car producer'. Quality at that Japanese plant exceeded the quality at all plants except one in Europe, a plant that required four times the effort of the Japanese plant to assemble a comparable car.[8] Assembly plants in Japan, as well as the US plants of Japanese automakers, enjoyed both higher productivity and higher quality compared with the domestically owned plants in Europe and in the United States, where one could find either high productivity or high quality, but not both. And quality was expensive for these plants to achieve – when it could be achieved at all.[9]

Relying on results obtained by other researchers,[10] the authors made another striking finding in the area of new product development. After various adjustments to normalize the survey data on 29 'clean sheet' product development projects reaching the market between 1983 and 1987 in the United States and Europe, they found that, on average, the

Japanese producers enjoyed a two-to-one advantage in terms of total engineering effort required and a savings of one-third in total product development time. What was remarkable about these findings was that lean product development methods *simultaneously* reduced the effort and time involved in manufacturing.[11]

How did the authors of *The Machine That Changed The World* account for the global variation in production and design performance? They concluded that the same machine that gave rise to mass production – the automobile – was now pointing the way toward a new model. That model, *lean production*, was a customer-driven system – producing only what customers wanted, when they wanted it, and at a price they were willing to pay.

## Customer-Focused

In a lean system, the customer provides an orientation for the full enterprise, representing what might be termed 'true north'. Customer needs and expectations act as a *pull* upon enterprise activities, from product design and manufacturing to after-market customer support.[12] This is not some *abstract* idea of serving the customer, but a set of disciplined work practices designed to give customers the right product or service at the right time and at the right price.

The customer pull in production operations is reflected in the elimination of in-process inventory and the building of products in direct response to customer orders. Increasing product variety and shortening new product-development cycle times are both ways in which a customer focus permeates the new product-development process. Contrast this with Henry Ford's classic statement that 'people can have any color they want, so long as it's black', a stance symbolic of the mass production mindset.

## Knowledge-Driven

Being customer-focused requires the ideas and effort of an entire workforce, because it is impossible to eliminate waste or add value effectively without the full input of frontline workers, engineering design team members, office staff, and all others who touch the product, develop designs, or deliver services. This recognizes the critical role of *people*, not just processes, in effectuating value – as highlighted in our Chapter 1 principle.[13]

Mass production presumes that innovation and improvement will come from a relatively small group of experts, with the rest of the workforce considered primarily as interchangeable cogs in the production and design machines – and as a cost. A key feature of lean thinking involves appreciating the entire workforce, the suppliers, and others as sources of knowledge, information, and insight regarding the elimination of waste and the creation of value. Consequently, it is essential to invest in training in technical and social skills (group process, communications, negotiations, leadership, and so on). Establishing disciplined or structured work processes is a common foundation for improvement efforts, with substantial support resources devoted to the implementation of improvement suggestions.

The full scale of knowledge-driven improvement efforts can be quite dramatic. For example, within two years of being established in the early 1990s, the Nippondenso components facility in Battle Creek, Michigan, had its approximately 750 employees (called 'associates') implementing an average of more than 7000 process improvement suggestions per year.[14]

A workforce and a cadre of suppliers who are supporting a knowledge-driven process will have expectations of being full partners in this process. Though it is not as widely appreciated as other aspects of lean, all leading lean operations are characterized by long-term partnerships designed to support knowledge-generating activities.

The lean thinking process is, therefore, customer-focused and knowledge-driven. But don't these two terms also apply to other systems change initiatives, such as Total Quality Management or Six Sigma? What makes the thinking 'lean'? Let's define two additional concepts, *eliminating waste* and *adding value*.

## Eliminating Waste

To be customer-driven, all forms of waste must be eliminated; these include overproduction, work-in-process inventories, and extra steps in accomplishing a task. Eliminating waste is important not just to cut costs, but also to improve quality, safety, and responsiveness to changing market requirements.

The link between lean and responsiveness is often not fully appreciated or understood. Yet, the elimination of waste can be a powerful way to shorten cycle times in both production and product development by eliminating all steps that both are unnecessary and do not add any value –

## The Seven Wastes

The 'Seven Wastes' are categories developed in relation to manufacturing, but they can be adapted for design operations or administrative operations.

| | | | |
|---|---|---|---|
| Overproduction | Inventory | Movement (motion) | |
| Waiting time | Processing | Rework | Transportation |

## The Five S's[15]

Similarly, the Five S's represent habits of personal discipline and organization that make it easier to see the waste.[16]

*Seiri* (organization) = Straighten or Simplify: organize tools, accessories and paperwork

*Seiton* (neatness) = Simplify or Sort: remove unnecessary items from the work area

*Seiso* (cleaning) = Scrub or Shine: repair, clean, and keep clean

*Seiketsu* (standardization) = Standardize or Stabilize: establish and maintain controls and standards

*Shitsuke* (discipline) = Sustain or Self-Discipline: strive for continuous improvement

and thus enhance responsiveness. In a lean enterprise, taking out time that does not add value is far more important than speeding up individual work processes or activities. In other words, lean is not a 'speedup' to work harder, but a deliberate approach taken to 'work smarter'.

Often, the words 'eliminate waste' are feared as code for eliminating jobs – and some initiatives under the banner of lean have indeed had this result. But as we noted above, the knowledge-driven nature of lean urges a focus on employees not as a cost to be cut, but as the source of ideas for eliminating waste. 'Waste walks', which literally involve walking around the operation and seeing forms of waste with new eyes, is still 'mass production' thinking if it involves only a handful of experts and managers.

That is why our definition of lean emphasizes *eliminating waste with the goal of creating value*, which applies to all stakeholders.

The knowledge-driven nature of lean goes far beyond pronouncements that 'employees are our most valuable resource'. It must show up in efforts to address pivotal issues such as job security and through investment in skills and capabilities.

## Creating Value

Every enterprise has many stakeholders: internal and external customers; a workforce; suppliers; shareholders (in most cases); and many other societal stakeholders, including communities and the general public. Each group of stakeholders has its own views – sometimes shared, sometimes complementary, and sometimes points of tension – regarding what represents additional value. For instance, customers and the workforce may both highly value quality. Society and the workforce may both value safety. Conversely, demands for immediate returns on investment by shareholders – what they value – may conflict with the long-term stability valued by the workforce and communities.

As we will see in Chapter 7, these many dimensions of value drive a transformation in our understanding of the concept of lean. For now, though, suffice it to note that lean thinking involves *learning to see value*. A powerful method for this is *value stream mapping*, where all 'value add' activities are traced in sequence through a given operation, and whatever does not add value is waste (in one form or another). Lean thinking, then, involves both eliminating waste and identifying improvements that will help create value for one or more stakeholders.

To complete our 'unpacking', let's look at two additional concepts from our definition: *dynamic and continuous*.

## Dynamic and Continuous

Lean thinking is dynamic – it has evolved over decades and will continue to evolve. And lean thinking is an ongoing process. The concept of continuous improvement (*kaizen*) has been a major thrust of the lean production system that began with Toyota and continues to be central to lean thinking.

In Japanese, *kaizen* means ongoing improvement based on knowledge from *everyone* – not just from experts, but also from managers and workers. Continuous improvement is a problemsolving process requiring the application of a wide array of tools, methods, and practices (for example, quality circles, total productive maintenance or TPM, suggestion systems, just-in-time, *kanban*, and labor–management and customer–supplier partnerships). The approach – which involves 'learning by doing' – stresses process-oriented thinking for the achievement of a continuous stream of improvements, enabled by giving workers many educational opportunities and by emphasizing teamwork. *Kaizen* suggestions for improvement are valued not just for their specific content, but also for the increased *capability* for improvement that such suggestions build in the organization.[17] However, the stress on continuous improvement does not mean that breakthrough innovation should be neglected. Indeed, 'both innovation and *kaizen* are needed if a company is to survive and grow'.[18] Some experts are already replacing the notion of continuous improvement with 'continual improvement', which has less of an incremental connotation.[19]

In the auto industry and other sectors, *kaizen* generally refers to incremental improvements. Ironically, in the aerospace industry, it has come to mean the exact opposite – reengineering or redesign. Aerospace readers may be familiar with or may even have been part of a so-called '*kaizen* event' – a one-time improvement that is far from the concept of *continuous* improvement.

Taken together, these elements of our definition represent a fundamentally different way of thinking. Consider the contrast with the mass production mindset, in which the focus might be on maximizing quantity, building 'buffers', increasing machine utilization, and reducing headcount. While quality, knowledge, continuous improvement, and the customer are valued to a high degree, they do not provide the overall orientation to the mass production system. Further, mass production involves a segmented form of thinking that encourages separation and that limits efforts to link across an enterprise and across value streams.

## Lean Thinking in its Historical Context

To appreciate fully the genius of lean thinking, it is important to understand the historical context: the shift from the agrarian system to the craft system; from craft to mass production; and from mass production to lean thinking. Table 4.1 summarizes the dominant modes of thinking associated with craft and mass production, along with some of the key elements of lean thinking presented earlier in this chapter.

The emergence and diffusion of successive industrial paradigms has not happened all at once. Each has involved evolutionary processes over relat-

**TABLE 4.1 | How craft, mass production, and lean thinking compare**

| | Craft | Mass Production | Lean Thinking |
|---|---|---|---|
| **Focus** | Task | Product | Customer |
| **Operations** | Single items | Batch and queue | Synchronized flow and pull |
| **Overall Aim** | Mastery of craft | Reduce cost and increase efficiency | Eliminate waste and add value |
| **Quality** | Integration (part of the craft) | Inspection (a second stage, after production) | Prevention (built in by design and methods) |
| **Business Strategy** | Customization | Economies of scale and automation | Flexibility and adaptability |
| **Improvement** | Master-driven continuous improvement | Expert-driven periodic improvement | Workforce-driven continuous improvement |

ively long periods, spanning centuries in the case of the craft system, nearly a century of mass production, and several decades in the case of lean thinking. Hybrid models often precede the clear dominance of any one model. For example, leading industrial enterprises in the 19th century have been characterized as a hybrid or 'late-craft system', with craft-shaped products that also featured interchangeable parts. And lean thinking itself has been evolving since the late 1940s, continuing today on a journey of global diffusion, adaptation, and refinement.

The world of mass production began to change in earnest as lean became known beyond Japan. But as the contours of this emerging paradigm came into view, its full nature and dimensions were still unclear. As noted earlier, the IMVP research team began to describe the emerging industrial model as 'lean production'. The 1990 publication of *The Machine That Changed The World* arose out of this intellectual ferment – and introduced the 'lean production' concept to an international audience.[20]

## Building Blocks for Lean Thinking: Womack and Jones

Our definition of lean thinking is designed to be both comprehensive and instructive. We give particular prominence to the knowledge-driven nature of lean and to the dynamic, evolutionary nature of lean thinking – in contrast to many other treatments of lean. In these respects, our definition builds on and extends the approach taken by James P. Womack and Daniel T. Jones in their book *Lean Thinking*,[21] one of today's leading sources for operationalizing lean thinking, so that it can be applied in practice.

The publication of *Lean Thinking* represented a significant jump forward in the evolution of this concept. Womack and Jones helped popularize lean concepts and contributed to the wider dissemination of lean ideas, making them easier to understand and implement across many industries. They began the conversation about lean as a way of *thinking*, stressing that it was not just about *doing*. Their five elements of lean (see below) put a brighter spotlight on *value* than ever before. And, in practical terms, Womack and Jones provided a framework for implementation of lean thinking. The book also elevated the concept of the value stream into the lean lexicon – a borrowing and broadening of the idea of the *value chain* introduced earlier by noted business writer Michael Porter.[22]

Womack and Jones presented lean thinking as an antidote to *muda* (waste), and as a way to convert *muda* into value. In their view, lean thinking encompasses five major steps.

### Specify Value

The starting point for lean thinking is 'value' as defined by the end customer. Womack and Jones explain value in terms of specific products and services, with specific capabilities, offered at specific prices to specific customers.

### Identify the Value Stream

A 'value stream'[23] is the set of all specific end-to-end and linked actions, processes, and functions necessary in transforming raw materials into a finished product delivered to the customer, and then in providing post-sales customer support. In mapping the value stream for a product, firms conduct an in-depth analysis of each individual action in that stream. Each action is classified into one of three categories: (a) it unambiguously creates value; (b) it creates no value but is unavoidable given the company's current capabilities; or (c) it creates no value and can be eliminated immediately. Actions in categories (a) and (b) are analyzed further through value engineering, in an effort to improve the action as much as possible and to eliminate unnecessary expenditures of resources.

### Make Value Flow Continuously

Once the wasteful actions along the value stream have been eliminated to the maximum extent possible, the next step is to make the remaining, value-creating steps 'flow'. The primary challenge is to discard the batch-and-queue mentality prevalent in mass production and to install small-lot production, with single-unit batch sizes as the ultimate goal. Flow is best achieved by eliminating traditional functional organizations and replacing them with integrated product teams organized along the value stream.

### Let Customers Pull Value

Conceptually, the customer 'pulls' the product from the enterprise, rather than the enterprise 'pushing' the product onto the customer. This 'pulling' action cascades upstream, all the way to the supplier network. A production system is organized according to the just-in-time principle, implemented by using the *kanban* system. Employment of total quality management roots out all defective work. JIT is supported by production smoothing, standardization of operations, reduction in setup times, single-piece flow, and rearrangement of production operations into work cells.

### Pursue Perfection

Companies that have implemented lean principles and practices find that there is no end to the process of reducing waste and continually improving products and services delivered to the customer. Consequently, the pursuit of perfection entails a continuous process of improvement in terms of removing waste and eliminating effort, time, space, and errors.

*Lean Thinking* by Womack and Jones still has its limitations, and it is certainly not the end of the lean story. For instance, the book does not fully explicate the concept of *enterprise*, thus risking a bounding of the value stream. Another limitation is that the book implies the notion of a lean champion, as opposed to the notion of an entire workforce embracing lean and incorporating it into the way jobs are done every day. Further, this framework understates the steps involved in what we term 'value identification' and constructing a 'value proposition' among stakeholders. Nevertheless, Womack and Jones have provided a powerful, core building block in the evolution of lean thinking.

**FIGURE 4.1** | **A timeline of the intellectual history of lean**

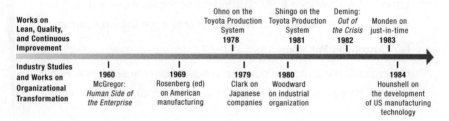

Even though the concept of 'lean' began to show up in the literature only in the late 1980s and early 1990s, this new mode of thinking evolved over many prior decades. (Figure 4.1 is a timeline of some of the intellectual history of lean.[24]) Let's return to Taiichi Ohno and put ourselves in his shoes as he began to think through a production system well suited to Japan's postwar environment.[25] Ohno faced many dilemmas, as we noted earlier. The domestic market was both small and fragmented, the workforce was in short supply, resources were scarce, land was quite limited, and little capital was available for investment. Clearly, the full mass production model exemplified by Ford's River Rouge facility would not work in the Japanese context.

Ohno set out to establish a totally different way of building cars, completely opposite from America's mass production system. That system had to produce only what the customer wanted – in the right quantity and variety, at the right price, and at the right time – and to deliver the quality the customer valued. This meant that Ohno had to supply highly varied and affordable products in relatively small runs to a market that placed a high premium on reliability.

The result was the birth of the Toyota Production System, later characterized as *lean production*: the capability to produce many models in small quantities in a way that would eclipse the mass production behemoths of the West in terms of cost, quality, and affordability. Ohno first introduced the idea of building only what would be supported by orders from the marketplace. Producing in response to orders actually placed by customers was true *customer pull*, driving the entire production system through a stockless production process. In making products that have value, all forms of waste – such as inventory and overproduction – were seen as an absolute evil and had to be eliminated from the production system.

The focus on the customer – the key to the Toyota Production System – was sharpened during a highly influential trip that Mr Ohno took to the United States in 1956 to tour General Motors plants. But his insights did not come from the auto plants. Rather, Ohno was struck by the supermarkets he visited,[26] where he saw the realization of a system through

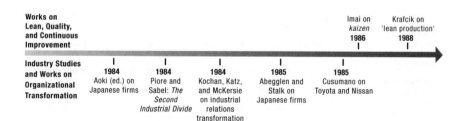

which the customer can get what is needed, at the time needed, and in the needed quantity.[27]

A related key insight was to think about production flow in the reverse direction: a later process would pull back on an earlier process to pick up only the right part, in the quantity needed, and exactly when needed. In an earlier process, the number of parts made would be only that number withdrawn by the next process downstream. This is the essence of just-in-time production, a pillar of the Toyota Production System. Making it work required a communication system that could indicate clearly how many parts would be needed, and when they would be needed, at each step in production: this was accomplished with the *kanban* (signboard or card) system.[28]

Every link in the production chain is tightly synchronized, making the 'pull' system possible.[29] Such a high level of synchronization, in turn, requires *production leveling* to achieve the benefits associated with a smooth production flow process, while also dealing with variability in demand.[30] The idea of production synchronization did not originate with Ohno, but can be traced to the Ford system.[31] Ohno had to figure out how to adapt the idea to many models in small quantities in response to variability in demand. The challenge was to achieve radical reductions in setup time – which was accomplished by Shingo, the creator of the 'single-minute exchange of dies' (SMED), who worked closely with Ohno.[32] Shingo asserts that the SMED system is a sine qua non of the Toyota Production System.[33]

'Autonomation' (*Ninbenno-aru-Jidoka*, or *Jidoka* for short, known as 'automation with a human touch' or 'people giving wisdom to machines') is another pillar of the Toyota Production System.[34] It is a sophisticated strategy that maximizes the capabilities of both workers and machines.[35] This is not a 'technology fix', but focuses attention on the interdependence between social and technical systems. To achieve a flawless just-in-time system, thousands of completely defect-free parts and components must flow to each subsequent process. Quality control, then, is a necessary precondition for just-in-time operations – thus overcoming a fundamental weakness of the mass production system.

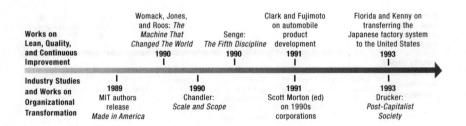

| Works on Lean, Quality, and Continuous Improvement | | Womack, Jones, and Roos: *The Machine That Changed The World* 1990 | | Senge: *The Fifth Discipline* 1990 | Clark and Fujimoto on automobile product development 1991 | Florida and Kenny on transferring the Japanese factory system to the United States 1993 |
|---|---|---|---|---|---|---|
| Industry Studies and Works on Organizational Transformation | 1989 MIT authors release *Made in America* | | 1990 Chandler: *Scale and Scope* | | 1991 Scott Morton (ed) on 1990s corporations | 1993 Drucker: *Post-Capitalist Society* |

The absolute elimination of waste in the Toyota Production System has perhaps not received the attention it deserves, beyond the obvious – and narrow – attention to how it minimizes cost.[36] Elimination of waste includes frontal attacks on its principal sources, which include overproduction,[37] waiting time, transportation, inventories, processing, movement (motion), and rework.[38]

Cost management is not confined to cost reduction, but covers enterprisewide activities across different departments aimed at improving overall profitability performance. This involves target costing, capital investment planning, cost maintenance, and cost improvement (*kaizen* costing). Thus, the new ways of thinking at Toyota that originated in the production operation ended up having implications for capital planning, performance metrics, and many other aspects of the enterprise.

Unlike the traditional mass production system, a Toyota-like lean production system puts a premium on workers as valuable assets essential to the overall success of the enterprise. The best Japanese producers, particularly Toyota and Nippondenso, have empowered workers by giving them wider discretion, actively seeking their help in developing the standardized work sequences they perform, having them take responsibility for maintenance, and expecting them to improve the production system by offering new ideas.

Here, two leading quality experts, W. Edwards Deming and Joseph Juran, became key advisors, introducing the concepts of Statistical Process Control (SPC) and productivity improvement. Instead of using full-time quality inspectors, frontline production workers were trained to take periodic samples of the production run and to track quality on charts. When these workers began to meet on a weekly basis to discuss their findings, the resulting 'quality circles' demonstrated the powerful impact of linking frontline knowledge and systematic data. This was fundamentally different from Ford's *exclusive* reliance on experts to analyze data and suggest improvements.

This *kaizen* process is thus linked to the concepts of quality control, total productive maintenance, error-proofing (*poka-yoke*), visual display of

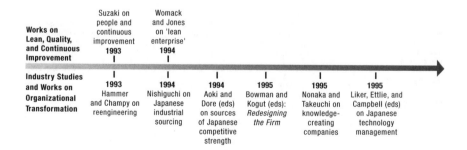

production status information (such as through *andon* lights) and other frontline tools. To foster the *kaizen* process, workers are given many educational opportunities, including classroom training in topics such as the company's management philosophy, leadership development, techniques of scientific management, *kaizen* principles, problem-solving, safety, and work standardization. The team concept is a key enabler of the *kaizen* process: members take direct responsibility for quality, cost, safety, and continuous improvement, while team leaders – although they have many of the same duties as traditional shop foremen – serve more as teachers and facilitators, and are able to perform the same tasks as other team members should the need arise.[39]

In contrast with the mass production model, the Toyota-like lean production system places heavy emphasis on forging stable relationships with a supplier network, based on trust, commitment, transparency, and mutual obligations and responsibilities.[40] It means operating with fewer first-tier suppliers, who are given greater responsibility and are integrated early into the design process. First-tier suppliers are given responsibility for managing lower-tier suppliers. Suppliers are selected not for low bids, but on the basis of their past performance. Dual sourcing is often practiced to stimulate competition among suppliers, while at the same time cooperative relationships govern bilateral links with individual suppliers. This is a delicate balance, with constant attention both to cooperation and competition.

The contractual vehicle employed, the so-called 'basic contract', establishes ground rules governing prices, quality, and delivery. Target costing, accompanied by value engineering, is typically employed to bring down supplier costs continuously. Suppliers are given incentives to reduce costs continually through the sharing of cost savings that can be plowed back to achieve greater efficiencies.

In sum, the lean production system that originated at Toyota represents an interconnected set of mutually reinforcing principles, practices, tools, and methods. It might be termed a 'virtuous circle', continuously driving out waste, improving quality, shortening cycle times, and meeting shifting

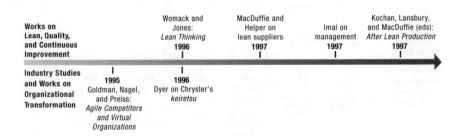

FIGURE 4.2 | The Ford production system

- Three pinion gears (components) linked to drive central gear – that is, operate the system

- All three must perform effectively to deliver the vision/goal – a holistic system that produces customer value

- As the processes (pinion gears) mature, the central gear becomes more fully engaged

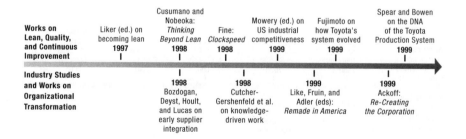

FPDS: Ford Product Development System

*Source:* Ford Motor Company.

customer needs flexibly and responsively. It has evolved over at least 30 years, and continues to undergo transformation. For instance, the first real step to introduce just-in-time production at Toyota took place in 1949–50. The *kanban* system was introduced companywide in 1962, affecting primarily forging and casting. In fact, it took another decade to establish *kanban* fully at Toyota. The company started handling the delivery of parts ordered from outside suppliers in 1963 and it took another twenty years to establish a just-in-time system across the supplier network.[41]

Today, this system is represented in different ways by a wide range of organizations. For example, Figure 4.2 features the 'Ford Gears', representing the Ford Production System. The advancing of lean principles at Ford, the original mass production benchmark, illustrates the diffusion of lean thinking across the auto industry.

The Ford model in Figure 4.2, the Toyota Production System, and similar models all focus on production, but suggest links to the larger value stream. As we will see in the next two chapters, the shift from a production focus to an enterprise focus is a significant challenge. In many ways, this expansion of focus is just one part of a larger evolution in lean thinking.

## The Cross-Cultural Diffusion of Lean Thinking

As lean principles have evolved over a long period, they have also diffused on a global basis.[42] A study of 'knowledge-driven work systems', which focused on both lean and sociotechnical work systems, revealed three very different strategies for the transfer of work systems between the United States and Japan.[43] In some cases, there was a 'piecemeal' strategy; for example, a firm or facility might adopt quality circles, but not the full range of related quality practices. The results are predictable: a flurry of new activity is followed by complications and disappointment, since most innovations are interdependent with other parts of the work systems.

Other cases featured an 'imposed' strategy: a change initiative at the entire system level is introduced, which avoids some of the problems associated with the piecemeal model, but creates new problems. For example, when Mazda first established operations in Flat Rock, Michigan, it attempted to import every aspect of how it operated back home in Hiroshima, Japan. The first few, complicated years saw inconsistencies

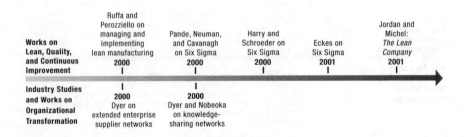

surface concerning relations with the workforce, in the supply chain, and elsewhere. Mazda eventually evolved toward the 'negotiated' model, which is the most complex to implement but is most likely to succeed.

Nippondenso in Battle Creek, Michigan, and NUMMI in California both adopted the 'negotiated model' from the outset, with the aim of creating a new, hybrid system. Negotiated interactions involved first ensuring a shared understanding of governing principles, such as elimination of waste and continuous improvement, but then allowing substantial flexibility in how these principles are applied in a given cultural context.

The global diffusion of lean principles and practices has reached the aerospace industry in several ways. Some aerospace companies are part of larger conglomerates that include automotive divisions or have suppliers that serve both the automotive and aerospace industries. In companies such as Textron or United Technologies, lean experiments in automotive divisions were then introduced to aerospace divisions through the rotational assignments of managers and other internal mechanisms for sharing leading-edge practices. In other cases, leaders in the aerospace industry read books such as *The Machine That Changed The World* and interact with consultants or other experts, which can prompt exploration of these ideas.

## Lean Thinking and Other System-Change Initiatives

The application of lean principles and practices represents a fundamental system change in a given operation or enterprise. It is, in fact, one of many concurrent or sequential change initiatives found in today's organizations, including total quality management (TQM), Six Sigma, reengineering, high-performance work organizations (HPWOs), and others – all terms that designate new business models pursued in recent years by a large number of firms seeking to gain competitive advantage. Sometimes, many such initiatives may even become interwoven.

Consider the recent experience with the C-17 (detailed in Chapter 8). Here was an aircraft that had to make dramatic gains in cost control and quality if it was to continue as planned as the US military's primary transport plane. Its success involved the application of quality tools and techniques, the establishment of a strong labor–management partnership, and the use of lean principles. When the C-17 earned the Malcolm Baldrige National Quality Award, it was celebrated as a total quality management success story. At the same time, union and management leaders have pointed to the HPWO partnership between Boeing and the Machinists union in St. Louis as an exemplar for jointly growing a business. Most recently, C-17 has been touted as a clear demonstration of the way lean principles and practices can transform an entire enterprise.

Which interpretation is correct? Is the C-17 a TQM story, a story of labor–management partnership, or a lean story? Of course, the answer is that all three interpretations are correct. Al Haggerty – a senior management champion for lean at Boeing – uses none of these terms when he comments that 'the key was "customer focus" and a full sharing of information, responsibility, and accountability between industry and the Air Force'.[44]

Though the many initiatives can all be interwoven together, as in the C-17 case, they are not the same. It is important to be precise about the linkages among lean and other related systems change initiatives.

The various system change initiatives used today share many common roots, and taken together represent an overall confluence of thinking.[45] They are initiatives that use many elements of lean thinking. Concepts such as quality circles and statistical process control evolved into TQM, which evolved further into Six Sigma. Lean thinking spawned agile manufacturing. Six Sigma and lean have much in common, particularly in terms of reducing variability and eliminating waste. And it is difficult to imagine lean thinking without the concepts that are central to HPWO. With the possible exception of business process reengineering, each of the change initiatives we discuss here embodies the principles of partnership and continuous improvement. Similarly, all of the initiatives build on the concept of teams and teamwork.[46]

## Lean Thinking and TQM

Total quality management programs took the corporate world by storm in the 1980s, and TQM continues to serve as an important means of meeting customer expectations (for example, product performance, reliability, durability, aesthetics, and perceived utility) by improving the efficiency of the organization – its products, processes, and services. TQM helped disprove an assumption that had emerged from mass production that productivity and quality are incompatible – that you cannot have both, since pushing for higher quality in a mass production system would mean falling behind in quantity and thus would cost more.[47]

Key quality principles came from work on quality control during World War II at Bell Laboratories in the United States, finding their way into Japan right after the war.[48] With the emergence of quality circles and a culture of continuous improvement, ensuring quality became an integral part of the emerging lean production system. But Japan's dramatically new approach to quality did not become apparent to US companies until about the 1980s, when the inroads made into the US domestic market by Japanese electronics and automotive producers highlighted the importance of a new way of thinking.

While today the term 'TQM' has receded – reflecting the reality that quality alone is insufficient to address the full scale and scope of required change – many of the principles associated with TQM have endured,[49] and are integral to lean operations.

## Lean Thinking and Reengineering

Reengineering, or business reengineering, was introduced in the early 1990s with the promise that it would revolutionize American business. The goal of reengineering was no less than to 'retire' the business principles and practices – going all the way back to Adam Smith's famous pin factory[50] – that set out the concept of a division of labor, and that had then led to the rise of the mass production system. Reengineering's leading proponents, Michael Hammer and James Champy, defined it as 'the fundamental rethinking and radical redesign of business processes to achieve dramatic improvements in critical, contemporary measures of performance, such as cost, quality, service, and speed' aimed at standing 'the industrial model on its head'.[51] It was not about fixing anything, downsizing, automation, or taking small and cautious steps; it was, rather, about starting all over again. At the heart of reenginering was the notion of a discontinuous process. Hammer and Champy even coined one of reengineering's enduring maxims: 'If it ain't broke, break it.'

Reengineering focused on business processes – collections of activities that turn inputs into outputs of value to the customer – rather than on organizations, structures, tasks, jobs, or people. Reengineering was thus devoted to the task of reunifying the tasks performed by corporations into coherent business *processes*.[52] That focus on process – shared by TQM – may be likened to value stream mapping, an important lean practice to eliminate waste and make the value-adding steps 'flow' in meeting customer requirements.

However, many applications of reengineering differ from lean thinking in a fundamental way. Reengineering sought breakthrough solutions by discarding existing processes and replacing them with new ones, which often included massive layoffs and other forms of organizational restructuring.[53] In essence, this approach optimized value primarily for senior leaders and shareholders. While lean thinking may produce major restructuring, it is oriented towards a different way of operating the enterprise – taking into account mechanisms for creating value from multiple stakeholder perspectives.[54] Lean thinking depends on and gives priority to building knowledge and capability, which directly contrasts with forms of reengineering that discount or disregard such factors.

## Lean Thinking and Six Sigma

In 1995, Jack Welch, the long-time chairman of General Electric, proclaimed that Six Sigma[55] was the most important initiative GE had ever undertaken. He likened it to the genetic code of GE's next generation of leadership.

What was it about Six Sigma that made it so compelling? The Motorola story helps provide an answer. In the early 1980s, Motorola was being battered by its Japanese competitors. By 1988, Motorola – in one of the most swift and dramatic corporate comebacks ever – was the first recipient of the Baldrige National Quality Award. Much of the success was attributed to Motorola's crusade for quality, which spawned its now famous Six Sigma initiative.

A simple idea drove this initiative: identify and reduce all sources of product variation – machines, materials, methods, measurement systems, the environment (or 'Mother Nature'), and the people in the process. It's an idea that can be traced to the origins of TQM – that is, it has its roots in the application of probability theory to statistical quality control.

At a technical level, Six Sigma aims (like lean) to achieve virtually defect-free production, where parts or components are built to very exacting performance specifications and a defect is defined as any instance or event in which the product fails to meet a customer requirement.[56] However, the importance of Six Sigma reaches beyond its narrow technical base. It is used as an integrative management tool – for instance, by providing a means for measuring performance across different processes and thus for measuring performance improvements across the enterprise.[57]

It also serves to connect performance measures at lower levels to higher-level corporate objectives, thus providing a broader management method. Six Sigma places special emphasis on tangible cost savings achieved by minimizing waste and use of resources, while increasing customer satisfaction through the successive improvement of quality (ultimately to a level of Six Sigma perfection).

Beyond generating immediate performance improvements, say its proponents, Six Sigma is a strategic tool for fundamentally changing the way corporations do business. In this respect, it is based on the concept of 'value entitlement' – that companies have a rightful claim to producing quality products at the highest profits, while customers have a similar claim to buying high-quality products at the lowest possible cost.[58] In practice, however, it is not always clear how Six Sigma can reconcile some diametrically opposed expectations. As we will see in Chapter 7, the construction of a 'value proposition' across multiple stakeholders is a pivotal and dynamic process that is not fully addressed within the Six Sigma framework.

How does Six Sigma relate to lean thinking? Clearly, the enterprise perspective and the use of many quality tools and principles are all consistent with lean thinking. Both also have roots in TQM and related quality principles.[59] Indeed, building Six Sigma capability will help increase customer satisfaction and bottom-line performance by reducing variation and eliminating waste throughout the enterprise, which represent key capabilities in the context of lean thinking.

There is a cautionary note, however. The implementation of Six Sigma involves successive levels of capability represented by the achievement of 'green belt', 'black belt', or 'master black belt' status. Each level is attained through leading a cost-saving project of successively greater magnitude. This risks a form of suboptimization in which the project cost savings may be achieved, but at the expense of unanticipated system consequences elsewhere. And there are deeper questions around whether Six Sigma levels of quality are being achieved with the right products and services. In this respect, Six Sigma may help to ensure that 'the job is done right', but it does not necessarily address whether it's the 'right job'.

## Lean Thinking and HPWO

Labor unions face a unique challenge when it comes to system change initiatives aimed at making substantial gains in organizational performance. They must ensure the success of the business while simultaneously

## Raytheon's 'Lean' Six Sigma Program[60]

Although we compare and contrast initiatives such as 'lean' and Six Sigma, the practical applications of these concepts often blurs the distinctions. Consider, for example, Raytheon's corporate Six Sigma initiative, which has lean principles and practices woven throughout.

Raytheon is a large, multi-program enterprise with annual revenues of approximately $17 billion. As did many aerospace companies in the 1990s, Raytheon underwent a transformation by acquiring several avionics and missile business units – Texas Instruments Defense, Hughes Aircraft, and E-Systems – to add to its base business of defense and commercial electronics and aircraft systems. And the company tapped Dan Burnham, formerly of AlliedSignal, as its new CEO.

Dan faced a challenging task: integrate multiple legacy organizations into an efficient lean enterprise. He chose to implement a Six Sigma program. At the kickoff Raytheon Leadership Forum in January 1999, Dan declared: 'Raytheon Six Sigma … is a whole new way to think about work. … It's going to touch everything that we do.' Raytheon Six Sigma centers on a unifying strategy integrating culture, customers, and tools to achieve customer satisfaction, productivity, growth, and shareholder value.

Dan Burnham appointed Bob Drewes as Vice President for Productivity to head up Raytheon Six Sigma. Both recognized the attraction of the Six Sigma name and tools to the investor community, but they also realized the power of lean thinking and its potential for enterprise transformation. They restructured the Raytheon program around five core principles adapted from *Lean Thinking* by Womack and Jones, Six Sigma, and their realization of the importance of the workforce: specify value in the eyes of the customer; identify the value stream and eliminate waste/variation; make value flow at the pull of the customer; involve, align, and empower employees; and continuously improve knowledge in the constant pursuit of perfection.

In 2000, Raytheon generated approximately $300 million in financial benefits from Raytheon Six Sigma. And in Spring 2001, Bob Drewes shared with the LAI consortium members what Raytheon had learned by applying its lean principles. He told us that leadership alignment is critical, and that business integration – of strategic and annual plans, goals, and performance measures – is essential. The principles must apply to 'everything' and the benefits must accrue not only to the shareholders, but also to customers and employees.

protecting against aspects of the change that might threaten the interest of their members.

The leading union in the aerospace industry, the International Association of Machinists and Aerospace Workers (IAM), has attempted to address this challenge through the development of what it terms the high-performance work organization.[61] While HPWO initiatives are not as well known as are TQM, reengineering, or Six Sigma, it is important to examine this type of initiative in relation to lean thinking because it brings out issues relevant to a key stakeholder – the workforce.

Prior to entering into an HPWO partnership agreement with an employer, the union seeks assurances of continued investment in a given operation for three to five years. Based on such an agreement, the union then commits to a full partnership in the creation of work teams and the application of improvement methods. This is consistent with lean notions of partnership, though such formal agreements about job security are not found in all lean implementation efforts.

There are a number of key elements of the HPWO process. These include establishment of a joint partnership agreement that provides enabling language to support workplace change initiatives, and communication of the agreement and the planned activities to the entire workforce. Further, there are needs assessments of skills, capabilities, and related matters, setting of appropriate roles and responsibilities to support the change process, continuing education to build needed skills and capabilities, and ongoing evaluation and improvement.[62]

Within this framework, many lean principles and practices can be utilized. Indeed, in some operations the individuals leading lean implementation and HPWO implementation have been co-located, and their efforts coordinated. The lesson to be learned from the HPWO experience involves the degree to which the workforce will be cautious about lean improvement efforts without mechanisms to address issues such as job security, investment in skills and capabilities, and the long-term viability of the operation. In surfacing these issues, the HPWO framework is really providing a mechanism for establishing what we call the 'value proposition', explored in detail in Chapter 7.


## Implications of Lean Thinking for the Aerospace Industry

In contrast to the auto industry, where lean thinking initially took form, the aerospace industry is characterized by much lower volumes, complexity greater by orders of magnitude, and higher degrees of cyclicity, as well as year-to-year instability. As we've noted in earlier chapters, the industry exhibits considerable diversity as well as a complex structure, with the defense and commercial sectors, aircraft and space sectors, and commercial aircraft and air transportation sectors closely intertwined.

Aerospace is characterized by a highly interdependent industrial and technological ecology, encompassing a deep as well as broad supplier base that fans out to many corners of the economy. The industry is both a significant source, and an important importer, of technological innovation, with a rich intellectual capital base and a highly skilled workforce. It produces products and systems, from fighter aircraft to spacecraft, that must operate in demanding environments. Beyond their staggering complexity and technological sophistication, these products and systems are expected to – indeed, they must – operate with zero failures. All of these factors point to an industry with a knowledge base of enormous complexity and broad competencies.

Aerospace systems have long lifecycles that span decades and involve the turnover of many generations of subsystems and components exhibiting rapid technological change – even though basic platforms may remain relatively stable over long periods. Given these attributes, what are the implications of lean thinking for the aerospace industry? And what about other industries?


## A Focus on Creating Value

First, we see that 'lean' has been an evolving concept, and will continue to evolve in the aerospace context. The idea of creating value, not just eliminating waste, has always been part of the discussion on lean. The aerospace experience brings it into even sharper focus for all industries.

## A Broader View of the Entire Enterprise

Second, lean has long been narrowly interpreted as focused on manufacturing. A full analysis of the evolution of lean thinking urges a broader view of lean, centered on the entire enterprise. Anything less than a holistic systems approach is bound to result in suboptimization.

'Improving the parts of a system taken separately is not likely to improve the performance of the system as a whole', notes one author.[63] The majority of product value in aerospace resides in upstream design and development (which, in the past, has taken many years, often more than a decade for military products) and in downstream sustainment operations (which typically span many decades). While manufacturing operations have also been the first area of focus in the application of lean thinking in the aerospace industry, it is increasingly clear that a focus across the *entire* business enterprise is essential.

## Transformational Change

Third, lean thinking means transformational change at a fundamental level – not merely a series of incremental improvements. This calls for the creation of networked learning and knowledge sharing to optimize enterprise value streams. Transformational change, by its very nature, is multidimensional, qualitative, and discontinuous.

Without vision, such change is like *looking for* rather than *using* a compass – and, therefore, requires transformational leadership capable of systemic thinking and fashioning an integrated change strategy. Put differently, a series of discrete, incremental *kaizen* events do not, in themselves, realize anything close to lean thinking's full potential – whether in aerospace or any other industry.

## Continuous Learning and Capability-Building

Fourth, lean thinking is a continuous process of learning and capability-building. Aerospace thrives on innovation, but has a mixed record when it comes to investing in workforce and organizational capability. Such investments are essential to the successful implementation of lean principles and practices in all industries.

A deeper lesson involves the link between lean thinking and technological innovation. Lean must be seen as more than a cost-cutting strategy, and it cannot be assumed to be a 'cost-free' approach. Indeed, as we discussed above, the aerospace sector points to lean thinking that is focused on the creation and delivery of 'value' to multiple stakeholders by bringing about a constant stream of innovations – something the industry has done so successfully in the past.

## Pushing the Limits of Core Lean Concepts

Finally, the aerospace context has pushed the limits of all the core lean concepts outlined earlier. Customer focus must be broadened to accommodate multiple customers. Synchronized flow and pull must be rethought to operate in the context of volatile markets and complex supply chains. Elimination of waste must be defined over product lifecycles that span many decades. Perfect quality is a given in the domains of both aircraft and space systems, but it must extend to new domains, such as computer software, and in the defense aerospace sector it must be achieved in the context of severe financial constraints. Flexibility and responsiveness must be achieved in the context of extensive government oversight and regulation. Partnerships between customers and suppliers, labor and management, and even among direct competitors, are essential despite the many forces that pull parties apart.

In sum, lean principles must be understood and implemented in the context of aerospace products for which the link between design, manufacturing, and sustainment has far-reaching implications in terms of life-cycle affordability and delivery of best value to customers and other stakeholders. Lean concepts must also speak effectively to the need for continuous technological upgrading of aerospace systems over many decades, taking advantage of rapid technological advances to enhance overall performance and mission effectiveness. These are issues that face *many* industries.

We will see these multiple extensions of lean thinking, as well as the tensions inherent in them, as we examine in the next chapter some lean 'islands of success' in the aerospace industry.

# CHAPTER 5

# Islands of Success

The journey to lean for the US Aerospace Enterprise began in earnest in the early 1990s, as industry and government responded to post-Cold War imperatives. Most organizations responded first by harvesting the 'low-hanging fruit' – opportunities that required minimum investment and that would yield quick results. Often, these resided on the factory floor, where it was felt that rapid improvements in production processes could be implemented. To be sure, there were *some* more far-reaching change initiatives – 'pilot projects' – where a measured industry or government investment could show progress and serve as a powerful illustration of new principles and practices. But going after the 'low-hanging fruit' was most common.

The first applications in aerospace of lean practices were in manufacturing, where the lessons from earlier initiatives in commercial businesses with large production volumes, such as autos and electronics, translated almost directly into the aerospace context. Efforts to reduce costs and cycle times concentrated on specific activities or locations on the factory floor and, to a lesser extent, on the factory suppliers, and introduced streamlined manufacturing flows through mechanisms such as fabrication cells, single-piece flow, and inventory reduction (all of which had been successful in the auto industry). Many involved teams of workers brought together to solve specific problems. These *kaizen* events – largely directed at the highly visible bottlenecks or inhibitors to factory flow – incorporated elements of 'Toyota lean', Six Sigma, or total quality management, and had some notable, if isolated, successes.

Regardless of scope, these change initiatives often relied on isolated champions who lacked the full leadership commitment needed to tackle the bigger challenge of organizational transformation from mass production to a lean paradigm. Consequently, most productivity improvements though lean principles and practices became (and remain) what we call 'islands of success' within the organizational units that pioneered them. In other words, they have failed to include entire value streams or to be inclusive of the entire enterprise.[1] Often, the monuments and misalignments we discussed in Chapter 3 are at the root of why success is not more encompassing.

In this chapter, we review several compelling illustrations of lean thinking.[2] These cases unambiguously demonstrate the applicability of lean ideas in the aerospace context, and should put to rest the question from the early 1990s (at LAI's founding) of whether practices from the automobile industry could be applied to the aerospace industry, with its greater complexity and lower production volume. In each case, though, the transformation to lean is incomplete.

Our concept that cases in this chapter are simultaneously success stories and islands depends on the breadth of their application of the lean initiatives. One dimension of breadth is the application across an entire value stream. Another is the application across a multi-program enterprise: people, engineering, manufacturing, suppliers, leadership, supporting infrastructure, and customers. The cases presented are, indeed, success stories, but they remain islands of success because they have fallen short of their full potential in one or both dimensions.

Our stories move progressively from very local efforts to more inclusive involvement in the product value stream or enterprise. In each case, multiple stakeholders came together and fundamentally changed the way they operated – with demonstrable gains to show for their efforts. We examine the common characteristics and challenges faced, including the challenges to building bridges from island to island to optimize an entire system. The last of our cases affords a look into genuine transformation across value streams and throughout a defined enterprise. This will prepare us for the next chapter, where we formally explore the concept of lean at the *enterprise* level.

Let's begin with a look at the C-130J Hercules, an example of success in one program, first as it overcame infrastructure and institutional monuments and then how it expanded improvements through the value stream.

## A Herculean Island: Transforming Production on the C-130J

In the late 1980s, the Lockheed Aeronautical Systems Company (now Lockheed Martin Corp.) established a lean enterprise strategic planning team headed by Don Meadows to help the company improve its performance and remove waste. The team concentrated first on eliminating work-in-process inventory waste by optimizing the process flow, making changes in a number of areas. The greatest benefit was realized on the C-130J Hercules, the newest-generation upgrade to the tactical airlifter workhorse which had been in continuous production since the mid-1950s.

The extrusions manufacturing shop – with its sawing, milling, routing, sanding, and deburring operations on standard extrusion stock – was one of Lockheed Martin's more mature areas, and handled some 20 000 part numbers, many for the C-130J. The area had some of the highest costs and lowest efficiencies. By 1994, the team had redesigned the area into what it called a 'focused factory', grouping products into small and large extrusions to improve flow and reduce inventory and matching management authority, control, and facilities to produce a given type of product.

The redesigned factory, using a random-access delivery system for components and tooling and a nightly scheduling system, improved store-to-stock throughput times from 65 to 11 days and reduced the work in process from 35 to 2 days.[3] Then, in early 1997, the operation was transformed to a 'one-piece-at-a-time' flow cell, whereby a piece travels uninterrupted through all processes needed to complete the part. The results have been phenomenal – reduction of throughput time from an average of 12 days to less than 3 minutes! Work-in-process was reduced by nearly 100 percent.

Initial factory improvements resulted from close coordination with raw-material suppliers and from the first steps taken towards internal factory control. However, the full management team was not supportive. 'The company really started its journey to lean about ten years ago', explained Bill Bullock, former President of Lockheed Martin Aero Systems, in 1999, 'but we didn't have the right people to do it.'[4]

There were further, impressive gains in 1997–98, including greater employee involvement and management support and the extension of improvements to the final assembly line. But why did these have only about a 1 percent impact on the price of Lockheed Martin's C-130J Hercules product in 1999?[5] Because although there were notable steps taken towards a lean transformation, the improvements were 'islands of success' isolated to specific cells. The efficiencies had not been fully exploited throughout the entire value stream – that is, the flow of product from raw material to finished form.

Still, Lockheed Martin continued its journey to lean. By 2000, many of the in-house fabrication centers were linked to the final assembly area of the C-130J with a *kanban* system. By then, demand at the final assembly line triggered the fabrication shops to make replacement parts. Inventory was reduced significantly – enough to eliminate a large parts storage area. With this further step, Lockheed linked 'islands of success' into an island chain representing a larger portion of the company's product value stream.

Over this period of ten to fifteen years, a progressively larger part of the Lockheed Martin enterprise became involved in lean improvements to the C-130J. But Lockheed Martin's transformation remains incomplete. Externally supplied parts are delivered to inventory rather than directly to the production line. The journey continues as Lockheed Martin works to link its suppliers directly into the final assembly line. Despite all the successes, however, a complete lean transformation awaits the application of lean practices to the *entire* value stream. Our next example illustrates well that need.

## A Byte-Sized Island: Improving Code Generation

Lean success stories go beyond the realm of manufacturing and can be found in other corners of a company, such as in the software domain. For instance, efficient code-generation techniques improve software quality by lessening defects and decreasing the time necessary to generate code. But from a lean standpoint, applying such techniques alone still represents an island of success, because code generation is only one part of a larger software development value stream.

Since the introduction of the autopilot, aerospace products have relied increasingly on information technology and software. Software, just one of many critical aerospace systems components, has become more dominant with each generation of products (see Figure 5.1). Software is also the main means by which aerospace systems can be upgraded to perform new functions or to correct problems that arise in operation. It comes as no

**FIGURE 5.1** | **Annual cost of DoD systems (all types)**

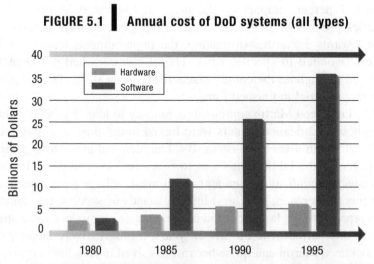

*Source:* Jose Menendez, 'Building Software Factories in the Aerospace Industry', MIT Master of Science Thesis in Technology & Policy and Aeronautics & Astronautics (February 1997).
Note: 'All types' includes weapon systems and management information systems.

surprise, then, that as aerospace systems benefit from software capabilities, they are prisoners of the software development process.

The US Air Force knows firsthand the burdens of software development, in particular the cost and time required for periodic upgrades of software in military aircraft programs. Consider that total avionics development times for four representative military aircraft systems ranged from 36 to 64 months from concept definition to customer delivery, with costs of $30 million to $100 million plus.[6] Imagine waiting more than five years for the next version of *your* computer's operating system!

In early 1998, Maj. Gen. Dennis G. Haines of the US Air Force Air Combat Command (ACC) at Langley Field, Virginia, launched a cost-cutting initiative for Operational Flight Programs (OFPs) – the name used for major software upgrades on USAF aircraft. His predecessor's efforts to cut software costs in half had been largely ineffective, despite isolated pockets of 'success', and the end user community was still dissatisfied. A three-man team – Maj. Fred Gregory, Lt. Col. Mark Fish, and Col. Jeff Sogard – took the task of mapping the process of software development for the ACC, visiting contracting companies and government System Program Offices to uncover the practical issues, and developing an action plan to achieve Maj. Gen. Haines' cost-cutting targets.

This effort coincided with the initiation of a research project at MIT to look at some of the same issues. Brian Ippolito, a graduate student and former Air Force captain and program manager for military software programs, had proposed the research project to LAI. The four men teamed up to take a comprehensive look at the software development process. What they found was revealing.

While there were improvements in the software development process, they were isolated to a limited portion of the total process – primarily in code generation. Major strides were being made in reducing time and cost for mission-critical code generation, while simultaneously improving quality, through automatic code-generation technology and other programming improvements. This finding corresponded with earlier LAI research that showed a 40 percent reduction in development time and an 80 percent improvement in quality for an engine controller using automatic code-generation technology.[7] And Airbus Industries improved overall quality through automatic code generation by an order of magnitude, even while seeing software grow in 'size' by a factor of five (see Table 5.1).

One of the most common misconceptions of software development is that the process is simply the generation of code, of '1s and 0s'. In fact, the effort required to deliver a software upgrade to an aerospace system requires many more areas of expertise. As evidence, consider that code generation absorbs

TABLE 5.1 | Automatic code generation reduces Airbus software encoding errors

| Aircraft | A310 | A320 | A340 |
|---|---|---|---|
| Flight Software (Megabytes) | 4 | 10 | 20 |
| Errors per 100 Kilobytes | 100 | 12 | 10 |

*Source:* J. Menendez. 'Building Software Factories in the Aerospace Industry', Master's thesis, MIT (1997).

as little as 10 percent or less of total development costs[8] – analogous to the small portion of manufacturing costs attributable to 'touch-labor'. There is a tightly coupled and highly complex relationship between coding and other steps (requirements generation, integration, testing, and so on). For example, government certification, technical orders, support equipment software changes, multiple aircraft sensor software changes, weapons software changes, and weapons and tactics trainers must all accompany a military aircraft software upgrade (see Figure 5.2).

The research team arrived quickly at an overarching recommendation – later incorporated into some policy directives – that a focus on code-generation improvement would produce only limited reductions in total development costs and in total program cycle time. It remains unclear whether the recommendation to expand the focus of software development

FIGURE 5.2 | Military avionics software upgrade value streams

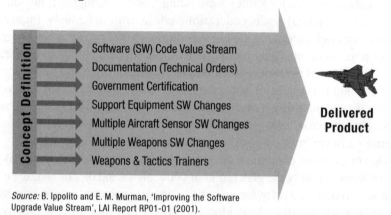

*Source:* B. Ippolito and E. M. Murman, 'Improving the Software Upgrade Value Stream', LAI Report RP01-01 (2001).

improvements *beyond* code generation has been addressed across military aircraft platforms.

Efficient code generation is a truly lean practice. But from a more holistic view, sandwiched between requirements derivation and system test (two key drivers of development time and cost), code-generation improvement has done little to limit *total* development costs or *total* program cycle time. The lack of solid software requirements at program initiation, coupled with 'in-process' changes to the requirements, drive total software program schedules and costs. For example, a study of ten recently completed aerospace software upgrade programs (including the four avionics programs in the study referenced earlier) showed that, on average, 23 percent of the software requirements required unplanned rework, at an average cost of 16 percent of the total software development cost.[9] That's more than the total cost of code generation.

Productivity improvements in code generation are a lean success story, but an island of success. Clearly, the perception of software development as nothing more than code generation has driven people to suboptimize software development as a whole. To expand the efforts of improvement, the industry must widen its efforts to focus on the broader value stream of software delivery.

The software development story illustrates one kind of barrier to moving beyond islands of success. Our next example shows that old habits die hard, and that success in one program can come right up against the barrier of old ways of thinking.

## A Better-Practice Island: Manufacturing F-22 and RAH-66 Electronics Using Commercial Practices

In 1994, an independent study conducted for Secretary of Defense William Perry identified 130 regulatory and standards-based cost drivers that contributed an estimated average cost premium of 18 percent to DoD goods and services.[10] This information, in the context of ongoing acquisition reform initiatives, motivated the F-22 Raptor fighter aircraft and RAH-66 Comanche helicopter programs to team with the Air Force Research Laboratory and TRW's Avionics Systems Division to test whether savings could be realized by leveraging the commercial electronics base.

In this case, a product already designed for military-qualified components (MILSPEC) had to be redesigned to use commercial components and to accommodate commercial production equipment and processes.

That came with a redesign cost, which TRW and the Air Force shared through a Lean Pilot Project, 'Military Products from Commercial Lines', an official program sponsored by the Air Force Research Laboratory's Manufacturing Technology Division.

The objective was to produce two electronic module assemblies on TRW's automotive computer-integrated manufacturing (CIM) system at its Marshall, Illinois, plant. First, the modules had to be redesigned to be compatible with this highly automated system, using commercial parts that could be employed at Marshall. Use of these commercial parts required a rigorous component test process to ensure that the components met the durability and reliability requirements of the baseline military parts.

The challenges, though, involve more than a simple switchover to commercial standards. Certainly, it is more economical to *start* a program with the intent to use commercial production facilities, but that means that from the outset program managers must be on board and willing to relinquish some of their control. Further, commercial parts used in commercial manufacturing houses must not only meet military requirements, but must be available over the lifecycle of the product. Approvals often involve additional effort on the program's part. Then there's the problem of volume: military products are usually produced in low volumes, and so in most cases they are inserted into commercial production when there are gaps in orders. This translates into a production schedule that is often not under the control of the program manager. Also, military programs are often more unstable as regards their requirements and production quantities than are their commercial counterparts.

The pilot project faced another obstacle: many commercial houses that supply parts do not want to deal with the DoD.[11] So, contracting practices had to be devised that would induce the large-volume electronic component suppliers to the Marshall plant to bid on this low-volume military work.

Despite all these obstacles, the commercially produced modules proved to be cheaper and were completed faster than the modules using MILSPEC's parts and procedures.

Chuck Ebeling, TRW's project manager, characterized the dramatic benefits: a 30 percent reduction in total procurement and manufacturing span time; a 50–70 percent reduction in product cost; and an order-of-magnitude improvement in product quality. Specific commercial–military comparisons highlighted a reduction on a per-unit basis of labor cost from nearly $12 700 to just over $5200 and a reduction in material from $27 300 to $5600, leading to a total cost of $10 900 compared with the military equivalent of $40 000.

Savings certainly accrued from using commercial standards. And this type of effort clearly could be more successful if employed at the start of a program. However, the obstacles facing program managers indicate why this is an island of success. There is a mismatch between the cycle times of military and commercial products, which makes it onerous for program managers to undertake such an effort across the entire avionics value stream. TRW's Marshall plant could have produced the entire requirement for all projected F-22 electronic modules in a matter of days, yet the F-22 is not projected to go operational until 2005 (a decade later). In the broader context of the entire F-22 or RAH-66 programs, the savings accrued from the manufacture of some electronic modules (that are directly adaptable to commercial manufacturing) is pocket change, viewed by many as hardly worth the effort. The commercial manufacturing of modules can be successful, but it requires a completely different perspective by the DoD relative to program development times and industrial base management.

The sharing of costs challenges several of the mental monuments we discussed in Chapter 3. In our next case, the F-16, success was restricted by cost- and skills-related barriers linked to the *institutional* monuments that govern organizations.

## An Engineering Support Island: The F-16 Build-To-Package Center

When problems are found on the typical aircraft production line, the solutions usually are included in the official product definition – the Build-To-Package (BTP). Even with minor changes initiated by operations, delays in passing changes through the necessary engineering checks and paperwork either hold up production or allow defective parts to proceed down the line, only to be reworked later at considerable expense.

Facing this typical situation, engineers at Lockheed Martin Aeronautics created the F-16 Build-To-Package Support Center. Previously, changes had to pass through several functions – engineering design, manufacturing planning, manufacturing engineering, tool planning, tool design, tool manufacturing, and various support groups – before final approval, which involved a great deal of travel for the paperwork and lots of waiting for that paperwork to rise to the top of each person's to-do list. Lockheed Martin's solution employed a classic value stream approach: the existing flow was mapped by following the paperwork package, identifying where it went and who touched it. The analysis led to creation of a new flow that was radically improved over several iterations.

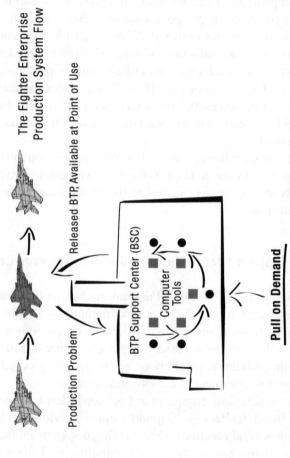

**FIGURE 5.3** | Lockheed Martin's BTP Support Center

The Fighter Enterprise
Production System Flow

Production Problem

Released BTP, Available at Point of Use

BTP Support Center (BSC)

Computer
Tools

**Pull on Demand**

•Canopy •Fuel Sys. •Fire Control Sys. •Harness Def. •Avionics •Elect Planner •TMP •MRP Planner
•Propulsion •Coproduction •Buyer •NC Programmer •Tool Design •Wiring Instl. •CRB •ECS Instl.
•Life Suppt •Process Control •Structures •Labs •M&P •Ldg Gear •PP&C •Parts Engrg
•Escape Sys. •Safety •Customers •DCMC •Stress •ECS Sys. •Arm Sys. •Scheduling •Hydraulics
•Equip Instl. •Program •PQA •Planner •Frac. & Fat. •Maintainability •Tool Mfg

*Source:* Gary Goodman, Presentation to LAI Product Development Workshop (January 2000).

Typically, change initiatives of this sort are 'beyond the factory floor' – that is, in the engineering design office, not at the point of production. Figure 5.3 shows the BTP Support Center created *on the factory floor*. Here's how it works. Technical expertise is pulled to the center, which is arranged in a series of engineering 'cells'. Each package passes through the cells in single-piece flow, without waiting. Modifications to the process support both the single-piece flow and the possibility of some tasks being performed in parallel, allowing scheduling improvement without the dangerous elimination of necessary steps, checks, or reviews. Communication, when necessary, is mostly face-to-face with co-located personnel, minimizing both delays and misunderstandings.

Lockheed Martin's approach has resulted in consistent, sustainable improvements: 40 percent fewer steps, 75 percent fewer handoffs, and a 90 percent reduction in travel distance. A 75 percent cycle-time reduction has had a major, positive impact on factory operations, eliminating delays and lifting from operations personnel the paperwork burden of initiating BTP changes.

The biggest barrier to continued success has been the struggle for over-stretched personnel – to function at full efficiency, the BTP Support Center needs priority access to personnel. When too many fires are being fought in other parts of the organization, efficiency at the center dips. The situation is made tougher by the pull of tradition: the typical responsibilities of three organizations – engineering, manufacturing, and quality control – have been fused into one.

For all its benefits, though, the BTP Support Center remains an island of success. It struggles internally to maintain critical personnel while traditional functional organization goals from the outside tend to subvert value stream and functional interactions. In addition, the concept, although proven, is costly to implement – which only fuels functional institutional barriers to its accomplishment.

The barriers to change in the US Aerospace Enterprise make the acceptance of even *proven* concepts challenging. In our next example, we see how *cultural* monuments get in the way.

## A Cultural Island: New Ideas and Methods for 777 Floor Beams[12]

Large jigs and fixtures represent substantial startup investments for complex assemblies, and one lean practice is to eliminate these to the extent possible. Conventional assembly uses heavy, rigid tooling to control alignment, weight, and uniformity, all critical to installation in freighter and passenger versions of commercial aircraft. Transport aircraft floor beams are very large indeed, and tooling alone can absorb as much as 20 percent of total production costs. Two suppliers of floor beams to the Boeing Commercial Aircraft Group (BCAG) – Boeing's own Wichita plant, responsible for the Boeing 767 floor, and Rockwell's Tulsa division, which supplied the Boeing 777 version – started down the path to eliminate this costly tooling. Let's look at both cases. While separated in time by only a year, they are separated culturally by perhaps a decade.

At the Wichita plant, where cost and schedule were important performance measures, new productivity techniques were introduced. Particular emphasis was given to statistical process control (SPC), and productivity performance was made highly visible to personnel through charts and computer terminals on the factory floor. It was an ideal site for a six-month internship for James Koonmen, an LAI student researcher. Jim's interest in tool-less manufacturing matched perfectly with the Wichita decision to form a team to prototype the use of laser-alignment techniques for the 767 floor beams to reduce dimensional variation and cut costs. The group was, in fact, an integrated product team (ITP)[13] involving engineering, manufacturing, manufacturing engineering, and quality control. Jim became a key contributor to the necessary analytical and design work.

Boeing set aside an area on the plant floor with a flat granite bedplate on which beams could be assembled, and with the configuration of lasers necessary to ensure alignment. The prototype worked: component fabricated parts had been designed successfully to have very tight tolerances and to provide for match points permitting accurate fit-up and laser targets. After six months, Wichita management saw the results, approved the process, and took a proposal to do the work in this way to Boeing's aircraft assemblers in Everett, Washington.

But the culture of the 767 program got in the way, and the proposal was rejected. The approach was too untried, and a new design from a remote production facility – despite being a *Boeing* facility – was questionable.

The 777 story could not have been more different. At the time, 777 floor beams were manufactured by the Rockwell International Aircraft Division in Tulsa, Oklahoma, under subcontract to Boeing. Rockwell Tulsa had been building floors for Boeing since 1967. Development of the 777 was aimed at adaptability and cost reductions, and the program had a management team that sought the latest methods to achieve those ends. This time, there was a different result.

It was early 1993, and Rockwell had just shipped the pilot set of 777 floor beams (rather than a completed floor unit, as in the past) to BCAG. They were the first floor beams to be made of a graphite composite material and had been assembled using a new tool-less precision assembly process. John Hoppes, an LAI student researcher, tells how Bob Emanuel – a production manager with Rockwell's 777 Floor Beam Fabrication Area – was worried whether they would fit. His concerns were shared by other Rockwell and Boeing veterans.

Bob nervously paced the metal platform of Boeing's three-story floor-unit assembly works in Everett as the first beam was lowered vertically into the fixture. The beam reached the proper position and was slowly turned 90 degrees to lock its 18 clips into the fixture's seat-tracks, with only a few hundredths of an inch between each clip and the track. Every clip turned snugly into place.

'It's just luck', commented the employees watching from the platform. But as the second, third, fourth, and fifth beams slid easily into place, skepticism gave way to astonishment. Floor beams don't fit like this, especially not on a first shipment. When the sixth and seventh beams turned into place as easily as the first five, everyone *knew* it was much more than luck. In that short time, precision assembly proved far superior to the assembly techniques used in the past, and established itself as the new assembly paradigm.

The story Bob Emanuel tells is the culmination of a much more revealing tale that began with the 777 design teams. Precision assembly aimed at eliminating hard tools, instead using locators on a part as an index point for a mating part. With a computerized three-dimensional modeling package called CATIA, Boeing designers could understand part fit, dimensioning, and stack-up tolerances as never before. Rockwell realized that its conventional assembly techniques, which relied heavily on handwork, would never achieve the Boeing level of precision. And since Rockwell would be responsible only for assembling the floor beams, and not the entire floor units as in the past, poor fit would be evident immediately during final assembly at the customer facility. Rockwell needed to develop an assembly technique that would provide parts with tighter tolerances, using fewer tools than ever before.

Working with the CATIA tools and Boeing's Design Build Teams in Seattle, Rockwell defined the surfaces, contours, or interfaces (called key characteristics) with the greatest impact on the product and assembly. Rockwell then found the upstream process that would most affect a given characteristic, and used SPC to reduce and monitor its variability. As a result, the 777 floor beam could be assembled like an erector set – all parts had full-size holes that allowed easy assembly, with no need for drilling, trimming, or other adjustments to achieve the proper fit. In comparison to a similar beam for the Boeing 747 aircraft, the Rockwell 777 floor beam takes about 47 percent less time to assemble, uses no hard tools, and requires only a table on which to do the assembly. In our lean terms, Rockwell slashed assembly time and added real value.

The contrast between the 767 and 777 stories offers insights into critical, yet ephemeral, components of success: openness to new ideas, involvement of suppliers and customers in the design process, a commitment to reducing variation through process improvements, and the use of enabling technology. The 767 story is that of technical success for an existing system within an existing culture, but without full stakeholder involvement – in this case, the decisionmaking Seattle organization. The 777 example of people willing to try new ideas shows the successful development and use of new methods with the full involvement of a joint design team and people on the manufacturing floor. The results were major savings in assembly time and the elimination of costly tooling.

These cases reflect the need for the involvement of all stakeholders and for receptivity to new ideas. Our next example adds the issues of encompassing the entire value stream to the mix of challenges.

## An Island Chain: The Pratt & Whitney Story

Aircraft engine manufacturers enjoyed record orders in 1991, but by late 1992 – reflecting the industry's cyclical nature – the bottom had fallen out of the market as international demand for new aircraft engines evaporated. This post-boom downturn hit Pratt & Whitney Aircraft Engines – 'battered by military and airline rollbacks'[14] – particularly hard. Executive discussions changed from 'how to invest profits to which facilities to close'.[15] As Peggy Ford, a company spokeswoman, told reporters: 'We have to resize our company for the smaller market.'[16]

Pratt & Whitney, then under Karl Krapek's leadership, refocused its energies to reduce costs, improve manufacturing performance, and increase competitiveness. The company's successful implementation of lean in two instances illustrates the ongoing challenges that often leave an island of success within the product value stream. And the Pratt & Whitney story also illustrates how, as time and continued efforts evolve, linking multiple islands of success into an island chain can continue the overall transformation to lean.

Massive changes got underway at the company's General Machining Product Center in East Hartford, Connecticut, transforming the facility between 1993 and 1994 from a departmental layout to a series of 36 manufacturing cells. At the peak, it was not uncommon to see two or three pieces of machinery moving down the main aisle concurrently, around the clock.

Once the dust settled from the layout change and cellular operations began, the results were dramatic. The top-performing cell saw huge reductions in lead times from eight to three weeks; the average number of pieces in process dropped from 273 to 77; travel distance went from 13 670 to 5800 feet; and average setup time shrank from 6 hours to 30 minutes. Quality improved from 1200 to 269 defects per million opportunities.[17] Once produced, parts were shipped to a warehouse to await shipment to final assembly operations. All this was accomplished with fewer machines and gauges and, hence, a commensurately smaller workforce.

There were problems brewing, however, in late 1996 and early 1997, when the right parts were not on hand as needed. When we took a look at final assembly operations, we found that shortages of the right parts accounted for 38 percent of the disruptions, quality-related issues for 13 percent, and the lack of people and equipment for 2 percent.[18]

The manufacturing system (Figure 5.4) consisted of suppliers (both internal and external) building parts and sending them to a central warehouse. Ideally, the assembly line got the parts from the warehouse according to the Manufacturing Requirements Planning (MRP) schedule. But, the system didn't always work, and it took a lot of informal communication to expedite or locate needed parts. Despite impressive gains in the General Machining Product Center and other areas such as the turbine blade *chaku-chaku* cell,[19] assembly operations were not seeing the benefits. Even as we were collecting our data, though, change was afoot.

We returned to engine final assembly operations in late 1998, and found that the military engine assembly line had changed from a departmental layout to a flowline that improved the way parts were provided to final assembly. This new system design, shown in Figure 5.5, still used MRP for scheduling. However, parts now bypassed a warehouse and went directly to the assembly plant from the component centers (which were responsible for both internally and externally sourced parts). A daily 'milk run' connected all component centers to the assembly plant.

'Lean' was evident throughout. To ensure a steady stream of parts, a special *andon* system had been added to alert management on the assembly line and at the component centers that the line might stop were a needed part not supplied. Cellular design within the final assembly area – with smaller cell areas and cell output contiguous with the next assembly station – allowed single-piece flow. Concurrently with the change to cells for the production of engine modules, the material center changed to providing kits for each engine module build. Carts supplying these kits acted as *kanban* containers to be rotated between the engine module build

**FIGURE 5.4** | **P&W manufacturing system design (early 1997)**

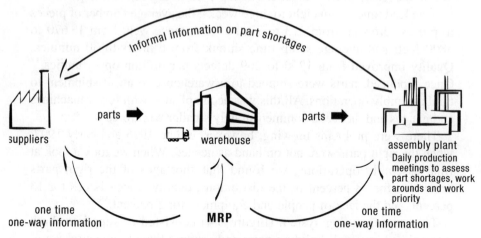

*Source:* LAI Report RP00-01 (August 2000).

**FIGURE 5.5** | **P&W manufacturing system design (late 1998)**

*Source:* LAI Report RP00-01 (August 2000).

area and the material handling area. By eliminating the parts warehouse and by linking final assembly and the parts fabrication centers, Pratt & Whitney succeeded in connecting several islands of success.

What we saw over five years of observing this lean transformation reinforces the notion that lean changes take time. Most striking was the growth in enterprise involvement. In the General Machining Product Center, a strong leadership team fostered a change from a functional organization to a product cell organization, using *kaizen* to involve factory floor workers in determining the new center layout and operational methods. To make the changes at the final assembly operations required coordination among internal and external suppliers, as well as companywide efforts to revamp material transportation, material presentation, and material management.

Changes like these require determined, long-term leadership from the highest levels. When that happens, small islands of success can be linked into an integrated chain of islands – ultimately encompassing a complete value stream.

Our next example, which points to the need for more widespread changes across a broad infrastructure, shows how the diffusion of success in one program can be hampered by infrastructure monuments in other programs.

## An Awakening Island: Diffusing Lean Practices to the Delta IV Launch Vehicle

What would cause a business decision to redesign a 4 million square foot facility to 1.5 million square feet *after* the plans, building contracts, and foundation materials for the plant had already been procured? A great deal of trust in new partnerships, leadership vision – and the principles of lean.

In early 1997, the McDonnell Douglas Company was designing the production facility for its new launch vehicle, the Delta IV. The planning team, looking for the right location for a facility large enough to house the vehicle component fabrication as well as the integrated assembly and checkout, found just such a site in Decatur, Alabama. It was an exceptional deal for both McDonnell Douglas and the city: a new facility, complete with huge incentives for the company and guaranteed jobs for Alabamans. The facility is ideally located to transport the nearly complete launch vehicles to Cape Canaveral by barge on the nearby Tennessee River, using state-provided docks. Launch vehicles that need to reach Vandenberg, California, use these same docks, traveling through the Panama Canal en route to the West Coast.

Later in 1997, McDonnell Douglas completed its facility design, which called for upwards of 4 million square feet of floor space, 10 integration and checkout lines, and 20 cranes to move the enormous vehicle pieces. This coincided with ongoing merger negotiations between McDonnell Douglas and Boeing – a partnership that would end up changing the circumstances of the Delta IV. While Boeing Commercial Airplane Group (BCAG) had been experimenting for some time with lean practices, the Delta program had little exposure to their potential.

A post-merger review of the Delta IV facility in November 1997 (with team members from BCAG) introduced the Delta IV people to their 'lean brothers'. It was suggested that Shingijutsu Co., Ltd. could provide some help to improve plant efficiency, as it had at BCAG. In early 1998, Delta

**FIGURE 5.6** | **Delta II and Delta IV integration flows**

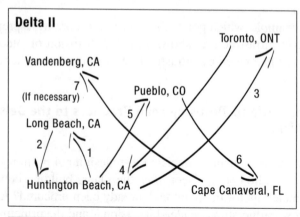

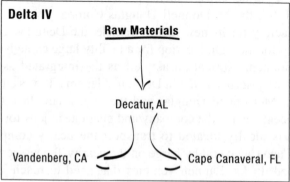

IV brought in the Japanese consultants – former Toyota production executives who became known as the 'Men in Black'.

In just three months, the facility design was overhauled under the watchful eyes of the Japanese visitors. The redesign would have been far more extensive, but a good deal of the factory was completed and couldn't be undone. The integration assembly and checkout line saw the most change, in three months evolving from the original design to a single pulse moving line with four cranes and 108 900 square feet.

This effort to minimize movement was not isolated to the factory floor. The Delta II program provided lessons about excessive movement during fabrication, leading to some major changes with Delta IV (as Figure 5.6 illustrates). With Delta II, raw materials traveled from facility to facility in the production of the launcher – a distance of nearly 8000 miles, all but eliminated in the Delta IV program. For the Delta IV, raw materials enter the Decatur facility and the entire vehicle is then assembled and transported to Cape Canaveral or Vandenberg via a dedicated dock on the nearby Tennessee River.

While these changes spell great success in getting lean, Boeing's major strides at the final assembly operations touch only part of the value stream. If it is to become more than an *island* of success, all the suppliers that provide the components and subassemblies to the final assembly operations need to be linked into this lean system.

The idea of 'linking' fits well with our next example. GE Lynn overcame its old mindset – a cultural monument of the past – to think about linking suppliers directly to the assembly line and delivering products to customers at their demand rate.

## An Island of 'Pull': Integrating Supplier and Material Management at GE Lynn

At the LAI 1998 Plenary Workshop, Ernie Oliveira described the lean transformation at the GE aircraft engine plant in Lynn, Massachusetts, that had unfolded over the previous six years. Ernie, the GE Lynn leader of manufacturing initiatives, explained the development of a manufacturing strategy aimed at gaining competitive advantage. He took us through the implementation steps that transformed the Lynn Engine Assembly Operations into an exemplar of lean aerospace production – a transformation enabled by changes to the manufacturing and assembly facilities, the materials management system, and the supply chain.

A key to success involved moving away from a departmental approach, in which functional departments serve multiple products, to grouping most resources needed for assembling a particular engine into one linear process flow. This means that the product moves a shorter distance, because each line is shorter and straighter. And because there are fewer units in these new product flow lines, delayed assemblies are more visible and get attention sooner. That reduces the buildup of work-in-progress. In short, Lynn has begun to operate at a pace dictated by customer demand.

The final key to the plant's lean production system involved a dedicated effort to build trust and open communication with suppliers and customers. An electronic data-exchange system allows GE to signal suppliers for replenishment and to pay the bills. Most impressive is a pull replenishment system established with suppliers of the highest-cost parts.

On the final assembly line, 100 percent on-time delivery (during our study) results largely from employing a system that features close coordination with suppliers through a *kanban* system, and a commitment to freeze requirements two weeks prior to the actual date parts are needed. The key to solving GE Lynn's most vexing problem – parts shortages – is in the pull linkage made with the internal and external supplier base (see Figure 5.7).

Through material 'stratification', the plant 'pulls' the high-dollar-value components of assembly while using a forecasting system to acquire the

### FIGURE 5.7 | GE Lynn supplier system

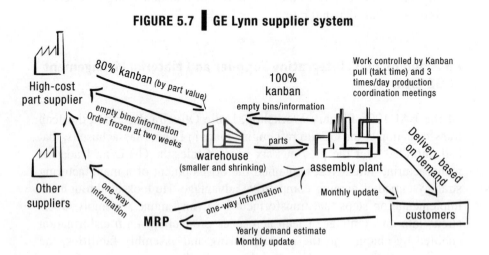

*Source:* LAI Report RP00-01 (August 2000).

lower-dollar-value components. GE Lynn implemented a special small-parts bin supply system to ensure the availability of inexpensive parts and thus to eliminate delays in engine assembly.

This assembly plant's effectiveness in implementing lean throughout its product value stream is impressive (see Table 5.2). GE Lynn was able to establish a system across high-cost and commodity suppliers that accomplished 100 percent deliveries to customers' schedule. Engines are completed, tested, and loaded directly into a customer truck every three days to match assembly requirements at the customer site.

GE Lynn is a success story: a concerted, three-pronged effort that combines manufacturing system transformation, material management, and supply chain integration to deliver engines to customers when needed. As champion of this transformation, Ernie Oliveira not only guided the management systems and infrastructure changes, but won over a unionized workforce to this new method of operation. GE has managed to involve critical on-site stakeholders: leadership, workers, material management, and suppliers.

The transformation process continued with the introduction of a moving assembly line in 2000. This and similar islands of success at GE's Raleigh-Durham, North Carolina, and Rutland, Vermont, plants highlight what can be achieved with these site-specific transformations.

Often, the key to success with change initiatives lies in breaking down the bureaucratic impediments to change, as the GE Lynn story illustrates. The JDAM story further highlights the importance of such efforts, particularly with respect to the government.

**TABLE 5.2** | **Lean manufacturing results at GE Lynn**

| Performance Metric | Improvement (Actual Average) |
|---|---|
| Inventory Turnover | 33% |
| Throughput Time | 35% |
| Quality (Internal – DPU's/engine) | 28% |
| Human Effort per engine | 17% |

*Source:* Data from LAI Plenary Workshop proceedings (October 14th–15th, 1998) and presentation by Ernie Oliveira, 'The Transition to Lean Manufacturing in Lynn Engine Assembly Operation, GE Aircraft Engines' (October 1998).

## A Mini-Enterprise Island: Joint Direct Attack Munition

Our next chapter reviews the implications of the term *enterprise* with respect to the full potential of lean practices. For now, let's look at a relatively narrow enterprise to see how the incorporation of lean practices provides important benefits for an entire program.

The Joint Direct Attack Munition (JDAM) program was established to provide a guidance system for 'dumb' bombs and to improve their accuracy fivefold.[20] This product was in high demand by the warfighting community because it afforded all-weather pinpoint bombing accuracy.

In 1993, Terry Little, the JDAM Program Manager, met with then USAF Chief of Staff General Merrill McPeak to discuss the program. At the time, the JDAM kits were planned to cost $40 000 apiece, but cost estimates were running higher – as much as $68 000. Terry remembers the General's reaction. 'He pounded his fist on the table and said, "By God, if it's one cent over, I don't want it."'[21]

Terry realized that he would not be able to manage this program in the traditional manner. And thanks to the establishment of the DoD's Defense Acquisition Pilot Program, he got his wish. With JDAM earmarked in 1994 as one of six such pilots, Terry could employ commercial practices, regulatory/statutory relief, and plain common sense to streamline his program. 'However, the greatest benefit of being a Pilot Program was the willingness of management to allow us to try new things.'[22] And try new things he did, for here was a program that could introduce lean practices from the start.

In the program's initial phase, a competitive procurement process yielded two contractors. Each contractor formed a multidisciplinary team, and then Terry and the rest of his program took these teams down a new path – he put government representatives on each, as well as at the contractor sites, and tasked them to be advocates for their teams throughout the competition. The communication and trust that evolved from this effort, combined with a reduction of requirements to six 'do or die' criteria and the establishment of a simple measure of cost, allowed each team to approach its design of the product in a completely different way.

Cost became the primary driver for the design, and the teams sought to integrate the design in order to reduce costs, rather than seek suppliers for specific components. This caused a change in the relationships between the prime contractor and its suppliers. Using commercial practices induced some suppliers who would not normally work with DoD to participate. Business relationships – and, more important, workshare (and therefore revenue) – among suppliers and the prime contractor had to be adjusted, while protecting proprietary knowledge. This was accomplished by including suppliers on the design teams so that they became a part of the tradeoff process that defined the minimum cost architecture for the product. Costs were reduced further by trading configuration control to the contractor teams in exchange for a lengthening of the warranty from 5 to 20 years.

The yield from these innovative approaches exceeded expectations. When the downselect to the Boeing team occurred, the proposed cost per unit had been slashed to $15 000. This represented a reduction in unit costs reported to Gen. McPeak in excess of 75 percent. Still, naysayers maintained it could not be done for less than the original estimates.

Two years later, government estimates for per unit costs were still only $24 400,[23] well below the original $68 000 estimate. In fact, after five years of production, the prime contractor has maintained the original $15 000 per unit cost commitment (in 'then-year' dollars).

Figure 5.8 shows other JDAM improvements in the past few years. Important also is that the design process created the conditions for lean surge production needed during the NATO Kosovo action to meet the urgent all-weather targeting needs of military planners and flight crew.

JDAM is a lean program enterprise. It brings together the entire product value stream to achieve 17 inventory turns per year (and some suppliers are poised to achieve more than double that number). It involves all of the stakeholders, from the USAF leadership down to the lowest-tier supplier. It integrates design, manufacturing, and product lifecycle support. True, the product is relatively simple, and – compared to a full airplane or space system – JDAM has few stakeholders. Yet, this does not detract from its accomplishments. But if JDAM is a lean enterprise, why do we characterize it as an island of success?

When viewed in its broader context, JDAM is an island – one program among many that DoD manages. As we explain in Chapter 6, that makes it a *program* enterprise within a *multi-program* enterprise. Although Terry Little incorporated the lessons learned from JDAM in the next program he managed, Lockheed Martin's Joint Air-to-Surface Standoff Missile (JASSM), most DoD programs march to the rules, regulations, and cultural cadence meant for a different time. These institutional and cultural monuments impede the more general application of the lessons learned from JDAM. But the approaches and results make this a benchmark case for the government and industry, as we explore in Part III.

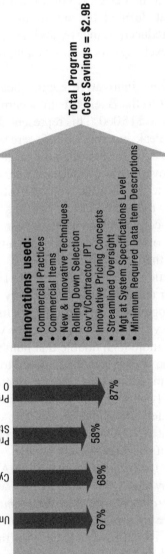

**FIGURE 5.8** Joint Direct Attack Munition (JDAM) improvements

**Total Program Cost Savings = $2.9B**

**Innovations used:**
- Commercial Practices
- Commercial Items
- New & Innovative Techniques
- Rolling Down Selection
- Gov't/Contractor IPT
- Innovative Pricing Concepts
- Streamlined Oversight
- Mgt at System Specifications Level
- Minimum Required Data Item Descriptions

Projected O & M Costs — 87%

Program Staffing — 58%

Cycle Time — 68%

Unit Cost — 67%

Benchmark

Reductions

*Source:* Based on Pilot Program Consulting Group 'Compendium of Defense Reform Performance – Affordable Defense for the 21st Century' (April 1999), prepared for the Office of the Under Secretary of Defense for Acquisition, Technology, and Logistics.

## Summing Up

We've made this point throughout the book so far, and it's worth repeating: aerospace faces difficult challenges in a complex environment. Our islands of success make clear, though, that the transformation process is not starting from scratch. For the past decade, various initiatives to reduce costs and cycle times, in quite different organizations, have enjoyed success. The common shortcoming is the inability to translate these successes to the *entire* value stream, or to be more inclusive of other functions or activities within the enterprise. In each case, success points to possibilities for additional lean activities, and in some cases we see a continuous expansion of lean. Yet, progress is painful and easily deflected or waylaid.

The islands of success we have described demonstrate the need to become lean throughout the whole enterprise. Each of our cases represents one group of activities within a more comprehensive entity – the factory is part of an entire manufacturing plant, for example, and the design group is part of a development project – but those who manage these activities perceive them narrowly as the enterprises whose bottom lines will reflect their success. A CEO, for instance, considers whatever contributes to pre-tax earnings; a program manager drives almost exclusively towards the successful completion of the program. Until everyone sees each organization as part of a total enterprise, and until lean islands of success are linked across that enterprise, *true* success with lean efforts will remain elusive.

As our examples over this chapter moved progressively to involve more of the value stream and broadened aspects of enterprise, we have tried to show how the important players came to a fuller recognition of the need to *extend the boundaries* of initiatives to improve the *real* bottom line. This is critical in navigating the pathways to revitalization of the US Aerospace Enterprise. Aerospace is a complex industry, and productivity or related changes in one area cannot be isolated from other activities. The application of this understanding – important well beyond aerospace – is the thrust of Chapter 6.

# CHAPTER 6

# Lean Enterprises

> Our entire enterprise will be a Lean operation, characterized by the efficient use of assets, high inventory turns, excellent supplier management, short cycle times, high quality and low transaction costs.

The words above describe one of three core competencies at the heart of a corporate vision statement – 'Vision 2016' – issued in early 2001 by Boeing, the world's largest aerospace company (Figure 6.1). When the concept of a 'lean enterprise' appears in the corporate strategy of a company whose history mirrors that of aerospace, it says something about the future direction of the industry as a whole.

What does it mean to be a 'lean operation'? What is a lean enterprise? How does this relate to the lean principles and practices introduced in Chapter 4, and the applications we saw in Chapter 5? What is involved in the journey to become a lean enterprise? Are there examples of lean enterprises in aerospace? These questions have been on the Lean Aerospace Initiative agenda since the mid-1990s, with hundreds of scholars, students, and practitioners working together on these issues. This chapter reports some of our findings and future projections, which were first signaled in Chapter 1 with Principle 3, in which we urged the adoption of an enterprise perspective.

One thing we've learned is that understanding and creating value for stakeholders is a critical aspect of being a lean enterprise – indeed, this topic is so rich that its full treatment is the primary focus of Part III of this book. Before we explore value for stakeholders, though, we need to delve more deeply into the concept of a lean enterprise. It is not a new concept. Many publications address lean enterprise topics,[1] and more are likely to appear. *The Machine That Changed The World*, the book that introduced lean terminology, has a chapter on 'Managing the Lean Enterprise'.[2] One of its authors, James Womack, founded the Lean Enterprise Institute,[3] which offers publications and services to organizations that wish to become lean. A web search for 'lean enterprise' results in hundreds of hits.

Despite so much information out there about lean enterprises, however, *most implementations of lean do not have an enterprise-level focus. As*

FIGURE 6.1 | Boeing's Vision 2016

## VISION 2016

*'People working together
as a global enterprise
for aerospace leadership'\**

**Boeing – Forever New Frontiers\***

### Core competencies

**Detailed customer knowledge and focus**
We will seek to understand, anticipate and be responsive to our customers' needs.

**Large-scale systems integration**
We will continuously develop, advance and protect the technical excellence that allows us to integrate effectively the systems we design and produce.

**Lean Enterprise \***
Our entire enterprise will be a Lean operation, characterized by the efficient use of assets, high inventory turns, excellent supplier management, short cycle times, high quality and low transaction costs.

### Values

Leadership

Integrity

Quality

Customer satisfaction

People working together

A diverse and involved team

Good corporate citizenship

Enhancing shareholder value

\*updated as of January 2001

*Source:* The Boeing Company.

Chapter 5 illustrates, most lean transformation efforts in aerospace, focused on 'low-hanging fruit' or with a 'factory floor' perspective, have been implementations of *kaizen, poka-yoke,* and *kanban.* This focus emphasizes cost cutting and risks suboptimizing one part of an operation rather than optimizing an entire enterprise. By contrast, ours is a holistic vision of *creating value for the entire enterprise.*

Discussions and action need to shift to that enterprise-level focus – which can mean many things. An individual program, such as the F-22, can be thought of as an entire enterprise. A corporation or a government agency can be thought of as an enterprise. Even the entire US aerospace industry can be treated as an integrated set of activities with the properties of an enterprise.

Before we can talk in detail about transformation to a 'lean enterprise', though, we need to define that term. Let's first clarify 'enterprise' so that we can get to 'lean enterprise'. Note that the concept of 'enterprise', much like 'system', is contextual in nature. For example, an avionics system could be viewed as a major system in its own right, as one subsystem in an overall aerospace system, or as comprising a number of smaller subsystems. This conceptual distinction has very practical implications. And just as a particular system and its associated interfaces and attributes must be carefully defined before the tools and methods of system engineering or system analysis are applied, one must be equally clear about the nature of the enterprise. There can be enterprises embedded within larger enterprises, each operating at different levels.

We define a 'lean enterprise' (in its most generic sense) as follows:

A lean enterprise is an integrated entity that efficiently creates value for its multiple stakeholders by employing lean principles and practices.

Lean enterprises systematically employ lean thinking. They are dynamic, knowledge-driven, and customer-focused – consistent with our definition of lean thinking in Chapter 4. As a result, they are responsive to change. A lean enterprise is continuously evolving with its environment, seeking improvement and perfection.

What are the enterprise processes in a corporation, a business unit, or a government agency that need to be transformed in order for it to be a lean enterprise? Figure 6.2 illustrates a generic process architecture for an enterprise, developed by a team of LAI consortium members to provide a common language and structural framework for discussions at the enterprise level. Many of these processes would be found in a more traditional mass production organization. Some, such as 'supply chain management', have connotations that go well beyond the traditional 'purchasing' function. In a lean enterprise, they *all* take on different roles.

In our generic enterprise architecture, traditional functional aspects of a business related to product or program execution are grouped under the label 'Lifecycle Processes'. These are the value stream activities that contribute directly to revenue generation for the enterprise through the creation of products, systems, or services delivered to the enterprise's customers. Our term reflects the lean view of an overall product lifecycle within which functions serve, as opposed to the more traditional paradigm that allows each function to suboptimize around its own operations.

The next set of activities – 'Enabling Infrastructure Processes' – includes many traditional corporate support functions. In a lean enterprise, though, they are reoriented to support the 'Lifecycle Processes'. This can involve a major transformation in the operation of most support functions.

FIGURE 6.2 | Generic multi-program enterprise process architecture

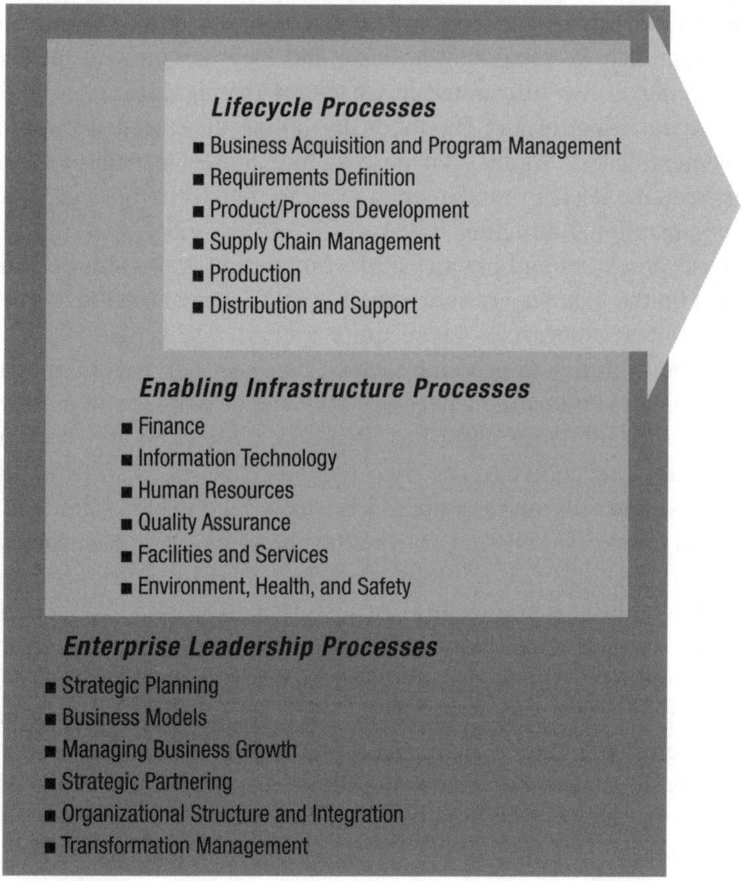

**Lifecycle Processes**

- Business Acquisition and Program Management
- Requirements Definition
- Product/Process Development
- Supply Chain Management
- Production
- Distribution and Support

**Enabling Infrastructure Processes**

- Finance
- Information Technology
- Human Resources
- Quality Assurance
- Facilities and Services
- Environment, Health, and Safety

**Enterprise Leadership Processes**

- Strategic Planning
- Business Models
- Managing Business Growth
- Strategic Partnering
- Organizational Structure and Integration
- Transformation Management

The final set – 'Enterprise Leadership Processes' – does not show up on traditional organizational charts, but these processes play a critical role in setting the direction for an enterprise transforming to lean.

The transition to lean is not a quick process, as so many enterprise leaders have been surprised to learn. Too often, leaders fail to come to grips early on with the *sustained* commitment needed to make bottom-line improvements. In particular, they consistently miss the human-oriented practices associated with lean principles. Consequently, the true transformational power of lean to unlock the potential of an *entire* organization is lost, and organizations realize only a fraction of the benefits. Hence, we find islands of success like those examined in Chapter 5.

We have yet to find an example of an aerospace enterprise that has been fully transformed into a lean enterprise. Within the last couple of years, however, we have begun to observe several organizations taking an enterprise approach to implementing lean, and they are showing performance improvements. We also noted in Chapter 4 the significant progress made by General Electric and Raytheon by taking an enterprise approach to implementing Six Sigma. Our observations make clear that an enterprise must redefine itself in fundamental ways to transform to a lean enterprise. Its organizational structure will be affected, as will essentially all of its business processes and practices. Most important, there will be a dramatic impact on the *behavior* of individuals at all organizational levels.

Aerospace enterprises faced quite a challenge in the 1990s as they began their journey to becoming lean. There was no 'Toyota' in aerospace from which to extract aerospace-specific lean principles and practices, and aerospace could hardly afford to spend a decade or more experimenting, observing, and codifying its own industry-specific lean principles and practices. The only feasible approach was to take overarching lean principles and practices, knowledge from the automotive and electronics industries, and the collective wisdom of academics and practitioners, and from there hypothesize a framework for lean transformation. Some companies did this on their own, while the Lean Aerospace Initiative afforded an opportunity for many aerospace stakeholders to work together.

Each part of this chapter builds in different aspects of our definition of a lean enterprise. First, we elaborate on 'lean principles and practices' at the enterprise level. We then turn to questions of implementation and progress. Later in the chapter we elaborate on 'integrated entities' and 'multiple stakeholders'. All this is the foundation for our focus in Part III on 'creating value'.

## The 'Whats' of a Lean Enterprise: Lean Principles and Practices

What are the principles and practices that characterize lean enterprises – especially in a field as complex as aerospace? Transformation efforts at Toyota had focused on manufacturing and supply chain operations, as had most scholarship on lean (including the seminal book *The Machine That Changed The World*). But manufacturing accounts for a much smaller proportion of the value associated with aerospace products than in automotive and other industries. So, are the lessons from the automotive industry applicable to aerospace, given the much greater product complexity, much lower volumes, much greater instability, and very

**FIGURE 6.3** | **Lean enterprise model architecture**

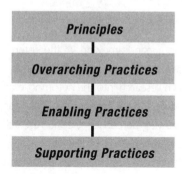

Principles

Overarching Practices

Enabling Practices

Supporting Practices

different customer base (with incentives that sometimes run directly counter to the concept of continuous improvement)?

To find the answers it is necessary to develop lean principles and practices for all of the enterprise functions shown in Figure 6.2 – in other words, to develop a broader, *enterprise* view of lean. Figure 6.3 presents the architecture for a lean enterprise model with a hierarchy of principles and practices, and Figure 6.4 details the model's principles, which state the high-level enterprise goals through the implementation of lean practices. In our view, these are the *core principles of a lean enterprise*. Two principles flow from the origins of lean introduced in Chapter 4. *Waste minimization* captures the ultimate goal of a lean organization to eliminate non-value-added activities, and thereby reduces the time and resources needed to produce a product or service that delivers value to the customer. *Responsiveness to change* captures the need for agility in responding to market opportunities (or, in the case of national defense, to changing threats) in order to produce the product or service when it is needed.

**FIGURE 6.4** | **Principles of a lean enterprise**

- Waste minimization
- Responsiveness to change
- Right thing at right place, at right time, and in right quantity
- Effective relationships within the value stream
- Continuous improvement
- Quality from the beginning

## LAI's Lean Enterprise Model (LEM)

In 1995, a team of MIT researchers, industry practitioners, and government officials set out to forge a lean framework at the enterprise level that would be appropriate across the many segments of the aerospace industry. Combining lessons from research into the automobile and electronics industries, many years' combined experience with a broad range of improvement initiatives, and LAI's growing aerospace-specific research findings, the team produced the Lean Enterprise Model.[4] The LEM is a synthesis of principles and practices, a hypothetical model of a generic lean enterprise.

The LEM framework – which is a more detailed version of the model we describe in this chapter – found quick acceptance from LAI consortium members, and an easy-to-read chart version turned up on office walls and in presentations across the country. The LEM has since become a standard reference for consortium members developing lean enterprise strategies.

One company used the LEM framework to assess the state of lean in multiple divisions after a period of mergers and acquisitions. A large military program enterprise used the LEM as a reference for lean practices and terminology across multiple organizations, including the government acquiring organization and the major contractors. In yet another case, the LEM Overarching Practices were used as criteria in identifying supplier candidates for long-term supply contracts. And a recent book from outside LAI elaborates on the LEM Enterprise Principles and Overarching Practices, adding strategies and tools for a generic manufacturing firm to become a lean enterprise.[5]

Four additional lean principles round out the model. *Right thing at the right place, at the right time, and in the right quantity* reflects the goal of every enterprise function performing as needed to meet customer demands.[6] *Effective relationships within the value stream* recognizes that people and organizations function efficiently when there is mutual trust and respect, sharing of information, and open and honest communication between employees, customers, suppliers, and partners throughout the entire value chain. *Continuous improvement* embodies the pursuit of perfection that is fundamental to lean thinking. *Quality from the beginning* recognizes the critical role of building in quality from the very outset, balancing the need to meet schedules with the expectation of continuous improvement.

It's important to note here that lean is not so much about the *individual* principles and practices as about their *effective integration and application* to meet the pull of customer demand, whether it be an external or an internal customer. As elementary as these principles may sound, their embodiment and application throughout the enterprise is far from simple. That's where the practices come in – in helping to identify what successful implementation will require.

Table 6.1 lists a dozen 'Overarching Practices' that support the principles we've just discussed. They are interdependent, and each must be adopted to some degree. For example, flow cannot be optimized without maintaining stability. Similarly, it takes a seamless flow of information to implement integrated product and process development. These Overarching Practices are at a high level, and enterprises need more detailed *enabling* and *supporting* practices that embody approaches for implementation in various enterprise domains.

Half of the Overarching Practices in Table 6.1 represent human-oriented practices. Notably, the original Toyota Production System recognized the key role of people:

> There are two major distinctive features of these [Toyota Production and *Kanban*] systems. One of these is 'just-in-time production', an especially important factor in an assembly industry such as automotive manufacturing. ... Second ... is the 'respect-for-human' system where the workers are allowed to display in full their capabilities through active participation in running and improving their own workshops.[7]

So, while the important, interdependent nature of the people-oriented aspects of lean practices and principles is not new,[8] the challenge of achieving gains across a defined enterprise continues to be an elusive goal for many organizations – largely because of the striking impact of human-oriented practices on process-oriented practices. In fact, many such human-oriented practices are *prerequisites* for process-oriented practices.

One human-oriented practice deserves special attention as a prerequisite: *Promote lean leadership at all levels*. The vignettes included in this chapter, the islands of success in Chapter 5, and the principles of lean thinking in Chapter 4 all support the observation that leadership commitment and alignment are critical to becoming a lean enterprise. Absolutely key are the overall enterprise leaders who drive lean practices and principles from the top of the organization, and the frontline leaders who make lean practices and principles an everyday reality.

**TABLE 6.1** | **Overarching practices of a lean enterprise**

### Human-oriented Practices

- Promote lean leadership at all levels
  *Align and involve all stakeholders to achieve the enterprise's lean vision.*

- Relationships based on mutual trust and commitment
  *Establish stable and ongoing relationships within the extended enterprise encompassing both customers and suppliers.*

- Make decisions at lowest appropriate level
  *Design the organizational structure and management systems to accelerate and enhance decisionmaking at the point of knowledge, application, and need.*

- Optimize capability and utilization of people
  *Ensure that properly trained people are available when needed.*

- Continuous focus on the customer
  *Proactively understand and respond to the needs of internal and external customers.*

- Nurture a learning environment
  *Provide for development and growth of both organizations' and individuals' support for attaining lean enterprise goals.*

### Process-oriented Practices

- Assure seamless information flow
  *Provide processes for seamless and timely transfer of, and access to, pertinent information.*

- Implement integrated product and process development (IPPD)
  *Create products through an integrated team effort of people and organizations that are knowledgeable about and responsible for all phases of the product's lifecycle, from concept definition through development, production deployment, operations and support, and final disposal.*

- Ensure process capability and maturation
  *Establish and maintain processes capable of consistently designing and producing the key characteristics of the product or service.*

- Maintain challenges to existing processes
  *Ensure a culture and systems that use quantitative measurement and analysis to improve processes continuously.*

- Identify and optimize enterprise flow
  *Optimize the flow of products and services, either affecting or within the process, from concept design through point of use.*

- Maintain stability in changing environment
  *Establish strategies to maintain program stability in a changing, customer-driven environment.*

## The F/A-18E/F Super Hornet: An Evolving Lean Enterprise

One of the US Navy's most recent aircraft production programs, the F/A-18E/F Super Hornet, provides a 'test' of whether our model of a lean enterprise corresponds to any lean enterprise within the US Aerospace Enterprise. An LAI case study of the Super Hornet Enterprise revealed remarkable alignment with the principles in our model and concluded that the F/A-18E/F is an 'evolving lean enterprise'.[9]

Five organizations today comprise the core of the Super Hornet Enterprise: Naval Air Systems Command (NAVAIR, the customer); Boeing Military Aircraft and Missiles Systems Group (the prime contractor); Northrop Grumman's Integrated Systems Sector (the principal subcontractor); General Electric Aircraft Engines (the engine supplier); and Raytheon Systems Co. (the radar supplier). The extended enterprise consists of more than 2500 suppliers, the end user Navy warfighter, and Navy and supplier maintenance and support personnel.

The environment in which the Super Hornet was to be developed was intense. The Navy had lost its Advanced Technology A-12 aircraft program, canceled by the Secretary of Defense. Many believed the credibility of NAVAIR and then-McDonnell Douglas was on the line. The Navy Program Executive Officer, Rear Admiral John Lockard, and his McDonnell Douglas counterpart, Vice President Michael Sears, were committed to executing the Super Hornet program in a radically new way to improve customer satisfaction, program efficiency, and employee morale. Many of the practices they instituted map directly to our 'Overarching Practices' in Table 6.1. For instance, they promoted lean leadership at all levels by delegating responsibility, accountability, and authority to integrated product teams (IPTs) through five levels of management. At the same time, this delegation promoted decisionmaking at the lowest appropriate level.

By creating a single management information system, with simultaneous and equal access for core enterprise members to cost and schedule data, they helped ensure seamless information flow. This seamless flow was further served by the use of weekly earned-value metrics for cost and schedule performance; by daily contact between customer and prime contractor counterparts, to ensure communication and to build credibility; and by a policy of open and honest communication among the team members, with expectations that they would request help when needed. The latter two helped to promote the 'Overarching Practice' of relationships based on mutual trust and commitment.

A common risk-management procedure, shared throughout the enterprise, aided implementation of integrated product and process development, as did the extensive use of lessons learned from the development of earlier Hornet models. And by adopting a mindset of 'the airplane is the boss' when deciding on benefits for tradeoff decisions, the enterprise kept a continuous focus on the product.

The Super Hornet's journey to lean continues. Rather than adopting the 'low-hanging fruit' approach, the program has tackled the challenging enterprise-level issues, including integration.

Our model of a lean enterprise provides a holistic framework for the 'what' of lean – the collection of interrelated and interacting practices that characterize a lean enterprise. But it doesn't reflect any order to implementing lean across the entire enterprise. How does a given entity actually transform into a lean enterprise? That is the focus of our next section.

## The Northrop Grumman ISS Journey to Lean

In 1999, Northrop Grumman made a strategic choice to adopt a lean *enterprise* approach for its Integrated Systems Sector (ISS), a major multi-program business unit of the company with about $3 billion in annual revenue from defense contracts. ISS adopted this enterprise approach under the leadership of Ralph Crosby, Jr, the ISS President.

Chris Cool, the ISS Vice President for Manufacturing, Quality and Lean, was tapped to develop a Lean Enterprise System and Operating Concept.

## FIGURE 6.5 | Northrop Grumman ISS lean enterprise system

*Source:* Northrop Grumman Corporation.

He employed the principles and practices we describe in this chapter. For ISS, lean at the 'shop floor and above' involves five operational steps: define value, map the value stream, establish the flow, implement pull, and strive for perfection. Figure 6.5 illustrates the system devised at ISS.

Has it made a difference? By the end of 2000, throughput times on the major ISS programs had been reduced by 21 to 42 percent – quite a significant improvement.

At an April 2001 LAI consortium meeting, Chris shared some of the lessons learned at ISS. 'The focus is always on customer value', Chris explained, describing the ISS view of lean as an 'enabler of competitive advantage'. He told us that the biggest challenges are 'learning to see and eliminate waste' and 'sustaining the change', and that 'the soft stuff is the hard stuff', meaning that much of implementing lean is about changing the organizational culture. He explained how focusing on 'time' forces everyone to think as an enterprise.

Chris also remarked on how a lean enterprise approach changes the organization's view of management. There must be an evolution, he told us, from the top-down approach where few are rewarded, to an environment of empowerment, with a fully educated workforce enjoying expanded incentives.

## The 'Hows' of Lean Enterprise Transformation

The issue of 'how' to transform an enterprise, applying lean principles and practices, raises a number of questions. What are the key success factors in implementing lean enterprisewide? Is there an ideal order in which transformation activities should be performed? How can a bottom-line impact be assured? And why do so many lean transformation initiatives fail?

One thing's for sure: leadership is critical, and what leaders must do overall is clear. One leadership model identifies 'setting the direction', 'aligning people', and 'motivating and inspiring' as the key factors.[10] Another describes the need for a 'shared vision' communicated and understood at every level of the organization.

> A vision is little more than an empty dream until it is widely shared and accepted. Only then does it acquire the force necessary to change an organization and move it in the intended direction.[11]

These ideas suggest several key elements of an enterprise transformation, which we call 'organizational change principles'. The business need for transformation must be clearly determined and articulated, and the need for dramatic change must be understood and conveyed throughout the organization. An overarching, prioritized transformation plan that is consistent with strategic business objectives, along with detailed implementation plans, must be developed. Resources must be provided to support the plan. All relevant stakeholders – including employees and union leaders, as well as external customers, suppliers, partners, and so on – must be involved in developing the transformation plan. Strategic goals and objectives consistent with the strategic vision must be established, with metrics for measuring progress in place and diffused throughout the organization. Senior leadership must be the champion of the change initiative, leading it personally, and must take an active role in monitoring progress, removing barriers, and motivating and providing incentives for both individual and team performance. The organizational structure must be aligned with the new vision, and change agents must be put in place to assist in making the transformation.

One approach to 'operationalizing' these elements is a 'roadmap' framework that translates the change principles into specific guidelines for lean enterprise transformation. Figure 6.6 presents a framework for the overall flow of action steps – part of three interdependent 'cycles' – necessary to initiate, sustain, and refine an enterprise transformation continuously, based on the elements described above along with additional lean princi-

**FIGURE 6.6** | Enterprise-level 'Transition-to-Lean Roadmap'

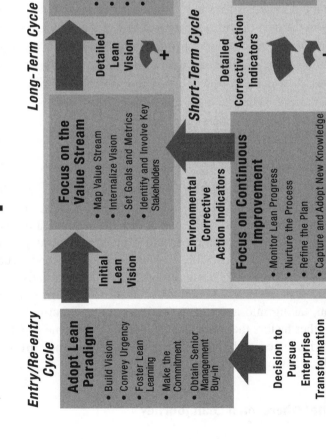

## LAI's 'Transition-to-Lean Roadmap'

When LAI brought together a group of scholars, industry practitioners, and government officials to develop a roadmap for transforming an enterprise to lean, the process surfaced a healthy give-and-take on how best to make the transition. What ultimately emerged was the 'Transition-to-Lean Roadmap' in Figure 6.6.[12]

Many LAI members were already on the lean journey when the TTL roadmap was being developed and tested. Notably, we found that different enterprises had started their journey in different boxes of the map (that is, in one or another 'cycle'), but without knowing what an overall map might look like. Most enterprises started at 'Implement Lean Initiatives' in the 'Short-Term Cycle' and found they had to go back to the 'Entry Cycle' and 'Long-Term Cycle' to gain leadership commitment and to understand enterprise value stream priorities. Others used the roadmap to validate or refine their own transition paths. No matter where the enterprise was, though, a roadmap helped to reveal choices that had already been made and to identify additional options for consideration.

ples and practices such as leadership, value stream mapping, stakeholder involvement, and customer focus. Special emphasis is placed on promulgating lean to the *entire* enterprise value stream, to avoid creating islands of success. The roadmap also pays particular attention to strategic issues, internal and external relations with all key stakeholders, and structural issues that must be addressed during a significant change initiative.

As with any such roadmap, it is important that each enterprise assess its own situation, taking into account its business strategy, current position, culture, and other factors that influence its journey to become a lean enterprise. Enterprises need to be able to figure out where they are on that journey – which is the topic of our next section.

### Assessing the 'Where' on a Lean Journey

A key element of enterprise transformation is to understand the organization's current and desired future state. To achieve a focus on the value stream, both the existing ('as-is') and future ('to-be') enterprise value streams must be defined and analyzed.

The answers to diagnostic questions about enterprise transformation linked to the 'Enterprise Leadership Processes' in Figure 6.2 assist leaders in making the assessment. Some relate to leadership and communication. For instance, do all senior leaders and management enthusiastically support a transformation to lean? Has a common vision of lean been communicated throughout the enterprise? Are lean change agents positioned and empowered to provide guidance and leadership for the lean transformation?

Other questions address the transformation plan and organizational structure. Is the enterprise-level lean transformation plan prioritized and

## The Value of Assessment

What do assessments uncover? LAI developed a tool known as the Lean Enterprise Self Assessment Tool[13] (LESAT) which employs a capability maturity model to measure the 'leanness' of an organization and its readiness for change. The focus is on the key integrative practices at the uppermost level of an enterprise.

In Spring 2001, ten US aerospace organizations participated in the testing of LESAT. Maturity stages were uneven, though most organizations were in their 'infancy' in addressing lean from an enterprise perspective. Nonetheless, several common themes emerged. Notably, the assessments confirmed that lean is a journey of years, not months. In every case, senior executive leadership, commitment, and involvement emerged as critical success factors in enterprise transformation – and we found that enterprises with leaders who personally championed lean practices achieved broader and more lasting results.

The assessment process helped initiate healthy discussion and debate over the strengths, weaknesses, and opportunities across each enterprise. More often than not, these discussions and the resulting actions proved more valuable than the LESAT score. In almost every case, the assessment process afforded the participants a more holistic understanding of the role of core, enabling, and leadership processes in delivering value across the entire value chain.

aligned with strategic business objectives? Have the value streams of all stakeholders been mapped, integrated and balanced? And has an organizational structure been implemented that focuses on core processes along the customer value stream?

Then there are questions related to overseeing implementation. Are senior managers actively involved in monitoring progress of lean implementation at all levels? And are lessons learned being captured in a consistent, systematic manner?

Any sound assessment of a lean transformation must also address Figure 6.2's 'Lifecycle Processes'. These are the processes that most directly determine the value provided to customers. The degree to which an enterprise is successful both in making these processes lean and in integrating them across the value stream is a measure of its effectiveness and efficiency. Some questions related to these processes included whether new business opportunities arising from lean-enabled capabilities are being fully exploited; whether product lifecycle data are being used to determine requirements and subsequent specifications; and whether customers and other lifecycle stakeholders (such as suppliers and manufacturing) are involved in product and process development.

The 'Enabling Infrastructure Processes' in Figure 6.2 might easily be overlooked as sources of value creation, since they enable rather than directly result in enterprise success. However, waste that is difficult to identify or quantify in these processes can have a negative impact on the enterprise as a whole. Enterprises transforming to lean need to assess how well the financial and accounting systems have been integrated with nontraditional measures of value creation, and whether common tools and systems are being used across the enterprise. They should explore how easily stakeholders can retrieve required financial information, and whether the information technology system is compatible with stakeholder communication and analysis needs. Further, they should determine the degree to which enabling infrastructure processes are aligned to value stream flow.

Among 'Enabling Infrastructure Processes' in a lean enterprise, for example, human resources (HR) plays a special role. The entire HR function needs to be redefined to support lean thinking throughout the enterprise. When HR recruits new employees for production, selection criteria must recognize that lean production requires a multi-skilled workforce capable of performing a wide array of tasks, many of which were performed by specialists under the mass-production paradigm. Likewise, HR must facilitate continuous just-in-time education and training consistent with the new lean paradigm. Similar modifications are necessary for all other HR functions, including employee benefits, incentives, and so on. Finance and information systems are other critical enabling processes.

Let's now return to our definition of a 'lean enterprise'.

A lean enterprise is an integrated entity that efficiently creates value for its multiple stakeholders by employing lean principles and practices.

Thus far in this chapter, we've focused on one part of our definition: 'lean principles and practices' and how they are employed. Part III of the book addresses value creation. The remainder of this chapter discusses what we mean by 'integrated entity' and 'multiple stakeholders' for the lean enterprise – terms that help elevate lean thinking 'beyond the factory floor'.

## Integrated Entities

The general definition of an 'enterprise' in the business literature roughly corresponds to what most people think of as a 'corporation'. But, as we noted in Part I, aerospace is a complex field involving a multitude of interconnected industry, government, educational, and nonprofit research organizations which collectively create some of the world's most sophisticated products and systems. Thus, any simple definition of an entity is bound to lead to an overly simplistic analysis of an aerospace lean enterprise.

We identify three distinct levels of aerospace enterprises based upon the level of entity being considered: *program* enterprises, *multi-program* enterprises, and *national and international* enterprises. Not surprisingly, they are interconnected and interdependent.

## Program Enterprises

The most elemental unit of aerospace business activity is the program, a collection of activities that produce a particular product, system, or service that is delivered to the customer and that generates revenue. Programs usually encompass the full range of 'Lifecycle Processes' listed in Figure 6.2, and a distinguishing characteristic of program enterprises is that they have accountability for cost, schedule, and performance of the product, system, or service.

Aerospace programs number in the hundreds, and vary in size from many billions of dollars, such as the F-22, Delta IV launch vehicle or C-130J airlifter, to hundreds of millions of dollars, such as the JDAM, to

**FIGURE 6.7** | **Program enterprise value stream**

those of a few million dollars.[14] The largest programs represent quite substantial enterprises, spanning many locations and a wide range of integrated activity. At the other extreme, programs that are conducted largely within one company may be too small to be considered enterprises.

Most programs feature one core value stream. Figure 6.7 illustrates this simple concept; the arrow represents a program's value stream, and as it progresses it leads to 'Value' being delivered to the end user or consumer. Value creation of program enterprises is taken up in Chapter 8.

## Multi-Program Enterprises

Business organizations and government agencies responsible for executing multiple programs are *multi-program* enterprises. Such enterprises provide the leadership and enabling infrastructure necessary for program execution (Figure 6.2). We address value creation in multi-program enterprises in Chapter 9.

We represent multi-program enterprises as a symbol (in the figure, an office or production facility) containing or intersecting program enterprises, and with multiple value streams, as depicted in Figure 6.8.

**FIGURE 6.8** | **Multi-program enterprise value streams**

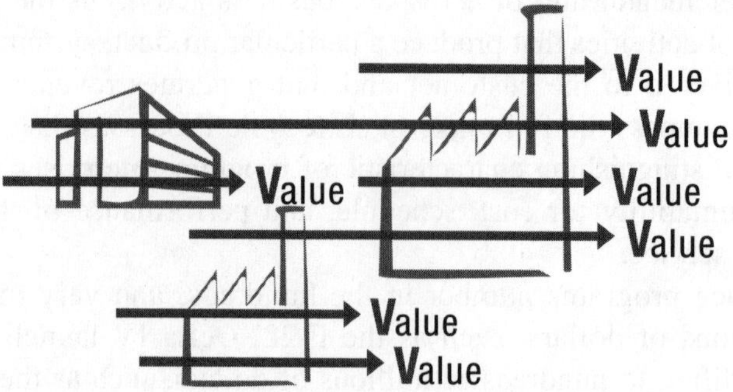

Remember, 'enterprise' is contextual. In its simplest form, a business enterprise could consist of a single division or business unit of a firm. The unit might produce an entire aerospace product, portions of a product, or contribute to multiple products. A distinguishing characteristic of business enterprises is that they have profit/loss accountability. A government enterprise in the aerospace context[15] is similar to a business enterprise in that it deals with aerospace products, systems or services, that it is composed of multiple sub-units, and that it can be part of larger government enterprises. A distinguishing characteristic of multi-program government enterprises is that they have budget authority to purchase products, systems or services.

## National and International Enterprises

It is unusual to extend the concept of enterprise beyond the multi-program level, but we find it helpful to do so as we address the challenges aerospace enterprises face on their journey to lean. In our context, the collection of *all* entities that contribute to the creation and use of aerospace products, systems, or services can be seen as a *national* or an *international* enterprise.

It is virtually impossible to consider aerospace isolated from governmental influences. Not only is the government a monopolistic customer for defense and some civil space products (government enterprises are the customers of business enterprises), but governments also fund research and development, establish policies for international trade, set environmental regulations, and certify commercial aircraft.

We characterize the US Aerospace Enterprise as including all *customers* (airlines, air freight carriers, military and civilian government agencies, general aviation, and satellite service providers), government *end users* (warfighting commands and civil space users), *manufacturers* (prime contractors, and multiple tiers of domestic and foreign suppliers), *infrastructure* (airports, military bases, maintenance depots, and air traffic management), and *related entities* (universities, professional groups, labor unions, laboratories, and support organizations). We address value creation for the US Aerospace Enterprise in Chapter 10.

The US Aerospace Enterprise, with its international customers and suppliers, is one national enterprise within the larger International Aerospace Enterprise (Figure 6.9). A growing number of aerospace companies are becoming global. Military systems are sold to many countries, sometimes resulting in portions of the system being manufactured or assembled outside of the United States through offset agreements. The newest tactical

**FIGURE 6.9** ▌ **National and international aerospace enterprises**

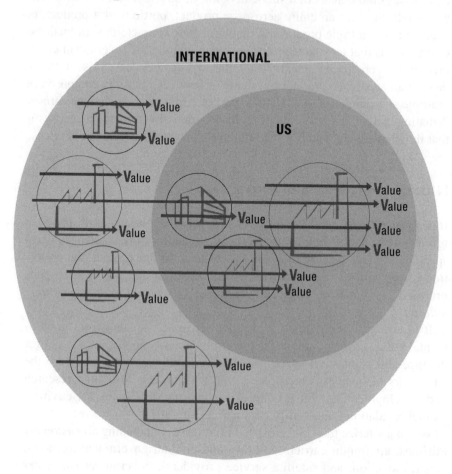

aircraft, the planned Joint Strike Fighter, is being funded and developed jointly by the United States and the United Kingdom, and has other international participants. And the International Space Station would not be possible without the participation of many nations and companies.

## Core and Extended Enterprises

For each of these three enterprise levels, a distinction exists between what we term the *core* and the *extended* enterprise. The core enterprise consists of entities tightly integrated through direct or partnering relationships. Less tightly coupled customers, suppliers, and government agencies encompass the extended enterprise – all the entities along an organization's value chain, from its customer's customers to its supplier's suppliers, that are involved with the design, development, manufacture, certification, distribution, and support of a product or family of products. In this definition, products include all of the goods and services that satisfy the customer's, and ultimately the end user's, needs.

The extended enterprise is the larger base for a given core enterprise. One might call the extended enterprise the 'enterprise of enterprises' supporting the aerospace 'system of systems' in delivering value to stakeholders.[16]

At which of these levels (program, multi-program, national/international) should the core or extended enterprises adopt lean principles and practices? The answer is: at all levels. The challenge is, and will be, to determine the appropriate lean practices and implementation strategies for the different enterprise levels. The interconnectedness and interdependence of aerospace programs suggested by Figure 6.9 illustrates that a piecemeal approach can lead only to piecemeal results, or further islands of success. This will become more apparent as our discussion unfolds in Chapters 8–10.

One could argue that it is solely industry's responsibility to become a lean enterprise, and not that of government. After all, industry most visibly creates and delivers value to the stakeholders. While this is basically true for business enterprises with little or no sales to government customers, it is a different story for military aircraft, missiles, and both military and civil space. There, the government customer has a significant impact on the overall program schedule, cost, and performance goals.[17]

For a program value stream to be lean, all critical elements of the value chain must become lean – particularly those upstream. If the government customer is not lean, the nation can realize only a portion of the benefits of adopting lean principles and practices. The JDAM we discussed in Chapter 5 provides an excellent case in point. It succeeded because the government program office adopted a lean approach. The same approach is required to ensure the success of the Joint Strike Fighter program. Government cannot expect a lean transformation within industry without the application of lean principles and practices in all branches of government as well. Education of government program managers, contract administrators and other acquisition personnel in lean principles and practices is *mandatory* if lean thinking is to be promulgated throughout the US Aerospace Enterprise.

## Suppliers Play a Critical Role in Extended Enterprises

Suppliers are critical to an enterprise perspective, as the aerospace industry examples make so clear. The aerospace industry encompasses a broad, deep, multi-tiered supplier base supporting both commercial and military sectors. Increasingly, these suppliers are called upon not only to supply parts, but also to participate in the design and development of new products, the continuous improvement of existing products, and field support for older products. These firms are also the most vulnerable to the instability and uncertainty characteristic of the aerospace industry.

Some suppliers are in the first tier of the industry, directly supporting, for instance, the airframers (fuselages, wings, vertical and horizontal stabilizers, landing gears, hydraulic systems, environmental control systems, interior cabin systems and components). Others provide engine components, accessories, and power systems, as well as electronic and electrical parts, components, and subsystems. Producers of rocket propulsion systems are unique in that they are both first-tier suppliers and system integrators in their own right.

Beyond the many first-tier suppliers, there is a wide range of second- and third-tier suppliers of commodities, forgings, and other component parts. Many of these firms have the option of pursuing businesses entirely unrelated to the aerospace industry. Depending on their specialization, these firms may be highly vulnerable to industry fluctuations or may be quite insulated from such influences by virtue of their more diverse customer base across different industries.

## Integration

To create value efficiently, various elements of any enterprise – processes, information, organizations, and enabling infrastructure – need to be appropriately linked and integrated. There is a great tendency for organizations to function as a group of 'silos', with each sub-unit (for example, purchasing or engineering) acting independently of the other sub-units. Often, sub-unit performance excels, but the enterprise as a whole fails to achieve its full potential. While the *necessity* of integration is undeniable, the *realization* of integration is quite difficult.

A full discussion on enterprise integration is beyond the scope of this chapter, but we offer a brief example for each of the enterprise levels to illustrate its importance.

At the program enterprise level, integrated product and process development (IPPD) has made a revolutionary impact on efficiency. IPPD includes the use of integrated product teams (IPTs), comprising all key stakeholders, which address organization integration. IPPD also includes the use of CAD/CAM systems to provide a single, integrated digital definition of the product being developed, as well as integrated information systems.

At the multi-program enterprise level, we've seen the emergence of corporatewide process councils in most of the large aerospace companies. These councils bring together groups across the enterprise involved in executing the same processes (for example, program management, engineering, and manufacturing). The councils develop standard processes across the company, building upon the best practices that exist within the various organizational units or from outside the company.

At the national enterprise level, the DoD instituted the Single Process Initiative (SPI) as part of the acquisition reform efforts of the 1990s. Prior to SPI, different DoD organizations had different process requirements for their contractors. A given contractor with multiple DoD customers would have to maintain multiple process standards that could be audited for compliance, an expensive and wasteful approach. Under SPI, a contractor facility was able to adopt a single process standard, which each DoD agency accepted.

## The F-22 Raptor Integrated Enterprise

Those responsible for the F-22 describe it this way: 'The future of the F-22 Raptor Enterprise depends on the innovations and contributions of every member of every IPT and each supply chain partner in transforming the F-22 program into a world-class Lean Fighter Enterprise. The Lean Fighter Enterprise, delivering the world's most capable weapon system is the goal. Achieving the Lean Enterprise means going well beyond customer expectations to secure the future and prosperity of the extended enterprise. F-22 people are the key. Application of lean enterprise concepts and tools is a key step in generating the requisite ideas and innovations.'[18]

The F-22 Raptor program is a good example of an integrated, extended program enterprise – one that embraces and cuts across numerous enterprises, many of them extended enterprises in their own right. Lockheed Martin Aeronautics Company serves as the prime contractor, in a teaming arrangement with Boeing's Military Aircraft & Missile Systems Group and with Pratt & Whitney. More than 1200 subcontractors or suppliers (some relatively small) participate in the F-22 program.

This first new fighter aircraft built in more than 25 years has been under development since the early 1980s. Its development has required the integration of an array of cutting-edge technologies – advanced aerodynamics, supercruise engines, fourth-generation stealth technology, and the most powerful avionics and computer systems – to ensure US air dominance well into the 21st century. Consequently, the program has presented a series of unprecedented technical and organizational challenges. This has called for the application of advanced design techniques, manufacturing systems, management methods, and coordination mechanisms across numerous enterprises.

A management council, comprising the leadership of the key stakeholders, provides an overarching management structure for the program, helping to establish common goals and objectives shared by all participants. The F-22 System Program Office (SPO) – the USAF program office responsible for all aspects of F-22 acquisition – and the major industry partners have worked together closely to shape policies and to translate them into action throughout the program. A dedicated centralized communication infrastructure system facilitates real-time coordination across enterprises.

The F-22 program pioneered the use of integrated product teams in defense acquisition programs – as a requirement by the Air Force customer – beginning in 1991, at the start of its engineering and manufacturing development (EMD) phase. The creation of many IPTs at the system, subsystem, and functional levels has enabled the full engagement of the end user, the Air Combat Command, and of major suppliers. Effective IPT functioning has required common requirements flowdown and integration of team outputs, accomplished through system integration at the program level, as well as through the creation of 'analysis and integration' teams at multiple levels.[19]

Computer-aided designs, as well as the use of common databases and solid modeling tools, have been critical to the aircraft's development. The IPTs have been able to perform early configuration and trade studies, to design for manufacturing and assembly, and to integrate design tasks across many teams. The engineering drawing release process, benefiting from the earlier F-16 experience involving the use of a single-piece flow build-to-package design release process (presented in Chapter 5), has resulted in significant reductions in both cycle time and engineering design rework. The program has benefited from timely and seamless information flow, real-time exchange of technical data, and effective coordination of myriad program-related interactions – design changes, schedule updates, financial transactions – among participating companies all across the country.

Affordability remains a key challenge for the F-22 program. An aggressive affordability initiative has been instituted by both the prime partners and throughout the supplier network, employing lean principles to reduce cost.[20] Previous success stories indicate the potential for cost savings in the future using creative incentive mechanisms that foster innovation throughout the F-22 extended enterprise, focusing on the supplier network.

In his keynote address to the April 2001 LAI Plenary Conference, Maj. Gen. Michael Mushala, the USAF Program Executive Officer for Fighter and Bomber Programs, underscored the central importance of affordability to the F-22 program. He stressed the critical need for the entire F-22 extended enterprise – encompassing the government, prime partners, and suppliers – to work together as part of a 'total team effort', with lean thinking as the 'absolute centerpiece', to ensure the program's future success.

## Enterprise Stakeholders

In any complex enterprise, whether it be autos, computers or aerospace, there is a large and varied number of stakeholders (Figure 6.10). Key among these stakeholders is the *customer* or *acquirer* to whom the enterprise delivers its products or services. In aerospace, customers include aircraft owners, air travel providers, government acquisition offices, and satellite service providers. These customers in turn deliver products or services to *end users* or *consumers* – the customers' customers – such as the traveling public, the warfighter, or the DirecTV™ viewer.

Customer focus is a key lean principle, and satisfying and even delighting both the customer and the end user is essential for enterprise success. Yet, a focus at the enterprise level highlights the importance not only of being oriented toward serving the customer, but also of recognizing that other stakeholders – shareholders, employees, unions, business partners, suppliers, and even society – are equally critical in the orientation of the activities of a given enterprise.

**FIGURE 6.10**   ❙   **Enterprise stakeholders**

## What Is a 'Stakeholder'?

Scholars have offered several definitions of 'stakeholder'. One defines a stakeholder as 'any group or individual who can affect or is affected by the achievements of the organization's objective'.[21] Another suggests that stakeholders generally include stockholders, employees of all types, suppliers, customers, governments, competitors, and activist groups, and notes that sometimes the 'general public' is included.[22]

Other scholars suggest that such definitions are not useful, because they lump all stakeholders – irrespective of the role they may play – into one category. Kochan and Rubinstein[23] list three criteria to identify the *saliency* of potential stakeholders: (1) the extent to which they contribute valuable resources to the enterprise; (2) the extent to which they put these resources at risk and would realize costs were the enterprise to fail or their relationship with the enterprise to terminate; and (3) the power they have over the enterprise. Stakeholders meeting all three criteria are *definitive*; others are *latent*.

Stakeholder theory examines individual preferences and efforts to satisfy as many of those preferences as possible, with the understanding that these individuals – and the groups they form – have particular relationships with the enterprise and with each other. The number of stakeholders can be very large, and with each new stakeholder involved in the enterprise the complexity of creating enterprise value will most likely increase.

In this book, we treat stakeholders generally as 'individuals'. It should be noted that each 'individual stakeholder' is actually a group; however, we assume for the purposes of this discussion that members of a given group share the same value system.

As we saw in Chapter 4, the customer represents 'true north' in the traditional lean paradigm. Even with a broader focus at the enterprise level, the customer can be a unifying force. The customer provides the ultimate means (revenue) for satisfying all the individual stakeholders. Although customer satisfaction is necessary, however, it alone is insufficient to guar-

antee long-term success of the enterprise. The roles of these multiple stakeholders who interact with, contribute to, and derive value from the enterprise must be considered. Any one of the other stakeholders can cause the
enterprise to fail, making it impossible to satisfy the customer.

*Shareholders* provide capital and expect a positive return on their
investment, enabled by ongoing innovation, growth, and profitability by
the enterprise. Satisfied shareholders are just as important as are satisfied
customers – a point made clear by the stark consequences of reduced
shareholder investment in aerospace and other sectors of the economy in
recent years.

*Employees* – senior management and the workforce – are another
group of stakeholders, contributing effort and knowledge within the
enterprise. This is the heart of value creation, which these stakeholders
provide in return for fair compensation, personal growth, pride, some
measure of employment stability, and various other tangible and intangible factors. Some employees may be represented by a *union*, yet
another critical stakeholder. Unions have their own internal governance
structures and must grapple with the decision to support lean transformation in a given enterprise.

*Business partners* provide risk-sharing capital and intellectual property,
and contribute to the enterprise's products or services in return for a
sustained portion of the value created by the enterprise. *Suppliers* provide
subassemblies, components, or services, and are concerned with mutually
beneficial relationships. The suppliers and partners are many and varied,
numbering in the thousands for a large aerospace enterprise. A lean enterprise depends on lean capability by all or most suppliers, which substantially enlarges the lean transformation task.

Finally, *society* is an important stakeholder with an interest that the
enterprise maintain the environment, provide job opportunities, support
the tax base, and serve as a positive force in the community, the country,
and even the global economy. Elected officials, agencies, regulators,
special-interest groups, or individuals – in the United States and abroad –
can represent society. As society's representatives, the media are an important stakeholder for aerospace enterprises: aerospace stories – a space
flight, an accident, a new product, a traveler's delay – appear almost daily
in newspapers and television.

Some of these other stakeholders will have specific agreements or
contracts. Others can be bound by unwritten, implicit 'social contracts'
that embody the mutual expectations and obligations that the different
parties bring to the enterprise.

## The Stakeholder Complexity of Aerospace Enterprises

Aerospace enterprises are characterized by the complexity of their stakeholders, often mirroring the complexity of aerospace products and organizational systems. Aerospace enterprises typically exhibit a high degree of interdependence among them, as well as a complicated set of relationships that bind them together – which makes it rather difficult to define stakeholder relationships in any meaningful way except in terms of specific programs.

The US Air Force F-22 Raptor program provides a good example. Lockheed Martin, the prime contractor, is teamed with Boeing and Pratt & Whitney. Together they work with 1200-plus subcontractors – accounting for more than 60 percent of the program cost. Meanwhile, Lockheed Martin and Boeing led two different teams of companies as primes developing the Joint Strike Fighter, competing for what is likely to be the biggest prize in the defense sector over the next several decades. Such multiple links and relationships among aerospace companies are not uncommon. The mutual interests that bring them together on one program may well pull them in opposite directions on others.

As if this were not complex enough, the picture also includes the many other key stakeholders that interact with these firms and further shape the patterns of complexity and interdependence. First, there is the US government, which is the primary customer for defense aerospace products. Government policies and regulations, acquisition practices, technology development efforts, and maintenance, repair, and overhaul operations supporting the existing military aircraft fleet all shape the design, manufacturing, and sustaining of defense aerospace products. More important, the government has actively shaped the very structure of defense aerospace firms, for example by promoting the consolidation of the defense industrial base. For example, the government launched the Evolved Expendable Launch Vehicle program, which represents the next-generation rocket technology for space launches, by setting up a 'winner-take-all' competition, shifting to a shared contract when it became clear that the losing bidder might not be able to stay in business (which would compromise the nation's future capabilities in this sector). Government regulatory policies have had a deep and pervasive impact on the structure and evolution of the entire commercial aerospace sector as well.

Customers for civil aircraft – many of whom are linked directly to foreign governments – represent a second set of stakeholders on the commercial side. These foreign governments also show up as customers for defense aerospace products through foreign military sales. Foreign governments also shape the industry through their demand for 'offset' arrangements, involving the procurement of certain parts, components, and services from their respective countries – sometimes not even tied to the original purchase. Essentially, these governments are looking to offset the cost of their purchases with job creation and skill-building in their countries. The desire for such support from other countries is understandable, but it does raise complex issues around the export of jobs and expertise from the United States.

To track performance and to guide continuous improvement, enterprises need to define and measure *stakeholder value*, not just shareholder value. Success is possible only when some balance is achieved in addressing the needs of *all* stakeholders, a challenge that usually entails difficult trade-offs. To equip an enterprise to provide value to all stakeholders is a tough and complex undertaking, but one that must be accomplished. We turn to this challenge in Part III.

## A Long Journey

The US Aerospace Enterprise journey to lean is underway. We've argued that lean demands an enterprisewide approach. The deconstruction of our definition of a lean enterprise makes clear that while there are broad principles and practices associated with lean, each enterprise must determine the appropriate priorities and actions needed to achieve its *own* goals. These actions, however, *must* be developed in the context of the *extended* enterprise, involving all stakeholders, and with an emphasis on integration with customers and key suppliers.

## The Critical Role of the Enterprise Leader

It is a massive undertaking to transform an aerospace enterprise – or any enterprise, for that matter – from a mass production orientation to one based on lean principles and practices. It will likely be the most comprehensive change initiative ever undertaken, and will touch every person and position in the organization. A change initiative of such magnitude and scope *must* be directed by the enterprise leader, whose personal involvement, understanding, and leadership are critical for success. This cannot be delegated – as several leaders and researchers have shown.

'The single most effective action in converting an organization to lean practices is for the CEO to lead the initial improvement activities', says Art Byrne, president and CEO of Wiremold Company (a firm that has made the transition to lean, and is widely referred to in the book *Lean Thinking*). 'Big changes require leaps of faith in which the CEO must say "just do it", even when "it" seems contrary to common sense.'[24]

Mike Rother, reporting on several lean transition efforts in the book *Becoming Lean*,[25] concludes: 'The notion that you can drive change to lean from the bottom is "pure bunk".'

Keith Allman, General Manager of Donnelly Mirrors, adds the following comment (reported in *Becoming Lean*): 'The transition to lean must be driven by knowledgeable and committed managers who understand it in their gut.'

Motivated by these and similar observations, LAI undertook to research the impact of leadership on systematic organizational change, seeking to quantify the critical role leadership plays in achieving results in a lean transformation.[26] This involved using a previously developed leadership 'index'[27] to survey aerospace organizations about factors such as creating a shared purpose, empowerment, strategy setting, and organizational change. The survey also asked about productivity, including outcomes in areas such as customer satisfaction, product and service quality, return on assets, and cycle time. There is a considerable spread in the results, but correlation is apparent between leadership involvement and results-based outcomes.

Further, lean transformation cannot be a standalone initiative for a given enterprise. It needs to be tightly coupled with enterprise business and strategic planning, and corresponding goals and metrics. And it must be tailored to meet the business needs and future direction of the organization.

Lean principles and practices are very much about people. They speak to the need to invest in training, the need to build trust and commitment, and the importance of delegating decisionmaking to the lowest appropriate level. For success, enterprise leaders must *capture the minds and hearts of the people and organizations* across the entire enterprise. This takes leadership – an essential ingredient.

The implementation of lean practices is not an easy journey, nor is it a quick one. It must become a way of thinking, a mindset for leaders at all levels of a given enterprise.

# PART III

# Creating Enterprise Value

When external factors force change, an industry has a choice – to adapt, transform, and prosper, or to pursue an outdated model, atrophy, and perhaps vanish. This is not a challenge unique to aerospace – history is full of examples of both choices – but it is a very real aerospace challenge. Nor is it a technology challenge, although there are plenty of challenging technology issues. What, then, is the real challenge? It is to provide enough *value* to key stakeholders so that the industry has a future role to play in society.

Chapter 7 lays out 'A Value-Creation Framework', conceptually simple and powerful, yet also requiring new ways of thinking and new methods and tools to implement. The framework's three interrelated phases – value identification, value proposition, and value delivery – need to be applied both iteratively and adaptively.

Chapters 8, 9, and 10 – 'Program Value', 'Value in Corporate and Government Enterprises', and 'Value at National and International Levels' – analyze the value-creation framework at our three levels of enterprise. We also address the interrelatedness and interdependencies of these enterprise levels.

Value is a powerful, but elusive, goal. Activities and entities that create no value survive only by policy or edict – a concept familiar to each of us as consumers. But in a field as complex as aerospace, who defines value and how can it be measured and tracked? How can the stakeholders be identified, and the value exchanges they expect be isolated? How can propositions be developed and fulfilled to deliver the expected value? And how can the expected value be delivered most efficiently? We address these questions in Part III.

Our value-creation framework provides the path to resolve the 'Higher, Faster, Farther' and 'Better, Faster, Cheaper' challenges of aerospace. Aerospace cannot wait decades to transform. Thinking based on yesterday's priorities will not carry aerospace – or any industry, for that matter – very far into the new century. The new mantra must be *lean enterprise value*, a holistic approach to the new challenges with a renewed focus on innovation.

To be sure, our value framework – logical and conceptually simple – lacks the test of time in aerospace. Its operationalization in the industry – and, more broadly, in society – is a formidable task, but a necessary one. In Chapter 11, 'Future Value', we affirm our view not only that insights from aerospace into lean enterprise value apply to many other industries, but that the five fundamental principles must be embraced.

# CHAPTER 7

# A Value-Creation Framework

Successful enterprises must not only do the job right: they must do the right job. Becoming lean, as traditionally defined, is important, but it is only part of the story. More important is to use lean concepts and approaches to *create value* for *all stakeholders* for *all enterprise missions*. That's the essence of our Chapter 1 principles.

Understanding 'value creation' is not difficult, but determining the specific actions to create value can be a complex challenge, especially in a changing world. For the US Aerospace Enterprise, the end of the Cold War forced a shift from the overriding demands for performance as the primary value of aerospace products. The focus has shifted in many aerospace domains to more of a market-based standard. The rise of global competition in the commercial sector has intensified this market-driven shift. In addition, resource constraints – from financial markets, from the public's reduced willingness to fund space exploration, and from the pull of the workforce to sectors other than aerospace – create obstacles to value creation.

As we've seen, the mismatch between these shifting realities and the existing institutional and infrastructure monuments further complicates matters. Government policies, legacy organizational structures, tradition, and a historical focus on 'hardware' rather than on end user capability all stand as barriers to enterprise value creation. Simply put, the predominant approach based on mass production no longer suffices.

The lean principles and practices we put forth in preceding chapters are a powerful alternative to that predominant approach. In Part II of this book, we saw that lean has typically been defined around the elimination of waste, with a primary focus on manufacturing operations. Many tools and methods support the systematic elimination of waste. But while each can be appreciated as an important accomplishment, they are all unfinished stories. More to the point, without appropriate attention to the principles of value creation applied at the enterprise level, the stories risk ending up limited in scope – as in our earlier islands of success – or even have unhappy endings. In contrast, we urge an enterprisewide focus on the elimination of waste *and* the creation of value. Some enterprises, including some in aerospace, are beginning to adopt this dual focus.

In this chapter, we present a framework developed to help better understand and succeed in value creation. The focus is on all three enterprise levels introduced in Chapter 6: the program enterprise, the multi-program enterprise, and the national or international enterprise. The challenges at each level are interdependent and often unique to specific situations.

There are no simple recipes for creating value. We present our framework as a guide for action, designed to trigger new insights and provide strategic orientation. The challenges are genuinely complex. Our aim is not to make them artificially simple, but to provide a way of thinking to make the challenges tractable.

The first hint at this complexity comes from the concept of 'value' itself. By definition, value is highly subjective – it depends on the vantage point and the specific time. Some outcomes will be highly valued by some and devalued by others. For instance, an end user receives no benefit from a requirement that a given program must provide management reports to the acquisition customer to show that things are 'on track'. To the end user, this looks like an added cost. The acquisition customer, though, values the information. Clearly, value to one stakeholder is not necessarily value to another stakeholder.

There is no single metric to track value, let alone value creation. Success or failure may only be fully evident in retrospect. Yet, value *must* be the focus. It encompasses both 'performance', the dominant focus of the Cold War era, and affordability, the dominant focus since the Cold War, as well as other attributes. Becoming lean is not the goal – it is just an enabler or a means to the goal of creating and delivering value. Success requires delivering value to end users and every other stakeholder. And creating value is a continual process, punctuated by negotiated agreements, unanticipated events, and complex economic, political, and social dynamics.

This framework and the rest of the material in Part III build on and extend the concept of lean. Throughout, we urge a disciplined approach to 'doing the right thing'.

## What is Value?

Our definition of value centers on exchanges that provide utility or worth and that result from some organizational action. Here, we are not concerned with the 'cultural values' of stakeholders, but with *how various stakeholders find particular worth, utility, benefit, or reward in exchange for their respective contributions to the enterprise.*[1] We also note that value is not fixed, but evolves with stakeholder changes in priorities, willingness to pay, and time horizons.[2]

The concept of 'true north' represents value in the broadest sense, and lean thinking teaches us to seek 'true north' – understanding what stakeholders need – to orient the enterprise. As Chapter 6 shows, there are *multiple* stakeholders in an enterprise, and each seeks *value*. Consequently, there are many exchanges in an enterprise – not just a single exchange of dollars for goods produced.[3]

Earlier we defined 'lean' around adding value and eliminating waste. Eliminating waste is a relatively simple concept, whereas providing value is harder. For one thing, *understanding* stakeholder value is not easy.[4] While the stakeholders can be identified in most cases, for many their view of value may not be identified with the value of the product, service, or improvement provided to end users. The value for these stakeholders is embedded in the value stream – as in the case of stakeholders in the finance and human resources functions of a business, who never get near the physical product, but add benefit all along the way.

The spectrum of enterprise stakeholders ranges from the workforce, to the business partners that provide capital, to the US public – through Congress, which provides ultimate authority for government programs and sets policy affecting multi-program enterprises (including many that are not in the 'defense' industry). To make things more complicated, stakeholder value expectations may change over time – sometimes evolving slowly and sometimes shifting dramatically. Additionally, the values of different stakeholders may conflict. Environmentalists, for instance, may object to specific manufacturing techniques that pollute the atmosphere, whereas industry may feel that the economic impact of addressing environmental concerns is greater than the actual environmental risks.

Value can be reinforced and extended through positive feedback cycles. For example, a success such as the Mars Pathfinder that captures the public's imagination produces renewed support for extraterrestrial missions. Engineers and scientists are excited to work on these missions and believe that they are making significant contributions as well as improving their technical skills. There also can be negative cycles when public opinion and policymakers question the value of space exploration, and the desire to pursue such activity dissipates. The workforce, the financial community, and even companies may feel that they would be better off engaging in nongovernmental programs.

In many situations, especially in aerospace programs, value cannot be defined around a single class of 'customer'. Often, there are many kinds of end users and potential beneficiaries of a given program. Consider the value associated with the construction, integration, and operation of the International Space Station. Whose value is it: that of NASA (the customer)? the astronauts (the actual operators)? scientists (the actual users)? the public who pays for the development and operation? or, say, the contractors who construct the space station, including all its subsystems and components (the people and organizations involved in actual construction)? In addition, international partners may not share the US perspective of value. Each of these entities has value that it adds to the project, certainly, but each also has its own stake that must be satisfied for continued participation.

The Space Station may be a particularly complex example, but it illustrates the many dimensions of value that can be driving a given enterprise. Focusing only on customer pull is clearly too simple. It may suffice in some sectors or some individual operations, but the application of lean principles in aerospace – and similarly complex industries – points toward a broader, multidimensional view.

So, how do we go about moving to a value focus? First, we recognize that value varies depending on stakeholder perspective, and that stakeholder perspective can vary over time. To some, value is building the product in the minimum amount of time for the minimum cost; to others, it is providing the right capabilities. Clearly, both are important. And it is equally important to provide the appropriate rewards and environment so that the critical stakeholders will be willing to participate in enterprise value creation. In sum, a value focus means orienting to the variety of stakeholders involved in an activity by identifying what they value and incorporating that understanding into the approach.

## Value Streams and Doing the Job Right

In Chapter 4, we saw the importance to lean implementation of identifying and optimizing the value stream. In their book *Lean Thinking*, Womack and Jones highlight the importance of eliminating waste from the value stream by making it flow continuously.

A value stream map identifies every action required to design, order, and make a specific product. The actions are sorted into three categories: (1) those that actually create value as perceived by the customer; (2) those which create no value but are currently required by the product development, order filling, or production systems; and (3) those actions which don't create value as perceived by the customer and can be eliminated immediately.

**Make Value Flow Continuously**. Once the third type of wasteful actions along the value stream have been eliminated to the maximum extent possible, the way is clear to go to work on the remaining, non-value-creating steps through the use of flow, pull, and perfection techniques.[5]

Tools such as value stream analysis are invaluable in 'doing the job right'. The value stream map is a tangible representation of how value is delivered. A typical approach is to map a process from beginning to end showing all the actions, buffers, and elapsed time.

Value stream mapping has proven to be a useful tool in eliminating waste to decrease the cost and time of producing products to meet customer demands. But mapping the value stream is not the complete story in value creation. Focusing value stream mapping on one process area or program rather than at the enterprise level can lead to optimization of a part at the expense of the whole. The enterprise 'big picture' may be missed. For example, there may be things going on along the value stream that could add value to another program in the future, but that are not directly related to the current product – and hence would be considered waste. Such narrowness of vision can reinforce the 'not invented here' syndrome.[6]

Product value streams do not directly represent values of all stakeholders. Hence, an action classified as unnecessary waste might ignore some stakeholders and lead to elimination of an action that provides value to others in the enterprise. Consider the difference between an engineer's direct added value to the project and the longer-term value associated with developing new skills or capabilities. For any one project or program, it may be hard to make a business case for the investment needed to learn how to use a new software platform, but over a series of assignments that may be money well spent.

Too many of the examples discussed in Chapter 5 remained islands of success, perhaps because of the lack of an enterprise focus. This is particularly true for innovations or improvements that could apply across multiple programs. Suppose the person working on a mechanical design has discovered how to use the CAD/CAM system in a unique way. If the engineer takes time to brief another program that would benefit, there is clear value added for the multi-program enterprise. But there is direct additional cost to the engineer's home program. This shows the danger of being too focused on applying lean principles to serve only an immediate end user. When the elimination of waste is narrowly focused around short-term cost cutting, there is a risk that value will be eliminated from the multi-program enterprise.

Another limitation of just being focused on 'doing things right' is that it is often static. While value stream mapping is completed and then left unchanged for a period of months or even years, *actual* value streams tend to evolve and change with time, and with stakeholder priorities and events. For example, process improvements guided by the *initial* value stream will require a *new* mapping of the process. Changes in technology may also drive significant process changes. For defense or civil aerospace, a new Congress every two years can mean new priorities that change a program significantly. In those programs, changes in the world geopolitical structure can have a strong impact on plans for a specific program. The F-22 program is a particularly high-profile example, having experienced major annual changes in its funding and projected production volume. Similarly, a change of CEO can drastically change a company's direction, rendering a value stream map obsolete.

Clearly, value stream mapping can play a very useful role in helping to identify areas that can be improved to 'do the job right'. But, when we take a more complete view of value, it's just as clear that these maps are not the total solution.

Creating value requires doing the right job as well as doing the job right. Of course doing the right job must be understood in context, and depends on the level of enterprise. At the program level, a given enterprise focuses on delivering the right product according to customer expectations. In a multi-program enterprise, the job is more strategic in focus. Concerns center on choosing the right markets and continuing to build enterprise capability, innovation, competitiveness, and financial strength. Chapters 8 and 9 explore these two areas in more detail. Chapter 10 explores the broader issues of value creation in national enterprises.

### Introducing the Framework

Creating value – with its two elements of doing the right job and doing the job right – is the cornerstone of a successful lean enterprise. But how does the enterprise address these elements? Simply exhorting people to 'create value' or 'deliver value' is inadequate. It requires systematic processes combined with instinct, leadership, vision, and even a dose of fortunate timing. To help increase the odds of success, we offer the three-phase framework for value creation in Figure 7.1.

Most lean improvement efforts, such as the use of value stream mapping tools, focus on the last phase of the model: value delivery (doing the job right). Insufficient attention is paid upstream to figuring out the

### FIGURE 7.1 | Value-creation framework

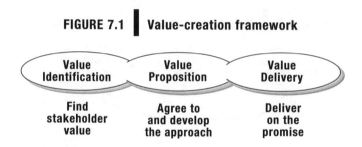

right thing to do in the first place – what we call value identification. Identified value will never be realized until all relevant stakeholders are aligned around one or more value propositions. And the impact of process improvement efforts aimed only at doing the job right will be constrained without the opportunity to raise the more basic questions about the underlying stakeholder proposition and the initial value identification.

This three-phase model emerged from early discussions on the material for this book. LAI research on what is termed 'lifecycle value' used the framework to examine findings and found excellent agreement with our model.[7] Lifecycle value of a product anticipates value over the entire lifecycle of a program, not just the low-cost bid to develop or build the product. This would include operations and sustainment costs, platform renewal costs, and other factors. Industry insiders are often skeptical of such initiatives, given the many forces that pull acquisition decisionmakers away from this lofty vision. Nonetheless, as we have seen in our studies, lifecycle value can provide the 'true north' orientation for programs such as the F/A-18E/F, 777-300, F-16, and JAS39. It was in the study of such initiatives that the first two phases of our framework – value identification and value proposition – became clear as necessary precursors to value delivery. Again, it is as important to do the right job as it is to do the job right.

These phases in value creation don't always follow neatly in a sequence, but they are conceptually distinct activities that are important to examine separately. They are iterative in nature, as Figure 7.2 illustrates. Seldom does a single pass through the three phases accomplish the task of developing a value stream that delivers value to all stakeholders. Additional stakeholders often emerge as the value proposition (discussed in detail later in this chapter) is developed. And iteration takes place among levels of the program enterprise, as well as between the program enterprise and the multi-program and national enterprises.

As stakeholder needs or external/internal constraints change, value creation will need to be reevaluated and appropriate changes made. Sometimes laws of nature intervene that make it impossible to create the

FIGURE 7.2 | Value creation iterates and adapts

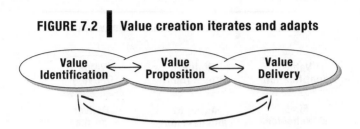

value stakeholders desire. As we will illustrate in Chapter 8 in the case of a single-stage-to-orbit reusable launch vehicle, the current state of technology can combine with the laws of physics to render a development infeasible – even when there is a perceived need.

We believe that this framework helps to make the value-creation process more visible. The remainder of this chapter discusses the framework in more detail, while Chapters 8–10 explore in depth its application at the three enterprise levels introduced in Chapter 6.

## Value Identification

The first phase in our framework involves identifying the stakeholders and their value needs or requirements – what negotiation theorists sometimes refer to as underlying 'interests'.[8] Economists might see 'utility functions' here. Importantly, many aspects of value identified in this stage involve reciprocal 'exchanges' that must take place between stakeholders even to identify the desired value. This is where determining the 'right job' begins. It can easily be the most overlooked activity.

The process commences with the identification of stakeholders.[9] Care should be taken to be sure that stakeholders with the greatest potential for both positive and negative impacts are identified. Too broad a definition of stakeholders – say, all pilots in the world – makes the task impossible. Missing a stakeholder whose participation would cause the 'wrong' outcome or inability to deliver on the promise is usually disastrous.

After the stakeholders have been identified comes a first attempt to understand what part of the project or process adds value for them and what kinds of exchanges are required to provide that value. This is quite complex. Stakeholders may be reluctant to be fully forthcoming on all of the dimensions of value that are important to them, lest they weaken their position in subsequent negotiations. Moreover, many stakeholders cannot fully articulate or even anticipate all of the dimensions of value that are important.

The sheer volume of research into how to conduct effective market analysis for consumer products offers evidence of this challenge. Can consumers know that they need something that isn't already available? Does an individual member of a stakeholder group speak for all stakeholders? And, in the defense context, can the military end user, trained in today's environment, truly speak to the needs of an unknown future war scenario? These are difficult issues and the solution won't be found simply by getting all the stakeholders together in the same room and 'working things out'. After all, focus groups and market surveys, though useful techniques, only go so far. It's necessary to construct *value propositions*.

## Value Proposition

The *value proposition* phase is where the needs of key stakeholders come together. Here, intangible values (such as job satisfaction), support of public policy, or an important enterprise need that was missed are either brought to the fore – or lost. In other words, constructing the value proposition may, as a process, help identify value.

The concept of a value proposition is not new, and the term appears extensively in current business literature.[10] The objective of the value proposition phase is to structure value streams based on the stakeholders' value propositions so that people, groups, and enterprises will contribute their efforts or resources to the value streams in those ways from which they can, in turn, derive value. This is critical to value delivery, since stakeholders will probably discontinue contributing when they receive no value.

These propositions are seldom based on a single outcome benefit – profit, for example – and cannot be fully expressed as a single attribute. They require taking into account a whole range of desires: for example, protecting the environment, meeting technical performance specifications, satisfying investor expectations, and providing a safe and exciting work environment.[11]

During this phase, different stakeholders structure explicit or implicit 'value exchanges' – sometimes referred to as 'agreements' or 'deals'. Clear examples of explicit deals abound, for most of them are formalized as contracts, which are physical manifestations of agreements between two or more parties. There are many implicit deals, as well. For instance, Congress might approve funding if it believes that the public supports a given project, but Congress might approve more funding if a project can relocate to an area with an especially high level of unemployment and, in doing so, help people (constituents) get jobs.

The agreements in themselves mean nothing until they are put into a structure to deliver on the promises. The fields of sociology, psychology, and economics tell us that the incentives in these agreements are pivotal.[12] Recent efforts aimed at 'acquisition reform' for government contracting are a vivid example of restructuring incentives better to match current realities. Instead of incentives that support going 'Higher, Faster, Farther', the shift is toward incentives that support being 'Better, Faster, Cheaper', such as by using commercial standards for many components.

Beyond aligning the incentives, the bargaining process itself matters. In some cases, one or more stakeholders play a strong 'forcing' role in constructing the value proposition, while others play much more of a 'fostering' role.[13] In constructing most value propositions, a combination of the two is involved – with many consequent dilemmas. For example, the value identification phase may surface a clear priority around taking a 'modular' approach so that a given product is designed at the outset to accommodate periodic upgrades – something to account for in the deal. Or, an integral part of the value proposition may involve long-term supply agreements. In a government program, there is forcing needed around government rules that require compliance with acquisition regulations. There will be fostering around joint efforts to achieve process improvements over time, as well as some forcing over how to distribute these gains. What is critical is that the bargaining process, the way the forcing and fostering takes place, can undermine or expand value creation in this phase of the overall process.

Part of the value proposition phase is to anticipate the sequence of actions that provide the value. For a program, it goes well beyond developing the program schedule and deliverables list. At the multi-enterprise program level, it takes into account how the actions interact with other value streams. It may look like a schedule, action item list, or traditional value stream map, but it must be much more to be effective.

Stakeholders need to be able to see that their value needs are met. Sometimes, this means additional tasks. For example, capturing the rationale for decisions during a long development process is important because it cannot be assumed that the same people who started the development are still around. Another example is the need to build additional information collection and sharing capabilities; this does not contribute directly to the end product, but serves the enterprise need for rapid access to information that supports management decisions.

## Value Delivery

The implementation phase, *value delivery*, is the most familiar in the context of lean practices and principles. Here is where value is delivered both to the various stakeholders who participate in the value stream and to the end user when the product, service, or improved capability is received. This is where all of the promises, both explicit and implicit, are kept.

Delivering value by conveying benefits to stakeholders requires the interconnected chain of activities that we call the 'value stream'. Excessive focus on delivering value to the end user or any other single stakeholder creates 'dysfunctional' value streams that ignore other stakeholders. Value delivery as we mean it depends on adding value at every step along the value stream.[14]

Beyond value stream mapping, other process improvement methodologies can be useful in the value delivery phase, such as Six Sigma, synchronous material flow, or in-station process control.

## Linking the Value-Creation Framework Across Three Levels of Enterprise

In the next three chapters, we illustrate the value-creation framework for all three levels of enterprise. We refer to the levels separately, but in reality they are highly coupled and interrelated. They are, in fact, like the layers of an onion; programs are usually embedded in one or more larger, multi-program enterprises (as shown in Figure 6.9). These are embedded in a yet larger national structure that imposes policies, constraints, and expectations.

Program, multi-program, and national enterprises have unique but related value needs. Table 7.1 summarizes the major aims of each phase for each level of enterprise. Value identification occurs at all three levels, though the focus becomes broader and less precise as the levels progress. Value propositions also become less explicit and more complex. And value delivery shifts from narrow implementation activities to broad transformation initiatives. In each case, however, a precise aim can be specified, which then gives focus to the value-creation activities.

## Summing Up

We began this chapter with the observation that a goal is not simply to become lean, but that lean is a means to effective delivery of this crucial

**TABLE 7.1** Value-creation model over three levels of enterprise

| Enterprise Levels | I. Value Identification | II. Value Proposition | III. Value Delivery |
|---|---|---|---|
| Program Enterprise (Chapter 8) | **Aim:** Identify value-add opportunities for customers and end users; assess implications for other key program stakeholders. | **Aim:** Construct a mutual gains agreement on value to be delivered among program acquirer, contractor, suppliers, and others; align incentives to focus on stakeholder value. | **Aim:** Implement lean principles and practices across the value stream – including product development, manufacturing, and sustainment. |
| Multi-Program Enterprise (Chapter 9) | **Aim:** Identify value-add synergies across programs; assess implications for internal and external stakeholders – including strategic partners, the financial community, and others. | **Aim:** Construct mutual gains agreements to develop current and future capabilities across the enterprise; align enterprise incentives to prevent suboptimization across programs. | **Aim:** Align enterprise support systems to enable lean implementation across multiple value streams – including information systems, financial systems, human resource systems, and others. |
| National and International Enterprise (Chapter 10) | **Aim:** Identify incremental and breakthrough opportunities to advance core enterprise missions. | **Aim:** Establish overall system incentives to ensure stability and foster innovation simultaneously. | **Aim:** Establish a flexible, robust institutional infra-structure oriented toward ensuring current and future capabilities. |

thing called value. We have seen that creating value can be understood in a systematic way, consisting of three phases that are repeated in an iterative way. Further, this process of value identification, value proposition, and value delivery occurs across all three enterprise levels.

In this context, we can now properly place the vast literature and even greater effort centered on lean transformation. Lean practices and principles are, in essence, almost all centered on efficient value delivery to a single 'customer'. In fact, lean capability in value delivery makes many value propositions and even new forms of value identification possible, so it is a powerful lever for action.

Focusing only on making value delivery efficient is a trap. It leads to an ever-increasing focus on eliminating waste – typically interpreted narrowly around cutting short-term costs. We urge that lean improvement efforts be grounded in the *larger* value-creation framework – with up-front attention to value identification and constructing value propositions. As our Chapter 1 principle states: *Deliver value only after identifying stakeholder value and constructing robust value propositions.*

This systematic approach to value is not a guarantee of success, but it does help to organize effort, increase alignment across levels, and reduce the risk of 'disconnects'. Its importance cannot be minimized. In many ways, this is the heart of the 21st-century challenge: to be unrelenting in the pursuit of something that is so hard to define or to quantify.

## CHAPTER 8

# Program Value

Programs are core building blocks of an extended enterprise, providing value in the form of capabilities, revenue streams, jobs, supplier contracts, and in numerous other forms. A program delivers a particular product, system, or service within the constraints of a cost and schedule, and can itself be thought of as an enterprise that cuts across many entities, including the prime contractor and its supplier network, partners, and customers (such as the program office if a government program).

A program can also be thought of as a value stream that encompasses the full spectrum of lifecycle processes, from the development of new business to requirements definition, design and development, manufacturing and sustainment – with supply chain integration throughout – as introduced in Figure 6.2.[1] The three-phase value framework we developed in Chapter 7 applies across this full spectrum.

Figure 8.1 illustrates how the three phases in our value-creation model apply to a program. The primary challenge in creating program value is to 'do the right job' *and* 'do the job right'. Even a well-structured program will have difficulty generating value from 'doing the wrong job' – that is,

**FIGURE 8.1** | **The pillars of program value creation**

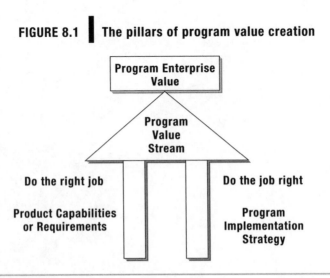

making the wrong product. And even the best product will fall far short of its potential if its value stream is poorly managed or not well integrated – that is, if the job is not 'done right'.

The figure shows the right product, and a set of stakeholders with the right capabilities, supporting the tasks necessary to produce value. It is in the value stream that value is created for both the end users and the participating stakeholders. Failure to achieve full value almost always comes back to poor execution in one or more of the three phases.

Aerospace programs have always faced this challenge of creating value. What is new is the environment in which these programs now operate. It is not unusual to take five to ten years or more to develop and field a new aerospace product, which might then have a lifetime exceeding fifty years. Over such long periods, the external environment, available technology, and market opportunities all change. This often results in radical changes in the way the end user will use the product, as well as in the needs of other stakeholders. Programs today must be flexible and adaptable, effectively integrating both mature and emerging technologies, anticipating and mitigating instabilities in funding and staffing, pioneering new business models, and operating in a global context. Some programs, such as the F-16, succeed in this environment. Others, as we will see in this chapter, do not.

This environment makes it difficult to identify value, which is part of finding the right job. It makes it more complicated to put together a value proposition – a plan not only to do the right job but also to do the job right.

## F-16 Falcon – Sustained Lifecycle Value Creation[2]

The Lockheed Martin F-16 was originally developed by General Dynamics in the 1970s as a lightweight, 'no-frills' fighter aircraft for the US Air Force.[3] When conceived, it reversed a trend towards 'bigger, heavier, more complex, and more expensive aircraft'. Although technical performance is a priority for any weapon system, a driving influence in the F-16 development was limiting the technical requirements to an acceptable level while keeping within funding constraints. The F-16's basic performance, however, is nothing short of impressive. No other fighter of its generation has the maneuver energy or instantaneous turn rate of the F-16 (both key measures of air combat capability). The F-16's lifetime record in air-to-air combat is 71 victories and no defeats.

F-16 value has been sustained as much by its adaptability to changes in the global environment and customer requirements as by its drive for affordability through implementation of lean practices. Considering sales performance as an indicator of customer acceptance, the F-16 has done better than any other free-world tactical aircraft. It is currently operated by or on order for 21 customers, with 46 repeat orders made by 14 of those customer countries. The F-16's success rate in open sales competitions is 67 percent over its lifetime, 75 percent in the 1990s, and 100 percent from 1996 to 2000.

The original system architecture – specifically the fly-by-wire avionics and flight systems structure – facilitates F-16 lifecycle value creation. It has maintained its flexibility over the course of many years. The original A/B models were outfitted with guns, Sidewinder missiles, and dumb bombs. The F-16 Multinational Staged Improvement Program led to the C/D model with intercept capability beyond visual range, day/night precision strike capability, and provisions for other advanced systems and weapons. The F-16 multi-role capability has led to it taking over many missions from other aircraft, such as national air defense from F4D and F-106 interceptors, suppression of enemy air defenses from the F-4G Wild Weasel, photo reconnaissance from RF-4C, and close in support and combat search and rescue from the A-10. It is also being employed in a number of non-combat roles – adversary aircraft in the training of USAF and Navy pilots, flight demonstration aircraft for the USAF Thunderbirds, flight test support aircraft for the Air Force, and a flying test bed for USAF and NASA.

In the early 1990s under the leadership of Gordon England, then General Manager of General Dynamics Fort Worth Division, the F-16 program responded to the affordability imperatives of the post-Cold War era. Adopting many of the lean practices we introduced in Part II of this book, the Lockheed Martin F-16 has maintained its sales price constant despite a 75 percent drop in its production rate – from 24 to 6 per month. Furthermore, its time from order to delivery has dropped from 42 to as low as 24 months. Some of the lean practices implemented include supply chain integration, flow optimization, focusing on core competencies, integrated product and process development, electronic work instructions, cellular manufacturing, and continuous improvement. The Build-To-Package Center introduced in Chapter 5 is a detailed example of lean implementation in the F-16 program.

The evolutionary development approach taken by the F-16 program has led to a system that – many years after the original conception – has become an example of sustaining value throughout the lifecycle.

In this chapter, we look at programs and their management and apply the value-creation framework outlined in Chapter 7 before moving in Chapters 9 and 10 to larger and more complex enterprises. We address value identification, value propositions, and value delivery. Each section includes concept definitions and examples, key difficulties and/or obstacles to success, and some tools for program managers. We conclude with a discussion of the need to adapt to change. By introducing a way of thinking about programs from a value perspective, we're laying the groundwork for understanding how programs fit into larger enterprises.

## Value Identification

For a program, value identification means understanding the value to be created by the program. Program value includes the value to end users of the product or service as well as the value to stakeholders participating in the program. We discuss these values in terms of identifying the needed capabilities of a product or service and identifying the stakeholders and the value they expect. Figure 8.2 maps the value identification tasks onto Figure 8.1's framework.

Product value – the capability to be delivered to the user over the product's lifetime – can be difficult to understand. Early in a product's lifecycle, especially if it is an innovative product, there is often limited

FIGURE 8.2 ┃ Elements of program value identification

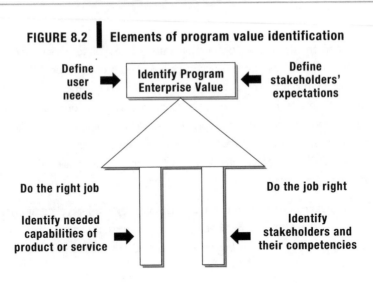

information on which to base an assessment of total user value. Unforeseen circumstances and possibilities could render a product less useful (and hence eliminate some of its value) or could cause unanticipated value to emerge that goes beyond the original vision of the product developers.

The transcontinental railroad provides a striking historical example. Its initial economic justification – east–west trade – was minor compared to the explosive growth and settlement it touched off, which exceeded the expectations of even the wildest visionaries of the time.[4] In aerospace, the F-16 was initially intended as a light, inexpensive defensive fighter and emerged as a versatile multi-role platform. The B-52 offers an even more extreme example. Over its long life, the B-52 has served as a high-altitude strategic nuclear deterrent and conventional bomber, a low-level nuclear bomber, and a standoff platform capable of precision tactical strikes with cruise missiles.

It's also difficult to determine the 'users' for whom value is created. For example, 'users' of a commercial aircraft include the airline that owns it, the pilots and flight attendants who operate it, the public that is transported in it, and the maintenance and support crew who keep the plane ready to fly. All are relevant stakeholders, with concerns about many different elements of product capability. Figure 8.3 provides a framework for understanding these facets of product value.[5]

The changes that continue to unfold in the business environment are also key factors to consider in the process of identifying value. In aerospace, for instance, there is an ongoing shift from an emphasis on perfor-

**FIGURE 8.3** | **Elements of product capability**

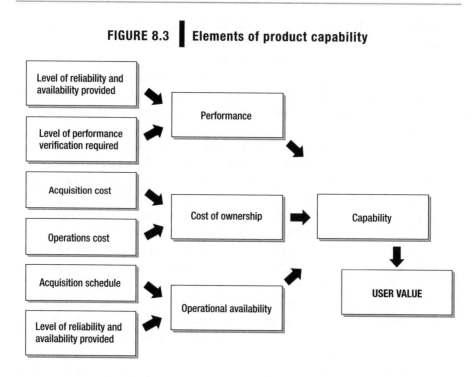

mance to a focus on total lifecycle value.[6] As Chapter 3 highlights, this is natural for an industry entering its mature phase. A feature of the transition to total lifecycle value thinking is that the emphasis shifts from defining the functions and characteristics of physical products to more expansive consideration of what will provide utility to the user of the product in operation. This broadens the focus to include less tangible features, including convenience, confidence, maintainability, and so on. In turn, this requires more attention in the product value identification phase to the product operating environment and the infrastructure necessary to provide full utility in long-term service.

Value identification also requires that consideration be given to whether the program is in a mature market, which has a more easily identified set of user needs, or whether it is introducing new technology or capabilities with the belief that the market will follow.[7]

Identifying the value to be received by other stakeholders is as important as identifying the value to be delivered to the end user. For example, it's crucial to identify the values of the workforce stakeholder – which, depending on the situation, may be more or less difficult. In tight labor markets, firms must compete to be the employer of choice, and what needs to be offered to correspond to what the workforce values may be clearer. In other cases, a firm might concentrate on what it needs in the way of developing skills and capabilities for the future in a given area, such as to support a shift in business strategy. Ideally, an enterprise perspective on value identification would link the two together, and link workforce capability development to program value stream requirements at each stage of a product's lifecycle.

For a program, others within the multi-program enterprise or even the national enterprise are often important program stakeholders. These stakeholders, by definition, have broader horizons than those focused solely within the program – for example, on the question of support for innovation beyond incremental improvements. From the program enterprise perspective, it may be that the product market does not require such support. But for the multi-program enterprise, such support may be central to retaining talent and capability needed for future value creation. And the public, Congress (directly in government programs, or indirectly by way of regulation), and the acquisition authority in a government program have direct interest not only in a specific program but also in how the program relates to broader goals. Policy considerations may even have important technical implications for a program.[8]

Failure to account for all key stakeholders can cause a program to fail. The value expectations of key suppliers, for instance, need to be identified along with those of a product's users. Consider suppliers of critical subsystems or components that must be available over a product's lifetime. A fabricator of components for a military product might have a commercial market that is much more lucrative than defense, and could choose not to supply the government or even the aerospace industry. Failure to identify the value of maintaining the attractiveness of the military market for such a supplier could result in the need for costly redesign should that supplier exit the market. This is particularly problematic today with information technology, where the market for consumer technology offers volume and profits far exceeding those of military markets.

As everything above suggests, there are many challenges in identifying value for a new or evolving program. There are also traps that, if not avoided, may doom a program to failure or stagnation. We offer three illustrations.

The 'preconceived solution' – often a solution that has worked in the past, and that has become institutionalized as a 'monument' – is one such trap.[9] Take technology solutions, for instance. Some researchers have found that technologies tend to be perfected at the very moment that they become obsolete[10] – an irony that often locks a firm into technologies because of its particular expertise.[11]

A second trap – in some ways a variant on the first – involves the powerful advocate with a vested interest in a specific design approach or solution to a problem. In the Reagan era, for example, the Strategic Defense Initiative was a specific solution advocated first by a cadre of thinkers at Lawrence Livermore National Laboratory, who were then joined by the President himself. They continued to push 'Star Wars' despite growing technological obstacles and a changing world situation.[12]

A third trap in value identification is the tendency to underestimate the difficulties in developing a new technology, especially if this occurs simultaneously with developing a new product or system based on that technology. New technologies may enable large gains in performance, or even entirely new capabilities, but 'pushing the envelope' is tough. Often the desire to exploit the possible advantages of new technologies leads to pressure to decrease the extra engineering margins sensibly applied to new technology applications, or to make aggressive assumptions about technology readiness. If assumptions are too aggressive, a program will, at

## X-33 – The 'Single Stage to Orbit' Challenge

The X-33 program, part of NASA's program for improved space access, is a relevant example of the traps in value identification. Putting payloads into orbit is real rocket science. Doing it cheaply and reliably has always been, and remains, a daunting challenge. Every pound of payload requires many pounds of fuel, structure, and control systems to gain orbital velocity. The laws of physics and current technologies do not permit any payload, no matter how small, to reach orbit with a single-stage vehicle using metallic structures with conventional rocket motors. Launch systems such as the Space Shuttle are 'staged', meaning that unnecessary weight in the form of the solid rocket boosters and, later, the large fuel tank are jettisoned once they are no longer needed.

The X-33 program was intended to pave the way for a single-stage-to-orbit (SSTO) vehicle that would replace the Space Shuttle. NASA's stated goals for Mission Affordability are: 'Reduce the cost of delivering payload to LEO [low Earth orbit] by a factor of 10 within 10 years, the cost of inter-orbital transfer by a factor of 10 within 15 years. Reduce costs for both by an additional factor of 10 within 25 years.'[13] But are these laudable goals realistic?

The X-33 attempt was based on a preconceived idea – a large, national-asset launcher, using an SSTO design. The concept was very risky given available technology. But the idea's powerful advocates took the position that there was (and is) a reasonable set of technologies that would make it possible. The result was a system that, although pursued competently and with the best of intentions, fell prey to all of the traps discussed here.

The X-33 vehicle, designed as a government–industry partnership, was to demonstrate the key technologies that would slash launch costs and open a wealth of new opportunities in the space business. But one study of technological readiness conducted before the granting of the X-33 contract to Lockheed Martin showed that the competing vehicles, which relied on conventional technology, used unrealistic mass margins to attain the mass fraction necessary for single stage to orbit.[14]

The winning Lockheed vehicle worked on the incorrect assumption that several advanced technologies, notably all-composite cryogenic fuel tanks and linear aerospike engines, would be ready with only a modest amount of technological development. Neither technology arrived on schedule, and the program was canceled after the cryogenic fuel tank failed its first major test.[15] This failure was typical of new technologies – things rarely work the first time. Although such failures were accepted during the early Cold War years as part of the progress towards a successful system (see Chapter 2), today's risk-averse environment is not so forgiving.

The program itself was reasonably structured, with technology demonstration preceding full-scale development. However, the SSTO problem in particular, and the low-cost launch problem in general, are physical challenges that, though perhaps not insurmountable, cannot be addressed simply by hoping that technologies will be developed faster than usual. Managed as a technology development program without a firm timetable and with a tolerance for learning from failure, the X-33 could have been a success. As advertised, it was not.

best, face schedule problems as technological roadblocks are cleared. At worst, a program will fail.

These traps provide a useful checklist of areas for further probing as stakeholders and their values are identified. Identifying all of the stakeholders is usually possible if the work is done. Developing a useful representation of their values is more difficult.

Many existing methods and tools aid program value identification. Where there is a clear definition of the product to be developed – such as an upgrade to an existing product, or a clearly stated need with a defined set of users – tools such as focus groups, surveys, or interviews are

## Creating Incentives for Value Creation in Government Acquisition

Open and honest sharing of information is particularly critical in the case of a government program. Can lean enterprise value creation be realized within the existing government procurement system? LAI research and case studies presented in this book provide a clear answer – yes![16]

While there are challenges that must be overcome on a program-by-program basis, no legal or administrative barriers have been found that prohibit acquisition based upon 'best value' principles. Education, frameworks and tools are needed to overcome these challenges and to support the transformation of the government acquisition system to achieve these goals.

A coalition of LAI stakeholders developed one such practical aid, the *Incentive Strategies for Defense Acquisition*[17] guidebook, which is organized around five questions for acquisition personnel to ask as they develop an incentive strategy: Why are we concerned with contractual incentives? What elements contribute to an effective incentive strategy leading to a successful business relationship that maximizes value? How do you build and maintain an effective environment for the successful business relationship? How do you build the acquisition business case? How do you build an incentive strategy that maximizes value? An electronic version links to further resources, references, and tools.[18]

useful.[19] Quality Function Deployment[20] – a structured process for capturing and prioritizing user needs – is targeted for these types of programs. Multi-Attribute Utility Theory[21] is another approach that is quite useful in facilitating the dialogue between the design team and the end user. These tools aid lean enterprise value by improving the efficiency and scope of the identification process.

One of the lean enterprise elements discussed in Chapter 6 is '*Effective relationships within the value stream*'. This recognizes that people and organizations function best when there is mutual trust and respect, sharing of information, and open and honest communication between all relevant stakeholders throughout the entire value chain. If stakeholders 'game' the identification of what they want from the program (for example, in hope of trading for concessions later in the program) an entire program infrastructure and approach may be set in ways that are inefficient – or worse.

Taking a lean enterprise perspective on programs points to a process of identifying value that builds on existing methods of identifying product value. Only *systematic* value identification leads to robust value propositions – the focus of our next section.

## Program Value Proposition

The essence of the value proposition is the understanding of the goals of the program and an implementation approach that will effectively deliver value to all stakeholders. At the program level, the value proposition formalizes program objectives, defines relationships between stakeholders, and structures the program to deliver expected value to stakeholders. Figure 8.4 shows the aims of this phase in terms of the value-based program enterprise structure proposed in Figure 8.1.

The first pillar in the figure, 'Do the right job', is formalized in terms of objectives for a product or service to be delivered (traditionally, this has meant documentation of product requirements). The second pillar, 'Do the job right', is formalized through written documents and verbal agreements. The content includes the definition, schedule, and responsibility for the tasks. There are contracts that formalize the relationships among elements of the program enterprise and define roles and responsibilities. Other agreements, usually informal, identify contributions and expectations between the program and stakeholders. These two pillars come together in the form of a program plan, which is the representation of that program's value stream. Traditionally, requirements, contracts, and a plan/schedule are *all* prepared, but often without sufficient attention to

**FIGURE 8.4** | **Elements of a program value proposition**

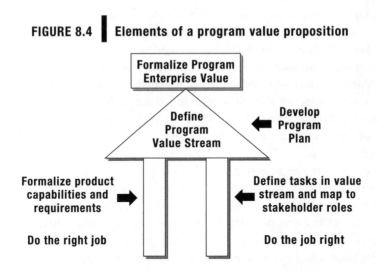

integration and without the benefit of a value perspective. A requirements document, a set of supplier contracts, and a program schedule do not combine to make a value proposition.

A value-based program plan is seldom a single document, in a large program: it comprises a hierarchy of documents. The prime contractor generally will have a plan with requirements that flow down to suppliers. These suppliers, in turn, have plans at levels of detail that depend on the size of their portions of the development. Also, plans evolve with the phases of the program. A plan for a new technology development might have far less documentation of product requirements and a less detailed task plan than for a full-scale production program. There is no simple formula for the amount of material or the level of detail to put in a program plan. What's important is to provide a mechanism to communicate and check that the program will deliver appropriate value to all stakeholders.

Many organizations use 'mission statements' to provide focus and direction. While often overly vague, if carefully worded and agreed upon by all parties, they can serve as the top level of a value proposition. Ideally, such a statement would be explicit and inclusive of all major stakeholders. The establishment of at least a tacit agreement among key stakeholders is characteristic of many successful programs mentioned in this book, and the trend is towards increasing inclusiveness and more explicit statements.

Many of the programs profiled in this book trace their success to an understanding between the program (as represented by the integrator) and the customer. Several others add the supply chain to this understanding.

We know of top-level mission program statements that have been made explicit, and are even signed by the stakeholders to indicate their commitment. Most of these are bilateral, between prime contractors and customers. Based on our observations, we offer an idealized version of such a program statement in the box opposite – not as a template, but as a thought provoker. It explicitly traces out the roles of many stakeholders and how they will interact with the program. It is generic – a real program would need to be more specific – but it does provide a set of basic principles to guide a value-oriented program.

We emphasize the importance of having a top-level focusing statement that is referred to constantly and reinforced by program leaders when communicating with stakeholders. Developing such a statement requires significant effort – especially if the program has many different, and perhaps conflicting, objectives. It requires a process that takes into account how the talents and capabilities of every stakeholder can be used to create value, and requires appropriate incentives to encourage full participation.

Referring again to Figure 8.4, a program cannot provide value if it does not deliver the capabilities required by the end user. Needed capabilities must be translated into identifiable functions and measurable parameters that can be designed, developed, and verified. Getting this right requires giving consideration to more than technical performance. Again, Figure 8.3 is a framework for capturing all the needs of a product end user, and can aid the development of the set of requirements documentation that becomes part of the program plan.[22]

Many textbooks and commercial standards provide guidance on the preparation and content of program plans.[23] However, they need to be augmented by a value-creation perspective, with attention to including various stakeholders, explicit and implicit relationships between stakeholders, information flow, and risk and uncertainty considerations.

An important aspect of the program plan is to define relationships and interactions between entities in the program. Many are spelled out in contractual documents. However, there is also a large number of less formal agreements. The multi-program enterprise may have strategic agreements in place that bind the program. These might be labor agreements with the workforce, tax abatement agreements with certain communities, or strategic alliances with other companies. There can also be supporting infrastructure or knowledge from the multi-program and national enterprise level that contribute to or constrain a program enterprise value proposition. These interdependencies will become more apparent in Chapters 9 and 10.

## A Hypothetical Program Mission Statement – The Top Level of the Program Value Proposition[24]

Our highest obligation is to the end users and customers of our products and services. We will meet or exceed key performance parameters. We will constantly strive for the highest possible quality and the lowest possible cost, to offer the best value to our customers. Customer orders will be delivered promptly. Customers agree to keep product requirements as stable as possible, working with us cooperatively to respond to changing needs and new opportunities. In the same spirit, we will strive to maintain a stable partnership with our suppliers, working with them to achieve mutual gains.

We will use open and honest communication with all our stakeholders – the individuals, companies, and organizations that make up the program. We will resolve disputes in a constructive manner.

We respect the dignity and value of our workforce. We will strive for fair compensation and rewards; we are committed to safe and pleasant working conditions. Our employees are expected to understand the goals of the program, and to contribute wholeheartedly to its success – working to the best of their abilities. Difficulties and shortcomings will be communicated honestly and resolved in a nonjudgmental way. Employees are encouraged to share ideas freely with coworkers and management – we are expected to listen and to engage the issues appropriately.

In all aspects of the program, we will act ethically and observe the letter and spirit of the law. We will do no harm to the communities in which we work, and we will be supportive of the efforts of the program stakeholders to improve and to support their families, communities, and society.

We will balance the needs of the program with the needs of the stakeholders involved in the project. The need for member companies to make a fair profit, for member organizations to meet their goals, and for individuals to develop their skills and move forward in their careers will be accommodated. The stakeholders will, in return, provide the program with the necessary resources, materiel, personnel, and time. Changes in program needs and/or available resources will be communicated clearly and in a timely fashion.

There may also be unstated or implicit agreements. For example, in addition to an explicit long-term partnership agreement between a prime contractor and a supplier, there also will be an implicit set of understandings around information sharing, communication, trust, and other intangibles. These less visible agreements are typically just as important as the explicit ones in generating lean enterprise value.

The organizational structure and the way program responsibilities are assigned to the organizational elements have a tremendous impact on how well the program will function. A complete program plan must show how different parts of the program pass *information*, as well as physical parts of the product. Equally important is defining how problems will be surfaced and solved between program entities.

An understanding of risks associated with delivering the product is an essential element of a sound program plan. Risk identification and management is always a problem, and it is impossible to identify unknown unknowns. In all programs, there are limitations on the resources that can be applied to avoiding potential problems that may never occur. Nevertheless, it is essential to have a planned, proactive, and ongoing risk-management approach that surfaces and evaluates issues before they become problems. This is especially so for technically complex products developed in an ever-changing environment.

As we move to consider the value delivery phase, we note that decisions made early in the program lifecycle have the greatest impact on eventual product capability – cost, schedule, and availability. Although the expenditure of resources in the early program phases is relatively small, this is the time when the greatest leverage exists. Figure 8.5[25] illustrates that decisions about the product architecture and the key design features made in the conceptual and preliminary design phases lock in two-thirds of the eventual cost of the product, even though these costs will not actually be incurred until the production phase.

There are a number of tools and methods that can aid in developing a value-based program plan for a lean enterprise. Organizational approaches such as integrated product teams (IPTs) help provide better understanding and communication among program enterprise stakeholders. IPTs are especially effective when the end user, the acquirer, and the suppliers are all equal members of the team. Integrated product and process development (IPPD) and concurrent engineering approaches are effective in organizing work to be as efficient as possible.[26] And having a good understanding of the design space and the relationship between cost and different levels of performance provides an important basis for negotiating

**FIGURE 8.5** | **The impact of early program phases on eventual product cost**

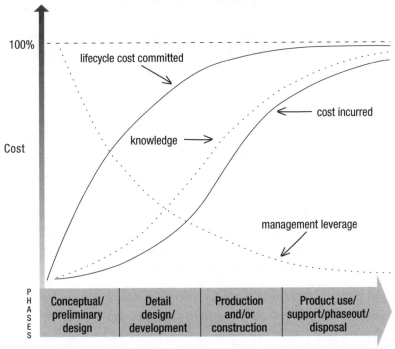

Source: Based on W. J. Fabrycky, *Engineering Economy*, © 1989. Electronically reproduced by permission of Pearson Education, Inc., Upper Saddle River, New Jersey. The figure is notional.

the balance between various end users, as well as the values of those executing the program.[27]

For program planning, tools such as PERT and Gantt charts are useful for developing master schedules and sequencing of tasks. More powerful methods are emerging based on the application of design structure matrices (DSMs), which provide a powerful visual and analytical tool to understand how the partitioning of work can affect not only the schedule but also the information flow throughout the program value stream.[28]

As we move to the next phase in our framework, it is absolutely crucial to remember that efficient application of lean principles and practices in the value delivery phase cannot overcome poor value-creation decisions in the preceding value proposition phase.

## JDAM – Program Value Creation through Early Supplier Integration[29]

The Joint Direct Attack Munition program discussed in Chapter 5 provides an excellent example of gathering stakeholders together to develop a program plan that addresses the value expectations of the customer and the suppliers.

A key enabler for JDAM value creation was *early* integration of suppliers in the product teams. One result was *architectural innovation* – a major modification in the system architecture – that led to lower costs, improved product performance, and value for all the stakeholders. This was made possible by proactively leveraging and integrating the technology base and knowhow of the supplier network early in the product development process. The *tacit* (that is, uncodified, experience-based) technical knowledge in the supplier network led to a product configuration that would have been impossible without such supplier participation.

After the contract award, detailed analyses indicated that increasing the levels of integration of various system modules could significantly reduce the cost of producing the overall system. This would be a significant shift from the original conceptual design, which consisted of a highly partitioned system architecture. The drive toward a more integrated architecture was especially significant for the electronics portion of the system, which represented a large percentage of total system cost.

Of particular relevance was the fact that suppliers were responsible for a major share of the electronics portion of the overall system. The electronics architecture had to be redesigned in order to achieve the desired greater level of integration, and supplier knowledge was essential for the task. Furthermore, greater integration also meant that some portions of the system, initially allocated to one supplier, might be reallocated to another. Hence, an increased level of integration meant that, if the desired cost reductions were to be realized, some trading of workshare among the suppliers would be necessary, along with changes in the levels of revenue they might expect. Thus, some would lose, others might gain; and for all to receive value, individual goals would have to be subordinated to team goals.

A policy of open and candid communications allowed suppliers to bring their knowledge and expertise directly to bear on the redesign. In one instance, some functions resident on a receiver module from one supplier were moved to an antenna module initially assigned to another supplier. This allowed the use of less expensive elements on the antenna module and reduced the production costs of the receiver module. Also, greater integration allowed the elimination of connectors and wiring harnesses, which not only reduced costs but also increased reliability. Other beneficial changes included reductions in heat-management requirements, inherent electromagnetic shielding, better design for manufacturing and assembly, greater vibration tolerance, and a reduced parts count.

*Goal-congruency*, an important unifying factor enabled through innovative contracting, linked the government advocacy team, the prime contractor, key suppliers, and subtier suppliers. Long-term program commitment by the government and complementary long-term relationships between the prime contractor and its key suppliers were established. The government also gave the prime contractor configuration control in return for an extended warranty. In turn, the prime passed design authority and configuration control down to the suppliers, greatly reducing reporting and oversight requirements. In a number of instances, commercial practices were substituted for military specifications and reporting requirements were substantially reduced. Finally, innovative contracting methods also served to protect proprietary commercial pricing methods and trade secrets of some of the suppliers.

## Delivering Program Value

The program has developed its value proposition, taking into account all key stakeholders. The actions necessary to deliver the product or service to end users have been determined, along with how they will be done, who will do them, and when they will be completed. This has all been made explicit and communicated to stakeholders. Now the program must *deliver* on the promise.

How does a program enterprise deliver value? The value proposition must be turned into action, and the program must efficiently provide the capability agreed to within the agreed-upon cost and schedule. The program must be ready to react quickly to make decisions and to address and solve problems. Stakeholders in the value stream need to execute their tasks well. Engineers need to do good engineering, software developers need to develop good software, and craftspeople need to produce excellent hardware. But more than that, there must be *continual* attention to finding and minimizing waste. And it must all be managed to improve the value delivered – also continuously.

Lean principles and practices apply directly to the value delivery phase. Lean programs must continually strive to deliver value more efficiently. As we've noted earlier, most lean applications to date have been limited to the factory floor, and hence are islands in the overall program value stream. To deliver maximum value, lean or related techniques must be applied all along the program value stream. Most important, they must be applied to the interfaces and interactions between 'traditional' functions on the value stream.

One key to improving value delivery in a program enterprise is to identify areas that require interactions across boundaries or areas, because it is at these 'crossings' that we find some of the greatest potential for problems and often long delays associated with problems that require rework. Concentrating on only one part of the value stream is suboptimal, as we saw in the Chapter 5 example of software development. Again, realizing lean enterprise value requires an enterprise perspective.

The curves in Figure 8.5 indicate that special emphasis on improving value delivery is needed in the product development phase. Most commitments are made at early points in the value stream; if early efforts require rework later on, the implications for ultimate value delivery can be quite substantial.

Within the value stream, it is arguably product development that, more than any other part, requires effective use of human capital. Much of this takes place in the form of interactions between individuals or groups of individuals. These interactions tend to be 'non-linear' and are often unstructured. They're also hard to see. Unlike design drawings, which can be inspected to analyze whether they meet stated requirements, it is nearly impossible to map the ways in which intellectual capital is actually deployed to develop those design drawings. However, examining information exchanges can help at least to identify sources of waste and to point to where information can be transferred through simple communications such as documents and where higher bandwidth is needed.

Integrated product teams, when implemented effectively,[30] greatly improve the use of human capital in product development. Researchers

## Creating Lean Enterprise Value in Product Development

Through LAI research, we've gained some important insights into creating lean enterprise value in product development.[31]

■ Each product may be unique, but product development processes are repetitive – thereby presenting a key opportunity for continuous improvement efforts.

■ Defining value is more complex the further away you are from the end user[32] – but this is where the leverage is also greatest (see Figure 8.5).

■ In product development, the focus is on the flow of information (comparable to the flow of materials in manufacturing), a flow that is often branching, non-linear, and iterative.

■ It's important to understand waste with respect to information, especially when information is handed off imperfectly from one function to the next.

■ Studies on wasted effort in processes point to 30–40 percent of charged time being wasted.

■ Worse, typically 60 percent of *tasks* are idle (that is, with no effort being charged to them) at any given time.[33]

■ Costs associated with this sort of intellectual work-in-process (that is, tasks that are waiting for information, answers to questions, or someone to take them up) are not currently accounted for, but this waiting represents a high percentage of program delays.

■ Advanced tools such as CAD and manufacturing design systems may enhance the efficiency of existing processes, but work best when they are embedded in *new* work processes tailored to their strengths.

have found that 'boundary objects' (models, prototypes, tools, and activities that allow sharing of knowledge and information across organizational and disciplinary boundaries) are needed to give team members a common reference.[34]

## Value Streams and Value Stream Maps

A value stream map is not the same as the program value stream represented by the program plan. A value stream map (of which there are many types) makes explicit the way the actions in the program plan are carried out. The program plan is the 'what'. A value stream map shows an aspect of 'how' the effort takes place. Value stream maps are important tools for understanding the current program approach. They are useful as a vehicle for training and improvement. But they are *not* the starting points for creating value.

An LAI study[35] surveyed program enterprises for best techniques in value stream mapping, specifically for product development processes, and found a wide variety. Sometimes, the map was the schedule showing sequences and times. At other times, the map showed process, outputs, and feedback. And in still other instances, the maps followed the physical product as it went through the build process. Our insight is that these are various ways of portraying a value stream, but we have yet to see a technique that captures the *whole* context of a value stream.

The research noted that traditional tools such as Gantt and PERT charts, as well as newer tools, were effective in capturing the value stream at a high level. At more detailed levels, Rother and Shook[36] maps for manufacturing and DSM techniques for product development and other information processing tasks were found to be effective. No clear best practices were found. The success of value stream mapping was found to depend on matching the techniques to the desired outcome and using value stream mapping in the context of overall lean efforts, rather than as an isolated tool.

For lean enterprise value creation, effective program management is needed in *all* the lifecycle processes of a program enterprise. As the resource expenditures increase in the value delivery phase (as indicated in Figure 8.5), program management becomes increasingly critical.

## Value Attributes for Program Management Best Practices

It's a daunting challenge to manage a program enterprise to deliver value to all the stakeholders. Learning and adopting the best practices from successful programs can help.

Two comprehensive LAI studies of a sample of aerospace programs have contributed practical and useful knowledge about best program management practices. The first[37] led to the creation of the *Incentive Strategies for Defense Acquisition* guidebook discussed earlier in this chapter. In the second, a combined study between LAI and the Swedish Lean Aerospace Research Program, more than a hundred practices were observed and codified into six value attributes evident in successful programs.[38]

- *Holistic Perspective* – both in terms of the entire system and its entire lifecycle.

- *Organizational Factors* – including cross-functional teams, organizational structure, and enterprise culture.

- *Requirements and Metrics* – developing, allocating, managing, and tracking requirements.

- *Tools and Methods* – modeling and simulation tools, system engineering and risk-management methods, and other process models for, among others, business practices and information systems.

- *Enterprise Relationships* – open and honest communication, mutual trust, and respect amongst the stakeholders.

- *Leadership and Management* – leading the program enterprise and interfacing with the multi-program and the national enterprise, as well as managing program enterprise people and processes.

Lean practices underlying these attributes, when applied to programs, can enable the creation of lean enterprise value.

## Adapting to Change

As we explained in Chapter 7, our value-creation framework is not a static, one-time executed series of phases. Aerospace programs – with their relatively long development cycles and product lifetimes – are subject to changing environments, changing technology, and changing markets, not to mention a changing workforce. This creates instability and obsolescence, but also opportunities for improvement and emergent value. Program enterprises must be adaptable if they are to survive.

Even a well-designed product and an effective program structure can fail to deliver value if external forces cause continual instability. When an LAI research project[39] surveyed 154 government and 106 contractor program managers to quantify the impact of instabilities on cost and schedule, the results were eye-opening. On average, these programs experienced annual cost growth of roughly 8 percent – year after year – due to instabilities. The most effective mitigating strategy for this problem was continuous, open, and honest communication between customer and supplier.

Without an effective framework for value creation, the cumulative impact of instabilities can be devastating – as the story of the C-17 transport program so vividly demonstrates. Here was a program on the brink of collapse, which then recovered by applying the value-creation framework. It was an amazing turnaround. The program not only survived, but also became a model for others, even going on to win the coveted Baldrige National Quality Award.

It is impossible to predict the unknown. But attention to how external events might affect a program is essential. One way to adapt to change is to recognize that complete definition of the value stream does not have to be a one-time event. While it is common to think of identifying the required capability at the beginning of the value stream, it is often necessary to adapt as time progresses.[40] Sometimes technology changes such that the original needs become obsolete. Or a capability may depend on technology that cannot be brought to maturity. Or you might just get lucky, and find technology or needs shifting your way.

As discussed earlier in the value identification section, large programs tend to have emergent properties. Part of this is external, due to shifting environments, but this can also be internal, especially in an innovative program. As the program progresses, more is learned about the actual design and implementation, and the product tends to evolve as it moves from concept to production. It is very difficult to prepare a plan at program initiation that will never require change during value delivery.[41]

## C-17: An Example of What Can Be Done with Cooperation[42]

The need for a replacement for the US Air Force's large C-5 transport aircraft led to the initiation of the C-17 program in the early 1980s, during the rapid Cold War buildup of the Reagan years. But by the end of the decade, the program was in peril, a victim of continual instability coupled with technical challenges and the changes brought about by the end of the Cold War.

The C-17 became a 'broken' acquisition program, with a troubled design and a unit cost of more than $260 million. After considerable effort, the design was stabilized, the average unit cost was reduced to $178 million for the final 80 aircraft in the planned 120 aircraft buy, and both the government customer and the contractor were delighted with the results. How did this happen?

Originally, a fixed price incentive contract was awarded in July 1982. Changes to the Program Management Directive, the official government statement of program objectives, occurred at least yearly during the 1980s. The relationship between the government and the contractor steadily deteriorated to a tense state.

A change of leadership was made in 1993. Lt. Gen. Ronald Kadish (then a brigadier general) was appointed head of the government SPO at Wright-Patterson AFB, and Don Koslowski became the program director of the C-17 at McDonnell Douglas. Together, they fostered an environment of mutual trust and respect, because they believed that this would contribute to information flow and would enable better decisionmaking on the C-17 program. The close communication and coordination between Kadish and Koslowski was a departure from previous program managers, and set the example for what they expected from their subordinates. They consulted each other when making decisions, listened to C-17 stakeholders who might have concerns or suggestions and, when they made a decision, subsequently supported its consequences.

After this environment was established, the C-17 enterprise engaged in a 'should cost' exercise to codify the vision of price reduction. That helped identify and communicate the core values of the stakeholders in the C-17 program. Government oversight agencies participated in the joint cost exercise, allowing the agencies to gain a better understanding of the methodologies involved in establishing the cost estimate. A model was developed that represented agreement of all involved stakeholders' implementation strategies to reduce the cost of a C-17 aircraft while satisfying those values. Each strategy used to reduce the price of an aircraft was the result of many discussions requiring effective communication to reach agreement among stakeholders.

During the joint cost exercise, the team had been challenged to identify which rules, regulations, or operating procedures, if eliminated, might provide a reduction in price and hence should be built into the contract. The most important additional provision accounted for rate fluctuation. As part of the joint cost model, a Variation in Quantity (VIQ) matrix was developed, which acknowledged one of the contractor's most important risks – the change to the planned purchase quantity for an annual production lot. Including the VIQ served two primary purposes: it allowed the government to respond quickly and accurately to questions from Congress concerning the funding impact associated with adjusting the production rate, and it quantified the contractor's risks associated with rate fluctuations.

Given the understanding of stakeholder values achieved through trust and communication within the C-17 enterprise, a viable value proposition was constructed that satisfied not only the government customer and contractor, but also labor, the financial community, the warfighter, the taxpayer, and the supplier base. Each stakeholder's core values were satisfied. The government received a highly capable aircraft system at a greatly reduced cost, and McDonnell Douglas earned up to an 18 percent profit, which was considered high by established government standards and more like commercial standards.

The lesson of the C-17 and the related guidebook[43] is to evolve from 'getting on contract' to a 'trust-based relationship'.

In a constantly changing world, no value proposition will ever be completely static. Usually, user desires must be continually balanced against the needs of other stakeholders.[44] The F-16 described earlier is an outstanding example of a program that has sustained value creation over a long period by adapting to the evolving needs of its users. The SST (described in Chapter 2) is a good example of a program that could *not* adapt. Here was a program that enjoyed stakeholder support in an era of technological expansion and national prestige building, but lost that support in a less economically buoyant, more politically ambiguous, and more ecologically conscious time. In the 'détente' era of the 1970s, the Cold War need for national prestige products lessened as environmental consciousness increased and consumer needs shifted from air travel as an activity of the 'jet set' towards a mass market.

Some programs have to find new value propositions. When the Cold War ended, the national consensus on the need for a prestigious, massively expensive Space Station that could be put to military use collapsed. The program survived several Congressional votes to kill it – each by one-vote margins – and then found an entirely new set of stakeholders, benefiting foreign cooperation, technology advancement, science, and, most recently, tourism. The Space Station program survived its near-death experience, but generated a different set of challenges – such as dealing with policies on a wider, *international* basis.

It is wholly appropriate to terminate a program – gracefully, if possible – that has truly lost stakeholder support. The termination strategy is vital to the health of the multi-program enterprises within which most program enterprises exist, preventing honest mistakes from mushrooming into costly disasters. Thriving innovation depends on a mindset that recognizes that not all programs *initiated* will necessarily *succeed*.

## Summing Up

The application of our three-phase value-creation framework at the program level builds on the principles of lean enterprise value we laid out in Chapter 1. Value *identification* encompasses identifying the value to be provided to the user, identifying other important stakeholders, and honestly communicating stakeholder needs. If done correctly, value identification leads to a robust value proposition – including product requirements and a program structure – that maximizes the benefits to all relevant stakeholders. The aim is a trust-based relationship backed by appropriate contracts and agreements. Then, with an enterprise focus, value is delivered all along the product value stream. The program must be adaptable, changing if necessary and taking advantage of emergent opportunities.

If a program is designed and managed well from this perspective, its likelihood of success will increase substantially. It must all be done through a process of eliminating waste with the goal of creating value – our definition of 'becoming lean'.

Our fourth lean enterprise value principle in Chapter 1 states: 'Address the interdependencies across enterprise levels to increase lean value.' In this chapter, we have made reference to critically important interactions between the program enterprise and the multi-program and national or international enterprises. These interactions include the competition for resources among programs, infrastructure, a workforce to support program needs, and instabilities imposed upon the program from changing national priorities or budgets – to mention a few. In the next two chapters, we look at these interdependencies from the perspectives of the multi-program and national enterprise, and consider the value-creation framework for these other enterprise levels.

## CHAPTER 9

# Value in Corporate and Government Enterprises

Creating value at the level of a corporation, government agency, or other multi-program enterprise has long been a challenge. But when companies such as Martin Marietta, McDonnell Douglas, Texas Instruments, and myriad less well-known enterprises are merging or restructuring, and once-familiar names have disappeared altogether, a new sense of urgency grows. How can value best be created at this level? The challenge is large, the stakeholders are many, and this is where multiple value streams come together – each with independent and sometimes conflicting goals.

## A Value Stream Approach to Understanding Enterprise Integration Challenges

Practitioners and scholars have long struggled with the conflicts, disconnects, and misunderstandings that often develop among supposedly collaborating organizations. Commonly, they attribute these to direct economic conflicts or to differences in culture. But the root cause probably lies elsewhere. It may have more to do with the way *value* does or does not flow through such an enterprise. More specifically, it may relate to the challenges of coordinating the multiple interacting flows of value in an enterprise. Each value stream has its own set of imperatives that cannot be ignored while constructing mutually agreeable value propositions across multiple value streams.[1] Hence, value streams are the key building blocks for the multi-program enterprise and key levers for organizational transformation.

As this chapter's title suggests, we focus here on bridging across multiple value streams in both corporate and government enterprises. In the aerospace industry these are often intertwined, yet these two types of enterprise can have marked differences. The corporate aerospace enterprise operates for profit and focuses its activity on the creation and support of products and/or services; the government enterprise is driven by political processes and acquires and uses aerospace products over a long and complicated lifecycle.

## Above the Level of a Single Program Value Stream

What differentiates a program enterprise from a multi-program enterprise? Size would seem to be a good indicator – but consider the F-22 air combat fighter program. The USAF is channeling revenue through that program at a clip of nearly \$4 billion per year, which rivals some of the Fortune 500. But F-22 program activity involves that one system, not the full range of stakeholders, capabilities, and values that drive the program's industry and government participants. Clearly, the F-22 is a program enterprise focused on delivering products oriented towards a single platform. In this chapter, we address enterprises containing many program value streams, each directed towards providing one or more distinct customers with value, and receiving compensatory value in exchange. Those are the characteristics of a multi-program enterprise. Figure 9.1 provides a generic illustration of such a multi-program enterprise, with its many programs, value streams, and intersections among both. It could be a large multi-division corporation, a government acquisition organization managing a portfolio comprising multiple systems, or a user operating a mixed fleet of aircraft.

As the figure shows, program value streams are a primary source of revenue, future capability, and other forms of value for corporate enterprise stakeholders. In exchange, the enterprise adds value to the program through the use of its resources and infrastructure, such as skilled people, plant and equipment, tools and processes, and relationships throughout a supplier network. It also provides coordination, resource allocation, and management to ensure that the programs receive the appropriate level of support as they create value.

Just how extensive are these enterprise value streams? The design, manufacture, testing, and deployment of modern aerospace systems take extraordinarily complex coordination and integration. A corps of experienced engineers, scientists, and skilled technicians is critical. The program as a whole involves test facilities remarkable in their sophistication – during development for typical aerospace programs, up to half of the engineering staffing resources required are for test engineering[2] – along with technicians and engineers who understand how to design, plan, execute and analyze sophisticated aerospace testing. And finally, there is the substantial ongoing investment in capital equipment, machinery, and facilities, not to mention the continual investment required to bring new technology into practical use.

Consider this example of the enormous variety of skills and functional organizations we're talking about: the corporate telephone book of one major aerospace company lists 45 000 organizational elements or func-

**FIGURE 9.1** | **Value exchanges in the multi-program enterprise**

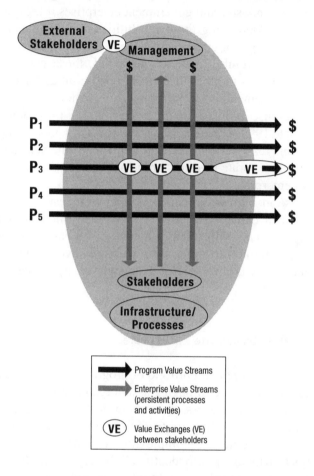

tional specialties. Each of these has its own budget. There are countless administrative activities, with the attendant skills needed for their essential functions. The same engineering or scientific disciplines show up repeatedly in different units, but each unit deals with different stakeholders, standards, regulations, and technologies. That requires that each unit possess *extensive* knowledge and experience.

Government research, acquisition, and test organizations are similar, bringing together large armies of people at a huge cost, whose knowhow is essential to designing, building, testing, and administering aerospace programs. This assemblage of infrastructure, technology, technical talent, skilled labor, facilities, and veteran program managers, administrators, and businesspeople comprise the capabilities and processes that constitute enterprise value streams. Maintaining these capabilities exacts a huge fixed cost on both industry and government enterprises if they are to function in this arena. Delivering these capabilities is a significant, ongoing management challenge for enterprise leaders.

The challenge is doubly difficult. After all, these capital-intensive capabilities compete with other investment opportunities for the attention of investors, who demand good performance. Investors were merciless in discounting defense industry share prices during the booming stock market of the late 1990s (Chapter 10 discusses why in greater depth) – and enterprise leaders respond to financial stakeholders, whether they be financial markets and corporate investors or the public and its representatives in a government enterprise.

An enterprise in a growing market is freer to invest in future growth through enhanced capabilities. But with so many defense enterprises facing unstable markets with ambiguous futures, it's easy to see why some might be more inclined to defer infrastructure investments and avoid creating stranded assets. In the interim, though, enterprise capabilities go idle, and may even atrophy.

## Identifying Value Across the Enterprise

As they assemble the optimal portfolio of programs, multi-program enterprise leaders identify value through classic organizational levers, such as strategy, structure, and process. As we saw in Chapter 8, it is difficult enough to align key stakeholders to deliver value within *one* program value stream – imagine the complexity of bridging across *multiple* programs. It's a challenge just to identify all the key stakeholders, let alone assemble them in one place to build a shared vision or common implementation strategy. At this level, the dilemmas are many and the choices are tough.

Consider what might seem a relatively simple question: what level of general and administrative (G&A) and overhead expenses should one program pay to sustain the overall enterprise? The enterprise certainly doesn't want to extract so much that it undercuts the program – that would be like 'eating the goose that lays the golden eggs'. At the same time, it cannot provide a supportive infrastructure *without* such overhead contributions. Then there's the question of what that infrastructure should be. Tough choices have to be made at a strategic level concerning the portfolio of programs to be supported; if every program is entirely unique, there are fewer opportunities to share resources and capabilities. And a lack of diversification in the mix of programs, while perhaps optimizing the multi-enterprise infrastructure, may not shield the enterprise from instability in markets, funding, and technology.

A key part of identifying value at the multi-program enterprise level involves periodically questioning where existing enterprise capabilities might be maintained by someone else and used only when needed – that is, moving certain functions or capabilities into what we introduced in Chapter 6 as the 'extended enterprise', which often works best through strategic partnerships and similar teaming relationships with other organizations. This allows the enterprise to focus on maintaining its core competency while letting the competitive marketplace define excellence in non-core domains.

Many aerospace firms and government organizations have made an effort to define more clearly their core competency, which has often resulted in their outsourcing long-held capabilities.[3] However, outsourcing requires the development of new coordination skills across supplier networks.

Identifying value at this level depends crucially on enterprise infrastructure – the support systems that cut across multiple programs. Multi-program enterprises need lean enterprise thinking focused on eliminating waste and creating value across multiple programs. This requires a form of cooperative action around areas of common concern for the enterprise with stakeholders who are beyond the boundaries of a specific domain.

In commercial product development, approaches that reuse knowledge or take advantage of common processes are considered best practices. These include modular design and platform strategies. In aerospace in general, and in military aerospace in particular, the search for common solutions is in a constant struggle with the need for product performance and the need to meet mission-specific requirements. Historically, mission performance has won out over commonality – the idea that a single product, service, or capability can be used to address a wide range of requirements. Highly visible failures in commonality, such as the TFX program (later known as the F-111), only reinforced the notion that commonality and meeting performance objectives are at odds.[4]

This lack of commonality is beginning to change with declining defense budgets and specific initiatives aimed at trading performance for cost-effectiveness (to achieve greater value within a realistic budget environment). Nonetheless, military users still tend to put mission performance first, opting for lower-cost alternatives when doing so wouldn't compromise that priority. Budgetary constraints don't mean that the threats are fewer or any less lethal. Additionally, the military budgeting process tends to isolate systems and organizations from one another, making it costlier for individual programs to seek common solutions. In the commercial aircraft domain, there is a spectrum of use of commonality strategies ranging from clear and consistently applied strategies to those demonstrating no common vision.

Let's look at two examples that highlight the critical part enterprise infrastructure plays in value identification.

## One Example: Identifying Value in Enterprise Maintenance Operations

Identifying common solutions in a multi-program enterprise is made more difficult by the fact that the pieces of the puzzle lie scattered across multiple organizational and cultural domains. That's what Leon Silva, a leading avionics engineer at Sikorsky Aircraft, discovered when he tried to find out how operations and maintenance (O&M) data could be fed back into avionics system design and development to reduce system lifecycle costs.

A rule of thumb is that the total lifecycle cost of an aircraft system can be broken into phases (as we showed in Figure 8.5). The *concept* and *engineering* phases consume roughly 10 percent of lifecycle cost (although decisions made then may ultimately define as much as 90 percent of the eventual lifecycle operational cost of the system as a whole). The *production* phase consumes about 30 percent of the lifecycle cost; and the operational phase accounts for the lion's share – roughly 60 percent. So, it makes sense to look for savings in the *operational* phase of the aircraft's lifecycle and to try to apply the lessons learned during the first phase.

When Leon sought out the maintenance records for five fleets of Sikorsky helicopters, totaling more than 350 aircraft, he was surprised to learn that his own company had very little in house. Aircraft *maintainers* fastidiously keep records on all maintenance work and procedures performed over the lifetime of each aircraft, but Sikorsky seldom kept duplicates for its own products. Fortunately, Leon found the maintainers more than happy to share their information.

Maintenance organizations also aggregate their records to identify trends in the operational behavior of a fleet of aircraft. This was quite helpful to Leon, although the maintainers acknowledged that they don't often use their data to suggest engineering changes (except in situations where a crisis demands immediate action). When the maintainers handed over huge bundles of paper documents, Leon noted the absence of a real infrastructure for communicating or analyzing the maintenance information.

Did it make a difference to look at these data in an effort to find evidence that lifecycle costs can be reduced? Does the benefit of reduced maintenance outweigh the cost of redesigning an avionics system? Many of the avionics subsystems Leon examined are relatively inexpensive by aerospace standards (about the cost of a single family home in most parts of the United States). When the aircraft that include these parts cost millions of dollars, and the cost of redesign, test, and certification of a component may cost many times that of the component itself, it might be tempting to live with the added maintenance burden.

Leon grappled with the economic justification for modifying an avionics system. He spoke with several users and maintainers to understand – from what might be termed a total enterprise perspective – how much an hour of maintenance really costs.[5] People could quote the direct labor costs of maintenance, but nobody knew the 'fully loaded' costs of an increased need for maintenance (or, if you will, lower product quality). Nobody knew the financial cost of an aborted mission due to the failure of a part. The operations people worried about the cost of a mission not being fulfilled relative to the rest of the organization's operations, but the maintenance people did not. The people with whom Leon spoke, diligent professionals all, were not avoiding the issues, but were dutifully carrying out their organizations' missions to the best of their ability. The enterprises of which they were part simply weren't designed to work together and solve such a problem.

The estimates Leon heard ranged from a few hundred dollars to a few thousand dollars per maintenance hour. Taking into account all aspects of enterprise operation, even using a conservative cost estimate for troublesome quality, the lifecycle impact of a relatively low-cost part can become substantial. In a number of cases, cost savings warranted a redesign of the avionics architecture.[6]

## Reaching Across Boundaries Within the Enterprise

Leon's story is meant to highlight more than the cost-effectiveness of replacing subsystems. It demonstrates the value of reaching across boundaries within the enterprise to share knowledge. Increased communication and knowledge sharing, while providing modest short-term benefits, can also lay the foundation for expanded business opportunities for industry providers as well as more reliable, lower-cost operations for users. Indeed, this type of product and service integration has become a significant growth area in the aircraft engines business. In the case of aircraft engines, as discussed in Chapter 3, the well-defined market need for service provides a clear incentive to overcome the effects of separate value streams. Without such a market 'pull', overcoming these effects takes more intentional identification of the overall value stream for the total enterprise.

Figure 9.2 illustrates how multiple provider and customer value streams might interact, and shows variations on how individual program agreements between customer and provider affect their respective enterprises and enterprise stakeholders.[7] In some cases, there is no agreement, as in the case of Program 1. Enterprise A stakeholders have identified a

**FIGURE 9.2** | **Multi-program enterprise value exchange relationships**

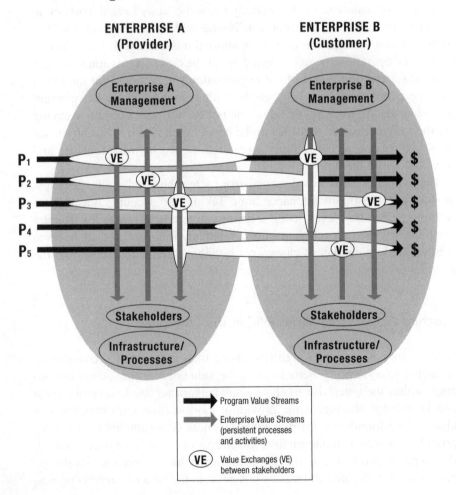

common value proposition, but there is no customer interest in the product or service (as was the case in the failed Northrop F-20 Tigershark venture described in Chapter 3).

Program 4's case is similar. Most stakeholder beneficiaries reside in the customer enterprise, with the key difference that the program is just attractive enough to motivate Enterprise A to stay engaged. This might be the case where a firm takes on a program, perhaps at an economic loss, to maintain a presence in a strategically attractive market segment (the High Speed Civil Transport was one such program). We explored the dynamics of such programs in Chapter 8. In Program 3, all stakeholders in both enterprises are behind the program, having identified a value proposition that satisfies their needs.

Inter-enterprise value propositions can also reach beyond a single program. The enterprise may find it desirable to identify common solutions across several programs that create economies of scale in production or economies of scope in use. Program 5 illustrates a familiar pattern, where a manufacturer seeks to develop economies of scope across multiple programs by using common infrastructure or processes.

Another problem in multi-program enterprises is competition for resources, especially for the most talented engineers – one of the most contentious competitions. Often, the compromise means assigning the most talented engineers to many programs; they are 'spread too thin' – one of the principal causes of poor program performance.[8] The level of design work and schedule slippage experienced in a program increases dramatically as the number of other program assignments for its staff increases. This is a problem not only for program managers but for the engineers themselves (who also are stakeholders). They find themselves pulled in too many directions simultaneously. Often they do not have time to manage their assigned work properly. Worse still, they have little or no time to devote to keeping current with technological developments and avoiding rapid burnout.

Program 2 illustrates the case where a customer organization develops a widespread consensus among multiple stakeholders that a given program has high priority within the customer organization and should be protected wherever possible. This strategy is common in the defense acquisition world (witness remarkably stable DoD budget shares for each of the three services over decades), and in the commercial aerospace world in the case of offsets and worksharing agreements.

## Another Example: Identifying Value in Spacecraft Testing and Operations

A further example illustrates how ubiquitous enterprise-level processes can have a substantial impact on the operations of individual programs. Consider the enterprise infrastructures required to support the spacecraft lifecycle value stream. To ensure that it provides the intended value to its stakeholders, a spacecraft must be designed and assembled; tested to validate its design and performance; launched into its operating location; and then controlled and monitored as it performs its mission. Significant enterprise infrastructure supports the ultimate value delivered to stakeholders.

Let's look first at testing. Spacecraft – high-value assets that are for the most part irretrievable once launched – must undergo significant system-level integration and testing to validate their performance. This consumes a large part of the development schedule and approximately 35 to 50 percent of total nonrecurring program costs.[9] It also requires dedicated test facilities. But while a great deal is learned about the spacecraft during the course of validating the design, relatively little of that learning seems to result in process improvements.

Annalisa Weigel, an LAI student researcher, conducted a study of 20 programs comprising 225 military and commercial spacecraft and examined more than 23 000 discrepancy reports generated during spacecraft system-level testing.[10] Roughly a third of the discrepancies involved anomalies that the testing process should uncover. Another third identified other anomalies in subsystems within the spacecraft that should have been detected during the testing of those subsystems. But most surprising was that the test equipment itself generated one-third of the discrepancies. Anomalies resulting from employees or operators and test equipment combined (shared enterprise infrastructure and resources) accounted for half of all discrepancies. And among those, enterprise infrastructure in commercial programs accounted for a much higher proportion of discrepancies than in military programs.

One conclusion from these data is that commercial enterprises, driven by the bottom line (and lacking government customer investment in dedicated test equipment), are less likely to invest in enterprise infrastructure and capability. Such infrastructure is like a 'tax' on the value stream a given program would generate, and, is thus a significant loss at both the enterprise and the program levels. Weigel's study estimated that individual programs spent roughly 10 percent of their product development time and saw profits reduced by the same percentage *per product* fixing problems found in system-level tests.[11]

A spacecraft, once tested and shipped, is launched into its operating environment. Many leave Earth from the US Eastern Range, known to most people as Cape Canaveral – the world's busiest spaceport, with a year 2001 manifest of thirty, mostly commercial, launches. Cape Canaveral is a national asset owned by the US government and operated by the Air Force. In line with US government policy, so-called 'excess capacity' (that is, beyond what's needed for US military and NASA missions) is provided to US commercial launchers at cost. Virtually all commercial launches using US launchers pass though this common infrastructure.

The operational capability of this national asset is critical as US firms work to recover their share of the commercial launch market lost after the Challenger disaster. Isn't it ironic, then, that there is such limited enterprise-level knowledge of how the capacity and dynamics of this facility would support achieving that goal?

David Steare, another LAI student researcher, developed a system dynamics model of the entire Cape Canaveral facility and infrastructure to understand better its ultimate launch capacity and potential constraints on realizing that capacity.[12] He found the capacity of the range to be between 49 and 54 launches per year. As with any system, though, queuing delays build up as capacity utilization increases towards its theoretical limit – the model predicts that wait time and launch delays will increase nearly four-fold. Most delays come from range crew rest requirements; other causes include big missions that monopolize the range assets, and 'range lock-down' (that is, the time between when the configuration of the range for a specific mission is frozen and when the mission is launched). Each factor represents a bottleneck in the flow of value that is governed by a common enterprise asset.

Here the asset owner – the US government – has no direct incentive to increase the enterprise capability because its *own* needs are being satisfied. Meanwhile, commercial launchers – which *do* have an incentive to drive down their launch costs by streamlining launch operations – are limited by the nature of the infrastructure upon which they must rely. This dilemma illustrates how the values and value streams of two major sets of stake-holders in the US national launch system are simultaneously interdependent and at odds.

Once the spacecraft arrives in space and begins on-orbit operations, it must constantly be monitored for anomalous behavior to ensure that it doesn't enter a situation that will result in the spacecraft being lost. A study by LAI student researcher Dave Ferris of on-orbit anomalies found that the vast majority (87 percent) were attributable to the operating infra-structure on the ground, rather than that of the spacecraft itself.[13]

We see two key points when we look more closely at the spacecraft value stream. First, spacecraft hardware is quite good. It is well designed and performs well once on orbit. Perhaps because of the visibility of hardware vis-à-vis infrastructure, the high cost of the spacecraft, and the low probability of being able to recover from a serious design or assembly flaw, spacecraft developers do a good job of producing space-craft. Second, a great deal of the activity supporting the realization of value with this high-performing hardware is shared enterprise infra-structure (and infrastructure that many would assume belongs to someone else's enterprise). Indeed, a failure during any stage of the spacecraft life-cycle can quickly halt *all* flow of value to stakeholders. A narrow focus on one's own value stream, while failing to understand how others' value streams may be interdependent with one's own, can profoundly affect all of the value streams.

We saw in earlier chapters how enterprises can search across traditional organizational, functional, budgetary, or cultural boundaries to identify stakeholders who share a common problem and who derive value from a common solution. We've also discussed the significant benefits that can be realized from the standardization of business processes across an enterprise – that is, by taking an enterprise perspective. Earlier examples reinforce the important role that enterprise infrastructures themselves can play in identifying stakeholders and their values, and in making possible the analysis necessary to understanding the benefits of enterprise-level action.

## Creating Enterprise Value Propositions

Once the potential value of an integrated or common perspective has been identified, along with the attendant stakeholders, an enterprise value propo-sition can be created. This defines the common unifying vision for all stakeholders and creates the conditions under which they all hope to gain value. It bridges individual program value streams to define the exchange between programs and the enterprise: what each expects from the other, and how each must adapt to accommodate the other's needs.

Developing the enterprise value proposition requires the skills and infrastructure needed to identify stakeholders, an analytical base to under-stand the values relative to one another, and the ability to negotiate and trade off multiple stakeholders' demands. Time, staffing, and resource availability underlie these capabilities, allowing stakeholders to complete the analyses and negotiations as they refine the value proposition. At the enterprise level, this capability is one that will be exercised on a regular basis as deals are constantly constructed and renewed. Consequently, *these are core enterprise capabilities.*

While enterprise leaders may try to structure the value propositions between enterprise and program value streams, they cannot control their likelihood of success. Ideally, enterprise value propositions seek to balance value between the enterprise and its stakeholders so that these stakeholders receive enough value to warrant their continued participation in the business of the enterprise. If the exchanges become out of balance and adjustments fail, one party may abandon the value proposition. Employees, for instance, may move on to other firms that have more attractive program prospects – as happened with aerospace engineering workers in Southern California during the 1980s Reagan defense buildup, and with computer and software workers in Silicon Valley in the late 1990s.

Applying lean principles and practices can have a substantial impact on the ability to create value propositions. For example, substantially reducing the cycle time for program development makes it possible to handle more programs, which creates new opportunities for a wide range of stakeholders.

There are three primary approaches to structuring an enterprise value proposition: hierarchical (or directive), architectural, and collaborative. Which one is most appropriate depends on the circumstances and the affiliation of the stakeholders. While there are many conceivable hybrids involving any or all three approaches, they are analytically distinct – as our detailed discussion below illustrates.

## Hierarchical or Directive Approach

When one authority controls all stakeholders, a hierarchical approach can be effective in driving creation of the value proposition. Hierarchies have defined reporting relationships, command and control structures, and 'rules of engagement'.[14]

In an age when innovation and agile adaptation to deliver value to customers are considered best practice, it might seem that imposing a hierarchical structure on an enterprise is a cure worse than any original illness. In general, though, and for most industries, *not* imposing some type of regime of centralized coordination can lead to at least two problems: an integrated enterprise perspective may be lost (illustrated by our earlier examples), and instability may arise (especially in multi-program systems). Instability occurs when a system's design causes it to respond unpredictably and undesirably to stimuli that are internal or external to the system. For instance, an unstable airplane would tend to depart from controlled flight (sometimes quite spectacularly) when hit by a gust of wind (external) or from an errant control input by the pilot (internal).

Instability might also result from a dramatic change in the size of a primary product market, from customer financial difficulties, or from troubles within the enterprise itself (such as a program running into a technical roadblock). In either case, it is the design or structure of the enterprise that prevents it from responding in a predictable or controlled fashion to the unexpected input. Just as the solution for an unstable aircraft is to use a flight control system that translates what the pilot wants the aircraft to do, so too does an unstable enterprise require a control system.

### Instability – An Enterprise Challenge

Most people have experienced feedback in a public address system. The microphone picks up, amplifies, and broadcasts sound through loud-speakers in a self-reinforcing feedback loop – an unintended, deafening screech. A good system design seeks 'error-proofing' so that the system continues to operate – even with degraded performance – when the unintended happens.

A multi-program enterprise presents an interesting system design problem, with built-in assumptions about planning, resource allocation, and program execution.[15] Often, the enterprise may operate beyond the bounds of those assumptions – which catches individual programs in the equivalent of an enterprise feedback loop. This instability wreaks havoc on program performance that can ripple through the multi-program enterprise.

To understand better the mechanisms of instability, a system dynamics model was developed at MIT to simulate a multi-program enterprise.[16] The results are consistent with program manager experience. They illustrate how the design of the enterprise structure for managing its program and capabilities portfolios can be critical, serving either to facilitate or to inhibit the contagious passing of one program's problems to other programs.[17]

Just how bad can this blight of instability be as it crosses the enterprise? One study of defense acquisition in the mid-1990s[18] found that programs, on average, experienced roughly 8 percent annual cost growth and around 24 percent schedule slip. In real terms, that means that a five-year development program would exceed its initially planned cost by some 47 percent, and take a year longer to execute. And instability's problems don't stop with immediate program performance. In the same study, defense contractors indicated that instability had caused the profitability of their programs to decline. They also indicated that the more unstable the program, the greater the proportion of suppliers of critical parts that might exit from the defense supplier base.

The workforce and skills base also suffers from instability.[19] Facilities facing higher levels of market, technology, organizational, or budget instability reported a significantly higher loss of people with critical skills than did facilities reporting lower levels of instability. Similarly, they reported a comparatively more significant decline in worker satisfaction.

What is to be done? Based on the insights gained from the studies in this area, the following practices may be helpful in alleviating instability:

- Use human resource practices such as cross-training, skills development, and increased worker participation to increase adaptability to unforeseen events.

- Exercise caution in allocating 'emergency' resources, such as overtime, to programs in a portfolio. Curing one program's ills may cause disproportionate damage in the rest of the portfolio.

- Keep priorities for program claims to resources relatively stable. Adjust the priorities only after making an impact assessment of the entire portfolio.

- Schedule programs with a buffer between the end of one and the beginning of the next to ensure that undiscovered quality problems and rework don't recall staff who have already been assigned elsewhere. This may be a good time to catch up on training and to capture lessons learned from the program for dissemination to other programs.

- When estimating a program completion date, use realistic assumptions about when people and other resources will arrive and begin making significant contributions.

■ Regularly update resource allocations across the portfolio as new information is obtained about all programs. This helps raise awareness about potential resource binds and also aids future planning.

■ Frequently review the portfolio for program cancellation opportunities early in the product lifecycle. Remove any programs that have little chance either of starting on time or of being completed before marketplace opportunities have evaporated.

One source of instability in programs is the existence of more programs at any one time than the multi-program enterprise can handle. Programs, which begin at a low scale of effort and expenditure, are destined to grow – and so the number of early-stage programs an enterprise can afford is always much larger than the number of later-stage, full-development programs. Beginning at the so-called 'fuzzy' front end of product development, there must be a process to reduce the number of programs as they progress and increase in size, and to ensure that the best concepts are developed.

Robb Wirthlin, a USAF officer and LAI student researcher who was part of a Headquarters Air Force team to study the service's requirements process, conducted an in-depth study of eight commercial and eight military organizations and identified best- and worst-case approaches to managing front-end processes. In general, the best-case approaches involved streamlined (or 'one-stop') decisionmaking authority throughout the process, with decisionmakers having the tools to make a regular assessment of the state of the enterprise portfolio relative to resource commitments and enterprise strategy. The best-case organizations also populated the processes with experienced people and provided resources to develop and maintain the tools and skills needed to conduct the necessary tradeoff analyses. The worst cases observed involved multiple handoffs between decisionmakers, had limited accountability for program or portfolio performance within any one decisionmaking domain, and had no way of ultimately tracking portfolio status. There was also limited material support, infrastructure, or capability for doing the needed analyses. Discontinuity of staffing assignments meant a lack of individual experience or long-term enterprise learning.[21]

## Why Is a Front-End Process So Important?

An ideal enterprise front-end process would accomplish several things. First, it would ensure adequate resources to stimulate the generation of ideas. For instance, some organizations provide a certain amount of time each week that scientists and engineers can devote to developing new product concepts or to maintaining technology incubators that supply what's needed for new product concepts to develop beyond the idea stage. Next, it would provide supporting infrastructure and processes that connect concept champions with other enterprise stakeholders who can bring their value perspectives to bear in shaping and developing the concepts. A senior decisionmaking body – representing the spectrum of key enterprise stakeholders and their values, and with the authority to authorize full enterprise commitment to a program – could screen out concepts that show the least promise, and authorize further development of the best concepts. Using more sophisticated analytic capabilities, the enterprise could map out the tradeoff space of a concept as it progresses through the process and develop the data necessary to construct a business case. With all tradeoffs complete, the architecture defined, and the business case developed, the senior stakeholder body of the enterprise would decide whether to commit to full engineering development.

*Stage gate* processes, one common approach for managing the front end of product development, work to limit the number of active programs ongoing in an enterprise to roughly as much as its infrastructure and processes can handle. They do this by means of well-defined decision points through which each program must pass in order to gain funding and resources to proceed to the next stage of its lifecycle. Because a program requires greater amounts of resources as it progresses, programs must be culled at each successive step in the process. Maps of stage gate processes resemble a funnel turned on its side: many programs enter the process, but few – ideally, the best concepts – emerge as final products.[20]

Many enterprise processes lend themselves to directive management. The most familiar examples to students of the lean paradigm come from manufacturing, and include concepts such as just-in-time inventory management and single-piece flow (these production examples also illustrate how the control algorithms for directive approaches in a stable environment can be relatively simple). There are clear advantages to using directive approaches for enterprise integration, and clear costs when they are not used. Directive approaches are neither easily executed nor mastered, however. When successful, though, they can be quite effective at aligning enterprise stakeholders with a value proposition that addresses all of their needs.

## Architectural Approach

In some cases, strong centralized control may not be desirable or possible, even if a single overarching authority exists for all enterprise stakeholders. This is a core challenge for multinational corporations, for instance, because of the size or scope of the enterprise, or both, or because the transaction costs of coordination may outweigh the benefits of integration and reuse. There are significant coordination challenges in running a monolithic organization that is spread across the globe, coupled with local requirements that often demand customization or adherence to local norms, preferences, or statutes. Success requires *adaptability*.

One way to provide for adaptability while leveraging enterprise capabilities is to define a template or architecture that provides a framework for collective action while also allowing local customization. This might involve prescribed communication standards and tools or even standardized enterprise processes, possibly through common reporting metrics or templates. Another approach is to establish product architectures that define work content. This section explores this latter example in detail.

Platform and modular designs are a familiar example of the use of product architecture to rationalize work and to leverage enterprise knowledge and processes across multiple customer demands.[22] Automobile manufacturers, for instance, reduce the cost and cycle time of new products in this way; many vehicles from a single manufacturer may share major components, such as a certain type of engine, as well as common subsystems or members of a product family, such as radios or fuel pumps. For instance, Ford's Lincoln LS Sedan, Thunderbird, and Jaguar S-Type Sedan are all derived from the same chassis (platform) but have different subsystems and bodies.

The architectural approach advantage is that it doesn't overly constrain enterprise capability to the point of stifling innovation and adaptability, thus fostering a stale product line and the 'not invented here' syndrome. In fact, a platform or modular approach can actually *enable* user-based innovation. Studies consistently show that sophisticated users provided with adaptable products make modifications that not only enhance functionality, but also enable leading-edge trends in the evolution of the product technology.[23]

The open-source software domain – perhaps best known for the Linux operating system – offers many compelling examples. Linus Torvalds developed the Linux kernel. Its open-source architecture allows programmer users the world over to enhance its functionality with additional software code.

The applicability of an architectural approach to enterprise coordination and value creation does have its limits. For instance, platform or modular strategies are problematic for products that operate where performance is constrained by the laws of physics.[24] Many aerospace products fit this category, and many do not. But even if a product's performance requirements demand use of an integrated design, enterprise processes can be rationalized using an architectural approach.

They define metrics and assess performance based on meeting strategic objectives. Senior management consistently emphasizes and reinforces the strategy to all enterprise stakeholders. And organization structure and resources are organized around product families to ensure adherence to the strategy. The structure of Toyota's development center is a prime example.[25] Supplier network stakeholders, for example, are committed to the product line strategy through strategic risk-sharing partnerships.[26]

Organizations that have mastered product line or platform engineering offer a number of insights into how this is accomplished. The aerospace industry provides several examples of where the success of some organizations relies on the extent to which they can reuse designs and design and test processes. The aircraft engine sector, for instance, relies heavily on product family design, with well-defined product family strategies that are communicated and uniformly enforced throughout the enterprise.

In sum, successful product family engineering doesn't happen by accident. The enterprise structure and processes largely define the outcome of the activities. But more important, to achieve these outcomes consistently and to do so well requires considerable effort. This requires enterprise-level commitment, organization, and very deliberate action.[27]

## Collaborative Approach

When no single overarching authority controls the behavior of all relevant enterprise stakeholders, collaborative approaches are needed, such as the

## Architecting Value Propositions
## Through Union Agreements

The collective bargaining process can be an important vehicle for architecting value propositions that involve the workforce in enterprise-level transformation initiatives. The most recent national agreement between the International Association of Machinists and Aerospace Workers (IAM) and Boeing carries forward language from a 1989 agreement and offers a good example of an architectural model aimed at delivering value to a particular stakeholder – the unionized workforce.

The two parties reached a contractual agreement in 1989 to support various joint training activities that would provide 'highly skilled workers capable of meeting individual and company goals'.[28] In 1992, Boeing established a national 'Quality Through Training Program' at a rate of 14 cents for every hour worked, with $14 million as a guaranteed minimum level of funding (in 1999, this formula generated $25 million). Between 1996 and 2000, the initiative provided educational assistance to more than 23 000 individuals, with vouchers covering the costs of approximately 35 500 courses. Additional programming and support has been provided through a 'Health and Safety Institute', a 'Layoff and Redeployment Assistance' initiative, a variety of supported classroom training courses, support for implementation of 'High Performance Work Organization' initiatives, and additional personal enrichment training.

Approximately half of the IAM's Boeing employees have benefited from the initiative, though it has only overlapped in a limited way with the lean transformation initiatives also taking place in the corporation – which illustrates a larger multi-program enterprise challenge. In delivering value to multiple stakeholders, initiatives aimed at serving customers or shareholders need to be aligned with those that serve the workforce.

development of standards. These standards, which may be proprietary or open, define key interfaces between major sub-elements of a system. Without defined standards, modular design would be impossible. The successful development of standards accounts for the success of the PC industry and the very existence of a firm such as Dell Computer Corp.

Our discussion focuses on open standards, which are important in this context because, for many performance-leveraging technologies in aerospace systems, business for the suppliers of these technologies in the actual aerospace market may represent only a small part of the total. In such cases, directive or hierarchical control regimes clearly won't work – the aerospace enterprise doesn't control the key stakeholders. Here, collaboration with other stakeholders in the development of standards can ensure that aerospace-specific requirements are met.

With the story of common large area displays (CLADs), Matthew Nuffort – a USAF officer and LAI student researcher – showed how using standards allowed a large group of stakeholders who shared a common problem to enjoy the benefits of a common solution.[29] Engineers at the Warner Robins Air Logistics Center noticed that displays on USAF E-3 airborne warning and control (AWACs) planes had a relatively high failure rate, and that maintaining the displays was increasingly difficult and costly. The original equipment was relatively advanced in the 1980s when it was procured, but supporting the dated technology was difficult because the military represented a limited market compared with the commercial sector and spare parts were difficult to come by.[30] The annual maintenance cost was roughly $4–$6 million for 500 displays, which amounted to about $8000 annual maintenance costs per display to support what was functionally a 19- or 21-inch computer monitor.

In the early 1990s, Bob Zwitch, an avionics engineer at Warner Robins, began looking for commercially available solutions to replace the aging and increasingly unreliable technology. He also began to wonder how many other users might be facing the same problem. Several other aircraft in the USAF fleet used a large number of functionally similar displays. Bob turned up some 15 000 such displays among users in all branches of the US military. Each user 'owned' only dozens or perhaps hundreds of the displays, but in aggregate the installed base was significant. Each, presumably, faced the same challenge with an aging product.

Great benefits came from shifting to commercial displays: about 60 percent less weight; 90 percent lower maintenance costs; and an eleven-fold rise in mean time between failures (MTBF). Power consumption dropped 30 percent, and display resolution and performance improved substantially. As many as eight new displays could be purchased for the same cost of replacing the legacy display. More important, commercially available replacements are available when needed. The savings to the AWACs program and the logistics community associated with that program alone justified the change; imagine the potential savings across the entire military enterprise. Across the DoD, up to $100 million per year in maintenance costs could potentially be avoided.

Key to Bob's success was the use of a neutral agent (one with no vested interest in the production and procurement outcome) to sort through the competing needs and define the best possible standard. Having one stakeholder with vested interests exerting undue influence over the process, to the detriment of other stakeholders' interests, could break the overall value proposition.[31]

In the case of CLADs, choosing an aerospace-unique solution was out of the question, because none existed. Many military aerospace systems currently face the same challenge. It will take more people like Bob Zwitch to survey the commercially available technologies, to compare them with the needs of a spectrum of military users, and to define a standard that meets the needs of all stakeholders.

The benefits of a standard should be self-evident – it reduces cost, effort, and so on – so that users have natural incentives to embrace it. Often, the more users that embrace a standard, the greater their individual benefit.[32] Because fights can erupt over competing standards, having an overarching authority that can convey legitimacy to the standard selected goes a long way. But that doesn't mean that aerospace enterprises should play passive roles in defining the standards that affect their products. On the contrary, by participating in and promoting the development of standards in key enabling technology areas, aerospace enterprises can ensure that they leverage technological advances occurring in other industries, while also maintaining a reliable source of components, parts, and subsystems.

## New Value Propositions Across the Supply Chain – Textron's LTA Initiative

Growing evidence from research over the past decade points to the critical importance of supplier integration into the extended enterprise as a basic source of competitive advantage.[33] Many firms have done just that; one such example is Textron's development of value propositions involving suppliers.

The Textron Corporation first launched its Long-Term Agreement (LTA) initiative in its Systems and Components Division, though it is now being implemented corporatewide. The initiative grew out of the corporation's '10X' lean initiative, developed to employ lean principles in an effort to realize gains by a factor of ten or more.

LTA was ied by the divisional procurement function, and the company used LAI's Lean Enterprise Model (see Chapter 6) to help identify potential improvement opportunities. The first step involved mapping the procurement process flow – how work was awarded to suppliers. The map revealed a significant amount of 'low-hanging fruit' – so, for example, Textron focused on things such as the excessive time it took to get requisitions out, developing an electronic system that puts orders directly into the buyer's queue. As a side benefit, the process enhancements led to a 50 percent reduction in the size of the procurement manual.

The second step involved implementing the 'Best Value Concept', which involves looking beyond initial price to consider the total cost of acquisition and ownership. The 'best value' selection method breaks down into four weighted components: quality (40 percent), price (30 percent), delivery (15 percent), and responsiveness (15 percent).

To implement this approach, Textron created 'Supplier Evaluation Teams' of buyers, quality engineers, and product engineers (supported by two full-time financial analysts). These teams began working daily with suppliers to look at the procurement process, to identify improvement opportunities, and to evaluate ways that both Textron and its suppliers could alter their processes to achieve better results.

To help open communication channels, Textron brought in customer representatives to meet with suppliers, and expanded annual supplier conferences to include more product lines. This helped convey customer requirements, and gave suppliers an opportunity to present improvement ideas to users downstream in the supplier chain. Today, these events are growing to include second- and third-tier suppliers. This communication also extends to design functions, where Textron engineers now have much more interaction with suppliers.

The third phase has been to implement LTAs linked to those suppliers who demonstrate success in achieving savings through the best value selection and supplier management process. Suppliers are rated according to the criteria above, as well as on their capabilities for continuous improvement, their continuous reductions in quality variability through the use of statistical process control tools, the degree to which they are 'team players' and engage in open communication, and the competitive advantage they afford Textron Systems. This supplier certification process has three levels – 'approved', 'certified', and 'preferred' – and LTAs are used only with the last two levels.

At a 1998 LAI workshop, Textron reported that the first year of implementation had produced 25 LTAs covering 118 parts. Most were five-year agreements; some were three years. Then, LTAs accounted for 73 percent (in dollars) of the group's procurement.

Gainsharing from continuous improvement is usually split down the middle: 50 percent of the savings go to the supplier, and 50 percent go to the end customer (who often prefers to take the savings in kind by placing additional orders).

Reflecting on the experience with the multi-year agreements, a leader from Textron's procurement function commented: 'The supplier base was always in trouble in the past. If you talked to an engineer about a problem, it was always [the supplier's] fault. That attitude has really changed.'

## Common Themes Among the Three Approaches

Whether involving directive control mechanisms or collaboration with many others, enterprise-level action can provide attractive benefits. Some common elements emerge. First, stakeholders often share the same challenges, and there is potential benefit in working together. At the same time, though, stakeholders come to the enterprise with vested interests, and care deeply about how collective enterprise actions affect their own programs or functions. Consequently, it is important to make the enterprise coordination process transparent to all stakeholders.

Enterprise leaders can bring the various stakeholders together by presenting a common, unifying vision of action. Whether it be a 'lean manifesto' or a challenge to land a human being on Mars, stakeholders need something that provides meaning and offers value to them while providing a reference that helps them determine and implement their own contributions towards that vision. The enterprise must be willing to support the development of the infrastructure and capabilities needed for the analysis, planning, and coordination of multiple activities and multiple stakeholders.

In some cases, supporting enterprise infrastructure development requires a leap of faith because it doesn't directly correspond to a program value stream or a primary enterprise revenue stream. Situations and stakeholders change over time, and so maintaining the ability to create the enterprise value proposition is a constant requirement. It takes continuous effort to keep the value proposition 'sold' to stakeholders.

Finally, enterprise participants have to deliver value *back to the enterprise*. They must be accountable, in some fashion, for enterprise performance. In the end, though, it often comes down to a few visionary change agents within the enterprise (at all levels) moving beyond narrow product or program performance thinking, beyond reducing costs in the system, to embracing value thinking to link together enterprise stakeholders through a viable value proposition.

## Delivering Enterprise Value

Readers associated with enterprises of one form or another may find much of what we've discussed thus far in this chapter familiar. Many books and articles on enterprise management address topics ranging from strategy to negotiation to R&D management to delighting the customer.

Perhaps what differentiates the aerospace enterprise case from most others is the nature of the products, the operating organizations, and the environments. Aerospace systems are complex, long-lived, interdependent systems, often designed to function within a system of systems requiring coordination across multiple stakeholder entities. Few consumer products will ever have the projected nearly hundred-year lifespan of a B-52 bomber (admittedly unique even among aerospace products), or will operate in as many diverse roles, missions, and functions, or will have been modified and upgraded as many times.

Consider that the foundations of modern digital computing were just being formalized in information theory at the time the B-52 first took flight. It is impossible to predict what the nature of computing will be two to three decades hence, when the plane takes its last flight to a desert bone-yard. Given nearly four orders of magnitude increase in the number of logic devices contained on one microchip over the last two decades, computer chips by then may contain as many circuits as the human brain.

The B-52 is also just one element in a diverse array of other aerospace systems that are needed in order to fulfill its own mission. A few of those systems are as old as the B-52 itself, but most are more modern. And without them, the B-52's probability of mission success would diminish dramatically. The venerable bomber is an apt metaphor for the diversity and complexity of value delivery in uses associated with aerospace products.

Creating enterprise value in such a complex context demands expanded definitions of enterprise. Take United Airlines, which operates a fleet comprising around twenty-five different models of commercial aircraft. Its customers, the flying public, expect to be transported to their destinations on schedule with a minimum of problems and at a competitive price. It is no small feat to coordinate more than 2300 flights each day with compli-cating factors such as connecting flights, weather, airport hub congestion, alliance partner operations, mechanical problems, crew shortages, and so on. Given all this, what are the boundaries of the enterprise involved in delivering value to the traveling customer?

Clearly, the airline plays a central role. The supporting infrastructure, including airports and air traffic control, is critical – as travelers are increasingly discovering. The upstream aircraft manufacturer plays an essential role in the airline's enterprise value streams and support capab-ilities. The product architecture and reliability, for instance, determine how much maintenance and repair infrastructure is needed. If every aircraft platform is a unique design, it may provide higher performance, but at the cost of a massive training infrastructure to train all the employees who must work with the diverse product array in the fleet. The same is true for spares inventory and location and, indirectly, for the short-term adapt-ability of the airline to changes in market demands on specific routes by reassigning aircraft and aircrews. Consequently, the upstream product architecture (and by extension, the upstream enterprise's organizational architecture) can have a significant impact on the downstream enterprise and the creation of value in use of the product. One particular element that stands out is the extent to which the upstream product architecture either enables or inhibits the standardization or streamlining of the downstream enterprise processes and/or infrastructure.

This point about defining the enterprise is made perhaps more strongly in a military organization such as the Air Force Special Operations Command

(AFSOC), which must be ready to deploy at any time to any potential trouble spot in the world and sustain operations there, perhaps under relatively primitive conditions (compared with most aerospace operations). AFSOC faces all the same issues as United Airlines relating to standardization of enterprise functions and infrastructure such as staffing, maintenance, support, spares, and so on. Because of the uniqueness of its mission and the specialized capabilities required, it must maintain its own dedicated enterprise processes and support infrastructures so that they can be deployed worldwide. Consequently, the enterprise mobility and logistics 'footprint' is critical, since everything needed for its operations has to be airlifted to a given site. The greater the diversity of the systems in the fleet that have to be supported, the more people who need to be trained to operate and support them, the more materiel that must be included in a deployment package, and so forth.[34] Redundancy or duplication in enterprise functions literally translates into weight, the age-old nemesis of the aerospace engineer (in this case, weight carried in the cargo hold of a transport).

The US Marines, while a larger force and tied to somewhat more conventional missions than AFSOC, are in many ways quite similar. The Marines must often deploy a complete operational infrastructure to harsh or forbidding locations, without the luxury of an extensive logistics lifeline. This constraint demands the use of enterprise structures and elements that support lean and efficient operations – and these in turn translate into an enterprise philosophy that places a high value on a streamlined support infrastructure. With a relatively fixed transportation budget, a lean operation is absolutely necessary to prevent the warfighting 'teeth' from being pulled by the demands of the logistics 'tail'.

Our earlier example of United Airlines speaks to the benefit of commonality, but it's all about different airplanes with passenger seats. What about commonality that's more counterintuitive – such as between helicopters that serve completely different functions? That challenge emerged with two aging pillars of the US Marines' airborne capability, the UH-1N 'Huey' utility and the AH-1W 'Cobra' attack helicopters.

The Cobra was derived from the Huey, and the two platforms originally shared about 75 percent common systems. But over the years, unique requirements drove upgrades and modifications to the airframes that reduced commonality to less than 40 percent. This, in turn, increased the logistics and mobility 'footprint' of operating these two platforms as they each began to require more unique maintenance and support capabilities, which also increased manpower and training requirements. Operational military capability – a direct measure of value to the warfighter and taxpayer – was significantly degraded because of these maintenance and support limitations.[35]

There were other challenges. With upgrades and new mission requirements over the years, the Huey had gained weight and was operating largely at or beyond its performance margins. The Cobra crew workload was becoming excessive with all the new weapons capabilities that had been added over the years. Clearly, it was time to modernize the fleet, but new aircraft would be prohibitively expensive.

The Marines chose to remanufacture both airframes with a focus on commonality in order to reduce logistics and manpower demands.[36] Taking an enterprise perspective, the Marines reasoned that commonality between the Huey and Cobra would make more sense because both aircraft deploy together in the same detachment on L-class amphibious assault ships. A major incentive for the Marines to pursue commonality was lifecycle cost, with projected savings of nearly $1.5 billion over the twenty-year anticipated lifecycle of the two platforms – compared with buying a mixed fleet of upgraded Cobras or AH-64 Apaches and new H-60s.[37]

Some elements of the two aircraft such as the dynamic systems, including engines, drive train, and transmission, are obvious candidates for commonality. But others seem not to make as much sense. Why would anyone put the same cockpit and flight control software in both an attack aircraft and a troop transport? The answer is simple – the value streams of the two platforms are intertwined by their common operation. From the perspective of the Marine Expeditionary Unit (MEU) enterprise, the value created by making them common outweighs the small additional costs imposed by commonality. For instance, the common cockpit reduces aircrew training costs and increases operating flexibility by allowing pilots to transition between aircraft types when circumstances allow. (Commercial airlines confront this challenge regularly and, in many cases, have made the same decision in their fleets.) The weapons fire control function in the common flight control software doesn't benefit the troop carrier, but it isn't used and costs nothing to keep in place – and in addition, there is now only one software installation in the fleet that maintainers need to manage. (Boeing used the same strategy on its 777 flight control software, although few of the aircraft were identically configured.)

The upgraded Hueys and Cobras will share common starting procedures and emergency procedures that will aid in cross-crew training and proficiency. The same mechanic will be qualified to work on both aircraft, with minimal requirements for additional training. Where components cannot be common between the two aircraft, the manufacturer is taking advantage of common manufacturing processes. For example, the cowlings will be manufactured using the same process on the same tool.

By focusing on the lifecycle operations of their helicopter fleet and their MEU deployment, the Marines were able to understand the enterprise implications of a seemingly straightforward procurement decision. In this process, the key enterprise stakeholders were given a voice and the full implications of their contribution to enterprise value were articulated.

A common thread in these examples is that to meet its enterprise objectives each enterprise must sustain operations of complex organizational and technical systems around the globe. Each of these enterprises, in some measure, encompasses the four missions of aerospace we introduced in Chapter 1. Their operations are diverse, complex, and demanding; must be sustainable over a variety of operating conditions; and must be predictable and reliable.

The airline traveler demands on-time arrivals and departures. The warfighter is perhaps even more demanding, given the coordination involved with military operations – the cavalry won't save the day if it rides over the hill five minutes too late. To achieve that level of operating capability under such demanding conditions, none of these enterprises can afford to waste resources in duplicated or ill-defined enterprise processes or infrastructure. These enterprises must also actively address how their own enterprise structures map onto other enterprises, and how other enterprises affect their ability to organize and streamline their own enterprise processes.

Enterprises respond to and address these demands by focusing continuously on streamlining and standardizing the enterprise processes. Commonality across processes and systems is key. Commonality can be thought of in a limited sense as the use of the same parts and equipment. However, the leading enterprises take the commonality vision further, making commonality a part of the enterprise culture, a way of thinking. They continually seek to identify similar challenges across multiple stakeholders that can be addressed by common enterprise solutions, whether these involve hardware, processes, or organization. The operational and functional behavior of the system serves as a guide in identifying both the relevant stakeholders and the boundaries of the search. There are lessons here for any complex industry.

Implementing the commonality vision involves reusing people's knowledge and organization processes. It leverages experience with existing products into new or derivative products to reduce cycle time and cost. It frees attention from the mundane aspects of operations to a focus on the exceptions. Achieving such a state is no trivial challenge. Many aerospace enterprises, especially those that are part of the military–industrial complex, are fragmented by organizational and functional boundaries and by budgeting processes that inhibit such enterprise coherence and integration.

## Summing Up

In addressing the enterprise integration we've been discussing, there are significant challenges to overcome. Even for an enterprise that is able to identify the appropriate stakeholders and boundaries of action, and that streamlines and standardizes processes and infrastructure where possible, significant challenges remain. These include whether there is a large enough market to sustain the capabilities and infrastructure that have been created. Enterprises in every industry need to ask: 'Are we in the right business in the first place, and does it make sense to optimize this specific enterprise?'

Even the most optimally structured enterprise can go out of business if there is an inadequate market for it to offer investors attractive returns on their invested capital. Given the extensive enterprise capabilities required to produce complex aerospace systems, there is a minimum market size below which there is no defensible case for remaining in business. No amount of enterprise efficiency can address that problem. Our next chapter looks at current trends in technology, demographics, and business – and what they mean for the future of the aerospace industry.

# CHAPTER 10

# Value at National and International Levels

Creating lean enterprise value at national and international levels represents a significant extension in the use of all three words: lean, enterprise, and value. Taking a lean enterprise approach to value creation is essential in addressing the challenges that are already emerging at the dawn of the 21st century – whether they involve addressing the limitations of the air traffic management system, pioneering commercial uses of space, or finding new ways to confront international terrorism. Our goal here is to foster a more intentional approach to lean enterprise value creation at national and international levels.

Normally, government, industry, and other stakeholders are not thought of in the context of a single, national-level enterprise. Similarly, national-level initiatives aimed at eliminating waste – such as government cost-cutting initiatives – are rarely linked to concepts of value creation or lean capability. While there are islands of success at these levels, where we see evidence of shifting the focus to lean enterprise value creation, these are generally in spite of – and viewed as a threat to – existing systems and infrastructure.

Each phase of the value-creation process poses significant challenges at the national and international levels. Value identification requires reaching beyond the bounds of aerospace enterprises to take into account alternative uses of society's resources. Value propositions are rarely contained in a single, explicitly negotiated agreement, but emerge as shared understandings among a vast array of global stakeholders. Value delivery takes into account future generations, not just current actors. Just as we've seen how the multi-program enterprise provides the context for value creation at the single program level, we will see here that enterprises at the national and international level provide the context for many multi-program enterprises.

The value created by the military and commercial segments of the aerospace industry has been central to our society: setting the global standard for defense products, dominating the balance of payments, driving technological innovation, and inspiring future generations. We are now in a period of reconstruction and redirection in which many dimensions of value are open for discussion, which begins with the four core missions of aerospace articulated in Chapter 1:

- enabling the global movement of people and goods;

- enabling the global acquisition and dissemination of information and data;

- advancing national security interests; and

- providing a source of inspiration by pushing the boundaries of exploration and innovation.

Success in each mission depends on a high-level process of value identification, value proposition, and value delivery. And at the national and international level, some very basic questions are posed: Will capital, labor, and other resources be devoted to any of these missions, or to other societal priorities? To other market priorities? Moreover, what role will *existing* aerospace stakeholders play in pursuit of the four missions? What role might be played by other sectors of society and the global economy?

In focusing on value creation at these levels, we address the defense and commercial aerospace markets separately, since the dynamics are quite different.[1] At the outset, it is important to review recent pivotal developments in the defense sector, where the value-creation crisis is perhaps most acute.

## A 'Crisis' in Defense Aerospace?

Since 1999, numerous studies, articles, and editorials have forecast the decline of the defense aerospace extended enterprise.[2] Is defense aerospace teetering on the brink of a slow and steady decline into dysfunction and reduced relevance?

The November 2000 Defense Science Board (DSB) study on the state of defense aerospace focused on the weak positions of defense aerospace companies in financial markets and warned that contractors' poor returns on invested capital were significantly damaging the industry's health.[3] Statements by executives (such as the one below from a company that exited the military aerospace business) captured the general mood of the study and the times:

The defense industry became unattractive through a process like the death by a thousand cuts. There was no one event that made the business unattractive but eventually things were screwed down so tight that it was no longer providing attractive returns. Moreover, the business no longer provided attractive cash flows and a company could no longer get cash up front for a large project. The government took all the savings from any operational improvements so that many capital investments would have had a negative return to the company had we employed the capital to achieve them.[4]

The DSB report also noted the looming problem in aerospace of attracting and retaining talented engineers and other technical people, attributing this to declines in R&D spending in the industry and the resulting dearth of 'interesting projects'. In March 2001, Congress chartered the Presidential Commission on the Future of the United States Aerospace Industry to determine a path forward. Its responsibilities include a study of the government's budget process and acquisition, contract finance, tax, and trade policies relative to the aerospace industry, an examination of the national space launch infrastructure, and a review of the state of higher education in the sciences and engineering. Had the aerospace crisis finally appeared on the national agenda?

The attention created by various reports and this commission will help raise public and policy awareness about the challenges facing the US Aerospace Enterprise. Policy and legislation may well be crafted to address some or perhaps many of the more pressing needs. But much more is needed – including, ultimately, a full recognition of the major shifts that have taken place in stakeholder values since the formative days of the aerospace enterprise. Without a 'total enterprise perspective' on the challenges facing aerospace, proposed remedies may serve only to support the existing monuments.

Following the lean enterprise value framework, any attempt to address the future of aerospace demands that three key questions be answered:

- What processes will *identify value* for key stakeholders at the national and international levels?

- What incentives, agreements, and supporting infrastructure are needed to address stakeholder interests (that is, to create the *value proposition*) in deploying societal resources?

- What institutional infrastructure and other enablers will help ensure *value delivery* to these stakeholders?

## No Value Proposition is Assured at National and International Levels

In 1989, on the 20th anniversary of the first lunar landing, President George Bush announced an ambitious endeavor called the Space Exploration Initiative (SEI). He challenged America to return to the moon to stay and to go to Mars by 2019, the 50th anniversary of Apollo XI. Perhaps in response to criticism that NASA was adrift, with no vision or goal for its future, perhaps also to address the disorientation that the United States suffered after the fall of the Berlin Wall, President Bush's call was for the American people to engage in an effort that would enrich the human spirit, enhance national pride, and inspire youth through ambitious, futuristic efforts. Unfortunately, though, the call was in vain.

By the end of 1990, it was clear that the hefty SEI price tag was encountering strong resistance.[5] Congress zeroed out Bush's first budget request for SEI funds (FY91). The next few years saw continued opposition as the federal budget deficit grew. A number of other scientific/technical 'megaprojects' on the national agenda competed with SEI for funding, and many were ultimately cancelled.

By 1992, NASA was reeling from budget attacks and the continued rejection of funding requests for SEI, which died quietly during the Clinton administration as NASA's 'Better, Faster, Cheaper' initiative stole the headlines with dramatic low-cost successes (and the occasional failures). SEI had been presented as the logical follow-on to Apollo, but several keys to Apollo's support were missing twenty years later (including the Cold War rivalry with the Soviet Union).

The underlying story behind the Apollo program and SEI is one of value. The Apollo program was possible because a broad base of stakeholders received value from it on a number of dimensions, and hence provided support. The SEI didn't fly – literally or figuratively – because its support base was too narrowly focused, with value delivered to too few stakeholders. The American public and its leadership were unwilling to foot the bill, because they saw more value in things other than space exploration.

A key message for aerospace – indeed, for other industries – is that no value proposition is assured, no matter the merits or apparent benefits. Aerospace, its products, and its contributions to society form but one facet of society's manifold needs.

## Value Identification

Lean enterprises at national and international levels must engage their stakeholders in an active process of value identification, which requires an understanding of economic, political, demographic, and social trends that may be difficult to identify. Success depends on having an appropriate, adaptable institutional infrastructure, and in the first place calls for clarity about the scope of the 'enterprise'. This requires a robust approach for identifying stakeholders, their values, and the evolving role they may play in the development of a value proposition.

To illustrate the process of value identification, we focus here on value from the perspective of three key stakeholders in national and international aerospace enterprises: investors, the public, and the workforce. In each case, there are significant tensions around the way value has been identified in past years, and there are significant opportunities if value can be better identified. Although aerospace is our focus, our comments on all three stakeholders have implications for other sectors of the economy.

### Investor Value

Investors are the primary source of capital, which is key to an aerospace enterprise's ability to create value across many stakeholders and to maintain capability to create future value. In fact, the financial and aerospace communities are interdependent and have untapped potential to generate mutual gains. Too often, though, they seem to be talking past each other.

What indicators help us identify investor value? The primary criteria are return on investment and risk. These are generally assessed in terms of healthy revenue streams and corresponding positive cashflow, a large customer base, and long-term profitable growth opportunities (which may come from new markets, product differentiation, and/or market segmentation within existing markets). Investors primarily express this value through the price they are willing to pay for a firm's equity shares or through bond valuations.

Since 1979, the aerospace industry has generated very good return to investors – some 17.3 percent (using Fortune 500 indices).[6] In fact, it is exceeded only by pharmaceuticals. The aerospace industry's performance on other basic financial measures (such as return on equity, revenue, and assets) since 1979 is consistent with that of a median Fortune 500 company – not at the top of the list, but not at the bottom either. In many ways, aerospace behaves like the other heavy manufacturing industries (autos, and farm and industrial equipment), although its aggregate financial performance is consistently superior to others in that category.[7] Based on high-level financial criteria, at least, aerospace industry performance is not as bad as many have thought in recent years.

The consolidation that occurred in the 1990s – encouraged by the need to reduce the excess capacity in the industry which had been propped up by Cold War spending (see Chapter 2) – significantly affected the financial valuation of aerospace firms relative to other investments. The financial performance of these firms suffered as they battled the multiple challenges of major restructuring to integrate acquired units and slimmer margins from their government customer, and sent some corporate debt ratings to junk-bond status. In essence, the investment community was signaling serious doubts about the value of aerospace investments during the most intense period of consolidation (though these doubts have since somewhat dissipated). Figure 10.1 puts the 'aerospace crisis' in an overall market context.

To understand investors' expectations for the aerospace industry's future, we need to address the civil and military aerospace businesses separately. On the civil side, early 2001 projections for revenue passenger-miles anticipated steady growth of nearly 5 percent per year through 2009, with the large jet fleet projected to grow by 3.4 percent during the same period.[8] The long-term impact of international terrorism on such projections remains to be seen, but even a slowdown in new airplane sales will still leave a market for spares, modifications, services, and infrastructure that is expected to be $1 trillion over the next 20 years.[9] After the past few years of volatility, the current projections for the commercial space sector point to a sizeable market with little growth.[10]

While the civil aerospace market is marked by recent increases in uncertainty, the military aerospace market has been a challenge for investors since the end of the Cold War.[11] The defense market may not be a high-

**FIGURE 10.1** | Aerospace's financial crisis in context

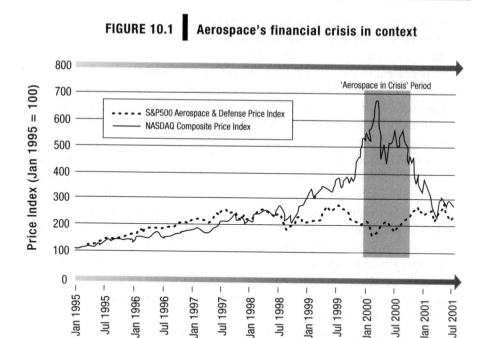

Source: Data from Thomson Financial Datastream.

growth area, but it is still quite large. But growth in the defense budget does not necessarily translate into growth in product sales for the aerospace industry. Operations and maintenance costs, along with those for personnel, are increasing faster than the overall top-line defense budget. The military has an enormous and aging capital equipment base that it needs to replace, update, or maintain – so there are potentially several different revenue streams the defense industry can tap for the future, and there are open questions around current work to be performed by private industry.

Clearly, the aerospace enterprise has provided value to investors in the past and has the potential to continue to do so. But the recent crisis of confidence with aerospace share prices and the resulting organizational turmoil signal the importance of reflecting the interests of the investment community in future value identification and value propositions.

## Public Value

The aerospace enterprise looks to the public for resources, revenue, and – at a fundamental level – the very legitimacy of its missions. The public –

in the form of its elected officials, government agencies, associations, and other entities – also provides regulation and the infrastructure that enables the use of aerospace products and services, from airports to air traffic management to the communication spectrum to space launch facilities.

How does the public express the value it derives from the US Aerospace Enterprise? Let's consider both direct and implicit measures of value.

In the civil sector, demand for products and services provides direct measures of public value. This includes demand for airline passenger-miles and space-based services such as telecommunications and direct broadcast entertainment – both related to aerospace's core missions to move people and goods and to transmit data and information. Also included is the public's willingness to invest resources in the nation's infrastructure for civil air transportation: the air traffic management system, airport facilities, and the institutional infrastructure supporting airline safety. The public's changing willingness to support large space exploration projects bears directly on another core mission – providing inspiration as we push the boundaries of air and space. The declining NASA budget reflects an important shift in this support.

In the defense sector, the value the public derives from national security is ultimately indicated by how much the public is willing to spend on it (as represented by federal budget allocations). Chapter 2 showed how defense's share of GDP has declined since the end of the Cold War. Figure 10.2 puts funding for national defense in perspective relative to other federal spending priorities for the last four decades – reflecting the reality of what provides value at the national and international levels. Defense discretionary spending has declined as a proportion of the total federal budget. Domestic discretionary spending has fluctuated, but remained within a range of roughly15–20 percent of the federal budget for some decades. During the same timeframe, mandatory program spending has nearly doubled.[12]

As Figure 10.2 shows, mandatory spending is putting the squeeze on the national discretionary budget (including defense and domestic spending). While priority will be given to national security, there are other strategic challenges facing society. Consider, for instance, the projected shortage of teachers, estimated at upwards of 2.7 million vacant positions by the end of the decade at the current rate.[13] Or consider the projected shortage of nurses and nursing home staff just as the United States reaches the cusp of a large surge of retirement in the population.[14] In addition, environmental and energy issues loom large. These are all pressing needs that compete with national defense (or space exploration and other aerospace-related activities, for that matter) for an increasingly constrained federal discretionary dollar.

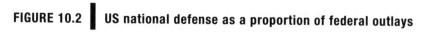

**FIGURE 10.2** | **US national defense as a proportion of federal outlays**

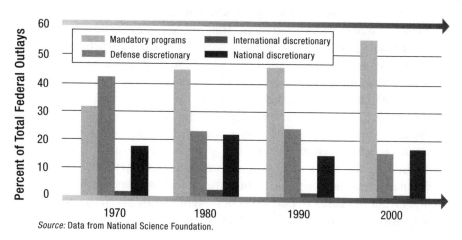

*Source:* Data from National Science Foundation.

Implicit measures of public value are found in investments that public or private enterprises make in future capabilities in the expectation that these will have value to the public. Let's consider public and private R&D spending across civil and defense sectors as an example.

Prior to 1980, aerospace was distinctly the largest performer of R&D in the United States; today, it is merely in the same pack with other industries, matched by motor vehicles and surpassed by computers.[15] This represents a dramatic decrease since the Reagan-era defense buildup. And since then, aerospace has made the least real gains in R&D funding relative to sectors such as chemicals, pharmaceuticals, computers, electronics, and motor vehicles. While typical R&D expenditures for all industries have grown almost sevenfold, and R&D spending in the service sector has grown an explosive forty times over, aerospace R&D has increased only slightly more than threefold. So, while aerospace still is a dominant force in US R&D (in absolute terms), the increasing R&D investments in sectors outside of aerospace suggest a comparatively more accelerated development of innovative capacity in those areas.

Interestingly, the ratio of company R&D funding relative to federal R&D funding is quite low for aerospace relative to other industry sectors. The same is true for the life sciences. Both aerospace and the life sciences have their current and future productive and innovative capabilities base tied to federal research funding priorities. In the life sciences, for instance, major federal policy priorities such the war on cancer, the fight against

AIDS, or the Human Genome Project – areas in which strong expressions of public value exist – have created standing armies of highly trained researchers, science knowledge bases, and technological infrastructures related to those specific activities. This illustrates the large role played by R&D funding in the development of the enterprise infrastructures discussed in Chapter 9. The development (or lack thereof) of these enterprise infra-structures, in turn, has implications for which technical paths an industry or nation can take into the future, as well as which paths are blocked.

What is clear is that lean enterprise value at national and international levels depends on sustained public support for investments in social and technical infrastructure. Neither the government nor private sector firms are making the kinds of investment necessary to sustain the increases in defense aerospace capability that the nation has enjoyed in the past. Significant increases in public support are unlikely, given the competition with other societal demands for limited budget dollars.

## Workforce Value

The 'human capital' associated with creating lean enterprise value is the most important input for the entire lean enterprise. As we stated in our Chapter 1 principles, it is people who effectuate lean value. Consequently, it is important to understand whether there are systematic factors that would affect the ability of the aerospace enterprise to continue to attract and retain the talented and highly skilled workforce it has traditionally enjoyed.[16]

In trying to understand workforce value, it is important to distinguish work content from work context. We discuss work *context* below; first, we address the work *content*, which is a significant source of motivation since it links to achievement, recognition, the work itself, responsibility, and growth or advancement.[17]

Aerospace has historically provided a challenging, novel, and stimulating environment in which to work. Where else can you work on a product that might travel halfway across the globe in a day, soar to the edge of Earth's atmosphere, or visit another planet? The challenges of 'Higher, Faster, Farther' still define the work done in this enterprise. Aerospace systems, and especially systems of systems, span a gamut of technologies, ensuring expo-sure for the technically inclined to a broader diversity of technologies and tools (many of them cutting-edge) than in just about any other field.

But many of these advanced tools and technologies were developed a generation ago – or more. Is there a new generation of technologies in the pipeline, emerging to challenge and inspire as these have done? Part of the answer lies in R&D spending, which as we've seen is declining in this industry.

What about another key part of work content – achievement? The concept of achievement suggests in part that one's actions have influence or impact, and in part that they achieve closure or completion to an activity. It's certainly easy to see that impact in aerospace, and the four core missions are testament to what aerospace has accomplished. Both the white- and blue-collar workforce in the defense aerospace sector responded to the nation's call to enable it to win the Cold War.

One indicator of accomplishment for aerospace, patents per employee, provides an indication of the potential for personal intellectual achievement, or 'making your mark in the world'. Here, aerospace ranks last among almost all high-tech industries. Aerospace also ranks last in sales per employee, another indicator of productivity.[18] Both affect the industry's ability to attract and retain its workforce.

The other element of achievement involves closure or completion, which depends to a great extent on product cycle times. Attaining a sense of closure can be difficult when a program takes years or even decades to complete, and the cycle time in defense aerospace has been increasing for a long time.[19] For instance, whereas the Lockheed P-80, the first operational US jet fighter, was designed and built in nine months, an employee could potentially have worked on the the USAF's current F-22 fighter aircraft program for twenty years or more by the time that it goes into production.

How does aerospace address an individual's need for recognition and responsibility? Work in aerospace, as in many other industries with large-scale endeavors, is most often a team effort. And generally speaking, the bigger or more complex the product, the smaller any one individual's contribution may appear to be. In this type of environment, it's difficult to win individual recognition – a challenge certainly not unique to aerospace.

Finally, does aerospace provide opportunities for growth or advancement? Civil aerospace is a mature market that is expected to grow steadily in the coming years, and thus to provide many opportunities for advancement. There are also occasional strategic initiatives that result in the creation of new businesses or markets, with attendant growth and leadership opportunities – an example is the creation of direct satellite broadcast systems in the civil space sector. In defense aerospace, though, the market is contracting while individual programs are becoming more costly. This results in fewer opportunities for program management or system-level engineering jobs, limiting advancement and learning opportunities.

What about *work context*, which includes organization policy or administration, supervision, interpersonal relationships, working conditions, salary, status, and security? Improperly handled, these work context matters can be a significant source of dissatisfaction.

First, there is the question of compensation. Lifetime earnings in aerospace compare well with those for similar employees in other sectors. Aerospace technical employees are among the most highly paid engineers and scientists (exceeded only slightly by electrical, computer, and software engineers). The real issue is that some of these rocket scientists are being drawn into other sectors of the economy at higher levels of compensation.[20]

Among the hourly workforce, organized labor plays a crucial role in the aerospace industry. In fact, aerospace is one of the most highly unionized industries in the United States. Some 40 percent of all production employees, or 20 percent of all industry employees, are represented by a union. The typical union aerospace worker earns wages 50 percent higher than does the average worker in manufacturing, and enjoys comprehensive benefits.[21]

Beyond the impact of unions on wages and other bargaining matters, labor organizations shape the work context in frontline operations and in strategic decisionmaking.[22] Through a combination of hard bargaining on issues of fair treatment and rewards, as well as partnership around training, new technology, and new work systems, unions have helped make jobs in aerospace production some of the best industrial jobs to be found anywhere. A key challenge for unions as a stakeholder is to expand their partnerships with management concerning the transformation of work systems, while still maintaining their independent role as workforce representatives. Both roles contribute to workforce value, but they are often in tension.

So, in reviewing aerospace's ability to deliver value to the workforce in both work content and work context, we find mixed opportunities and challenges. The biggest challenge for defense aerospace may indeed be the 'intellectual capital crisis' that has been on everyone's mind: a significant (and the most highly experienced) cohort of people is ready to retire from both the government and the private sector; there have been few production workers accepted into worker apprenticeship programs in the past half-dozen years; and the downsized military no longer provides the number of potential experienced employees that it once did. These factors point to a discontinuity in the process of transferring the experience base to a rising generation of leaders, engineers, and skilled craftspeople. That also coincides with the squeeze between investment and the higher cost associated with creating the systems through which that working knowledge is transferred.

This is all happening in the context of a mature technology base. Each new increment of performance costs more to achieve than did the prior way of working, resulting in fewer systems being created, and less frequently

## Understanding Intellectual Capital

Intellectual capital (IC) is a primary source of innovation, productivity, and competitive advantage for organizations. It includes the skills and experience of the workforce; the structures, policies, and procedures; the tools and technologies in use; and numerous intangible relationships. But it is poorly defined and difficult to measure.

Investing in intellectual capital, as in physical capital, builds capability to create value. One MIT study tracked commercial aircraft design programs over two generations and found a strong link between the currency of skills and practices and program performance.[23] Programs that had significant disruptions in staffing, or churning due to natural attrition and career advancements, tended to have more problems in meeting program goals.

To some extent, intellectual capital can be captured and preserved in tools and databases, though these are relatively static in nature. Training and prototyping exercises help develop and preserve a subset of design team skills. Ultimately, however, when it comes to intellectual capital, the study found that these are weak substitutes for practical experience.

Limited opportunities to gain experience in practice, brought about in part by technology maturity, can have serious implications for maintaining a productive and innovative skill base. As a result, policymakers must consider investments in intellectual capital when making choices about supply (size of the productive base) and demand (number of likely new programs). Such choices go to the heart of value-creation capability at national and international levels.

(and in less opportunity to generate new experience). In the end, there may not be enough challenging new work to attract and maintain a critical mass of experience in the workforce – and therefore, to maintain the intellectual capital base essential to the capability to design and produce future systems. With that erosion in capability come future losses in productivity. Lower productivity means system price increases, potentially offsetting gains achieved through productivity improvements from lean and other initiatives.

## Core Competencies for Value Identification

Even if the importance of value identification is appreciated, is there sufficient capability to do it well? Here are some competencies or capabilities that are required.

- *Stakeholder identification* – Understanding current and future stakeholders, including those without identifiable representatives.

- *Current-state data analysis* – Analyzing stakeholder interests/values.

- *Future-trend data analysis* – Projecting future trends; considering complex system interactions.

- *Verification/interaction* – Facilitating interactions among stakeholders to shape understanding and perceptions of current and future states.

Aerospace truly is at a crossroads. Our review of the values of three key stakeholders suggests the possibility that each, to varying degrees, may choose to disengage from aerospace. The same can be said for other stakeholders, such as suppliers, communities, and universities. Robust value propositions at the national and international level – which effectively address stakeholder interests – are crucial in determining the extent of participation by key stakeholders.

## Creating the Value Proposition

Value propositions provide orientation and direction to lean enterprises at national and international levels. Skillfully crafted, value propositions harness future visions, resources, incentives, and other factors to address the identified sources of value for relevant stakeholders. Constructing value propositions at this level requires a unique combination of interactive and institution-building capabilities – working with stakeholder interests as the central focus.

There never was a single Cold War value proposition. Rather, many national- and international-level value propositions emerged – a series of interrelated understandings concerning acquisition policy, R&D investment, international offset agreements, and other matters. Looking back, we can easily see the many ways in which diverse stakeholders at these levels all found value in aerospace. And we can now see the many ways in which the process of finding value has been disrupted.

The construction of value propositions at national and international levels happens in many ways. In some cases, individual leaders will drive their creation based on bold leadership visions. In other cases, value propositions are embodied in legislation or treaties, which are usually highly visible. Consider, for example, the legislation creating NASA or the recently established Presidential Commission on the Future of the United States Aerospace Industry. Though very different in scale and scope, each involves an act of Congress, with specific mandates, funding, and other agreements clearly specified.

Other value propositions, much harder to see, are no less important. For example, there has been a longstanding (and only partly discussed) national value proposition in the United States in which workforce skills and capabilities are viewed as largely a private matter between employers, employees, and unions. This contrasts with the many European countries that view such matters as central to national policy.

We have explored in earlier chapters the dynamic nature of value propositions at program and multi-program enterprise levels. The same is true at national and international levels, though the overlay of national interests at this enterprise level heightens the global significance of the developments. Consider the construction and evolution of value propositions within the European Airbus consortium.

When Airbus first came together thirty years ago, it was primarily a mechanism for pooling resources across national companies in order to gain overall market share. This involved reaching complex internal agreements or 'value propositions' regarding the distribution of responsibilities to each country. There was a centralization of marketing, customer support, and management activities, while the respective national companies retained control of design, engineering, and production of the elements of the aircraft allocated to them. This value proposition was designed to build a single, integrated product family, while maintaining employment and capability in the member countries. It also preserved the integrity of the various companies in these countries, each an important source of national pride. In its early years, the company lost out in bids to sell airplanes beyond the European market, causing some observers and even some members of the consortium to question whether Airbus was a viable value proposition.

In time, however, Airbus built a family of products and demonstrated an increasing ability to innovate – as illustrated by the first digital, fly-by-wire aircraft, and the concept of common cockpit configurations across the entire product line. Still, there were substantial costs and inefficiencies associated with running business operations on a distributed, consortium basis. Thus, the announcement on June 23rd, 2000, of a new integrated structure for Airbus was more than just a corporate restructuring – it was a fundamental change in the value proposition for many stakeholders. In its official history, the company explains that it has 'outgrown the consortium' structure that 'was well adapted to pooling skills and resources in order to establish a position on the market' and that it 'needed a new corporate organization that would centralize management control over every aspect of the business'.[24] Following this announcement, Airbus placed day-to-day control of all aspects of its operations under a single management team.

Consider what is involved in this value proposition change. The proposition shifted to emphasize efficient centralized operations and to de-emphasize national autonomy, distributed or redundant capability, and other factors. While it took just six months to bring the management operation together physically at the centralized headquarters in Toulouse, France, it will take much longer for the new value proposition to drive decisions and action fully in every aspect of Airbus operations.

In writing this book, we've worked carefully not to confuse the 'value' identified and delivered to stakeholders with the 'values' held in a given society. At this level, however, the two *do* become entwined. This was evident as we looked back at the Cold War value proposition centered on going 'Higher, Faster, Farther' than the Soviet Union. It is also visible in the centralization and restructuring of the Airbus consortium, where 'efficiency' is replacing 'autonomy'. If we think of US aerospace as an enterprise at the national and international levels, we begin to see the many tensions around changing the value propositions.

In military acquisition, for example, there is a deeply embedded value placed on competition as a means of fairly and effectively distributing military aircraft contracts. This may only be feasible in the US context, where there are sufficient companies to engage in a 'fly off' competition, and where there is a market big enough to support multiple contenders. But even in this context, there are many complicating implications of this underlying assumption. The key point here is that at national levels the lean enterprise mindset urges that such assumptions and implications be explicit, so that the tensions are understood and addressed.

We find another example of a set of national and international value propositions in tension in what is termed the 'offset' process. When US companies contract with a foreign country that is purchasing aircraft, there are often provisions for part of the purchase price to be 'offset' through an agreement to locate some part of the production of aerospace components in that country. Here the value proposition involves a trade of substantial export income for the development of new skills and capabilities in a given country. While this may make sense in the context of any one contractual agreement, the cumulative effect can have unintended consequences.

Today, when you visit the production facilities for the F-16 fighter in Fort Worth, Texas, there may be aircraft being produced for several countries. On a loading dock not too far from the production line sit struts or other component parts built in those respective countries, each sequenced for a particular aircraft, while the same component may be arriving from domestic suppliers or other countries for the next few aircraft in line. As this story is multiplied across many different products, the net effect has been a constant increase in aerospace component imports over the last twenty years.

Beyond the technical implications of a value proposition that involves offset agreements, there are human capital implications, as in so many other industries. The *global* workforce may provide a defined enterprise with additional human capital, but it also represents a diluting of the available work and the opportunities to build capability and experience for the existing workforce in the United States. There are tensions at the national level when defense-related joint ventures, strategic partnerships, and other linkages become cross-national – for instance, in contracting with ex-Soviet aerospace companies or Indian software companies.

At the national level, when it comes to the aerospace workforce there are core issues around institutional infrastructure. Earlier, we noted that some workforce value propositions, though unstated, are still very important. These include the understandings among government, industry, professional associations and unions, communities, and other stakeholders around their respective investments and other contributions to attracting, developing, and retaining an effective aerospace workforce. It may be that there are no appropriate economic or social mechanisms to address effectively the gaps we identified when undertaking value identification with the workforce. For instance, there may be a need for regional or national initiatives, training centers, and other institutional mechanisms centered on developing a 21st-century aerospace workforce.

MIT's Aero/Astro Department faced a microcosm of these issues in the early 1990s as it embarked on a strategic planning process. It quickly identified key gaps in its skill mix, such as the lack of professors with expertise in aerospace software systems and other emerging domains. A closer look raised complicated questions, however, since traditional aerospace education was not necessarily going to be appropriate to produce

## Studies and Commissions as Change Mechanisms at the National Level

Given the many dynamics we've been discussing, the charter for the Presidential Commission on the Future of the United States Aerospace Industry includes a commitment to study two aspects of international trade and technology export: '(a) the extent to which the current system for controlling the export of aerospace goods, services and technologies reflects an adequate balance between the need to protect national security and the need to ensure unhindered access to the global marketplace; and (b) the adequacy of United States and multilateral trade laws and policies for maintaining the international competitiveness of the United States aerospace industry.'[25]

It will require a lean enterprise value perspective to address effectively the interdependent human capital issues that are woven in with the US stance with respect to the value propositions that presently govern international trade and technology export. These are not only 'make or buy' decisions for the nation around 'core competencies', but also choices about just how many opportunities will exist for aerospace engineers, technicians, and others to develop skills in ways that we know are important and in ways that may become important.

National-level commissions, from the earliest days of the industry, have played a critical role in helping to construct value propositions. They help generate public awareness and opinion, or even legitimize bold new directions. Such commissions may include representatives of many key stakeholders, but they may be limited by their very nature in advancing the interests of all stakeholders with the sort of intensity and vigor needed to produce robust agreements. They are, therefore, an important mechanism in initiating the interplay of interests that can occur in a Congressional debate with legislation on the line, or in the bargaining for national contractual agreements, or in other national-level forums.

## Core Competencies for Constructing Value Propositions

The core competencies or capabilities required for constructing durable, effective value propositions include the following:

- *Mutual-gains bargaining skills* – Surfacing and framing complex issues around mutual gains, without becoming trapped by positional bargaining dynamics.

- *Structuring agreements and incentives* – Drafting self-regulating language (in mission statements, enabling legislation, contractual agreements, and other reciprocal understandings) that balances specificity and flexibility.

- *Institutional structuring* – Architecting new institutional arrangements, restructuring existing arrangements, and creating forums, consortia, and other mechanisms for dialogue, action, and continuity.

- *Moral and ethical foundation* – Building bridges between stakeholders with different degrees of power, divergent perspectives, and other complex dynamics.

such a faculty, nor were career development criteria, teaching rotation assignments, and other institutional arrangements necessarily going to be appropriate to people coming from very different backgrounds, such as information technology. This set of issues illustrates the mix of formal and informal value propositions that must be renegotiated in addressing the shifting nature of the aerospace workforce.

## Value Delivery

Value delivery at national and international enterprise levels is the effective and efficient deployment of societal resources to address identified stakeholder value in the context of existing value propositions. At these levels, markets often represent the most efficient and effective mechanisms for allocating resources among societal stakeholders. But markets sometimes fail. Governments and institutions must step in to ensure that stakeholder interests are identified and addressed in a value proposition, so that value is efficiently and effectively delivered – mindful of the risk that an appropriate intervention at one time may become a monument later on (as we saw in Chapter 3). Thus, value delivery at national and international levels involves establishing, sustaining, and periodically transforming legal, economic, and social structures or processes. These dynamics unfold in distinctive ways in the civil and defense sectors of aerospace.

## Civil Aerospace

The delivery of value in the civil aerospace sector occurs largely through the give and take of markets. This is where goods and services are bought and sold, as well as where capital and labor give their relative valuation of individual enterprises. Because the interactions between key stakeholders are market-based, resource allocation leading to value delivery in civil aerospace is largely a self-correcting process.

Success for individual aerospace enterprises operating in the civil sector depends, to a great extent, on strategy and execution. From the lean enterprise value perspective, strategy is 'doing the right job', while execution is 'doing the job right'. Both activities fall within the responsibilities of enterprise leadership in their stewardship and accountability to enterprise stakeholders. High-performing organizations do emerge over time.

Many stakeholders in US civil aerospace are prepared to let markets decide the fate of multi-program enterprises, with government intervention largely limited to matters of safety, air traffic management, and some degree of retraining for displaced workers. However, underlying the broad movements of markets are national legal and economic structures, regulatory environments, government- and other stakeholder-defined rules (within which the markets themselves operate), as well as various treaties and agreements governing interactions between nations. In fact, the role of government has loomed large throughout the long history of civil aerospace, even when it seemed that markets were determining the fortunes of individual actors. This involvement dates back to the financial support of the mail service (which effectively created and subsidized a passenger service), and continues to the present role of government in maintaining the infrastructure, public safety standards, and other dimensions of operations.

Even in the civil sector, a close look reveals that governments and other institutions play many important roles with respect to value delivery. Beyond the roles they play in structuring the rules for markets and providing infrastructure, governments are also major consumers of civil aerospace products. For instance, the US government first contracted for the Evolved Expendable Launch Vehicle (EELV) as a means of reducing the cost of access to space for government missions. In this case, however, a second role of government emerged when it became apparent that the commercial space launch market was potentially much larger than the government market. The government then shifted its role to that of minority partner, essentially providing seed funding for development and then letting market dynamics determine the ultimate investment and pricing policy for this new generation of launch vehicles.

These types of strategic choice by government are quite complex. In the first half of this century, government was busy creating infrastructure, subsidizing operations, and funding basic research in technical disciplines such as aerodynamics. One could well have asked then: 'Why would the private sector bother to underwrite the birth of this new transportation technology when steamships and railroads deliver more people and goods farther and faster than do aircraft, while delivering a better return for investors?' In the past, and still today, we find that government played a critical role in value delivery by bearing risk that markets could not justify.

## The Government's Role in Creating the Civil Aerospace Sector

America has an uneasy coexistence with industrial policy. It's seen as necessary, but best avoided. What constitutes effective industrial policy when it can't be avoided? The early days of aerospace provide useful insights. In a difficult business environment, the US aircraft industry delivered its first aircraft to the US Army in August 1908. Complaints from the industry led the government to establish the National Advisory Committee for Aeronautics in 1915 to advise the government on the industry's health and to conduct supporting research. Langley Memorial Aeronautical Laboratory was established in 1917, where aerodynamics research would produce engine cowlings and airfoils – leading to rapid and dramatic gains in aircraft performance.

World War I significantly challenged the young aircraft industry, first to meet the enormous demand for aircraft (more than 14 000 aircraft were delivered before the Armistice), and then to cope with surplus aircraft that flooded the market at the end of hostilities. Some planes found use when the Army began national airmail service in 1918, but the design and condition of the aircraft, and unregulated operators, made aviation dangerous. The service was also slow to catch on with the public. The Air Mail Act of 1925 opened airmail service to competitive bidding and encouraged passenger service, stimulating market demand for newer aircraft designs tailored to civil needs. But several government commissions during the early 1920s identified numerous safety and infrastructure inadequacies.

In 1926, the government addressed the problems with legislation that created the Bureau of Air Commerce in the Commerce Department to oversee aviation affairs; mandated safety regulation through pilot licensing and aircraft certification; established radio, air navigation, and airport facilities; provided mapping and weather information; and established control over the national airspace, including air traffic control. Other legislation reformed military procurement: it employed multi-year production plans to increase stability; ended direct government competition with industry in aircraft production and maintenance; and limited ruinous price competition in the competitive bidding process.

Aviation's fortunes improved dramatically. Lindbergh's crossing of the Atlantic captured public imagination. Increased safety and newer aircraft designs encouraged the public to embrace air travel. In 1928, civil aircraft sales exceeded military sales for the first time since the war. During 1928–29, aviation holding companies were the darlings of the stock market, with some trading at P/E ratios of 100.[26] But by 1934, the limitations of the prior airmail policies became evident when just three of the large aviation trusts held 90 percent of postal contracts. The new Air Mail Act of 1934 opened up competition again for airmail contracts and prevented single corporations from controlling both aircraft producers and operators, thereby removing market distortions caused by industry concentration and the expanding demand for new airliners. The DC-3 rolled out in December 1935 and was the first aircraft that allowed airlines to turn a profit solely on the basis of passenger service.

> The relationship between the industry and government in the early years was strained many times; government was hardly 'pro-industry'. But the judicious use of market creation, incentives, regulation, and privatization not only allowed the industry to become self-supporting, but also laid the technical foundations that would be built upon in winning World War II.

In many civil aerospace markets, of course, government's role in value delivery is much more limited. There are large, well-defined markets for many aircraft and spacecraft products and services. Investment decisions can be based on reasonably accurate assessments of risk, reward, and projected revenue streams. Large producer firms provide reasonable assurance of job stability to the labor markets. In such a mature environment, markets can, in the near term, efficiently allocate resources for R&D for new product innovation, product realization, operations, support, and even for enabling infrastructure. Over the longer term, however, the information that markets rely on for allocation decisions may not exist, requiring governments and institutions to step in. In recent years, the United States has seen the time horizon for private-sector-sponsored R&D shrink, largely because of market-based financial pressures. Here we would urge that government has a continuing role in ensuring that long-term basic research generates the breakthrough technologies that create new markets.[27]

Government and other institutions at national or international level can be effective in creating or shaping markets only if they have lean enterprise value principles. While governments and other institutions are not as nimble as are markets in changing to meet new demands, they do have adaptive mechanisms – a core competency required for a lean enterprise at this level. In addition to various commissions, study panels, and lobbying mechanisms, there are also deliberate initiatives by government to adapt itself to meet new needs. For example, the National Performance Review (or 'Reinventing Government') initiative during the 1990s did address some of the government monuments and misalignments that impair value delivery. We should note, however, that this initiative was less focused on the role of government in value identification – reflecting the fact that while many lean process improvement methods may be employed, a larger *enterprise* orientation is lacking.

Government and other institutions bear an important responsibility to fund basic research to identify and develop technologies that represent fundamentally new ways of executing the core missions currently served by the US Aerospace Enterprise. Hard questions need to be asked, such as: what would be required to realize a tenfold increase in productivity, with increased safety, in the global transport of people and goods? Or: what would be required to provide true global access to information at a hundredth of the current cost? R&D funding could then be targeted to address such questions. There is also a key role for government and other national or international institutions in reexamining and redefining norms and expectations around experimentation, risk-taking, and how failures are addressed. Current norms disproportionately punish occasional failures, stifling the learning and experience that result from pioneering work. Ultimately, it is when government and other institutions at this level operate as lean enterprises that they are best able to contribute to value creation in what is ostensibly the free-market environment of civil aerospace.

## Defense Aerospace

In recent years, doing the job right in defense aerospace has involved action by government as the customer, in partnership with its suppliers. The government has worked to meet its military needs in a constrained budget environment by enacting acquisition reform, by encouraging supplier base rationalization (for example, through corporate consolidation), and by working with its suppliers to make productivity gains. Defense contractors have, in turn, merged with one another and begun to institute lean practices such as those in our Chapter 5 islands of success.

The government, though, has yet to realize fully the potential of business process reforms within its own operations and in its relationships with the private sector. Of particular importance are the many monuments and misalignments that limit the ability of government as a stakeholder to apply lean enterprise value principles to its own operations and to reexamine fundamentally the ways in which it identifies stakeholder values and constructs value propositions.

To date, acquisition reform initiatives have emphasized cost reduction by employing commercial-like practices. Technology policy has also stressed greater use of commercial technologies. Neither type of initiative, though, has been conceived based on lean enterprise value principles. For example, policies fail to address the movement of companies and parts of the workforce entirely out of the aerospace sector. Key parts of stakeholder value identification and value proposition development remain incomplete.

Accounting practice reform is a core challenge if government is to operate as a lean enterprise.[28] Without the ability to track its own organizational and budgetary performance, identifying changes to enable 'doing the job right' will be impossible. There is more work to be done in diffusing the lessons learned from acquisition-reform pilot programs throughout the enterprise and in institutionalizing them in practice.

It doesn't take a lean enterprise perspective to see that the DoD also has more facilities and inventory than it needs, or that some portions of this are no longer relevant to the defense challenges it faces. But it will take the appropriate identification of stakeholder value and the construction of robust value propositions to address these issues in a way that will best ensure the long-term delivery of value. In other words, the rationalization of existing military operations should not be approached just as a cost-cutting exercise, but must focus on value creation.

With respect to doing the right job, it is clear that national military strategy must constantly adapt to meet changing threats to national security. Military operations are no longer dominated by the massive land battles of Central Europe that drove Cold War planning. Of 253 recent US Marine Corps overseas deployments, 238 (94 percent) involved urban operations.[29] Other threats to national security have emerged. The estimated economic losses – damages and lost work time – from the 'Code Red Worm' computer virus in 2001 were about $1.2 billion, while the 'I Love You' computer virus was estimated to have caused almost $9 billion in damages in 2000.[30] Terrorism, until the September 2001 attacks on the United States, was considered a deadly nuisance but not a sufficient reason to reexamine national security policy at a fundamental level; as of this writing, some $40 billion has been legislated in direct response to the attacks on the World Trade Center and the Pentagon, and another $15 billion has been earmarked to assist US airlines in the face of lost revenues due to the attacks – thereby putting a whole new economic cost on terrorism. These are non-trivial concerns, and they illustrate the importance of lean enterprises in addressing the emerging, asymmetric threats facing the nation.

At the national level, it is not sufficient to address the government separately from defense aerospace contractors. Both are inextricably linked in defining what will be the right job. Consider the proposed acquisition of the Joint Strike Fighter. Some estimates place the eventual stream of JSF business at up to $400 billion for 4000 aircraft produced for US and international customers.[31] Clearly, this is not a contract to miss. But it is also regarded by some as the last piloted fighter aircraft the United States will

## Exploring New Paradigms for Defense Aerospace

During the Gulf War, Americans saw numerous video clips of precision-guided munitions tracking into and destroying their targets. It would have been easy to assume that there was no safe place to hide from air strikes. But years later, when NATO launched an air campaign in Kosovo, the world watched as air strikes failed to stop Serbian paramilitary units from entering ethnic Albanian villages, expelling or killing the residents, razing their houses, and then moving on to the next village. The chief problem: the targets were small, mobile, and able to hide amidst 'collateral'.

This problem is not new – coalition air forces spent considerable effort (with limited success) hunting mobile Iraqi SCUD launchers during Desert Storm. Mobile targets remain difficult to find, track, and attack safely from the air, particularly in urban environments. The challenge becomes particularly disconcerting when one considers the range of unconventional and potentially deadly threats facing the military – and society.

Given limited funding and competing interests within the government and the military itself, how should the nation approach the activities at every enterprise level that address and eventually achieve solutions to such problems? In one example, the Defense Science Board outlines 'grand challenges' that focus attention – and effort – on needed capabilities. These include: 'Bioshield' (real-time detection, characterization, response, and attribution of conventional and unconventional biological threats); 'No place to hide' (ubiquitous, intrusive, and inescapable target sensing); 'Fast Forward' (rapid, decisive US force application); and 'Cognitive C4' (agile, secure, and available computer, command, control, and communications systems).[32]

With their focus on solving pressing national security problems by identifying needed capabilities rather than specific solutions, these grand challenges provide an interesting perspective on creating a vision for value propositions at the national and international level. Support for, as well as contributions to, these capabilities could come from a broad spectrum of societal stakeholders rather than narrowly defined incumbent interests –

with the advantage that some challenges might benefit from emergent technologies with potential commercial application. Targeted government funding and policies offer the potential to encourage development of or to leverage investments in growth markets that are intrinsically attractive to investors. The far-reaching vision and potential use of emergent technologies also ensures the attraction of the best and brightest people to solve these problems – while developing the intellectual capital base needed to address future needs.

develop in the foreseeable future. Viewed in isolation as an aircraft platform, it is a dead-end business (albeit a very large one that will last for some decades to come). Recent combat experience has shown that linking individual aircraft through command and control systems, including integrated software, sensors, and communication equipment, can dramatically improve combat performance in existing systems. The application of information technology networks linking individual military platforms represents an emergent technology. But compared with the JSF, contracts for such systems may be worth only tens or hundreds of millions of dollars, possibly a few billion for very large-scale projects. In other words, the less visible systems for integration may have much greater impact relative to the investment, but they have not been given the same prominence as being 'the right job' to work on.

Without a lean enterprise value orientation, it will be hard to shift DoD-defined incentives away from the current bias toward incumbent technology (such as the piloted fighter aircraft).[33] A defense contractor would be foolhardy to ignore such a sizeable potential revenue stream. A particular revenue stream might not lead to where either the customer or its supplier needs to be to address future threats. This is a core value delivery dilemma in defense aerospace at the national enterprise level.

Looking to the future, the government faces important strategic choices in meeting national defense needs and sustaining a robust defense infrastructure. Table 10.1 illustrates three generic investment strategies which indicate different potential paths into the future.

The 'invest in present assets' strategy prioritizes current operational expenses (operations, maintenance, and keeping aircraft in the air and the troops fed) over modernization. Here there is an underlying assumption that

**TABLE 10.1** Sustaining defense capabilities to deliver value: three generic strategies

| | Invest in Present Assets | Invest in Evolution | Invest in Revolution |
|---|---|---|---|
| **Primary Activity** | Maintain and sustain the existing inventory. | Produce replacements for the current generation of technology. | Emphasize R&D for breakthrough advances in technology. |
| **Rationale** | Current technology has proven itself capable of defeating likely threats; meet immediate operational force structure needs instead. | Incremental improvements to existing systems will stay a step ahead of threats likely to emerge in coming years. | Prepare for emerging unconventional threats; address the things the military still can't do routinely from out of harm's way. |
| **Primary Beneficiaries** | Maintenance infrastructure (US government maintainers); current warfighters. | Production infrastructure (production workers, producers); investors. | Research infrastructure (engineers and scientists); public potentially benefits from technology 'spinoffs'. |
| **Primary Liabilities** | Long-term growth in maintenance costs may diminish resources available for modernization efforts. | Potential for creeping obsolescence and inability to meet emerging needs as dynamic capabilities atrophy. | Creative destruction creates casualties; usually incumbent vested interests (existing institutional stakeholders). How is future investment reconciled with meeting current needs? |
| **Primary Activities** | Operations & maintenance; Service Life Extension Programs. | 'Build-to-package'; block upgrades. | Basic and applied research; new program starts. |

US military weapon systems have dominated all recent challengers and will probably continue to dominate conventional adversaries for some time to come. At current utilization rates, the equipment can be maintained, can perhaps have its operating life increased through a service life extension program (SLEP), and can continue to be used for years to come. Using this approach, the B-52 is projected to be nearly 100 years old when it retires.

The 'invest in evolution' strategy acknowledges that current equipment is quite capable against current threats, but also recognizes that maintenance costs increase with age and that threats evolve.[34] Moreover, the industrial base must be 'kept warm' with a steady stream of business to prevent the capability to design and produce future systems from being lost. The solution to these multiple constraints is to continue to produce current designs, with incremental or evolutionary upgrades in subsystems to keep them capable against evolving threats. This is a politically robust strategy that meets a variety of existing stakeholders' needs. But it risks a steady stream of tradeoffs in which key new opportunities go unexplored.

The 'invest in revolution' strategy places priority on developing advanced or breakthrough technologies that can 'leapfrog' beyond existing systems. In the process, the nation stays well ahead of any potential threats and avoids incurring the sunk costs associated with continuing to maintain the large existing military force structure beyond its economically feasible life. This strategy also refreshes the technology and intellectual capital base for the US Aerospace Enterprise by supporting a new era of technological ferment with its attendant development and organizational growth. It requires, however, the ability to adapt value propositions constantly to emerging opportunities.

Each strategy has its strengths and weaknesses. The 'invest in present assets' option meets current needs but shortchanges the capability needed to create future systems. The 'invest in evolution' option maintains that capability, but may not produce the radical innovation necessary to address an asymmetric threat. Both play to current strengths, and are therefore vulnerable to perpetuating existing monuments. The 'invest in revolution' strategy may be very costly, offers no guarantees that a new capability will emerge (think of the billions of dollars spent on the 1980s-era 'Star Wars' program, with no fielded capability), and carries a risk of gaps in current capabilities.

While we can't predict where policymakers and other stakeholders will head in the future, we are persuaded that all three strategies depend on lean enterprise value capability. Each highlights different stakeholder values and each features distinct value propositions that require effective and efficient value delivery. The strategy may be subject to debate, but the need for lean enterprise capabilities is clear.

Implementing commercial acquisition practices or starting to use commercial processes are important first steps, but meet only part of the challenge. There are much deeper issues around the increasing gap between military and non-military technologies, and the underlying knowledge base in these two sectors. Armed conflict and military operations are among the most adaptive of social activities. This is especially troubling as modern battlefields become less and less segregated from civilian populations. How does the vast assemblage of military capabilities, interests, and infrastructure close the gap between the direction of development defined largely during the Cold War and the evolving interests of society? It is a process that will unfold over the course of years and even decades. And to begin, debates about value delivery must be reoriented to ensure appropriate value identification and robust value propositions.

For defense aerospace to operate as a lean enterprise, it must start at the earliest stages of military system lifecycles, where warfighters define their roles, missions, and ultimately the systems that will enable them to accomplish those missions. While warfighters are by nature very innovative, and have in recent years done more experimentation through 'battle labs' and advanced concept technology demonstrators, these efforts, taken at the national and international level, are largely piecemeal. They have yet to achieve the level of a new value proposition between key stakeholders.

---

### DARPA: A Model for Future Technology Advances?

Established in 1958 in response to the Soviet launch of Sputnik,[35] the DoD's Defense Advanced Research Projects Agency's primary mission is to prevent technological surprise by funding cutting-edge research in high-risk, high-payoff areas of defense technology.

Focused on national defense, its impact on the commercial sector has been phenomenal, accounting for roughly half of the major innovations that drive information technology today: the internet, the graphical user interface and mouse, networking protocols, operating systems, programming languages, semiconductor technology such as RISC and VLSI, computer graphics, and CAD. The return to society on the initial investment is on the order of 100 000 percent.[36] Many high-tech firms, including Sun Microsystems,

Silicon Graphics, and Cisco Systems, trace their roots back to DARPA projects. Wireless telecommunications relies on Gallium Arsenide semiconductor and networking technologies developed by DARPA.[37] On the military side, the DARPA legacy includes stealth aircraft and precision-guided munitions. Current efforts suggest that there are even more breakthrough technologies in the pipeline.

An engine of social and economic change, DARPA has remained effective for more than four decades by focusing on future challenges while avoiding being captured by monuments of its own making. It has a limited permanent staff, with a temporary, multidisciplinary supporting staff on each project that disbands once a project is complete, leaving the defense sector or commercial marketplace to take on further development. Most technical work is done by world-class scientists and engineers drawn from universities, corporations, and government labs. They serve as program managers on a temporary basis, refreshing both the staff and the sources of ideas every three to five years. This process is not without critics: some 85 percent of DARPA projects fail, and concern has been expressed that DARPA's focus has shifted to meeting near-term demands of military relevance.[38]

The history of DARPA highlights the high payoffs possible from developing radical new technologies away from the core demands of the enterprise. But even the most promising emergent technology may be too radical for adoption by mature organizations if it's 'not invented here'. This points to a key element in overcoming existing monuments in mature organizations: what's needed is not only a means (like DARPA) for generating radical ideas, but also an aggressive formalized process for substituting those new ideas into existing roles, missions, or markets. Markets do this naturally. Hierarchies, such as the military, must learn to do it deliberately.

In the face of these trends and our understanding of the values of the key stakeholders, there are opportunities to create convergence between the needs of warfighters and the values of the greater society. In this regard, it is the 'invest in revolution' strategy that generates the most opportunities. Here we find the potential for developing remote sensing

## Core Competencies for Value Delivery

Value delivery from a lean enterprise perspective requires several core competencies or capabilities.

- *Establishing the appropriate legal, economic, and social structure* – Creating mechanisms for regulation, investment, technical assistance, and other enablers for program and multi-program enterprises.

- *Ensuring adaptive capability* – Aligning and periodically transforming key legal, economic, physical, and social structures.

- *Extending the principles of lean value delivery* – Adapting lean principles pioneered at the program and multi-program levels to interactions at national and international levels.

technologies; for extending the ability to digest enormous volumes of information and to extract exactly what is needed; for harnessing the power of our emerging understanding of biological systems; for communicating ubiquitously across vast networks and geographies; and for other areas of technology that address pressing challenges not just to warfighters but also to many other societal stakeholders. These opportunities represent areas of technological ferment where there is not only high risk but also high payoff potential – areas that can benefit from government's role in funding development, seeding markets, and leveraging private-sector outlays. The technical workforce would benefit from new challenges and the potential to develop skills in broader demand across society. Investors would benefit mostly through the development of new growth markets and through scale production. Without a lean enterprise capability, though, each of these opportunities runs the risk of being obstructed by existing monuments, with value delivery never fully being realized.

## Summing Up

We see value in adopting a lean enterprise perspective at national and international levels. This is the key to aligning the interactions of government, industry, and other stakeholders to ensure the best uses of society's resources. Without the willingness of all parties to see themselves as part of a shared enterprise, aerospace will always be captive to partisan and piecemeal dynamics.

In urging that we think of aerospace – or any other sector, for that matter – as a national or international enterprise, we are not suggesting that there will be automatic or easy agreements among stakeholders about common views of value or concerning value propositions. Stakeholders are not 'one big happy family'. Rather, ours is a vision that urges full and creative interaction among common and competing interests across many different stakeholders. These interactions are complex and sometimes contentious. But the very process of identifying and delivering value depends on elevating the debate to an enterprise level. With value well identified and value propositions well crafted, it becomes possible to determine whether value delivery should happen primarily through market mechanisms or whether other institutional arrangements – public or private – will be required.

At the outset of this book, we observed that the nation looks to aerospace for major contributions to the achievement of four core missions. In focusing on the global movement of people and goods, we have seen the need for enterprise-level mechanisms to manage the respective roles of markets and government in enabling civil aviation and its infrastructure. In considering the global acquisition and dissemination of information and data, we have seen that some key stakeholders reside outside what we have traditionally thought of as the aerospace industry, and that this fact requires all involved to take an expanded view of the enterprise itself. In addressing national security interests, we have seen the limits of the Cold War mindset and the need for fundamental changes in infrastructure and operations to deliver value in a new era. Finally, in discussing the source of inspiration that exists when participants push the boundaries of exploration and innovation, we have identified fundamental questions about the consequences of there being limited opportunities to work on new and exciting systems.

Taken together, the lens of lean enterprise value helps us to see how value creation has become misaligned at national and international levels. Moreover, we see the potential power that resides in well-defined mechanisms for value creation at this level. In aerospace, we single out the pivotal role that can be played by government as an enterprise integrator – enacting its roles as customer, regulator, and enabler of infrastructure from a lean enterprise value perspective. But the responsibility does not reside exclusively with government. All stakeholders have key roles and responsibilities in sustaining dynamic, lean enterprise value creation at national and international levels. These implications, as we will see in the next chapter, reach to many sectors of the economy in addition to aerospace.

Our core concepts of 'lean', 'enterprise', and 'value' provide powerful levers by which a mature industry can uncover and capture hidden potential, and embark on a path of continual renewal. The core missions motivating aerospace will never be routine, and nor will the industry that is dedicated to these missions – provided that it maintains its focus on creating lean enterprise value.

## CHAPTER 11

# Future Value

Every industry and sector of the economy has its core missions – ways in which it affects the operation, stability, and future potential of society. For aerospace, those core missions involve the global movement of people and goods, the global acquisition and dissemination of information and data, advancing national security interests, and providing a source of inspiration by pushing the boundaries of exploration and innovation. In every case, whether for aerospace or some other sector, future success in fulfilling core missions depends on establishing the capability to deliver lean enterprise value on a consistent basis.

Nearly every sector of the US and many other national economies also features a broad range of improvement initiatives – some linked to lean principles and practices and some tied to other, related concepts concerned with quality and continuous improvement. In each case, there is the risk that improvement efforts will become dominated by a narrow, cost-cutting mindset. The experience in aerospace highlights the importance of a broader focus on the identification and delivery of value across key stakeholders in a defined enterprise.

Building on our insights from aerospace, we illustrate here the broader applicability of our framework. As we review the five principles of lean enterprise value we introduced in Chapter 1, we suggest ways that they apply in industries as diverse as pharmaceuticals, automobiles, personal computers, and steel.[1] Of necessity, this is a high-level analysis, focusing on broad trends in these sectors. But not only does it help to illustrate the framework, it also reveals the interconnected nature of the five guiding principles and a challenge that faces all sectors and all industries – creating future value.

## Five Guiding Principles for Lean Enterprise Value

Rooted in nearly a decade of research, our five principles of lean enterprise value provide an orientation for any enterprise – whether at the program level, the corporate or government-agency (that is, multi-program) level, or even the national and international level. In introducing the five principles in Chapter 1, we defined the term 'lean' as 'eliminating waste with the goal of creating value'. The link between 'lean' and 'value' is not new, yet we found many aerospace facilities and enterprises where systematic efforts to eliminate waste were *not* linked to an equally systematic focus on creating value. Even the use of value stream mapping as a tool has too often become an effort to find areas of excessive cost, which is but one dimension of value. We use the term 'lean value' to get past the baggage that has become associated with the word 'lean' in too many settings.

The importance of shifting the focus to 'lean value' is not limited to aerospace. For example, although lean concepts are now on the agenda of virtually every auto company, many plants and organizations continue to focus narrowly on cost-cutting versions of lean. Preliminary results from the third worldwide automotive assembly plant study by MIT's International Motor Vehicle Program (IMVP) suggests that car and truck assembly plants have split into two groups.[2] One set of plants reports continuous progress in improving quality and reducing cost. The second set seems to be reducing cost at the expense of quality. The initial interpretation of these IMVP results is that they directly reflect the divergent outcomes associated, on the one hand, with a narrow cost-cutting interpretation of lean, and, on the other hand, with a broader focus on creating value.

Building on the importance of creating value, our first principle restates a simple truth:

---

### *Principle 1*

#### CREATE LEAN VALUE BY DOING THE JOB RIGHT
#### *AND* BY DOING THE RIGHT JOB

---

This may seem simple, but we find many aerospace facilities that devote considerable resources to improving 'flow' along a value stream without being equally systematic in asking whether it is the right value stream. Closer examination reveals just how much value can be derived from asking the 'upstream' questions. It is a difficult task, but necessary.

The importance and the difficulty of 'doing the job right' and 'doing the right job' can be found, for example, in the pharmaceutical industry. Here is a highly regulated, complex industry where value has historically been centered on the ability of research and development labs to patent new medications, and on the ability of marketing functions to promote the innovations. The expiration of an entire generation of patents has created the need to search for new products and services, generating hard questions about the second part of our first principle – doing the right job. At the same time, enabling legislation in the form of the Waxman-Hatch Act[3] and other factors have given rise to makers of generic drugs which generate value primarily through manufacturing efficiencies, raising difficult questions about the first part of the principle – doing the job right. Moreover, the emergence of biochemistry as a field and the ability to create new, synthetic chemical entities has opened up entirely new ways to research and produce medicine (involving both aspects of Principle 1).[4] Most traditional pharmaceutical companies today face hard choices around allocating resources to finding new products, improving manufacturing process efficiencies, and shifting to new biochemical methods. While these choices are rarely framed as *interconnected* aspects of achieving *lean value*, it would be a great mistake for this industry to approach the challenges in a piecemeal fashion.

In the personal computer industry, we have witnessed more than a decade of stunning success associated with 'doing the job right'. Gains in microprocessor speeds continue at an extraordinary pace, enabling the use of new generations of software and new applications for PCs – in many respects, the equivalent of the 'Higher, Faster, Farther' mantra in aerospace. While yet further gains in the speed of computer chips are likely, they may not translate into substantially increased value for most home and business users. In addition, there is a growing migration of software products and applications to the internet, which may further erode the value associated with gains in chip speed.

How is the industry responding? Many firms, reflecting a classic maturity dynamic, are focusing on cost cutting and efficiency gains. There are even firms exploring ways of operating as semi-virtual businesses – without their own fabrication operations – as a way to improve efficiencies.[5] However, replacing 'faster is better' with 'cheaper is better' doesn't fully engage the deeper value issues associated with doing the right job.

What would it be like to work in an organization that embraces our first principle? To start, there would be an open flow of information around strategic business decisions aimed at doing the right job, as well as information on continuous improvement efforts aimed at doing the job right. Similarly, there would be shared visions centered on both aspects, and clear ways for all employees to contribute. Our idea may seem basic, but we are astounded by how few large or medium-size organizations attempt to apply this principle in any other than a piecemeal, disconnected way.

Our three-phase model for value creation is also deceptively simple. It is easy to state the three phases – identify value, construct a value proposition, and deliver value – but actually establishing the systematic disciplines to do each of these is a great challenge.

## *Principle 2*

### DELIVER VALUE ONLY AFTER IDENTIFYING STAKEHOLDER VALUE AND CONSTRUCTING ROBUST VALUE PROPOSITIONS

The successful delivery of value is possible only when based on the answers to these questions: Who are the key stakeholders? Have we identified value for each? Was the value proposition properly constructed?

The importance of these questions reaches well beyond aerospace. The emergence of personal computers, for example, reflected the identification of new forms of value, which then required very different value propositions among customers, manufacturers, and suppliers, as well as new forms of value delivery. IBM's early lead in developing the personal computer was challenged by new approaches to value identification by Apple, Microsoft, and others. Dell Computer Corp., among others, redefined value delivery. Now, value propositions linking multiple stakeholders are emerging as a core source of competitive advantage for e-business initiatives on the internet. Indeed, the voice of the consumer, magnified through the internet, might even be characterized as a co-producer in value identification.

Our approach to value creation also has implications for government operations beyond the defense aerospace sector. Consider the experience with government deregulation over the past few decades – from telecommunications to airlines to banking to trucking[6] to energy. In each case, the logic in Congressional debates focused narrowly on two stakeholders – customers and producers. The identification of value to other stakeholders (such as the workforce and the suppliers) was reduced to ideological views that the 'market' would serve their interests. While there is continuing public debate on the degree to which deregulation has served society, it is very clear that there have been substantial, unanticipated, and devastating consequences for some stakeholders. This illustrates the necessity of taking into account the interests of *all* stakeholders if a value proposition – in this case, for deregulation – is to be viable in the future.

Elevating the focus to the enterprise level is another deceptively simple principle. The importance of avoiding 'chimneys' or other forms of suboptimization is not new. Yet most improvement efforts are limited to a particular part of an enterprise – such as manufacturing or product development or sales and marketing. Further, such efforts are often conducted as isolated '*kaizen* events' which may produce measurable savings, but which may not generate needed systems change. Even where significant gains are made, these often prove vulnerable to leadership turnover.

The challenge here lies in the fact that most organizations do not fully operate at the enterprise level. As a result, leaders must first assert the very *existence* of 'enterprise' – creating enterprise-level structures, strategies, and processes – in order to realize lean value fully.

## *Principle 3*
### FULLY REALIZE LEAN VALUE ONLY BY ADOPTING
### AN ENTERPRISE PERSPECTIVE

Retail banking, which faces the challenge of rising above piecemeal solutions to take an enterprise perspective, provides us with a telling illustration. This industry has invested heavily in information technology to automate 'back office' functions such as check processing, and today offers an ever-growing set of financial services to customers through existing and new service delivery systems such as PC banking.[7] But the proliferation of services offered has come at a significant additional cost, and implementation has been highly variable across branch office operations. Here is a sector that stands to benefit considerably from adopting an enterprise perspective.

Healthcare is an industry where we find what might be considered a *partial* enterprise structure emerging. The rise of health maintenance organizations and other managed care structures represents the creation of enterprise connections among what were previously more decentralized operations. However, shareholder interests – with comparatively less representation of patient and workforce interests – continue to be the dominant focus of value creation.

Interestingly, while the auto industry pioneered concepts of lean production, the drive to the enterprise level is no more advanced in the US auto sector than in US aerospace. US auto companies are just beginning to structure responsibilities across enterprise value streams and to address the enterprise infrastructure needed to support lean transformation. Of course, creating these new structures is only a first step. The establishment of enterprise-level patterns of interaction and of lean enterprise mindsets remains a significant challenge across most automotive companies. In particular, there is a need to create the enterprise-level infrastructure that can sustain lean transformation even as leadership changes.

Addressing interdependencies across enterprise levels is *not* a deceptively simple proposition: this is a complex idea from the outset. Experience in aerospace teaches that any program enterprise depends on the supportive systems – social and technical – that reside at the multi-program enterprise level. This is as true for a government agency as it is for a corporation. Indeed, we particularly highlight the importance of attending to these interdependencies in government operations.

## *Principle 4*
### ADDRESS THE INTERDEPENDENCIES ACROSS ENTERPRISE
### LEVELS TO INCREASE LEAN VALUE

The institutional infrastructure and other enablers at national and international levels are essential to the long-term vitality of any sector of the economy. Market solutions may be the most efficient, but markets rarely function perfectly and imperfections can increase over time. The construction of value propositions that address what economists call 'externalities' and other market imperfections frequently requires government intervention, or attention through other institutional mechanisms.

We see the importance of connections from the program level to the multi-program level in, for example, the case of consumer power tools. In this sector, legislation requiring double insulation in all power tools changed the enterprise environment. This meant the redesign of entire product lines. Had the focus been only at the level of the product line – what we have termed the program level – this could have led to enormously increased costs.

Black & Decker, though, responded with a fundamental reexamination of its manufacturing and product development functions. The company created a standard platform for the design of all its products, with common motors, ergonomic features, and other advantages – all supported by a new integrated organizational structure under a single vice president of operations. In this case, there was linkage across *levels* by connecting individual product lines at the multi-program level, and linkage across *functions* by connecting manufacturing, product development, and marketing. The results were a *reduction* in the price of the products (reflecting new efficiencies across product lines) combined with significant gains in the marketplace, which ultimately established this integrated product line approach as a new standard for consumer power tools.

Connecting multi-program enterprises at national and international levels is more complicated, but the impact can be just as far-reaching. Consider the experience with the ISO 9000 quality standards, which have become a global baseline for companies establishing internal supplier certification programs, and have also become an initial benchmark for continuous improvement efforts. These quality standards, developed by the International Standards Organization,[8] have become a valued part of the infrastructure for many sectors of the economy. The standards began as a European effort to facilitate trade as part of an integrated European economy. The global nature of markets soon drove the application of this standard in North America, the Far East, and other parts of the world. The standard has evolved to include ISO 9001 and other iterations, as well as a companion array of environmental standards beginning with ISO 14000. The establishment and evolution of these standards can be understood as national- and international-level value propositions that facilitate interactions at the program and multi-program enterprise levels.

The US steel industry affords an instructive look at crisis, success, and continuing challenge: one that illustrates not only the importance of our first three lean enterprise principles, but also the necessity of adopting our fourth principle. In the 1980s, the steel industry declined from its status as a global industrial powerhouse, long considered one of the largest, most modern, and most efficient in the world, and became a leading cause for concern highlighted in the *Made in America* call to action.[9] Foreign competitors demonstrated dramatic new efficiencies through a combination of new technology and process improvements – all gains in doing the job right. Then, the rise of so-called mini-mills and other specialty producers in the United States demonstrated the gains possible through new approaches to doing the job right *and* doing the right job.[10]

During the past decade, many of the industry's integrated steel producers have successfully restructured their organizations and operations. They have also achieved technological innovation through more effective management of R&D resources, process improvements, and acquisition of technology from suppliers, customers, and even competitors – all gains from operating at the enterprise level. As a result, the industry has become considerably more competitive and profitable.[11] Yet, the devastating effects of a recent global decline in demand suggests that the steel industry will require deeper attention to interdependencies at national and international levels, and that the journey to creating lean enterprise value will require yet more fundamental changes in this sector.

Our final principle is the key to unlocking the potential in adopting all of the others. Too much of the literature on lean and other system change initiatives focuses on new processes and procedures, with insufficient attention paid to the pivotal and fragile dynamics involved when people fully embrace and drive a dynamic mix of continuous improvement and quantum leaps in innovation. As we have noted earlier, this reaches far beyond statements proclaiming people as the most valuable resource. It involves establishing mechanisms to appreciate and develop knowledge and capability properly, and across an entire workforce.[12]

## *Principle 5*
### PEOPLE, NOT JUST PROCESSES, EFFECTUATE LEAN VALUE

MIT-based researchers highlighted the 'neglect of human resources' more than a decade ago, citing it as an underlying cause of US industrial weaknesses. Rejecting the notion that Americans had somehow lost their work ethic, the researchers found fault with many of 'the institutions that educate Americans for work'.[13] As we have seen from the aerospace experience, the challenge reaches well beyond educational institutions to encompass the broad range of workplace and societal institutions needed to attract, to retain, and to develop a 21st-century workforce.

The economic impact of innovative human resource practices has been well documented in many sectors of the economy. It is increasingly clear that piecemeal innovations have little impact, but that integrated 'bundles' of practices can have dramatic impacts on cost, quality, schedule, and so on.[14] Within a lean enterprise value framework, these bundles of practices represent enterprise-level mechanisms to enable the contribution of people to creating lean enterprise value.

Our experience through MIT's Lean Aerospace Initiative is of mechanisms that can engage people across many different organizations. A sense of shared vision and mission has been fostered by the networks of people on various collaborative research and implementation teams, combined with executive leadership groups and participants at various public events. A study that we commissioned with a noted organizational culture expert found that the consortium structure – as a learning network – promotes new forms of interaction by bringing together powerful combinations of customers and suppliers, workers and managers, scientists and government officials, and even direct competitors.[15]

The study also identified a continuing need to bridge highly different perspectives and expectations in order to realize fully the value made possible by the consortium structure. Academia often concentrates on data collection and analysis; industry members are more interested in implementation toolkits or 'how to' guides; and government members, with their contractual mindsets, are most concerned with program deliverables, schedule, and cost reduction. Forging a structure and a method of operation that engage each member group is essential to delivering value to all. The matching of expectations to capabilities among all stakeholders is a lesson that applies at any level of enterprise.

Powerful as these forms of interaction are in generating value, we have seen the frustration that arises when they run up against monuments, misalignments, and other barriers. Motivating this book has been our excitement in new insights about lean enterprise value, combined with a sense of urgency about enabling people at all levels to put these insights into practice.

## Conclusion

The fundamental natures of markets and work are changing. In a global, knowledge-driven economy, interdependence is on the rise. This creates new opportunities and new sources of tension among stakeholders. In aerospace and in other sectors of the economy, the capability to create lean enterprise value holds the key both to pursuing these new opportunities and to addressing these emerging tensions.

The transformation to lean enterprise value is not happening all at once, but it is under way. Financial markets that welcomed successive rounds of corporate downsizing a few years ago are now asking tougher questions about the impact of such cuts on corporate capability. Manufacturers and suppliers that previously engaged in arm's-length competitive struggles are now exploring long-term strategic partnerships. Unions and employers are joining together to establish high-performance work systems. In these situations, difficult decisions about eliminating waste do not go away, but the value driving such decisions has the potential to provide greater focus.

Looking ahead, we see ever more clearly the importance of properly identifying value for all relevant stakeholders, constructing robust value propositions, and consistently delivering value to multiple stakeholders. For aerospace and other sectors of the economy, success depends, in critical ways, on creating lean enterprise value – not just for today, but with a commitment to creating future value for generations yet to come.

# PART IV

## Appendices

Appendices

# Lean Aerospace Initiative Member Organizations (October 2001)

## Airframe

Boeing Commercial Airplane Group
Boeing Military Aircraft & Missile Systems Group
Boeing Phantom Works
Lockheed Martin Aeronautics Company
Northrop Grumman Integrated Systems
Raytheon Aircraft Company
Sikorsky Aircraft Corporation

## Avionics/Electronics

BAE Systems North America
Northrop Grumman Electronic Systems
Raytheon Company
Raytheon Systems Company
Rockwell Collins, Inc.
Textron Systems Division

## Propulsion, Power Systems and Controls

Curtiss-Wright Flight Systems, Inc.
Hamilton Sundstrand Corporation
Parker Aerospace
Pratt & Whitney Military Engines
Pratt & Whitney Space Propulsion
Rolls-Royce North America, Incorporate

## Space

Boeing Space and Communications Systems Group
GenCorp Aerojet
Lockheed Martin Missiles & Space
Northrop Grumman Electronic Space Systems
Spectrum Astro, Incorporated
TRW Space & Electronics Group

## US Air Force

Aeronautical Systems Center
Air Force Research Laboratory, Materials and Manufacturing
   Directorate, Manufacturing Technology Division
Space and Missile Systems Center
Electronics Systems Center
Secretary of the Air Force, Office of the Assistant Secretary for
   Acquisition
F-22 System Program Office
Joint Strike Fighter Joint Program Office
C-17 System Program Office
Flight Training System Program Office – Joint Primary Aircraft Training
   System

## Other Government Entities

US Department of the Navy, Naval Air Systems Command
US Department of the Army, Aviation and Missile Command
US Department of Defense, Office of the Under Secretary for
   Acquisition, Technology & Logistics
Defense Contract Management Agency
National Reconnaissance Office
US National Aeronautics and Astronautics Administration

## Invited Participants – Labor

International Association of Machinists and Aerospace Workers

United Auto Workers – International Union of Automobile, Aerospace and Agricultural Implement Workers of America

## Invited Participants – Industry and Government

US Department of Defense, Ballistic Missile Defense Office
Defense Systems Management College
Institute for Defense Analyses
Aerospace Industries Association

# APPENDIX B

## LAI Supported Students Completing Theses

Eric Achtmann
Lt. Comdr. Mike Anderson (USCG)
Michelle Antonelli
Michelle Bakkila
Joshua Bernstein
William Blake
Tyson Browning
Ernest Campbell
Jim Chase
Cynthia Cook
Stacey Cowap
Lt. Steve Czerwonka (USCG)
Sawan Deshpande
2nd Lt. Dan Dobbs (USAFR)
Basak Ertan
Pradeep Fernandes
Capt. David Ferris (USAF)
John Hoppes
Alex Hou
Christina Houlahan
Ted Hsu
Brian Ippolito
Marm Kilpatrick
David Lackner
Malee Lucas
Frederic Mahoue
Capt. Ross McNutt (USAF)
Jose Menendez

2nd Lt. Rich Millard (USAF)
Sean Morgan
Jeffrey Munson
2nd Lt. Matt Nuffort (USAF)
Rocco Paduano
Andrew Parris
Rob Perrons
Renata Pomponi
Mike Pozsar
Mitch Quint
Luis Ramirez-de-Arellano
Vicente Reynal
Marco Roman
Jim Schoonmaker
Alexis Stanke
David Steare
Todd Stout
Abhinav Taneja
Melissa Tata
David Tonaszuck
Khusrow Uzair
2nd Lt. Mandy Vaughn (USAF)
Myles Walton
Andrew Wang
Annalisa Weigel
2nd Lt. Loren Werner (USAF)
Capt. Rob Wirthlin (USAF)
Capt. Brandon Wood (USAF)

## Other Graduate Students Participating in LAI

Domenick Bertelli
Henrik Bresman
2nd Lt. Carmen Carreras (USAF)
Gary Crichlow
Lt. Col. Rob Dare (USAF)
Heidi Davidz
Marisi Dennis
Jason Derleth
Boback Ferdowsi
Bethany Foch
Maj. Chris Forseth (USAF)
Steve Frey
Cory Hallam

Sean Hitchings
Sandra Kassin-Deardorff
Angie Kelic
Aaron Kirtley
Jacob Markish
Dina Mayzlin
Michelle McVey
Rhonda Salzman
Joshua Schuler
Nirav Shah
Larry Siegel
Justin Talbot-Stern

## Other Graduate Students Whose Theses have Contributed to LAI

Geoff Andrew
Michelle Beckert
Mike Bravo
Colleen Charles
Tim Cunningham
Donna Doane
David Driscoll
James Falco
Samuel Garbo
Eugene Hamacher
Christopher Hernandez
Gregory Herweg
James Koonmen
Ramakrishna Mantripragada

Patrick Maurer
Angela Negron
Karl Pilon
James Robbins
Richard Rosson
Hope Rubin
Parag Shah
Leon Silva
Robert Slack
Eric Sorenson
Susan Spencer
Paul Thompson
Yu Feng Wei

# Notes

## Chapter 1

1 J. P. Womack, D. T. Jones, and D. Roos, *The Machine That Changed The World: The Story of Lean Production* (New York: Rawson Associates, 1990).

2 General M. A. McPeak, 'Ensuring Technology Preeminence of the US Air and Space Forces', Presentation at the Air Force Chief Scientists Group Dinner, Andrews Air Force Base, MD (January 5th, 1994).

3 J. P. Womack and D. T. Jones, *Lean Thinking* (New York: Simon & Schuster, 1996).

4 The idea of constructing a theory often sounds abstract and may be seen as separate from practical realities. In fact, a sound theory can be both useful and accessible – far more valuable than simple exhortations to 'turn things around'. In this section of the chapter, we outline principles that we use as touchstones throughout the book. While not a full theory, these principles have the potential to serve as steps in that direction.

5 A. de Saint-Éxupéry, *Citadelle (The Wisdom of the Sands)* (Paris: Gallimard, 1948).

6 J. Utterback, *Mastering the Dynamics of Innovation* (Boston: Harvard Business School Press, 1996).

7 W. K. Clark, *Waging Modern War: Bosnia, Kosovo and the Future of Combat* (New York: PublicAffairs, 2001).

8 This began with the 1915 founding of the National Advisory Committee for Aeronautics (NACA), the predecessor agency to the National Aeronautics and Space Administration (NASA).

9 MIT Labor Aerospace Research Agenda, 'The 21st Century Aerospace Workforce', Presentation to the LAI Executive Board (May 2001).

10 These numbers are based on an analysis by the strategic resources department of the International Association of Machinists and Aerospace Workers.

11 Booz·Allen, Hamilton, 1999 study cited in 'The New Industrial Reality: Ensuring America's Future National Security. DoD Briefing (May 2000).

12 Utterback (1996).

13 Named for former US Secretary of Commerce Malcolm Baldrige, the award was established in 1987 to recognize excellence by US organizations in improving national competitiveness.

## Chapter 2

1 S. Weiss and A. Amir, 'The Aerospace Industry', in *Encyclopedia Britannica* (Chicago: Encyclopedia Britannica, 1999). This article was a source for a number of historical facts used in the preparation of this chapter.

2 The plane was grounded after one year of service due to catastrophic flight failures, but returned to commercial operations in 1958 after improvements in fuselage resistance to metal fatigue.

3 As a percentage of GDP, however, defense expenditures have declined from a Korean War level of 10 percent to the present 3 percent.

4 W. A. McDougall, *The Heavens and the Earth: A Political History of the Space Age* (New York: Basic Books, 1985).

5 B. R. Rich and L. Janos, *Skunk Works* (Boston: Little, Brown & Co., 1994).

6 The CAB and CAA were the predecessors of today's Federal Aviation Administration.

7 Rich and Janos (1994), pp. 51–3.

8 Aerospace Industries Association, *Aerospace Facts and Figures 1999/2000* (Los Angeles: Aero Publishers, 2000).

9 AT&T developed the first active communications satellite, while Hughes was concurrently developing a geosynchronous satellite that became the model for Comsat.

10 R. McNutt, 'Reducing DoD Product Development Time: The Role of the Schedule Development Process', PhD dissertation, MIT (1999).

11 National Research Council, *Funding a Revolution: Government Support for Computing Research* (Washington, DC: National Academy Press, 1999).

12 Hitch, who served as the DoD's comptroller under McNamara, was the principal developer of PPBS. One present author recalls seeing huge charts on Pentagon walls diagramming the PPBS process, bearing titles such as 'Charlie Hitch's Wonderful Ice Cream Machine'.

13 'Payload fraction' is the fraction of the total weight of an airplane that can be devoted to 'useful' purposes such as passengers, baggage, or freight. Supersonic aircraft have higher drag than do subsonic aircraft – such as the 747 – and hence burn more fuel per mile. This makes SSTs more expensive to operate and also reduces the percentage of the total weight available for useful purposes.

14 J. Costello, *The Concorde Conspiracy* (New York: Scribner, 1976).

15 Airbus Industrie was originally formed in 1970 as a *groupement d'intérêt économique* (GIE) under French law. So-called 'economic interest groups' make possible the cooperation of various firms in the areas of research, buying and selling, and production. This legal framework enabled the consortium's member companies to focus on the Airbus joint effort as a group, while allowing them to pursue other non-competing projects independently.

16 Based on US Government Accounting Office, 'General Aviation: Status of the Industry, Related Infrastructure, and Safety Issues', GAO-01-916 (August 2001).

17 R. D. Launius and H. E. McCurdy, *Spaceflight and the Myth of Presidential Leadership* (Urbana, IL: University of Illinois Press, 1997).

18 Committee on Armed Services, House of Representatives, Hon. Les Aspin, Chairman, 'Operation Desert Storm Examined: Conduct of the War in Southwest Asia', Interim Report (Washington, DC: 1992).

19 Aspin (1992).

## Chapter 3

1 Utterback (1996) – see *Note 6, Chapter 1*.

2 We are introducing here an analysis based on the industry as a whole, and the figure includes firms making all aerospace products, including aircraft, spacecraft, launch systems, engines, and avionics. The evolution of each *individual* component of the aerospace industry may be different, and we leave that analysis to future research studies.

3 M. L. Tushman and P. Anderson, in 'Technological Discontinuities and Organizational Environments', *Administrative Science Quarterly* **31** (1986), 439–65, distinguish between competency-destroying and competency-enhancing discontinuities – that is, those changes that destroy and make obsolete the current way of producing a product versus those changes that do not destroy competency but that innovate and improve on existing competencies.

4 Since the late 1980s, there have been several 'wakeup calls' regarding a US manufacturing crisis, including in aerospace. For a seminal example, see M. L. Dertouzos, R. K. Lester, R. M.

Solow, and the MIT Commission on Industrial Productivity, *Made in America: Regaining the Productive Edge* (Cambridge, MA: The MIT Press, 1989).

5 In civil aviation, *only* small, innovative companies have been making planes, often classifying them as experimental to avoid liability problems (see Chapter 2). Recent changes in the law have spurred growth due both to pent-up demand and to accumulated innovations.

6 P. P. Shah, 'Network Destruction: The Structural Implications of Downsizing', *Academy of Management Journal* **43**:1 (February 2000), 101–12; R. Dewitt, 'Firm, Industry, and Strategy Influences on Choice of Downsizing Approach', *Strategic Management Journal* **19**:1 (January 1998), 59; W. F. Cascio, C. E. Young, and J. R. Morris, 'Financial Consequences of Employment-Change Decisions in Major US Corporations', *Academy of Management Journal* **40**:5 (October 1997), 1175–90.

7 S. R. Fisher, 'Downsizing in a Learning Organization: Are There Hidden Costs?', *The Academy of Management Review* **25**:1 (2000), 244–52.

8 W. B. Scott, 'People Issues are Cracks in Aero Industry Foundation', *Aviation Week & Space Technology* (June 21st, 1999), 65.

9 W. B. Scott, 'Launch Failures Cripple US Space Prowess', *Aviation Week & Space Technology* (May 3rd, 1999), 32.

10 J. Klein, Presentation to the Lean Aircraft Initiative Plenary Workshop on 'Continuous Improvement and Job Security', MIT Sloan School of Management (December 12th, 1995).

11 See comments in two books: M. Hammer, *Beyond Reengineering: How the Process-Centered Organization is Changing Our Work and Our Lives* (New York: HarperBusiness, 1996); and M. Hammer, *The Agenda: What Every Business Must Do to Dominate the Decade* (New York: Random House/Crown Business, 2001). In the latter, Hammer opens with a reflective look at his past 'take-no-prisoners, burn-it-down-and-start-over approach to making businesses better', and states: 'I was wrong.' Still committed to dramatic change, he notes that there is no single solution, and that there are significant considerations around what we term 'intellectual capital'.

12 Often, the motivation has been to reduce costs or save resources by offloading operations, functions, and activities previously performed in-house.

13 In 1989, the Chrysler Corporation initiated a new method of working with suppliers: the company would choose suppliers early on and give them significant, if not total, design responsibility. See J. H. Dyer, 'How Chrysler Created an American Keiretsu', *Harvard Business Review* (July–August 1996), 5. The delegation of greater responsibility to key suppliers with increased accountability resulted in improved on-time delivery, higher quality, and significant cost reductions.

14 W. Stowers, Presentation at the Boeing Suppliers Conference, Seattle, Washington (October 1st, 1998). Stower is Vice President, Procurement, Boeing Military Aircraft and Missiles Systems.

15 C. H. Fine, *Clockspeed: Winning Industry Control in the Age of Temporary Advantage* (Reading, MA: Perseus Books, 1998), p. 69.

16 Fine (1998), p. 163.

17 The Joint Direct Attack Munition (JDAM) program, for instance, reduced the number of military specifications from 87 to zero and cut procurement costs by 50 percent (Chapter 5 details other improvements). There were also notable successes in the Joint Primary Aircraft Training System (JPATS) and the Commercial Derivative Engine (CDE). See Pilot Program Consulting Group, 'Compendium of Pilot Program Reports' (1997) and 'Defense Reform Performance: Affordable Defense for the 21st Century' (April 1999), available at http://www.acq.osd.mil, the website of the Deputy Under Secretary of Defense for Acquisition Reform.

18 MILSPECs are themselves a monument – a collection of specifications used for designing and procuring military hardware that were vital to standardizing and assuring quality in wartime, and useful in the Cold War for the same reasons, but which now stifle innovation and drive up costs. They are not discussed at length in this chapter because they represent a monument that has been tackled: their mandatory use has been removed from the procurement rules.

19 Department of Defense, Memorandum from the Under Secretary of Defense, Acquisition and Technology (June 3rd, 1998). ISO 9000, which has become the internationally accepted system of rating quality management and assurance, refers to a series of quality standards established by the International Standards Organization (ISO) based in Geneva, Switzerland.

20 D. S. Goldin, Statement before the US Senate Subcommittee on Science, Technology, and Space of the Committee on Commerce, Science, and Transportation (March 22nd, 2000). Goldin is the NASA Administrator.

21 Mars Climate Orbiter Mishap Investigation Board, 'Report on Project Management in NASA' (March 13th, 2000).

22 K. Lewin, *Field Theory in Social Sciences* (New York: Harper & Row, 1951).

23 E. A. Cohen, 'Defending America in the Twenty-first Century', *Foreign Affairs* **79**:6 (November/December 2000), 40–56. Cohen writes, 'Following the logic of the so-called Bottom-Up Review of the early Clinton administration and then the 1997 Quadrennial Defense Review, American forces now aim at fighting two "Major Theater Wars" (MTWs) – presumably against North Korea and Iraq. ... The two-MTW strategy requires almost the same force structure as did the Base Force; a dispassionate observer would be hard-pressed to see much difference between the two. And neither strategy suffices today.' The 'Base Force' to which Cohen refers is the force planned in 1989–90 as a cautious post-Cold War force, somewhat smaller than the peak Cold War force, but with similar structures – in Cohen's words, 'a stopgap to remain until the Russian threat was clearly gone'.

24 M. Duffy, 'Rumsfeld: Older But Wiser?', *Time* (August 27th, 2001), 22.

25 In this context, 'defense programs' includes everything from weapons to software to field rations.

26 McNutt (1999) – see Note 10, Chapter 2. McNutt used the following source: J. M. Jarvaise, J. A. Drezner, and D. Norton, *The Defense System Cost Performance Database: Cost Growth Analysis Using Selected Acquisition Reports* (Santa Monica, CA: The RAND Corporation, 1996), MR-625-OSD. The data were current as of December 1994.

27 This business unit was sold to Boeing and is now Boeing Space and Communications Group.

28 This business model is described in more detail in Chapter 9.

29 Professor Charles H. Fine describes this type of amplification of business cycles as the 'bullwhip effect'; it is seen in many industries, but is particularly severe in commercial transport aircraft. See Fine (1998) – Note 15, Chapter 3.

30 J. P. Womack, 'Working Toward Hassle-Free Solutions', *Aviation Week & Space Technology* (January 1st, 2000), 52.

31 BRAC commissions are referred to by the year in which they were constituted. There have been four as of this writing: in 1983, 1991, 1993, and 1995. They have included representatives from members of each of the armed services, who made recommendations to the Secretary of Defense on base closures. The Secretary determined what list to send to Congress via the President. Congress was then empowered to accept or reject the complete list. This process was designed and initiated to insulate Congress and the White House from the political issues that might be construed from closing any particular base.

32 Dr William Ballhaus, Lockheed Martin's corporate Vice President For Science and Engineering, in an interview for the MIT Department of Aeronautics and Astronautics 1999

strategic plan: 'The engineering workplace has changed. The context for engineering has changed. Graduates must be able to adapt to the dramatic shift in the industrial working environment with: 1) a good grasp of engineering science fundamentals; 2) a good understanding of the design and manufacturing process; 3) a multi-disciplinary system perspective; 4) ability to think both critically and creatively; 5) flexibility and ability to adapt to rapid/major change; 6) curiosity and a desire to learn – for life; and 7) a profound understanding of the importance of teamwork.' *See also:* The Boeing Company, 'Desired Attributes of an Engineer: Participation with Universities' (1996), at http://www.boeing.com/companyoffices/pwu/attributes/attributes.html.

33  Accreditation Board of Engineering and Technology (ABET), *Criteria for Accrediting Engineering Programs: Effective for Evaluations During the 2000–2001 Accreditation Cycle* (Revised March 2000); MIT School of Engineering Committee on Undergraduate Education, 'Eight Goals of an Undergraduate Education' (Cambridge, MA: 1998); E. F. Crawley, 'The CDIO Syllabus: A Statement of Goals for Undergraduate Engineering Education' (Cambridge, MA: MIT CDIO Report #1, January 2001).

34  Sometimes workers recognize a monument – and the need to address misalignment – well in advance of management. It was the US labor movement that urged the government to adopt a strategic approach to 'defense conversion' more than a decade before the end of the Cold War. That voice, though, went unheard. See International Association of Machinists and Aerospace Workers, 'Defense Conversion Adjustment Demonstration Program', Narrative Report to the US Department of Labor, ETA (January 1st–April 30th, 1994), Grant No. Q-4058-33-00-87-60.

35  It's worth noting that several large facilities have been reduced drastically not because of a rational assessment of whether they might still be needed, but because the real estate they sat on became very valuable. For example, Lockheed sold its Burbank, California, property, which included an airport. And in the Silicon Valley, Lockheed sold large portions of its Sunnyvale, California, property. The buildings were demolished to make room for an e-business industrial park.

36  Briefly stated, value-based designs are those that maximize stakeholder utility for minimum resources, without early overspecification of requirements.

37  D. Patillo, *Pushing the Envelope: The American Aircraft Industry* (Ann Arbor, MI: The University of Michigan Press, 1998).

38  The $600 hammer was immortalized in the 'Hammer Awards' given out as part of then Vice President Al Gore's 'Reinventing Government' program to reward government waste-cutters. There have been some analyses suggesting that the $600 hammer is a myth. Rather, according to these analyses, a $15 hammer purchased as part of a bulk Pentagon acquisition of spare parts was recorded in the accounting system as one item along with hundreds of dollars of 'overhead'.

39  To the historical cost of production, the military buyer adds an arbitrary additional percentage of profit. This intrinsically limits the return available to the contractor. Program budgets are reviewed and budgeted on an annual basis. If an annual review is based on historical cost, any cost reductions become the new cost basis and profits are reduced proportionately. Consequently, there are few incentives for suppliers to invest in cost reduction, and little likelihood that cost reduction will become a significant source of increased profits that will attract investor interest.

40  L. Thurow, in *Building Wealth: The New Rules for Individuals, Companies and Nations in a Knowledge-Based Economy* (New York: HarperCollins, 1999), identifies the ability to accept risk as a key advantage that has reestablished the United States as the world's economic leader.

## Chapter 4

1 T. Ohno, *Toyota Production System: Beyond Large-Scale Production* (Portland, OR: Productivity Press, 1988), p.3.

2 M. Imai, *KAIZEN: The Key to Japan's Competitive Success* (New York: McGraw-Hill, 1986), p.1; W. E. Deming, *Out of the Crisis* (Cambridge, MA: Center for Advanced Engineering Study, 1987), 7th edn (originally published in 1982); J. Juran et al., *Juran's Quality Handbook*, 5th edn (New York: McGraw-Hill Professional Book Group, 1999).

3 Imai (1986).

4 Y. Monden, *Toyota Production System: An Integrated Approach to Just-in-Time* (Norcross, GA: Engineering & Management Press, 1988), 3rd edn, p. xiii.

5 J. F. Krafcik, 'A New Diet for US Manufacturing', *Technology Review* (January 30th, 1989), 28–36. See also an expanded version of this article in the *Sloan Management Review* (Fall 1988). Both articles are based on Krafcik's work at MIT. *See also:* J. F. Krafcik, *Comparative Analysis of Performance Indicators at World Auto Assembly Plants*, MIT Sloan School of Management Master's Thesis (1988). According to Daniel Jones, then an IVMP leader, all of the researchers struggled with terminology before the 'lean' designation took hold. (Personal conversation on August 24th, 2000.)

6 Womack, Jones, and Roos (1990) – see *Note 1, Chapter 1*.

7 Quality was defined as the number of defects per 100 cars traceable to the assembly plant, as reported by owners in the first three months of use. See Womack, Jones, and Roos (1990), p. 86, Figure 4.4.

8 Womack, Jones, and Roos (1990), p. 89.

9 Womack, Jones, and Roos (1990), p. 93.

10 K. Clark and T. Fujimoto, *Product Development Performance: Strategy, Organization and Management in the World Auto Industry* (Boston: Harvard Business School Press, 1990).

11 Womack, Jones, and Roos (1990), p. 111 (see also the tabulated results given on p. 118, Figure 5.1).

12 In Chapter 7, we introduce multiple dimensions of value – suggesting that customer pull must be considered concurrently with the pull that comes from shareholders, the workforce, and society.

13 This critical role of people in a production system was highlighted in a unique framework first presented by H. Shimada and J. P. MacDuffie, 'Industrial Relations and Humanware', MIT Sloan School of Management Working Paper (September 1986).

14 W. Lin, 'Identifying the Determinants of a Kaizen-suggested System and Assessing its Impact on Plant-level Productivity: A Pooled Cross-Sectional and Time Series Analysis,' PhD dissertation, Michigan State University School of Labor and Industrial Relations (1995).

15 T. Osada, *The 5 S's: Five Keys to a Total Quality Environment* (Portland, OR: Productivity Press, 1991); H. Hirano and M. Rubin (illus.), *5S for Operators: 5 Pillars of the Visual Workplace* (Portland, OR: Productivity Press, 1996).

16 W. L. Duncan, *Total Quality: Key Terms and Concepts* (New York: AMACOM, 1995).

17 J. Cutcher-Gershenfeld, M. Nitta, B. Barrett, N. Belhedi, S. Sai-Chung Chow, T. Inaba, I. Ishino, W. Lin, M. L. Moore, W. Mothersell, J. Palthe, S. Ramananad, M. E. Strolle, and A. C. Wheaton, *Knowledge-Driven Work: Unexpected Lessons from Japanese and United States Work Practices* (New York: Oxford University Press, 1998), p. 81.

18 Imai (1986), p. xxxi.

19 Deming study groups adopted the shift to 'continual', and it is now used by various quality improvement professional organizations.

20 As the discussion over lean unfolded in the United States, a similar concept emerged in the early 1990s – 'agile manufacturing'. Production – reducing cycle time and enabling

customization of product features – is central to the agile approach, with less focus across the enterprise. In contrast to lean thinking's 'flow' and 'pull' concepts, agile manufacturing is oriented toward building the adaptive capability to find and respond to new opportunities for growth. While there is an emerging literature, the evidence of this approach's impact is still limited in comparison to lean. See N. Gindy (ed.), *First International Conference on Responsive Manufacturing* (Nottingham, England: University of Nottingham, 1997), pp. 17–18; S. L. Goldman, R. N. Nagel, and K. Preiss, *Agile Competitors and Virtual Organizations, Strategies for Enriching the Customer* (New York: Van Nostrand Reinhold, 1995); J. C. Montgomery, 'The Agile Production System', in J. C. Montgomery and L. O. Levine (eds), *The Transition to Agile Manufacturing: Staying Flexible for Competitive Advantage* (Milwaukee: ASQC Quality Press, 1996).

21  Womack and Jones (1996) – see Note 3, Chapter 1.

22  According to M. E. Porter, in *Competitive Advantage: Creating and Sustaining Superior Performance* (New York: The Free Press, 1985), 'value chain' is the basic tool for conducting a systematic analysis of all of the activities (and their interactions) that a firm performs, in order to understand the sources of competitive advantage. The value chain is embedded in a larger 'value system' that encompasses value chains associated with suppliers, channels, and buyers. A firm's particular value chain (and the way it designs, produces, markets, and supports its products) is shaped by its own special history, strategy, implementation approach, and the underlying economics of the activities themselves.

23  Discussions of value streams and value chains often have an underlying assumption of congruence or alignment of all stakeholders in support of a clearly defined customer. In fact, as we pointed out earlier, there may be multiple customers and multiple stakeholders – all involved in a complex mix of power relations and associated with multiple value streams that change over time. In this context, the principles of value stream alignment are no less important, but much more difficult to achieve. Indeed, today's evolving market and industrial environment calls for new forms of customer-supplier integration to address the challenges of demand variability and the opportunities associated with information technology. These emerging developments will continue to advance the frontiers of what we term *lean thinking*.

24  D. McGregor, *The Human Side of the Enterprise* (New York: McGraw Hill, 1960); N. Rosenberg (ed.), *The American System of Manufactures: The Report of the Committee on the Machinery of the United States 1855, and the Special Reports of George Wallis and Joseph Whitworth 1854* (Edinburgh: Edinburgh University Press, 1969); Ohno (1988); R. Clark, *The Japanese Company* (New Haven: Yale University Press, 1979); J. Woodward, *Industrial Organization: Theory and Practice*, 2nd edn (New York: Oxford University Press, 1980); S. Shingo, *A Study of the Toyota Production System from an Industrial Engineering Viewpoint*, rev. edn, A. P. Dillon, trans. (Portland, OR: Productivity Press, 1989); Deming (1987); Y. Monden (1988); D. A. Hounshell, *From the American System to Mass Production, 1800–1932: Development of Manufacturing Technology in the United States* (Baltimore: Johns Hopkins University Press, 1984); M. Aoki (ed.), *The Economic Analysis of the Japanese Firm* (Amsterdam: Elsevier Science Publishers, 1984); M. J. Piore and C. F. Sabel, *The Second Industrial Divide: Possibilities for Prosperity* (New York: Basic Books, 1984); T. Kochan, H. Katz, and R. McKersie, *The Transformation of American Industrial Relations* (New York: Basic Books, 1984); J. C. Abegglen and G. Stalk Jr, *KAISHA: The Japanese Corporation* (New York: Basic Books, 1985); M. A. Cusumano, *The Japanese Auto Industry: Technology and Management at Toyota and Nissan* (Cambridge, MA: Published by the Council on East Asian Studies, Harvard University, and distributed by the Harvard University Press, 1985); Imai (1986); J. F. Krafcik, 'Triumph of Lean Production', *Sloan Management Review* **30**:1 (1988), 41–52; Dertouzos, Lester, Solow, and the MIT Commission on Industrial Productivity

(1989) – see Note 4, Chapter 3; Womack, Jones, and Roos (1990) – see Note 1, Chapter 1; A. D. Chandler, *Scale and Scope: The Dynamics of Industrial Capitalism* (Cambridge, MA: Belknap Press, 1990); P. Senge, *The Fifth Discipline: The Art and Practice of the Learning Organization* (New York: Doubleday/Currency, 1990); Clark and Fujimoto (1990); M. S. Scott Morton (ed.), *The Corporation of the 1990s* (New York: Oxford University Press, 1990); M. Kenney and R. Florida, *Beyond Mass Production: The Japanese System and its Transfer to the US* (New York: Oxford University Press, 1993); P. Drucker, *Post-Capitalist Society* (New York: HarperBusiness, 1993); K. Suzaki, *The New Shop Floor Management: Empowering People for Continuous Improvement* (New York: Free Press, 1993); M. Hammer and J. Champy, *Reengineering the Corporation: A Manifesto for Business Revolution* (New York: HarperBusiness, 1993); J. P. Womack and D. T. Jones, 'From Lean Production to the Lean Enterprise', *Harvard Business Review* (March–April 1994), 93–103; T. Nishiguchi, *Strategic Industrial Sourcing: The Japanese Advantage* (New York: Oxford University Press, 1994); M. Aoki and R. Dore (eds), *The Japanese Firm: The Sources of Competitive Strength* (New York: Oxford University Press, 1994); E. Bowman and B. Kogut (eds), *Redesigning the Firm* (New York: Oxford University Press, 1995); I. Nonaka and H. Takeuchi, *The Knowledge-Creating Company: How Japanese Companies Create the Dynamics of Innovation* (New York: Oxford University Press, 1995); J. K. Liker, J. E. Ettlie, and J. C. Campbell (eds), *Engineered in Japan: Japanese Technology-Management Practices* (New York: Oxford University Press, 1995); Goldman, Nagel, and Preiss (1995); Womack and Jones (1996) – see Note 3, Chapter 1; Dyer (1996) – see Note 13, Chapter 3; J. P. MacDuffie and S. Helper, 'Creating Lean Suppliers,' *California Management Review* **39**:4 (1997), 118–51; M. Imai, *Gemba Kaizen: A Commonsense, Low-Cost Approach to Management* (New York: McGraw-Hill, 1997); T. Kochan, R. Lansbury, and J. P. MacDuffie, *After Lean Production: Evolving Employment Practices in the World Auto Industry* (Ithaca, NY: Cornell University Press, 1997); J. K. Liker (ed.), *Becoming Lean: Inside Stories of U.S. Manufacturers* (Portland, OR: Productivity Press, 1997); M. A. Cusumano, K. Nobeoka, and K. Nobeoka, *Thinking Beyond Lean: How Multi-Project Management Is Transforming Product Development at Toyota and Other Companies* (New York: Simon & Schuster, 1998); K. Bozdogan, J. Deyst, D. Hoult, and M. Lucas, 'Architectural Innovation in Product Development through Early Supplier Integration', *R&D Management* **28**:3 (July 1998), 163–73; Fine (1998) – see Note 15, Chapter 3; J. Cutcher-Gershenfeld et al. (1998); D. C. Mowery (ed.), *U.S. Industry in 2000: Studies in Competitive Performance*, National Research Council, Board on Science, Technology, and Economic Policy (Washington, DC: National Academy Press, 1999); J. K. Liker, W .M. Fruin, and P. A. Adler (eds), *Remade in America: Transplanting and Transforming Japanese Management Systems* (New York: Oxford University Press, 1999); T. Fujimoto, *The Evolution of a Manufacturing System at Toyota* (New York: Oxford University Press, 1999); R. L. Ackoff, *Re-Creating the Corporation* (New York: Oxford University Press, 1999); S. Spear and H. K. Bowen, 'Decoding the DNA of the Toyota Production System', *Harvard Business Review* (September–October 1999), 97–106; S. A. Ruffa and M. J. Perozziello, *Breaking the Cost Barrier: A Proven Approach to Managing and Implementing Lean Manufacturing* (New York: John Wiley & Sons, 2000); J. H. Dyer, *Collaborative Advantage: Winning through Extended Enterprise Supplier Networks* (New York: Oxford University Press, 2000); P. S. Pande, R. P. Neuman, and R. R. Cavanagh, *The Six Sigma Way* (New York: McGraw-Hill, 2000); J. H. Dyer and K. Nobeoka, 'Creating and Managing a High-Performance Knowledge-Sharing Network: The Toyota Case', *Strategic Management Journal* **21** (2000), 345–67; M. Harry and R. Schroeder, *Six Sigma* (New York: Currency, 2000); G. Eckes, *The Six Sigma Revolution* (New York: John Wiley & Sons, 2001); J. A. Jordan, Jr and F. J. Michel, *The Lean Company: Making the Right Choices*, Society of Manufacturing Engineers, 2001.

25 We will not be reviewing the thought process associated with the development of all aspects of the Toyota Production System – though similar stories could be told for other developments.

26 Ohno (1988), p. 84.

27 Ohno states that his visits to supermarkets – which were quite different from Japan's turn-of-the century methods of merchandising – helped him to see better the waste associated with overproduction. To Ohno, the idea of the US supermarket also connected just-in-time production to value. To have value, products had to be offered at a lower price to be competitive with imported foreign models, and consumers should derive pleasure from their purchase. Of course, nothing would be achieved if lower prices meant poor-quality materials. See Ohno (1988), p. 84.

28 Shingo (1989).

29 Ohno (1988), pp. 4–5.

30 This amounts to minimizing the variance in the production levels in two consecutive periods. Production smoothing, in turn, requires production balancing across and among numerous processes, based on what is termed 'takt time': the available production time divided by the rate of consumer demand (consumption). For further details, see Monden (1988), pp. 75–87.

31 The Ford system featured synchronization of production flow, where workstations were synchronized physically by linking them via continuous conveyer belts. This worked particularly well for single-model production. See Womack, Jones, and Roos (1990), p. 27.

32 Shingo (1989), pp. 43–58.

33 Shingo (1989), p. xxiii. This is consistent with the view of Ohno (1988), who notes that Toyota's slogan was 'small lot sizes and quick setups' (p. 95). As a result, Toyota produced many models, in small lots, in a mixed-model assembly operation. While Ford separated assembly and parts fabrication, Toyota linked them directly. Also, while Ford used one-piece flow in the assembly process, with parts produced in large lots, Toyota performed all production in small lots. See Shingo (1989), p. 94.

34 Ohno (1988), p. 6; Shingo (1989), p. 58. *Jidoka* has two meanings, written with two different ideograms: 'automation' in the usual sense of changing from a manual to a machine process; and 'automatic control of defects', generally the preferred meaning, which closely approximates 'automation with a human mind'. See Monden (1988), pp. 224–5.

35 In essence, many of the benefits of full automation are achieved through the use of relatively low-cost machines designed to detect problems, leaving the correction task to human workers with skill and knowledge to undertake real-time troubleshooting and problem-solving. The actual implementation of autonomation involves a full array of methods, ranging from stopping the production line when abnormalities occur to training workers to monitor production and correct problems. Thus, autonomation, or pre-automation, is the stage before full automation, making optimal use of both worker and machine capabilities. See Shingo (1989), pp. 58–61.

36 Shingo (1989), p. xxi.

37 As Shingo (1989, p. xxi) notes: 'Overproduction is generally considered undesirable and many people regard it as an evil and make efforts to minimize it.'

38 Fujimoto (1999), p. 111.

39 See Krafcik (1988, 1989).

40 In the mass production model, relationships with suppliers are typically arm's-length, adverserial, short-term, and transaction-based.

41 Ohno (1988), pp. 31–5.

42 Studies have found broad diffusion of Japanese work practices without convergence on a single lean model. See Kenney and Florida (1993); Kochan, Lansbury, and MacDuffie

(1997). The researchers, who are associated with MIT's International Motor Vehicle Program, studied firms in Japan, the United States, Canada, Germany, the United Kingdom, Italy, Spain, Sweden, and Australia.

43  Cutcher-Gershenfeld et al. (1998).

44  Comments to the authors in 2001 by Allen C. Haggerty, who retired in 2001 as Vice President of Engineering at Boeing Military Aircraft & Missile Systems.

45  For example, the concepts of worker participation and partnership or the principles of variance reduction and continuous improvement were all codified in important ways during World War II. See F. E. Emery and E. L. Trist, *Towards A Social Ecology* (London: Plenum Press, 1973).

46  J. Cutcher-Gershenfeld et al., 'Japanese Team-Based Work Systems in the United States: Explaining the Diversity', *California Management Review* **37**:1 (Fall 1994).

47  P. Crosby, *Quality is Free: The Art of Making Quality Certain* (New York: Mentor Books, 1979).

48  The work at Bell Labs focused on statistical process control (SPC) principles. These ideas were carried to Japanese industry by Japanese engineers, learning from Gen. MacArthur's staff during the post-World War II reconstruction. During this period, W. Edwards Deming – an American statistician and management expert whose principles became widely embraced by many Japanese companies – played a central role, as reflected in the creation of the annual Deming Prizes for contributions to product quality and dependability (established by the Union of Japanese Science and Engineering). See Deming (1987), pp. 1–4.

49  Including statistical process control, systematic problem-solving by groups, and designing quality in (rather than inspecting it afterwards).

50  Adam Smith's *The Wealth of Nations* opens with a famous passage describing 'the trade of the pin-maker', in which ten workers turn out 48 000 pins per day precisely because of their 'division of labour' – they each specialize in one of the tasks associated with pin production. Smith contrasts this output with the very small number of pins – perhaps as few as one – that would be turned out by a single laborer working alone. See A. Smith, *The Wealth of Nations* (New York: Alfred A. Knopf, 1991; orig. pub. 1776).

51  Hammer and Champy (1993), p. 32. For further readings on reengineering, see M. Hammer, 'Reengineering Work: Don't Automate, Obliterate' *Harvard Business Review* (July–August 1990), 104–12; and J. Champy, *Reengineering Management: The Mandate for New Leadership* (New York: HarperBusiness, 1995).

52  Hammer and Champy (1993), pp. 2–5, 35.

53  Hammer and Champy (1993), p. 49.

54  Reengineering, which stresses starting anew with a clean slate, may have created a mindset of unwittingly pursuing radical *one-time* breakthrough changes, much to the detriment of continuous improvement. To put it another way, it is not clear that the reengineering movement ever resolved the central conflict between the imperative for radical change, which it espoused, and the importance of evolutionary organizational learning based on cumulative creation and sharing of *tacit knowledge* through a process of experimentation, adaptation, and diffusion of lessons learned. Further, *successful* radical change requires a coherent set of governing priciples and clear measures of success. Early signs of trouble may have been evident when Hammer and Champy (1993) noted in their 'manifesto': 'When a company is taking its first steps toward reengineering, no one really knows exactly where it is heading; no one really knows exactly what it will become; no one really even knows which aspects of the current company will change, let alone precisely how' (p. 154). Moreover, radical change means setting into motion a chain reaction of interrelated changes throughout an organization. However, beyond the somewhat offhand acknowledgement that 'change ripples into other parts of the organization' (p. 181),

reengineering lacks the fundamental *systems thinking* tools embedded in lean approaches to fundamental change. For these and other reasons, many of the companies that have launched reengineering efforts have failed – a stark admission by Hammer and Champy towards the end of their book (p. 200) and in subsequent public forums.

55 Eckes (2001), pp. 1–5; Pande, Neuman, and Cavanagh (2000), pp. 41–9.

56 See Pande, Neuman, and Cavanagh (2000), p. 28. The construct of *standard deviation* (denoted by the Greek letter $\sigma$, or sigma), a measure of dispersions around the mean, underlies Six Sigma as a statistical concept. Reducing variation to the Six Sigma level means reaching a performance level of 99.99966 percent perfection. The sigma level is also used as a measure of the manufacturing capability of individual enterprises, denoted by $c_{pk}$ – the manufacturing capability index that gauges the degree to which the system can produce defect-free products. For example, the Six Sigma level of performance corresponds to a $c_{pk}$ level of 2. For a more technical review, see M. J. Harry and J. R. Lawson, *Six Sigma Producibility Analysis and Process Characterization*, (Reading, MA: Addison-Wesley, 1992); and Eckes (2001).

57 General Electric and several other organizations use Six Sigma as a structured management tool, following a five-phase 'DMAIC' cycle: *define* customer requirements and develop a map of the process to be improved; *measure* key indicators of effectiveness and efficiency and translate them into the concept of sigma; *analyze* the causes of the problem requiring improvement; *improve* generate, select and implement solutions; and *control* ensure that improvement is sustained over time. See Eckes (2001), p. 10. This process is grounded in the well-known Deming Plan-Do-Check-Act cycle (PDCA), which describes the basic data-based improvement process.

58 Harry and Schroeder (2000).

59 Pande, Neuman, and Cavanagh (2000), pp. 41–9.

60 The material in this vignette is based on D. Johnson, Organizational Effectiveness Consultant at Raytheon (Wichita), at the Presentation at the LAI Lean Learning Workshop (October 31st–November 1st, 2000); R. W. Drewes Presentation at the LAI Plenary Conference (April 10th–11th, 2001).

61 International Association of Machinists and Aerospace Workers, 'Ten Steps to Achieving a High Performance Work Organization Partnership'. At the union's website, the following ten-step process is outlined: 1) on-site familiarization; 2) HPWO partnership planning session; 3) joint communications strategy; 4) design HPWO model and implementation plan; 5) draft HPWO partnership agreement; 6) conduct HPWO partnership education program; 7) implement the HPWO partnerships strategy; 8) establish continuing education; 9) negotiate an HPWO agreement; and 10) monitor/evaluate HPWO partnership.

62 The UAW and other unions representing aerospace workers have drafted similar enabling language, which can serve as a powerful enabler for lean thinking. But caution must be urged: management and unions have a mixed track record when it comes to delivering on commitments made as part of strategic-level partnerships. Corporate restructuring has sometimes undercut specific worksite HPWO agreements. See B. Barrett (with input from other members of Labor Aerospace Research Agenda), 'Fostering Workplace Innovation and Labor–Management Partnership: The Challenge of Strategic Shifts in Business Operations', LARA Case Study (2000).

63 R. L. Ackoff, *Re-Creating the Corporation* (New York: Oxford University Press, 1999), p. 49.

## Chapter 5

1 C. R. Cook and J. C. Graser, 'Military Airframe Acquisition Costs: The Effects of Lean Manufacturing' (Santa Monica, CA: RAND, 2001), RAND Study MR-1325-A. This study exam-

ines how to incorporate new DoD acquisition and manufacturing environments, notably lean manufacturing, into historical cost-estimating relationships or methodologies. Assessing the state of lean implementation in the military aircraft industry in 1998, the study concludes that while nearly all manufacturers had embraced lean, 'lean implementation tended to be very localized within particular functions or on pilot projects'. None had implemented lean practices from the beginning to the end of the value stream, or even 'wall to wall' within a factory. The authors today believe that implementation of lean practices continues to progress slowly, and that most lean successes remain in localized areas or functions.

2  Most of these cases have been presented at LAI conferences or in other venues.

3  Based on information in J. C. Hoppes, 'Lean Manufacturing Practices in the Defense Aircraft Industry', Master's thesis, MIT (1995), pp. 56–82.

4  S. Kandebo, 'Lean Thinking Spurs Culture Shift at LMAS', *Aviation Week & Space Technology* (July 12th, 1999), 56–9.

5  The *Aviation Week* article cited above reports a drop of about $500 000 in the average price of the C-130J. Assuming an average selling price of $50 million per unit, the bottom-line impact is about 1 percent.

6  B. Ippolito and E. M. Murman, 'End User Involvement in Establishing Software Requirements for Aerospace Software Systems', INCOSE 2000, Minneapolis, MN. (July 2000).

7  J. Menendez, 'Building Software Factories in the Aerospace Industry', Master's thesis, MIT (1997).

8  B. Ippolito and E. M. Murman, 'Improving the Software Upgrade Value Stream', LAI Report RP01-01 (2001).

9  Ippolito and Murman (2001).

10  Coopers and Lybrand, 'The DoD Regulatory Cost Premium: A Quantitative Assessment' (December 1994), as reported in the 'Acquisition Reform Benchmarking Group (ARBG) 1997 Final Report' (June 30th, 1997).

11  A survey conducted by the Institute for Interconnecting and Packaging Electronic Circuits (IPC) and LAI found that only 10 percent of respondents had heard of the beneficial contractual changes stemming from the Federal Acquisition Streamlining Act (FASA) and the Federal Acquisition Reform Act (FARA). The survey results also indicated that there were contractual barriers to commercial success, such as cost accounting standards (CAS), Truth in Negotiations Act (TINA), and unique reporting requirements. The major objection of the suppliers was government restriction on profitability and the requirement to provide cost and pricing data. See M. Heberling, J. R. McDonald, R. M. Nanzer, E. Rebentisch, and K. Sterling, 'Using Commercial Suppliers – Barriers and Opportunities', *Program Manager* (July–August 1998), published by the Defense Systems Management College.

12  Based on information from J. P. Koonmen, 'Implementing Precision Assembly Techniques in the Commercial Aircraft Industry', Master's thesis, MIT (1994); and Hoppes (1995).

13  The following criteria must be met for a team to be an Integrated Product Team (IPT): the team must have a finite mission to develop a product or process; membership must be cross-functional and include all functions with an impact on the product during its life-cycle (including, at times, customer and supplier representatives); there must be defined and measurable performance outcomes; and the team must function at a single program level. Adapted from J. Klein and G. I. Susman, 'Lean Aircraft Initiative Organization and Human Resources (O&HR) Survey Feedback – Integrated Product Teams (IPTs)', LAI White Paper (April 1995), Lean 95–03.

14  R. Weisman, 'Quarterly Loss is Pratt's First in Half-Century', *The Hartford Courant* (October 23rd, 1992), p. B1.

15  Hoppes (1995), p. 114.

16 Associated Press (November 30th, 1992).

17 Hoppes (1995), pp. 114–30.

18 L. R. de Arellano, A. Chambers, and J. T. Shields, 'Summary of Research Conducted in the Engine Sector', LAI Report RP00-01 (August 2000).

19 The *chaku-chaku* cell was the lean solution to the turbine blade root-grinding process in Pratt & Whitney's North Haven, Connecticut, facility. Womack and Jones (1996), pp. 174–80 – see Note 3, Chapter 1.

20 The JDAM guidance system, commonly referred to as a kit, is an all-weather guidance package to be added to 1000 lb and 2000 lb bombs in current inventory. The kit, which includes an inertial navigation system augmented by Global Positioning System (GPS) for updates, attaches to the bomb and directs it to the target through controlled tail-fin movements.

21 C. Ingols and L. Brem, 'Implementing Acquisition Reform: A Case Study on Joint Direct Attack Munitions (JDAM)' (July 1998), p. 6. The authors are from Corporate Classrooms in Cambridge, Massachusetts, and worked under contract to the Defense Systems Management College and Boeing.

22 Pilot Program Consulting Group (1997) – see Note 17, Chapter 3.

23 Pilot Program Consulting Group (1997).

## Chapter 6

1 See, for example: Abegglen and Stalk (1985) – see Note 24, Chapter 4; J. P. Womack, 'The Lean Difference: Building a High Performance Enterprise', *Prism* (First Quarter 1992), 103–11; J. P. Womack and D. T. Jones, 'From Lean Production to the Lean Enterprise', *Harvard Business Review* (March–April 1994), 93–103; T. Fujimoto (1999); Dyer (2000); Dyer and Nobeoka (2000), 345–67 – see Note 24, Chapter 4.

2 Womack, Jones, and Roos (1990), pp. 192–222 – see Note 1, Chapter 1.

3 http://www.lean.org/.

4 S. I. Weiss, E. M. Murman, and D. Roos, 'The Air Force and Industry Think Lean', *Aerospace America* (May 1996), 32–8.

5 Jordan and Michel (2001) – see Note 24, Chapter 4.

6 At the factory level, this might be 'single-piece flow' – where a defect-free part is delivered to its point of use when needed, without creating inventory or causing parts shortages. The same 'just-in-time' principle must apply to all enterprise support activities, such as hiring, financial information services, build-to-packages, and maintenance.

7 Y. Sugimori, K. Kusunoki, F. Cho, and S. Uchikawa, 'Toyota Production System and Kanban Systems – Materialization of Just-In-Time and Respect-for-Human Systems', *International Journal of Production Research* **15**:6 (1977), 553–64.

8 There has been extensive research, as well as a long history of initiatives and action, centered on the issues of leadership, trust, decisionmaking, learning, and other related aspects of the 'Overarching Principles' we term 'human-oriented' in our model. See Emery and Trist (1973); McGregor (1960) – see Note 24, Chapter 4; Cutcher-Gershenfeld et al. (1998) – see Note 17, Chapter 4.

9 A. Stanke, 'F/A-18 E/F – An Enterprise Achieving Life Cycle Value', presentation at the LAI product Development Implementation Workshop (September 22nd, 2000).

10 J. P. Kotter (ed.), *John P. Kotter on What Leaders Really Do* (Boston: Harvard Business School Press, 1999).

11 B. Nanus and W. G. Bennis, *Visionary Leadership: Creating a Compelling Sense of Direction for Your Organization* (San Francisco: Jossey-Bass, 1992).

12 LAI, 'Transitioning To a Lean Enterprise: A Guide for Leaders', Vols I, II, and III (2000).

13  LAI, 'Lean Enterprise Self Assessment Tool (LESAT)' (2001).

14  The Department of Defense categorizes programs in different levels. According to 1998 guidelines, *ACAT I* programs have Research, Development, Test and Evaluation (RTD&E) funding greater than $135 million with procurement funding greater than $640 million. *ACAT III* programs are below *ACAT II* levels.

15  We do not intend to characterize *all* the various bodies that comprise a government as government enterprises. We are restricting the types of government agencies discussed in this chapter to those that are principal players in the US Aerospace Enterprise.

16  Scholars in recent literature have addressed the critical role of the extended enterprise in achieving enterprise success. For instance, Dyer (2000) provides insight into Chrysler's success prior to their merger with Daimler-Benz in working with their extended enterprise to implement lean practices, and thereby outperforming Ford – which had concentrated in implementing lean only within the core enterprise.

17  See, for example, McNutt (1999) – see Note 10, Chapter 2.

18  Lockheed Martin Aeronautics Company, The Boeing Company Military Aircraft & Missile Systems Group, Pratt & Whitney, and the F-22 System Program Office (SPO), *F-22 Raptor 21: Achieving the Lean Enterprise, the F-22 Lean Toolkit Guidebook*, F-22/F119 2001 Enterprise Conference, Stone Mountain, Georgia (May 1st–3rd, 2001).

19  By design, the (then) Lockheed F-22 program and the F-22 System Program Office (SPO) had a similar organizational structure to ensure teamwork and close communications. Four major IPTs were created: Air Vehicle, Engine, Support System, and Training System, where each major IPT comprised a number of lower-level IPTs for specific subsystems. See M. D. Williams, *Acquisition for the 21st Century: The F-22 Development Program* (Washington, DC: National Defense University Press, 1999), pp. 80–91.

20  For example, based on extensive value stream mapping, Lockheed Martin has committed significant capital resources to the design of the F-22 final assembly to develop a fully integrated lean assembly process, in addition to consolidation of business systems and core functions. Pratt & Whitney, similarly, has stressed consolidation of operations and has achieved substantial cost savings through targeted initial investments. Also, key suppliers have actively pursued the implementation of lean principles to meet affordability targets.

21  R. E. Freeman, *Strategic Management: A Stakeholder Perspective* (Boston: Pittman, 1984).

22  C. P. Dunn and B. K. Burton, 'Stakeholder Interests and Community Groups: A New View', Proceedings of the International Association for Business and Society Annual Meetings (1996).

23  T. A. Kochan and S. A. Rubinstein, 'Toward a Stakeholder Theory of the Firm: The Saturn Partnership', *Organization Science*, 11:4 (July–August 2000), 367–86.

24  Liker (1997) – see Note 24, Chapter 4.

25  Liker (1997). Rother teaches at the University of Michigan and is manager of Manufacturing Outreach for the University of Michigan's Japan Technology Management Program.

26  D. M. Tonaszuck, 'The Impact of Leadership on Systematic Organizational Change', Master's thesis, MIT (2000).

27  Nanus and Bennis (1992).

## Chapter 7

1  This is consistent with the definition of value provided in W. B. Rouse and K. R. Boff, 'Strategies for Value: Quality, Productivity and Innovation in R&D/Technology Organizations', *Systems Engineering* 4:2 (2001), 88.

2  See A. J. Slywotsky, *Value Migration: How to Think Several Moves Ahead of the Competition* (Boston: Harvard Business School Press, 1996).

3 Current business literature focuses 'value' and 'value creation' on growth-generating strategies that increase the market capitalization of firms, enhance shareholder value, or increase customer satisfaction. See T. L. Doorley III and J. M. Donovan, *Value-Creating Growth: How to Lift Your Company to the Next Level of Performance* (Jossey-Bass: San Francisco, 1999); J. M. Donovan, R. Tully, and B. Wortman, *The Value Enterprise: Strategies for Building a Value-Based Organization* (Toronto: McGraw-Hill Ryerson, 1998); R. E. S. Boulton, B. D. Libert, and S. M. Samek, *Cracking the Value Code: How Businesses Are Creating Wealth in the New Economy* (New York: HarperBusiness, 2000). An account of IBM's recent transformation takes a somewhat different approach, with central emphasis on the customer: see J. W. Cortada and T. S. Hargraves et al., *Into the Networked Age: How IBM and Other Firms are Getting There Now* (New York: Oxford University Press).

4 Rouse, who focuses on the multi-program enterprise, makes the point that value is different things to different stakeholders, and notes the continual challenge of finding the 'sweet spot' among all enterprise expectations. He lists key questions (p. 85) – useful in our framework – to address the challenges of value successfully. See W. R. Rouse, *Essential Challenges of Strategic Management* (New York: John Wiley & Sons, 2001).

5 Womack and Jones (1996), pp. 37–8 – see *Note 3, Chapter 1*. Emphasis in original.

6 It should be noted that value stream maps can quickly become cumbersome and time-consuming to create for a complex product with many different participants. A recent LAI research study concluded that techniques to map complex enterprise value streams are immature and have achieved limited success. Several different tools are used, but the study found no single best practice. Specific technique is not as important as company mindset. See R. L. Millard, 'Value Stream Analysis and Mapping for Product Development', Master's thesis, MIT (2001).

7 A. Stanke, 'A Framework for Achieving Best Lifecycle Value in Aerospace Product Development', Master's Thesis, MIT (2001).

8 The noted book *Getting to Yes* urges that a focus on 'interests' rather than 'positions' will significantly increase the ability of parties to achieve mutual gains. See R. Fisher and W. Ury, *Getting to Yes: Negotiating an Agreement Without Giving In* (Boston: Houghton Mifflin, 1981). Later authors specifically termed this as an integrative process of 'creating value'. See D. Lax and J. Sebenius, *The Manager as Negotiator: Bargaining for Cooperative and Competitive Gain* (New York: The Free Press, 1986).

9 Employment relations scholars, for example, point to a focus on the workforce and other key stakeholders as necessary for achieving mutual gains. See, for example, T. Kochan and P. Osterman, *The Mutual Gains Enterprise: Forging a Winning Partnership Among Labor, Management and Government* (Boston: Harvard Business School Press, 1994).

10 Homans, most likely the originator of the concept of the value proposition, states it generally to explain social behavior. See G. C. Homans, *Social Behavior: Its Elementary Forms* (New York: Harcourt Brace Jovanovich, 1974). D. Bovet and J. Martha, in *Value Nets: Breaking the Supply Chain to Unlock Hidden Profits* (New York: John Wiley & Sons, 2000), define the value proposition as 'the utility a company provides through its products and services to the customer whom it chooses to serve'. Cortada and Graves et al. (1999) offer a similar definition: 'a general statement of customer benefits that a business delivers'. They elaborate further in describing the value proposition of Southwest Airlines (low price and convenience), its 'positive value attributes' (pricing; direct purchasing; frequent departures; first-come, first-served seating; best baggage handling record; and uncongested airports), and its 'negative value attributes' (no refunds for lost tickets; frequent flyer restrictions; no premium services; no meals). They also point out that choices about what attributes *not* to provide can be just as important as the specific attributes offered. Analysis of value attributes, along with value propositions, provides key

strategic insights into identifying and servicing particular markets and dominating specific market niches.

11 See R. L. Keeney and H. Raiffa, *Decisions with Multiple Objectives: Preference and Value Trade-offs* (Cambridge, England: Cambridge University Press, 1993). This classic on complex value problems was first published in 1976.

12 See, for example, R. Axelrod, *The Evolution of Cooperation* (New York: Basic Books, 1980); W. Poundstone, *Prisoner's Dilemma* (New York: Doubleday, 1992).

13 See R. Walton, J. Cutcher-Gershenfeld, and R. McKersie, *Strategic Negotiations: A Theory of Change in Labor-Management Relations* (Boston: Harvard Business School Press, 1995).

14 Rouse and Boff (2001) distinguish between the next user and the *end* user (p. 89).

## Chapter 8

1 There is an extensive literature on the structure and timeline of programs. K. T. Ulrich and S. D. Eppinger, in *Product Design and Development* (New York: McGraw-Hill, 1995), identify distinct phases of concept development, system-level design, detailed design, testing and refinement, and production. More formal is Institute of Electrical Engineers, *IEEE Trial Use Standard for Application and Management of the Systems Engineering Process* (New York: February 28th, 1995). A recent attempt to use frameworks for understanding the flow of information is 'Output from the 1998 Product Development Value Stream Workshop: A Framework for Understanding Information Flow in the Product Development Process', LAI Working Paper WP01-01 (2001).

2 Material for this vignette is drawn from T. Clancy, *Fighter Wing* (New York: Berkley Books, 1995); Lockheed Martin Aerospace Corporation (2001); 'The Shingo Prize for Excellence in Manufacturing, 1999 Achievement Report, Lockheed Martin Tactical Aircraft Systems' (1999); and personal communications with Lockheed Martin personnel.

3 General Dynamics was purchased by Lockheed in 1993, which subsequently merged with Martin Marietta in 1995. See Chapter 1, Figure 1.3.

4 S. E. Ambrose, *Nothing Like It in the World: The Men Who Built the Transcontinental Railroad 1863–1869* (New York: Simon & Schuster, 2000).

5 Adapted from R. A. Slack, 'The Lean Value Principle in Military Aerospace Product Development', LAI Report RP99-01-16 (1999).

6 E. M. Murman, M. Walton, and E. Rebentisch, 'Challenges in the Better, Faster, Cheaper Era of Aeronautical Design, Engineering and Manufacturing', *The Aeronautical Journal* (October 2000), 481–9.

7 There is a large portfolio of techniques for identifying user needs and mapping them to product requirements. The best-understood tools apply to new products developed in response to 'customer pull' (we explore these later in this chapter). Other products can be developed by 'technology push' – where a company has a unique competency in a particular useful technology and applies that technology to a wide variety of markets. The tools become less applicable as one considers truly innovative products or products with unexpected or emergent use. Champions can enhance the probabilities that such products will find a market. An LAI doctoral student found that the activity of a champion or a subject expert is more likely to result in technology application than is deliberate policy. R. Pomponi, 'Organizational Structures for Technology Transition: Rethinking Information Flow in the Integrated Product Team', PhD dissertation, MIT (1998).

8 See, for example, A. L. Weigel and D. E. Hastings, 'Interaction of Policy Choices and Technical Requirements for a Space Transportation Infrastructure', 5th International Conference on Technology, Policy, and Innovation, The Hague, Netherlands (June 27th–29th, 2001).

9 This problem, discussed in Chapter 3, predates today's aerospace industry. See E. Morison, 'Gunfire at Sea: A Case Study of Innovation' in *Men, Machines and Modern Times* (Cambridge, MA: MIT Press, 1966).

10 Utterback (1996) – see Note 6, Chapter 1. See, in particular, Chapters 3 and 7.

11 C. M. Christensen, *The Innovator's Dilemma* (Boston: Harvard Business School Press, 1997).

12 For a detailed, although perhaps not unbiased, exploration, see W. Broad, *Teller's War: The Top-Secret Story Behind the Star Wars Deception* (New York: Simon & Schuster, 1992) and W. Broad, *Star Warriors: A Penetrating Look into the Lives of the Young Scientists Behind Our Space Age Weaponry* (New York: Simon & Schuster, 1985).

13 As of this writing, this is Goal #7 of NASA's Aerospace Technology Enterprise. See http://www.aero-space.nasa.gov/goals/index.htm.

14 National Academy of Engineering, Committee on Reusable Launch Vehicle Technology and Test Program, National Research Council, *Reusable Launch Vehicles: Technology Development and Test Program* (Washington, DC: National Academy Press, 1995).

15 NASA George C. Marshall Space Flight Center, 'Final Report of the X-33 Liquid Hydrogen Tank Test Investigation Team', Huntsville, Alabama (May 2000).

16 LAI research has identified the essential role of trusted relationships and open sharing of information between the government and its prime suppliers in achieving 'win–win' outcomes for six major programs. The value-creation frameworks for these programs are aligned with the model introduced in Chapter 7. See S. A. Cowap, 'Economic Incentives in Aerospace Weapon Systems Procurement Thesis', Master's thesis, MIT (1998).

17 J. Mandelbaum (team leader) et al., *Incentive Strategies for Defense Acquisition* (Fort Belvoir, VA: Defense Acquisition University Press, 2001).

18 http://www.acq.osd.mil/ar/doc/incentivesguide-0201.doc.

19 See, for example, A. Griffin and J. R. Hauser, 'The Voice of the Customer', *Marketing Science* **12**:1 (Winter 1993).

20 J. Hauser and D. Clausing, 'The House of Quality', *Harvard Business Review* **66**:3 (1988), 63–73.

21 Rouse (2001), pp. 79–84 – see Note 4, Chapter 7; J. Warmkessel and N. Diller, 'Applying Multi-Attribute Utility Analysis to Architecture Research for the Terrestrial Observer Swarm', Digital Avionics Systems Conference, Daytona, Beach, Florida (October 14th–18th, 2001).

22 The set of documents that provides the basis for the specification, design, building, and testing of the product, including external interfaces and operational and support requirements.

23 See, for example, Institute of Electrical Engineers, *IEEE Standard for Software Project Management Plans* (New York: IEEE, 1998), IEEE Standard 1058-1998; H. Eisner, *Essentials of Project and Systems Engineering Management* (New York: John Wiley & Sons, 1997).

24 Based loosely on the Johnson & Johnson corporate credo (see www.jnj.com). J. C. Collins and J. I. Porras, in *Built to Last: Successful Habits of Visionary Companies* (New York: Harper-Collins, 1994), postulate that a source of J&J's excellent performance is the seriousness with which the company takes its credo, and the fact that they actually use it as a guide to day-to-day management decisions. In the terms of our value-creation framework, J&J uses the credo as a template for the value proposition of every program in which the firm engages.

25 Based on W. J. Fabrycky, *Engineering Economy*, © 1989. Electronically reproduced by permission of Pearson Education, Inc., Upper Saddle River, New Jersey. The figure is notional.

26 Early evidence indicated that these techniques can be effective, but are not magic bullets. Rather, properly implemented, they are necessary – but not sufficient – organizational

tools. See C. M. Hernandez, 'Challenges and Benefits to the Implementation of Integrated Product Teams on Large Military Procurements', Master's thesis, MIT (1995).

27  J. Warmkessel and B. Kaliardos, 'Architecting Space Systems', Proceedings of the International Council on Systems Engineering (INCOSE), Melbourne, Australia (July 1st–5th, 2001); H. McManus and J. Warmkessel, 'Creating Advanced Architectures for Space Systems: Product and Process', AIAA Space 2001-4738, AIAA Space 2001 Conference Proceedings, Albuquerque, New Mexico (August 2001).

28  For further discussion of DSM, see web.mit.edu/DSM; and S. D. Eppinger, 'Innovation at the Speed of Information', *Harvard Business Review* **79**:1 (January 2001), 149–58. T. R. Browning, in 'Modeling and Analyzing Cost, Schedule, and Performance in Complex System Product Development', PhD dissertation, MIT (1998), expanded the DSM capability to sequence tasks to include their potential cost and schedule risk, along with a probability that they will require rework due to errors found later in the downstream work.

29  Based upon K. Bozdogan, J. Deyst, D. Hoult, and M. Lucas, 'Architectural Innovation in Product Development through Early Supplier Integration', *R&D Management* **28**:3 (July 1998), 163–73.

30  J. Klein, Presentation at LAI Implementation Workshop on High Performance Work Organizations, Los Angeles (February 5th–6th, 1997).

31  Much of the emerging understanding used here has been developed by the LAI Product Development Team in a series of workshops and resulting whitepapers. A 'virtuous circle' of industry and government efforts, pilot applications, academic studies, and exchange meetings accelerated the process. Research efforts often catalyzed change in the projects they were studying, as the lean understanding of the sources of value was brought to bear on new problems. The results have been captured in working papers (see the working paper referenced in Note 29; see also H. McManus, 'Outputs of the Winter 2000 Workshop on Mapping the Product Development Value Stream', LAI Working Paper WP00-02 (January 2000)); more important, the community has established a tacit consensus on how lean is applied to product development.

32  J. Chase, 'Measuring Value in Product Development,' LAI Working Paper WP00-05 (March 2000).

33  N. R. Joglekar and D. E. Whitney, 'Where Does Time Go? – Design Automation Usage Patterns During Complex Electro-Mechanical Product Development', presentation at the LAI Product Development Workshop (January 2000); H. McManus, 'Outputs of the Summer 1999 Workshop on Flow and Pull in Product Development', LAI Working Paper WP00-01 (January 2000).

34  P. Carlile, 'A Pragmatic View of Knowledge and Boundaries: Boundary Objects in New Product Development', forthcoming in *Organization Science* (2002); J. I. Bernstein, 'Multidisciplinary Design Problem Solving on Product Development Teams', PhD dissertation, MIT (2001).

35  Millard (2001) – see Note 6, Chapter 7.

36  M. Rother and J. Shook, *Learning To See: Value Stream Mapping to Add Value and Eliminate Muda* (Brookline, MA: Lean Enterprise Institute, 1999).

37  W. L. Harris Jr, 'Economic Incentives for Production Programs: Policy Recommendations', Presentation to the LAI Executive Board (May 4th, 1999).

38  A. Stanke, 'A Framework for Achieving Lifecycle Value in Product Development', Master's thesis, MIT (2001).

39  E. Rebentisch, 'Preliminary Observations on Program Instability', LAI Working Paper 96-03 (1996).

40  See J. A. Highsmith III, *Adaptive Software Development* (New York: Dorset House Publishing, 2000).

41　The DoD Milestone approach has the element of adaptation since each phase builds on the last phase. But often the phases are very long, sometimes years apart, with many internal milestones. Within a phase, any alteration to the plan may be a contractual issue. This is changing; the latest version of DoD 5000, the standard that specifies the phases and specific requirements for DoD programs, allows 'evolutionary acquisition' strategies that provide for concurrent or iterative development.

42　This case study is based on material from Cowap (1998).

43　Mandelbaum et al. (2001).

44　In a workshop held as part of the Spring 2001 LAI plenary conference, successful aerospace industry program representatives contributed to a panel discussion of how their programs are working to deliver on their value proposition. Panelists responded with the following observations. Complete resolution to stakeholder expectations and needs may never truly be accomplished; it is more a process of constant negotiation where leadership plays a key role in questioning decisions continually and in reinforcing a value focus. One way to make progress towards agreement on program expectations is to bring the customer perspective into tradeoff decisions. Striving to deliver a balanced best-value product rather than a best technical product is facilitated by a team-based organization that utilizes structured processes. Anticipate sources of variation, identify where flexibility can be incorporated effectively and efficiently, and incorporate a robust design to minimize the impact of changes. Tools such as Quality Function Deployment, risk analysis, and cost versus schedule 'bull's-eye charts' are useful in managing the identification of changes as they come along. Finally, know your customer, understand that there's rarely a set answer, and embrace change as an opportunity.

## Chapter 9

1　P. R. Carlile and E. S. Rebentisch, 'Into the Black Box: The Knowledge Transformation Cycle', forthcoming in *Management Science* (2002), Special Issue on 'Managing Knowledge in Organizations: Creating, Retaining, and Transferring Knowledge'.

2　Based on one author's experience in the industry.

3　Examples include Boeing military aircraft operations in St. Louis, which outsource much of their fabrication; US government privatization of services such as payroll and cleaning; and the long-term US Air Force process of outsourcing engineering to contractors.

4　See R. J. Art, *The TFX Decision: McNamara and the Military* (Boston: Little, Brown & Co., 1968).

5　'Hour of maintenance' is a metric typically tracked by usage and maintenance organizations. We used it as a surrogate for cost since it is readily available.

6　It should be noted, however, that the immediate savings are modest – especially from the perspective of a leader responsible for a multi-billion dollar enterprise.

7　For ease of illustration and discussion, all programs of Provider A are considered to have a common Customer B. Previous chapters have highlighted how the complexities of the aerospace industry make such simplistic arrangements uncommon.

8　B. Lucas, E. Shroyer, B. J. Schwartz, and G. Noel, 'The Wrong Kind of Lean: Over-Commitment and Under-represented Skills on Technology Teams', LAI Working Paper (2000).

9　Percentages provided by The Aerospace Corporation for commercial communication satellites and by The Boeing Corporation for Global Positioning System satellites. Presented in A. L. Weigel and J. M. Warmkessel, 'Cross-Industry Characterization of Spacecraft Integration and Test Discrepancies: Transforming Discrepancies into Product Development Improvements', AIAA Space 2000 Conference, Long Beach, California (September 2000).

10 System-level testing represents testing on the 'ready to launch' spacecraft configuration. For more information, see A. L. Weigel, 'Spacecraft System-Level Integration and Test Discrepancies: Characterizing Distributions and Costs', Master's thesis, MIT (2000).

11 Weigel and Warmkessel (2000).

12 D. H. W. Steare, 'Space Launch Operations and Capacity Modeling: A System Dynamics Methodology for Advanced Analysis of the U.S. Eastern Range', Master's thesis, MIT (2000).

13 D. Ferris, 'Characterization of Operator-Reported Discrepancies in Unmanned On-Orbit Space Systems', Master's thesis, MIT (2001).

14 Of course, the challenge with using bureaucracies as a model for enterprise integration is that they often *stifle* innovative behavior, since they are designed largely to inhibit individualist behavior.

15 These assumptions are generally based on a 'rational' view of organizational behavior with respect to forecast accuracy, how staff act, and how resources are allocated. For more discussion of rational system assumptions, see W. R. Scott, *Organizations: Rational, Natural, and Open Systems* (Englewood Cliffs, NJ: Prentice-Hall, 1987).

16 G. Herweg and K. Pilon, 'System Dynamics Modeling for the Exploration of Manpower Project Staffing Decisions in the Context of a Multi-Project Enterprise', Master's thesis, MIT (2001).

17 The following examples illustrate the enterprise behavior generated by the model, which experienced program managers have probably witnessed first-hand. For instance, when a program runs into trouble, extra resources are often applied to help it 'get well'. These resources – people, equipment, money – have to come from somewhere else in the enterprise, and it's often another, lower-priority program. If a program takes longer to complete than planned, it means that the resources it would have freed up for reassignment to another program are still being used. Other programs then must slip their start date or execute at a slower rate until the needed resources are made available. When the portfolio contains one particularly large high-priority program, other, smaller programs tend to get starved of resources as even small deviations from the larger program's plan can mean significant changes in resource allocations to the lower-priority programs. Some of these smaller programs can never complete because they never reach the critical mass of resources and capabilities needed. It would have been better just to cancel them and free up their resources for other programs.

18 E. Rebentisch, 'Preliminary Observations on Program Instability', Lean Aerospace Initiative White Paper #Lean 96-03 (October 1996). The study was based on more than 154 survey responses from US government program offices and more than 106 survey responses from defense contractors. The program managers identified the extent to which various factors introduced instability into their programs, and attributed cost and schedule deviations to budget changes, technology problems, requirements changes, or other sources. The programs reported that their instability came, on average, as much from changing requirements or technical problems as from budget cuts.

19 J. Cutcher-Gershenfeld, T. Kochan, and B. Barrett, 'The Impact of Instability on Employment', Labor Aerospace Research Agenda Presentation to LAI Plenary (March 2001). These findings are based on a national random sample of senior leaders in 196 aerospace facilities – most with multiple programs.

20 See, for instance, R. G. Cooper and E. J. Kleinschmidt, 'Resource-Allocation in the New Product Process', *Industrial Marketing Management* 17: 3 (August 1988), 249–62. See also A. Khurana and S. R. Rosenthal, 'Integrating the Fuzzy Front End of New Product Development', *Sloan Management Review* **38**:2 (Winter 1997), 103–20.

21 J. R. Wirthlin, 'Best Practices in User Needs/Requirements Generation', Master's thesis, MIT (2000). This study contributed to LAI policy recommendations submitted to the USAF in May 2000 outlining how it could improve its requirements development process.

22 C. Y. Baldwin and K. B. Clark, *Design Rules: The Power of Modularity*, Vol. I (Cambridge, MA: The MIT Press, 2000).

23 E. von Hippel, *The Sources of Innovation* (New York: Oxford University Press, 1987).

24 Point designs – that is, designs optimized around a constrained or narrowly defined set of criteria, rather than a general or broad set – have dominated aerospace systems in the past. The mature nature of many aerospace vehicle technologies lends itself to rationalization of the design process.

25 See M. A. Cusumano and K. Nobeoka, *Thinking Beyond Lean: How Multi-Project Management Is Transforming Product Development at Toyota and Other Companies* (New York: Free Press, 1998).

26 See Bozdogan, Deyst, Hoult, and Lucas (July 1998) – see *Note 29, Chapter 8.*

27 For more on the organizational issues associated with the use of architectural strategies, see Cusamano and Nobeoka (1998). See also M. Beckert, 'Organizational Characteristics for Successful Product Line Engineering', Master's thesis, MIT (2000).

28 T. Kochan (with input from other members of the Labor Aerospace Research Agenda), 'A Decade of Learning: IAM/Boeing Joint Programs', Labor Aerospace Research Agenda Case Study (2000).

29 M. R. Nuffort, 'Managing Subsystem Commonality', Master's thesis, MIT (2001).

30 When the military goes out to buy the parts specified in the original designs, the suppliers have often moved on to making the new technology. This problem is known as DMS, or diminishing manufacturing sources.

31 An agent who engineers the standard or specification and is also the producing source is likely to be biased to select an engineering solution that matches that agent's own internal production capabilities, design philosophy, or specific sub-vendor relationships. If the standard is engineered independently using a true open architecture design and a modular approach, the standard/specification should allow the user to buy items openly and competitively into the future. This allows for price competition and technology insertion when it is appropriate to the user.

32 This is because of network externality effects. See M. L. Katz and C. Shapiro, 'Network Externalities, Competition, and Compatibility', *American Economic Review* **75**:3 (June 1985), 424–40; M. L. Katz and C. Shapiro, 'Technology Adoption in the Presence of Network Externalities', *Journal of Political Economy* **94**:4 (August 1986), 822–41.

33 See, for example, K. B. Clark, 'Project Scope and Project Performance: The Effect of Parts Strategy and Supplier Involvement on Product Development,' *Management Science* **35**:10 (October 1989), 1247–63; M. A. Cusumano and A. Takeishi, 'Supplier Relations and Management: A Survey of Japanese-Transplant and U.S. Auto Plants', *Strategic Management Journal* **12** (1991), 563–88; J. K. Liker, R. R. Kamath, S. N. Wasti, and M. Nagamachi, 'Integrating Suppliers into Fast-Cycle Product Development', in J. K. Liker, J. E. Ettlie, and J. C. Campbell (eds), *Engineered in Japan: Japanese Technology Management Practices* (New York: Oxford University Press, 1995), pp. 152–91; Dyer (1996), 1–11 – see *Note 13, Chapter 3.*

34 See Nuffort (2001).

35 Generally, a detachment of six attack helicopters and three utility helicopters is part of the air component of a Marine Expeditionary Unit. Because of the logistics burdens and manning requirements imposed by the lack of commonality between the two aging aircraft, MEU operations had been limited to deployments of four attack helicopters and two utility helicopters, thereby limiting combat capability.

36 This decision was controversial at the time, because some felt that a variant of the H-60 Blackhawk – more than 1500 of which were being operated by the Army, Navy, Air Force, Coast Guard, and several other nations – would save money for the government through economies of scale in procurement, shared maintenance, and support burdens.

37 Roughly half of the savings can be attributed to reductions in the cost of new equipment, spares, training and support equipment, and the like. The rest can be attributed to life-cycle costs of operations and support, including personnel, training, support infrastructure, and the additional airlift capacity required to fly in combat spares and support equipment.

## Chapter 10

1 The differences (detailed in Chapter 2) lie in the concentration and market power of buyers, the allocation of risks and rewards and financial models, and the definition of products and technologies. The military market, characterized by a customer that may be the only one for the product, plays a commanding role in the product definition, assumes the major part of the risk of fulfillment (and accordingly limits the rewards), and compensates the provider as work is completed rather than when the product is delivered.

2 In addition to reports cited, see, for example, several articles by W. B. Scott in *Aviation Week & Space Technology*: 'People Issues Are Cracks in Aero Industry Foundation' (June 21st, 1999), 63; 'Industry's Loss of Expertise Spurs Counterattack' (March 13th, 2000), 60; and 'Worries Deepen Over Dearth of Technical Talent' (April 23rd, 2001), 32.

3 Defense Science Board, 'Preserving a Healthy and Competitive US Defense Industry to Ensure Our Future National Security – Final Briefing' (November 2000).

4 Cited in Defense Science Board (2000).

5 A late-1989 NASA internal study estimated a $200–$500 billion cost for this program, but that section of the report was deleted before publication.

6 Most investors don't invest in industries, but rather in individual firms. An industry-level measure provides a general indicator of how highly an industry is perceived by capital markets to be innovative.

7 In return on revenues (income/revenues), return on assets (income/assets), and return on shareholders' equity (income/shareholder equity) – all defined by the Fortune 500 listing – aerospace is consistently superior to other heavy-industry firms and consistent with Fortune 500 median firms. Aerospace asset utilization (revenues/assets) is superior to many sectors, and is consistent with the general high performance of heavy manufacturing industries.

8 Federal Aviation Administration, 'FAA Aerospace Forecasts Fiscal Years 2001–2012' (Washington, DC: US Government Printing Office, March 2001). The regional/commuter fleet is forecast to grow by 2.9 percent and revenue passenger-miles are forecast to grow by 7.5 percent through 2009.

9 J. H. McMasters and R. M. Cummings, 'The Demise of Aerospace – Part 2 [We doubt it]', *Flight Journal* **6**:4 (August 2001).

10 Federal Aviation Administration's Associate Administrator for Commercial Space Transportation (AST) and Commercial Space Transportation Advisory Committee (COMSTAC), '2001 Commercial Space Forecasts' (Washington, DC: US Government Printing Office, May 2001).

11 The US government is no longer a primary driver of revenues in the aerospace industry. In 1985, 63 percent of total industry sales were to the US military, 27 percent to other customers, and 10 percent to NASA. By 1998, these proportions had changed to roughly 30 percent, 60 percent, and 10 percent, respectively. The same proportionate switch

between government and civil sales occurred in Europe. While commercial export sales of military aircraft account for some of that shift, growth in civilian markets accounts for much more.

12 'Historical tables, Budget of the United States Government, Fiscal Year 2002' (Washington, DC: US Government Printing Office, 2001). Domestic discretionary spending includes money for federal law enforcement, general government, education and training, science and technology research and space exploration, energy, natural resources, housing, agriculture, and transportation. Mandatory spending, authorized by permanent laws, includes entitlements such as Social Security, Medicare, veterans' benefits, and income, as well as interest on the national debt.

13 W. J. Hussar, 'Predicting the Need for Newly Hired Teachers in the United States to 2008–09' (Washington, DC: US Department of Education, National Center for Education Statistics, 1999).

14 'Who Will Care for Each of Us?', Panel on the 'Future of the Health Care Labor Force in a Graying Society', Nursing Institute, University of Illinois at Chicago College of Nursing (May 2001).

15 Data for this discussion of R&D come from National Science Board, 'Science and Engineering Indicators – 2000' (Arlington, VA.: National Science Foundation, 2000).

16 See, for example, Defense Science Board (November 2000); Scott (1999; 2000; 2001); and J. R. Harbison, General T. A. Moorman Jr, M. W. Jones, and J. Kim, 'US Defense Industry Under Siege – An Agenda for Change', Booz·Allen & Hamilton Viewpoint (2000).

17 For more explanation of the factors that shape job content and job context, see F. Herzberg, 'One More Time: How Do You Motivate Employees?', Harvard Business Review (January/February 1968).

18 Aerospace productivity has grown at a rate of 2.6 percent per year since 1979, compared with a productivity growth rate of 3.7 percent for utilities, 3.9 percent for the Fortune 500 median firms, 4.3 percent for pharmaceuticals, and 8.1 percent for computer and office equipment manufacturers (all based on Fortune 500 data). However, aerospace productivity increases do exceed those of other heavy manufacturers, notably industrial and farm equipment (2.3 percent) and autos (1.5 percent).

19 McNutt (1999) – see Note 10, Chapter 2.

20 National Science Board (2000), p. A-147.

21 E. Rebentisch, 'Creating Value Across the Enterprise: Pathways to a Robust and Prosperous US Aerospace Enterprise', LAI Position Paper (April 2000).

22 This three-tier framework – with relations at the workplace, in collective bargaining, and at strategic levels – derives from the analysis by T. Kochan, H. Katz, and R. McKersie, The Transformation of American Industrial Relations (New York: Basic Books, 1994).

23 W. G. Andrew, 'Do Modern Design Tools Utilized in the Design and Development of Modern Aircraft Counteract the Impact of Lost Intellectual Capital within the Aerospace Industry?', Master's thesis, MIT (2001).

24 www2.airbus.com/media/review.asp.

25 Public Law 106-398, Section 1092.

26 Patillo (1998) – see Note 37, Chapter 3.

27 MIT President Charles M. Vest has consistently raised the concern that the federal government is not providing enough funding for basic research. Basic research provides the foundation for long-term economic growth and creates the human capital to fulfill that growth. See, for example, Vest's testimony before the Joint Economic Committee of the US Congress (June 15th, 1999) and before the House Subcommittee on Acquisition and Technology (April 10th, 1997).

28 See several US Government Accounting Office reports: 'Financial Management: An Overview of Finance and Accounting Activities in DOD', GAO/NSIAD/AIMD-97-61 (February 19th, 1997); 'High-Risk Series: Defense Financial Management', GAO/HR-97-3 (February 1997); and 'Major Management Challenges and Program Risks: Department of Defense', GAO/OCG-99-4 (January 1st, 1999).

29 Lt. Col. K. Birkholz (PMA-276M), 'Impact of Commonality on the H-1 Acquisition', Presentation at LAI Plenary workshop (April 10th, 2001).

30 CNN, 'Code Red Worm Spreads, Pentagon Reacts: Rate of Outbreak Believed to Be Subsiding,' http://www10.cnn.com/2001/TECH/internet/08/01/code.red/index.html (August 1st, 2001); CNN, 'Cost of "Code Red" Rising', at http://www1.cnn.com/2001/TECH/internet/08/08/code.red.II/index.html (August 8th, 2001).

31 D. A. Fulghum, 'USAF's Joint Strike Fighter Price Estimates Jump 10 percent', *Aviation Week & Space Technology* (December 4th, 2000), 41.

32 Defense Science Board 1999 Summer Study Task Force (D. Latham and V. L. Lynn, co-chairs), *21st Century Defense Technology Strategies*, 'Vol. II: Supporting Reports' (Washington, DC: Defense Science Board, March 2000), p. xii.

33 This pattern of customers creating market incentives that perpetuate a mature technology (and its incumbent producer) occurs in numerous industries; see Christensen (1997) – Note 11, Chapter 8. Often, an emergent technology supersedes the mature technology before the incumbent producer can respond effectively. In this case, the government customer defined the market, its structure, and the incentives when it established the requirement for a new piloted aircraft and its acquisition strategy.

34 Congress of the United States, Congressional Budget Office, 'The Effects of Aging on the Costs of Operating and Maintaining Military Equipment' (August 2001). This report puts maintenance cost increases at 2–3 percent per year, but other studies claim that aging aircraft are much more expensive to maintain.

35 'DARPA Over the Years', at http://www.darpa.mil/body/overtheyears.html (April 18th, 2001).

36 M. Dertouzos, 'An Open Letter to DARPA', *Technology Review* **104**:8 (October 2001), 50.

37 Defense Advanced Research Projects Agency, 'DARPA Technology Transition' (January 1997).

38 D. Talbot, 'DARPA's Disruptive Technologies', *Technology Review* **104**:8 (October 2001), 42–50.

## Chapter 11

1 In looking at other sectors of the economy, we draw on a wide range of industry-level studies. We look back to *Made in America*, perhaps the best known of a series of assessments in the late 1980s that were highly critical of weaknesses in US industrial competitiveness. See M. L. Dertouzos et al. (1989) – Note 4, Chapter 3. We also draw on a report by the National Research Council Board on Science, Technology, and Economic Policy that was written as a much more optimistic counterpoint to *Made in America*. See Mowery (1999) – Note 24, Chapter 4. Also helpful are a variety of working papers and reports from among the 18 industry centers supported through the Sloan Foundation at 13 different universities.

2 Personal correspondence with IMVP Director John Paul MacDuffie.

3 The Drug Price Competition and Patent Term Restoration Act of 1984 (known as the Waxman-Hatch Act) authorized the US Food and Drug Administration to establish procedures to approve generic applications of drugs first approved after 1962, greatly increasing generic drug availability. The law also set up a process to extend the patents of new drugs to compensate for the time lost because of FDA review and approval procedures.

4 See S. C. Stallings, R. H. Rubin, T. J. Allen, C. M. Cooney, A. J. Sinskey, and S. N. Finkelstein, 'Technological Innovation in Pharmaceuticals', MIT Program on the Pharmaceutical Industry Working Paper 59-01 (May 2001).

5 R. C. Leachman and C. H. Leachman, 'E-Commerce and the Changing Terms of Competition in the Semiconductor Industry', University of California, Berkeley/Sloan Foundation Competitive Semiconductor Manufacturing Program Working Paper No. 50 (October 2000).

6 For a detailed discussion of trucking deregulation, see M. H. Belzer, *Sweatshops on Wheels: Winners and Losers in Trucking Deregulation* (New York: Oxford University Press, 2000). For a discussion of how the industry has redefined its value creation and delivery process, see A. Nagarajan, J. L. Bander, and C. C. White III, 'Trucking', in Mowery (1999), pp. 123–53.

7 F. X. Frei, P. T. Harker, and L. W. Hunter, 'Retail Banking', in Mowery (1999), pp. 179–214.

8 See Note 19 in Chapter 3 for additional information on the International Standards Organization.

9 Dertouzos et al. (1989), p. 278.

10 R. S. Ahlbrandt, R. J. Fruehan, and F. Giarratani, *The Renaissance of American Steel: Lessons for Managers in Competitive Industries* (New York: Oxford University Press, 1996).

11 R. J. Fruehan, D. A. Cheij, and D. M. Vislosky, 'Steel', in Mowery (1999), p. 75.

12 See, for example, C. A. O'Reilly III and Jeffrey Pfeffer, *Hidden Value: How Great Companies Achieve Extraordinary Results with Ordinary People* (Boston: Harvard Business School Press, 2000); and Cutcher-Gershenfeld et al. (1998) – see Note 17, Chapter 4.

13 Dertouzos et al. (1989), p. 81.

14 See, for example, C. Ichniowski, K. Shaw, and G. Prennushi, 'The Effects of Human Resource Management Practices on Productivity', *American Economic Review* (June 1997), 291–313; Kochan and Osterman, (1994); J. Cutcher-Gershenfeld, 'The Impact on Economic Performance of a Transformation in Workplace Relations', *Industrial and Labor Relations Review* **44**:2 (January 1991).

15 E. H. Schein and D. Digenti, 'LAI Learning Assessment: Putting R in Lean', Unpublished report (July 18th, 2000).

# INDEX